▶ *Messengers of the Right*

POLITICS AND CULTURE IN MODERN AMERICA

Series Editors:

Margot Canaday, Glenda Gilmore, Michael Kazin, Stephen Pitti, Thomas J. Sugrue

Volumes in the series narrate and analyze political and social change in the broadest dimensions from 1865 to the present, including ideas about the ways people have sought and wielded power in the public sphere and the language and institutions of politics at all levels—local, national, and transnational. The series is motivated by a desire to reverse the fragmentation of modern U.S. history and to encourage synthetic perspectives on social movements and the state, on gender, race, and labor, and on intellectual history and popular culture.

Messengers of the Right

Conservative Media and the Transformation of American Politics

Nicole Hemmer

PENN

University of Pennsylvania Press
Philadelphia

Published by
University of Pennsylvania Press
Philadelphia, Pennsylvania 19104-4112
www.upenn.edu/pennpress

Printed in the United States of America on acid-free paper
10 9 8 7 6 5 4 3 2 1

A Cataloging-in-Publication record is available from the Library of Congress
ISBN 978-0-8122-4839-5

For my dad

Contents

Part IV. Adaptations

Preface

"My project this summer is to get you to vote for George Bush."

My father's declaration, made one June day in 2004 as we were driving into town, did not surprise me. I was back in Indiana for my annual visit, and my dad and I had spent every day since my arrival wrangling over American politics: the war in Iraq, the marriage equality referenda, the impending election. Raised conservative, I had slowly slid to the left as my dad drifted further right. But that divergence ended up drawing us closer together. Political debate became the secret language of our relationship, the way we conveyed love, respect, disagreement, and admiration. So there was nothing extraordinary about an afternoon spent debating politics. Yet I remember every contour of that particular conversation—the conviction in my dad's voice, the soft hum of traffic, the breeze stirring the Ohio Valley's stagnant summer air—because of what he did next.

He turned on the radio.

Our conversation was replaced with the sound of the *Rush Limbaugh Show*, and then the *Sean Hannity Show*. Wherever we went that summer, the radio offered up a steady stream of conservative talk. I found it both grating and captivating, a heady mix of personality and passion and politics. During ad breaks we feasted on each segment's arguments and insights, dissecting the surprisingly wide variety of philosophies and logics (and illogics) at play. In addition to engaging from my own adversarial perspective, I observed my dad's response as a sympathetic listener. He absorbed some arguments, rejected others, and refashioned still others to fit with his life experiences. This dynamic interplay confounded the common stereotype of talk-radio listeners as sponges soaking up the host's message. It was compelling stuff. And while it didn't change my vote, it did change my life—and led to the book you're reading now.

Some months later, while skimming through back issues of the *Nation* magazine, I spotted an article called "Hate Clubs of the Air." It began, "Right-wing fanatics, casting doubt on the loyalty of every president of the United States since Herbert Hoover, are pounding the American people, this Presidential election year, with an unprecedented flood of radio and television propaganda." The article's existence refuted everything I thought I knew about conservative media. The long-accepted narrative said that the modern conservative movement started with intellectuals in the 1950s, took root in organizations in the 1960s and 1970s, and won political influence in the 1980s. Only then did a powerful and influential conservative media apparatus emerge, first in talk radio and then in cable news. Yet here was a liberal journalist disparaging right-wing radio and television in 1964. I had to find out more.[1]

With this discovery, I made my way into the archives. There I uncovered a network of activism far broader and far more influential than I had expected. Beginning in the late 1940s and 1950s, activists working in media emerged as leaders of the conservative movement. Not only did they start an array of media enterprises—publishing houses, radio programs, magazines, book clubs, television shows—they built the movement. They coordinated rallies, founded organizations, ran political campaigns, and mobilized voters. From the archives they emerged as a distinct group that I call "media activists," men and women (but mostly men) whose primary sites of activism were the media institutions they founded. While they disagreed profoundly on tactics and strategy, they shared a belief that political change stemmed not just from ideas but from the proper expression and diffusion of those ideas through ideological media sources. Unlike fellow conservatives who worked for mainstream periodicals and broadcasters, these media activists believed independence was vital to their work—that they needed to develop their own publishing houses, their own radio programs, their own magazines if they were going to truly change American politics.

This idea of conservative media activism no doubt resonates with anyone who has followed U.S. politics in the past few decades. Americans are accustomed to thinking of right-wing media as integral to contemporary conservatism. In 2009 Rush Limbaugh topped polls as the de facto leader of the Republican Party. Tea Party rallies in 2009 and 2010 featured Fox News personalities and popular radio hosts. But these well-known figures comprise the second generation of media activists. *Messengers of the Right* tells the story of the little-known first generation. It explains how conservative media became the institutional and organizational nexus of the movement, transforming audiences into activists and activists into a reliable voting base. It follows broadcaster Clarence Manion, book publisher Henry Regnery, and magazine publisher William Rusher as they evolved from frustrated outsiders in search of a platform into leaders of one of the most significant and successful political movements of the twentieth century.

Manion's and Regnery's stories start in the 1930s. Both held positions within the New Deal—political conversions abound in *Messengers of the Right*—but ultimately broke with the Roosevelt administration over foreign policy. In the meeting rooms of the America First Committee, these men spoke out against intervention and began building relationships that would launch their media careers. Regnery joined *Human Events*, founded by a number of former America Firsters in 1944 as the war began winding down. In 1947 he left to start his own publishing company. Manion remained in mainstream politics until 1954 when he was fired from the Eisenhower administration over his support of the Bricker Amendment (a national-sovereignty proposal). Both began using new media platforms to make arguments against the New Deal, the war, and containment, their independence rooted in the belief that there was a concerted effort by the mainstream media to block out conservative ideas. They criticized bipartisanship as well as what they saw as an ingrained liberal bias in media and the academy. Rusher remained part of Republican politics until the mid-1950s, when Eisenhower's censure of Joseph McCarthy convinced him that not even Republicans would take a tough enough stance against communism. Soon these media activists found themselves called to organize grassroots conservatives and to enter electoral politics. Originally intent on building mouthpieces, they ended up building a movement.

Conservative media activism has not been absent from the many histories of modern conservatism. George Nash's classic *The Conservative Intellectual Movement*, written in 1976, is rife with right-wing writers and journalists and editors. Rick Perlstein's 2001 book *Before the Storm*, a history of the conservative movement to 1964, begins with a chapter on the Manionites, named after right-wing radio host Clarence Manion. There are at least three biographies of William F. Buckley Jr., the wunderkind founder of *National Review*. Media-centered activists appear again and again in histories of conservative economic thought, grassroots organizing, and political campaigning. Yet no one has studied them as a coherent network of activists or looked at what it meant for the movement that media activists were its architects.[2]

The consequences of their leadership were profound. First and foremost: media activists crafted and popularized the idea of liberal media bias. This concept—that established media were not neutral but slanted toward liberalism—not only shaped the movement but remade American journalism. We have grown so used to this claim that it is hard to comprehend just how radical an idea it was in the 1940s and 1950s. After all, this was an era when institutional neutrality was considered the special genius of the American system. In a world roiling with the terrors of fascism, totalitarianism, and communism, American politicians and intellectuals celebrated the technocratic state and its attendant institutions as spaces free from the passions and pitfalls of ideology. To wit: two years after the publication of Harvard sociologist Daniel Bell's 1960 book *The End of Ideology*, President John F. Kennedy declared that the major domestic challenges of the era "do not relate to the basic clashes of philosophy and ideology, but to the ways and means of reaching common goals." His belief in a national consensus pursued through dispassionate management rather than ideological clashes was a broadly shared faith.[3]

Shared, that is, by those who saw themselves as part of what historian Arthur Schlesinger Jr. in 1949 called "the vital center." Schlesinger (who wrote Kennedy's 1962 speech) chastised those on both the left and the right who did not hew to this agreed-upon middle, which viewed New Deal domestic policies and liberal anticommunism as the only viable Cold War position. This consensus was, paradoxically, understood as both liberal and nonideological. Such an understanding could only be sustained from within the vital center. Viewed from the progressive left or the conservative right, the neutrality of the vital center was a farce. Activists on the left and the right found themselves tarred as extremists and ideologues, politically illegitimate in a post-ideology age. Both sought to expose the ideological agendas of these purportedly neutral institutions, attacking the press's claims of objectivity, the universities' claims of neutrality, and the government's claims of technocracy. But it was conservatives who had the greatest impact, convincing not just the right but a plurality of Americans that mainstream institutions were biased in favor of liberalism.[4]

For conservative media activists, the concept of "liberal bias" was both a lived reality and a rhetorical argument. It was central to their understanding of institutions as inherently ideological. They embedded their ideas about media in the organizations they founded and the political campaigns they led. They taught a generation of conservatives to reject nonconservative media and to seek out right-wing news sources. In the process, they made this habit of conservative media consumption part of what it now means to be a conservative in America.

This reliance on ideological media also reshaped the conservative relationship to ideas. The story I tell about conservative media activism from the 1940s through the 1970s is not just one of media spreading political ideas but media opening a battle over how best to assess what is true and what is not. Conservatives took up this battle against the dominant journalistic mode of midcentury America: objectivity. Some have argued that "objectivity" describes a set of professional practices rather than a coherent worldview, but this understates the power of objectivity as a concept. Objectivity was more than a set of professional values—it was a claim about the best way to understand the world. In midcentury, American journalists who were invested in the ideal of objectivity claimed the trueness of their stories could best be evaluated by how well they adhered to standards of disinterestedness, accuracy, factuality, fairness, and, less overtly but no less importantly, their deference to official information and institutional authority.[5]

Conservative media activists advanced an alternative way of knowing the world, one that attacked the legitimacy of objectivity and substituted for it ideological integrity. That attack was embodied in their notion of "liberal media bias," which disputed not just the content presented by mainstream journalists but the very claims they made about their objective practices. This was a battle over fundamentals, a struggle over how best to gauge the trustworthiness of information. Media activists weren't suggesting there existed a world of objective media that they rejected and a world of ideological media that they promoted. They were arguing there was no such thing as nonideological media, that objectivity was a mask mainstream media used to hide their own ideological projects.

In making this claim, conservative media activists in midcentury America provided their audiences—readers, listeners, and viewers—with a different way of weighing evidence: a different network of authorities, a different conception of fact and accuracy, and a different way of evaluating truth-claims. That evaluation relied not on the source's impartiality but on the assumed biases of the writers, editors, and publishers involved in the media enterprise. The assumption that all media outlets were biased and were engaged in the same type of ideological warfare allowed conservatives to develop a robust approach to absorbing contrary evidence. When an outlet like the *New York Times* criticized a liberal policy, conservative media activists presented it not as evidence of the paper's even-handedness but as evidence of the policy's failure. *Even the liberal* New York Times *had to admit. . . .* Thus evidence that seemed to undermine the charge of liberal bias could be reinterpreted to support it.

Media bias was not the only artifact of the conservative claim that institutions were inherently ideological. Through their critique of an entrenched liberal establishment, the first generation of conservative media activists developed an oppositional identity that enabled conservatives to identify as outsiders. They cultivated what we can usefully think of as an "elite populism," which allowed media activists to speak as representatives of an oppressed minority (and by the mid-1960s, an oppressed majority), despite their access to traditional sources of economic, social, and political power. Theirs was not simply a story of grassroots activists agitating for change or a story of well-placed elites manipulating the masses. Rather, the work of media activists sat at the intersection of these two factions.

Elite populism was a distinguishing feature of conservative media activism from the start. Though the "elite" part was seldom in question, the "populist" part took a while to fully develop. When their activism was simply a matter of formulating arguments and creating a sense of conservative identity among far-flung readers and listeners, it didn't particularly matter if they represented a minority. Populism flavored their work but functioned largely as a linkage to the past. This first generation of media activists saw themselves operating in a populist tradition that extended back to the American founding. They compared their work to that of Thomas Paine, raising the cry of revolution while laying the groundwork for a fundamentally new type of government, and to that of William Lloyd Garrison, demanding an end to slavery at a time when abolitionism was considered at best eccentric and at worst seditious. Drawn to iconoclasts, media activists constructed a lineage that was as radical as it was conservative. If the establishment was liberal, then they would dedicate themselves to demolishing it.

But with Barry Goldwater's landslide loss to Lyndon Johnson in the presidential campaign of 1964 it became painfully clear these activists would have to forge a conservative majority. Populism offered a way forward because it allowed them to build a bridge between conservative elites and ordinary Americans based on their shared experience of exclusion. And there was a factual basis for these claims. Conservative media activists faced real barriers in the 1950s and 1960s because their politics were considered too radical. They lost political positions, became targets of investigation, and were often mocked, misrepresented, or ignored by mainstream figures—"laughed away as extreme right-wingers," as Buckley put it in a 1955 television appearance.[6]

For people used to being gatekeepers, this exclusion was doubly frustrating. Seeking to influence both voters and politicians, pressured by both audiences and donors, media activists pointed to their education and connections as evidence of the injustice of their exclusion. They wondered, *How can we, university deans and well-heeled lawyers and Ivy League grads and party insiders and CEOs, have been shunted aside because of our political beliefs?* Yet unlike most groups excluded from power, these conservative activists had extensive resources to challenge their exclusion. This blend of populism and power helps explain the tremendous success of a movement that began on the fringes of American politics, as well as the right's ability to maintain an outsider identity in the face of that success.[7]

Finally, the influence of media activists ensured that, as modern conservatism grappled with the tensions between ideological purity and political pragmatism, the scale would always be weighted toward purity. That purity would always win out may sound like an odd claim, given Buckley's famously pragmatic declaration that he would support "the most right, viable candidate who could win." But Buckley also ran a quixotic campaign for mayor of New York City in 1965 as the most right, *least* viable candidate. The two can be reconciled by the timing of the Buckley dictum, which he used to explain *National Review*'s support of Richard Nixon during the magazine's flirtation with pragmatism in 1968. By the time Air Force One touched down in Beijing four years later, opening China and alienating conservatives, the flirtation with pragmatism-first politics was over, and the scales tipped back toward purity.

As the Buckley dictum suggests, conservative media activists acted as mediators between the base's flights of fancy and the realities of two-party politics. In the process they policed the boundaries of conservatism while helping steer the Republican Party to the right. But they understood their role as distinct from party politics. In this regard, William Rusher was fond of reminding his colleagues at *National Review* that "there is a real and necessary difference between the role of tablet-keepers like ourselves and that of a political leader . . . who must persuade substantial majorities to go along with him." For most media activists—including Rusher himself—the pragmatism of party politics was a force against which to struggle rather than a reality to accept.[8]

With the second generation of media activists this preference for purity became more pronounced, especially as Republican politicians began to attune themselves to right-wing media as proxies for the party's base. Though Richard Nixon began the process of courting conservative media activists in the late 1960s, by the 1990s Republican politicians had become markedly more sensitive to the judgments of media personalities. Conservatives, who in midcentury had been only one of many factions within the Republican Party, were now the party's base. Conservative media activists thus gained substantial influence over Republican politicians, influence that led many officeholders to choose ideological integrity over political pragmatism.

We often take for granted the close relationship between conservative media and conservative political success. But as the experiences of Rusher, Regnery, Manion, and other midcentury media activists suggest, that's a mistake on two fronts. First, as *Messengers of the Right* shows, there was a long postwar tradition of conservative media activism in a time when partisan politics repeatedly disappointed the right: from Eisenhower to Goldwater to Nixon, media activists tried—and failed—again and again in their attempts to transform politics. And second, by the 1970s the first generation of conservative media was in decline: out of power, out of money, and out of influence. Thus on the eve of conservatism's most important electoral victory—the election of Ronald Reagan—conservative media activism was largely defunct. The second generation would not arise until Reagan left office.

When the second generation did arise, its success did not always benefit the GOP. This dynamic led conservative commentator David Frum to declare in 2012 the Republican Party had a "followership problem" radiating from its media. While asserting both the right and left had created "alternative knowledge systems" driven by ideological media, he argued that "the Republican and conservative knowledge system does seem more coordinated than the liberal system—and even further removed from reality." Yet Frum located the genesis of that problem in the twenty-first century. Understanding why the conservative knowledge system is more developed and cohesive—and why Frum could plausibly argue that the Republican system is the same as the conservative one—requires us to grapple with a process started not by Rush Limbaugh or Fox News but by activists in the 1940s and 1950s.[9]

It's to their story that we now turn.

Part I

Networks

Chapter 1

The Outsiders

Pride. There was no better word to describe how Clarence Manion felt as he rolled into Lowry Air Force Base in August 1953. The Summer White House, the press called the base, because of the man Manion was there to meet. It was a remarkable day for the former law school dean. In just two short years, Manion had climbed his way from an academic post in South Bend, Indiana, to the inner sanctum of Washington political life. He had a best-selling book, a steady lecture schedule, and a Rolodex filled with some of the richest and most well-connected men in America. And now, just a month after his fifty-seventh birthday, he was in Denver to meet with President Dwight Eisenhower. At that meeting, Eisenhower would announce Manion's appointment as chair of the Commission on Intergovernmental Relations (CIR), a committee set up to investigate waste and redundancy in federal programs. For someone like Manion, who longed to be a political power-player, it meant that he had finally arrived.[1]

Six months later, it was all over.

The rapid unraveling was caused, in large part, by Manion's ambition. Though he would never let on—Manion was not given to voicing self-doubt or disappointment—the chairmanship of the CIR was not really the position he wanted. When Eisenhower won the 1952 election, Manion's name had been floated as a potential secretary of labor or even a possible Supreme Court appointee. The chairmanship was a much, much smaller role. Still, it was a hard-won prize, given Manion's history of thwarted political ambitions. Throughout the 1930s he had lobbied Indiana's Democratic Party

Figure 1. Clarence Manion, 1961.
Chicago History Museum.

for a nomination to Congress, but his efforts were repeatedly blocked by
savvier political rivals. In the 1940s he was appointed dean of Notre Dame
Law School but found the university setting too far removed from political
life. Even when he began to make a name for himself in the early 1950s,
leaving behind Notre Dame for a new career as a public speaker, he faced
unexpected challenges. He had to scramble to safeguard his reputation,
battling persistent rumors that he had been fired from Notre Dame for his
extremist politics. Whenever these accusations reached his ears, he pulled
out his Dictaphone and his mimeographed letters of support, then rattled
off a well-rehearsed demand for retraction. Not that he thought it would do
much good; as he constantly lamented, "A lie can travel seven leagues while
the truth is getting on its boots."[2]

Given that history of frustrated hopes, Manion had reason to be pleased
but not fully satisfied with his new post at the CIR. He planned to make the
most of the opportunity, to use it to prove both his dedication to small-gov-
ernment principles and his loyalty to Eisenhower. Leveraging his status as a
member of the administration, he crisscrossed the country to campaign for
a less interventionist government, both at home and abroad. Scarcely a week

passed without a television appearance, a radio interview, or a mention in the papers of record.

As it turned out, Manion was a skilled pundit but a poor politician. Rather than sticking to general political principles, he stumped in support of specific policies—things like selling the Tennessee Valley Authority and curbing the president's treaty-making powers. The problem? The policies he supported were policies Eisenhower strongly and publicly opposed. Manion had badly overstepped. By the start of 1954 Washington was awash in rumors that his days in D.C. were numbered. In mid-February, a front-page *New York Times* article detailed problems with the commission, discussing at length the "cloud of controversy" hovering over Manion. Eisenhower requested his resignation a few days later. Just like that, Manion's days as an insider were over.[3]

After decades of effort, Manion had made his way into the ranks of America's political elite—only to find himself forced back out because of his controversial policy stances. He was not the only one. Nearly every conservative media activist in the 1940s and 1950s had a similar story to tell. The founders of the newsweekly *Human Events* were refugees from the *Washington Post*, the *New York Post*, and the *Christian Science Monitor*. Writers for *National Review* were largely Ivy League trained with stints in party politics, government offices, and academia. Radio broadcasters came from similarly well-heeled backgrounds. Manion was dean of Notre Dame Law, Dan Smoot of the *Dan Smoot Report* worked for the FBI.

From these perches future media activists established connections with some of the wealthiest and most powerful people in the United States. They navigated the elite levels of American society in different ways, as Democrats and Republicans, as New Dealers and America Firsters, as students and enlistees and politicos and journalists. Yet despite their divergent paths, in the immediate post–World War II era they found themselves at the same spot. Dissatisfied—dismayed—by the course the country was on, these activists transformed themselves into media figures offering an alternative vision of a radically more conservative America. In the process, they went from insiders to outsiders, elites with traditional sources of economic, social, and cultural capital suddenly shut out of the halls of power.

To understand why conservative media activists took such circuitous intellectual and political odysseys requires taking a step back. Way back, in this case, to the turn of the century, when both politics and media in the

United States were undergoing a period of epochal change. The watershed moment was 1896, the year Clarence Manion was born in Henderson, Kentucky, a small town nestled along the flood-prone Ohio River. That year, the six-year-old People's Party, a party populated by southern and western farmers, nominated William Jennings Bryan as their candidate for president. Known more commonly as the Populists, members of the People's Party had spent two decades organizing for economic change, first through the Grange and then through the Farmers' Alliance. Their grievance: though they toiled to produce the raw materials for the industrial economy—the fibers for textile mills, the food for cities—every passing year they sank deeper into debt. High cargo rates, usurious bank loans, and disastrously low commodities prices seemed to the Populists not a misfortune but a conspiracy by bankers, merchants, and railroad companies to rob the producing classes of the fruits of their labor. Having spent the better part of twenty years educating farmers, organizing voters, and experimenting with alternative institutions, the Populists finally entered party politics in the 1890s.[4]

As the grassroots movement morphed into a political party, it relied on the power of media, particularly the newspapers of the Farmers' Alliance. In printing their own newspapers, the Populists joined a vibrant tradition in American journalism. Most newspapers in the nineteenth century were party papers, reliant on the patronage of a political party for support. As such, they reflected the positions and passions of their sponsors. This model of party-sponsored publishing was not solely an American one; across Europe newspapers followed the partisan model of publishing. Although American newspapers were shifting toward the commercial model in the late nineteenth century, distancing themselves from overt party ties, papers still typically identified with one of the major parties.[5]

But not all political issues were taken up by the major parties. Movements shut out of two-party politics had to create media of their own. Abolition of slavery was a radical position in 1831 when William Lloyd Garrison founded *The Liberator*, his antislavery broadsheet, in which he declared, "I will be as harsh as truth, and as uncompromising as justice." Likewise, the suffrage movement, religious awakening movements, and the temperance movement all had lively media arms. Prohibitionist Carry Nation published the *Smasher's Mail* and *The Hatchet*, Amelia Bloomer edited the abolitionist and temperance paper *The Lily*, and women's rights activists Susan B. Anthony and Elizabeth Cady Stanton founded *The Revolution* under the motto "Principles, not policy; justice, not favors."[6]

Operating out of this tradition, the Populists used what they called the reform press to strengthen and advance their movement. Like antislavery advocates before the Republican Party was founded in 1854, Populists had neither political representation in the two major parties nor support from existing media. As one historian of the Populist press explained, "Mainstream newspapers viewed farmers as naïve, unsophisticated, unintelligent troublemakers." Ridiculed or dismissed in local papers as well as national magazines like the *Nation*, Populists had to rely on their own media to circulate information about the movement, to reinforce farmers' political identity, and to legitimate the movement—functions media activists would perform for the conservative movement a half century later. So central was the reform press to the political movement that in 1891 Charles Macune, the bright and charismatic leader of the Farmers' Alliance's southern wing, formed the National Reform Press Association (NRPA) to represent the Populist papers, which numbered well over a thousand nationally. The NRPA was as short-lived as the Populist Party itself, which was more or less incorporated into the Democratic Party in 1896, but its formation signaled the centrality of alternative media to political movements acting outside the main currents of politics.[7]

Clarence Manion, born into an actively Democratic family in the months just prior to the 1896 election, absorbed the ethos of Populism much as the party did. Son of an Irish immigrant, Manion's father, Edward, split time between his grocery store and his father's hotel. In 1880 he married Eliza Carroll, who would give birth to Clarence sixteen years later. Outside work and family, Edward Manion had a penchant for politics. In 1883 he won a seat on the city council, a position he retained by waging hotly contested reelection campaigns year after year. The politics of the Manion home left deep impressions on Clarence. He remained a lifelong Democrat, even as the party liberalized. He embraced small-p populism in his celebration of small businesses over monopolistic corporations and in his belief that outside and outsized forces were poised to strip Americans of their liberties at the first opportunity. Government, however, was seldom in his crosshairs before the 1940s, and he often echoed the Populist sentiment that a strong government was necessary to countervail the forces of wealth and business in society.[8]

The People's Party waned after Bryan's loss, but the reform impulse soon reappeared in the Progressive movement. Progressives differed from Populists in significant ways: more likely to be found in cities, more literary, more elite than popular. But like the Populists, the Progressives saw a need to strengthen the federal government, to strip away the influence of corporations and remake the government into a powerful protector of the public interest. They faced a major obstacle, though: decades of Gilded Age individualism, enshrined in Horatio Alger novels, preachers' sermons, and the social sciences, had turned Americans against any sort of government intervention in society and the economy.[9]

Enter the scribes. To change popular attitudes about the proper role of the federal state, a group of writers set about investigating and exposing the conditions of industrial America. Taking advantage of the world of cheap paper that emerged in the late nineteenth century, these Progressive writers found wide audiences in the country's wealth of mass-market magazines and newspapers. Thanks to Theodore Roosevelt, they became known as muckrakers, a name they embraced despite his less-than-flattering intentions. Their investigative journalism, notable for its polished literary style, represented a significant development in America media at a time when journalistic style and values were in flux. Technological developments gave birth to low-cost newsprint in the 1880s and 1890s, opening the market for mass sales. Newspaper entrepreneurs made those sales through sensationalist headlines, graphic images, and exaggerated (even invented) details. This "yellow journalism" peaked around the time Manion was born, culminating in the frothing circulation battles between Joseph Pulitzer and William Randolph Hearst. Muckrakers borrowed yellow journalism's tendency toward titillation and emotionalism but added to it a sense of social responsibility and literary aspiration. They also drew from the work of earlier literary activists like Nellie Bly, whose undercover investigations of mental institutions led to major reforms in the late nineteenth century.[10]

The muckrakers' advocacy journalism marked one of the new directions for news in the waning years of the 1800s, the strand from which founders of conservative media would draw. The other major development of the era came in direct response to tabloid-style journalism. In 1896, the year Manion was born, Adolph Ochs bought the *New York Times*. In order to differentiate the struggling newspaper from its more popular counterparts, he dedicated it to objective reporting. While the word "objectivity" wouldn't come into common use until the 1920s, its hallmarks—"accuracy, fairness, impartiality, independence, and responsibility to the public welfare"—were present in the paper's reporting from the start of Ochs's tenure.[11]

As journalism professionalized in the first half of the twentieth century, those qualities of objectivity became central to newspaper, and later radio and television, reporting. Reportage, analysis, and opinion developed into separate modes of journalistic writing, even migrating to different parts of the newspaper. It was in this era that the opinion and op-ed pages emerged. Papers were still known for their political leanings (often tied to the politics of their owners and publishers, a form known as "personal journalism"), but they were independent of political parties and, at least in theory, corralled their political preferences in the opinion section. The public appetite for political analysis gave rise, by the 1910s and 1920s, to in-house and syndicated columnists. This analysis was bylined, labeled, and generally confined to sections of the newspaper separate from reported pieces. Even as conventional just-the-facts reporting began to yield to more interpretative analysis, a process well underway by the end of the 1930s, interpretative journalism retained objective reporting's style: impersonal narration, an emphasis on fairness and accuracy, and deference to official sources and institutions.[12]

Objectivity was always more a goal than a reality. Still, the pursuit of this goal shaped journalistic practices and norms for much of the twentieth century. The objectivity standard defined mainstream newspaper reporting by the 1930s, reaching the height of its influence in the 1950s and 1960s. Just as impassioned political stances had been pushed aside in favor of the technocratic policies of the postwar era, so too had emotionalism and advocacy in journalism taken a backseat to what philosopher Thomas Nagel later called the "view from nowhere." It was then, in that era when journalists were cleaving most closely to objectivity, that conservative media activists launched their campaign to discredit and ultimately replace it.[13]

Ochs's objectivity standards may have come to dominate newspaper reporting, but muckraking was the journalistic style that most shaped politics in the early twentieth century. Muckrakers were key to implementing the sort of government changes Progressives sought. Their arguments swayed public opinion in favor of new government programs, allowing politicians to advance bills like the Pure Food and Drug Act that had languished in Congress for years. Republican Theodore Roosevelt, who confidently pursued a sweeping national agenda when he entered office after William McKinley's assassination, was the first beneficiary of their activism. He strengthened the federal government, particularly the executive branch, and often relied on the public outcry stirred up by muckrakers to fortify his positions.[14]

So widespread was the progressive impulse in America that it appeared likely to shape the platform of both parties for a generation. This seemed especially true in 1912, when the Democrats named Woodrow Wilson, the reform governor of New Jersey, as their presidential nominee. But events in the Republican Party would interrupt the legacy of reform established by Roosevelt. Believing that William Howard Taft, his vice president and successor, was insufficiently reform minded, Roosevelt bucked tradition and ran for a third term. When he failed to secure the Republican nomination, he bolted the GOP and formed the Progressive Party. In November, Wilson won, Roosevelt took second, and Taft, the sitting president, lagged behind in third, topping only the Socialist candidate, Eugene V. Debs.[15]

Those wayward Progressive-Republicans who backed Roosevelt didn't reconcile after the election but merged instead with the Democrats. Because of the splits, rifts, and realignments of that election, Henry Regnery, who was born in 1912, entered a world in which the Democratic Party was newly minted as the party of progressive reforms, while the Republican Party tacked conservative. Like most postwar conservative media activists, Regnery grew up in an era when the federal government grew visibly and rapidly. In his autobiography he noted the political significance of his birth year, "the year in which Woodrow Wilson was elected president, an event that had a profound effect on American society, and in the end contributed to the partial destruction of Europe." But those events seemed quite distant from the bucolic Chicago suburb of Hinsdale where Regnery grew up. After making his fortune in the textile industry, his father, William, moved first to Chicago and then to Hinsdale, where he and Henry's mother raised their five children. As Chicago grew Hinsdale quickly moved into the modern era, a change signified for Regnery by the conversion of the family's chicken yard into a tennis court.[16]

More than any political party, Germany and foreign affairs shaped Regnery's worldview. "World War I was a difficult time for my father," Regnery recalled, reflecting on the challenges facing the son of German immigrants as the United States moved from neutrality to war against Germany and the other Central Powers. William Regnery fumed over anti-German propaganda in the United States during the war and viewed the Versailles Treaty as "an abomination." Regnery inherited both his father's skepticism of American intervention and his affection for the family's ancestral land. After graduating with a degree in math from MIT, Regnery traveled to Germany. He arrived in the country in August 1934, the same month Adolf Hitler merged the offices of chancellor and president and became führer of the Third Reich. Yet Regnery's reminiscences of the two years he spent studying economics in Bonn focused as much on Beethoven and Mozart as they did on Hitler's consolidation of power. That was a purposeful choice: "As foreign students we were well aware of the Hitler regime, but it seemed far removed from us. . . . Although the ugly business of anti-Semitism had started it was not then particularly evident, and life on the whole seemed quite normal." Regnery returned to the United States in 1936, moving to Cambridge to study as a graduate student under economist Joseph Schumpeter.[17]

While Regnery was born into Woodrow Wilson's world, he came of age in a brief period of Republican dominance. The expansion of federal power in the twentieth century was not linear, and the return of Republicans to the White House in 1921 (a few years before William Rusher was born in Chicago) made it clear the progressive impulse was not the only—or even the predominant—force in American politics. For Warren Harding, Calvin Coolidge, and Herbert Hoover, the Republican presidents of the 1920s, government had few responsibilities other than creating a favorable environment for business. That, they believed, could best be accomplished through noninterference (except in the case of labor unions, which required a fair amount of state and federal power to undermine). So it was that Silent Cal could claim "the chief business of the American people is business" and express a desire to shrink the government to the point that, if it shut down, "no one would notice for six months."[18]

This was not Teddy Roosevelt's Republican Party.

It was, however, Bill Rusher's.

William Rusher was born in Illinois in 1923, the grandson of a miner who worked in western Indiana. Hailing from the land of Eugene Debs, the perennial Socialist candidate for president in the 1900s and 1910s, Rusher's grandfather was a labor leader, a socialist, and a populist radical. That last bit would pass on to his grandson, who split off the leftism but clung fast to the idea that a single person could effect momentous change, could transform the very way people understood their relationship to the government. Though his family removed to Brooklyn when Rusher was just a toddler, he forever considered himself—city-dwelling, intellectual, soft-handed bon vivant that he was—a midwesterner at heart.[19]

Except when it came to foreign policy. The Midwest was the stronghold of American anti-interventionism, but the Rushers were New York Republicans: readers of the *Herald-Tribune* (where Rusher's father worked

Figure 2. William Rusher, 1984. Copyright Nancy Kaye Photography.

in sales), opponents of the New Deal, supporters of Wendell Willkie and intervention. Rusher expressed a keen interest in politics from a young age, involving himself in school government and the Republican Party. As the GOP went, so went Rusher—which was not necessarily the best direction in the 1930s and 1940s if one saw politics as a path to power. By the time Rusher was old enough to follow politics, the Republicans were out of power in a big way.[20]

For twenty years after 1932 Democrats ran the show. Bad news for a Young Republican like Rusher, but for Clarence Manion and Henry Regnery, the growth of New Deal governance and Democratic power meant new opportunities. After World War I interrupted his pursuit of a master's degree, Manion accepted a post at Notre Dame, where he taught history while working toward his law degree. He left South Bend for a few years to go into private practice but returned in 1925 to teach constitutional law.[21]

Politics, though, was never far from Manion's mind. Especially the issue of Prohibition, which by the mid-1920s had devolved into a political embarrassment and law enforcement quagmire. Manion, a devoted Wet, opposed Prohibition not only for its inefficacy but for the philosophy of government behind it. In "What Price Prohibition?" one of many pieces he wrote for the

Notre Dame Lawyer, Manion framed his opposition to Prohibition as a matter of the state's subservience to the individual. For him, government existed only as "an agent," "a necessary evil," "a parasite." It certainly did not exist to regulate personal morality. In seeking "to secure the State's help in getting sin out of people's souls," prohibitionists blurred the lines between moral law and civil law, distorting the proper functions of both. Manion, though never much of a drinker, preferred inebriated sin to sober state power. "A few honest citizens drunk on beer are to be preferred to an army of corrupt officials drunk on arbitrary power. It is better, far better," he concluded, "that all law-made morality end than that all God-made liberty die."[22]

In the 1920s, Manion and the Democratic Party stood on the losing side of the Prohibition issue. When Al Smith—a Wet, a Catholic, and a Democrat with whom Manion closely identified—lost his bid for the presidency in 1928, Manion realized his ideas and politics were out of step with the prevailing sentiment. So he took his arguments out of the pages of the *Notre Dame Lawyer* and into more popular outlets, hoping to channel public opinion in a new direction. His letters and articles appeared in a number of midwestern newspapers. At the same time he launched *The Independent Citizen*, a monthly magazine "devoted to the interests of 'the little fellow' in business and politics," undertaken by "militant old-fashioned individualists." The project revealed Manion's libertarian streak, as he went beyond denouncing bigness to advocating individualism.[23]

Manion didn't just want to influence the public conversation, though. He wanted to exercise power. With the Democrats back in the game in the 1930s, he tried again and again to secure a nomination—for the House, the Senate, anything—from the Indiana Democratic Party. As part of an effort to raise his profile in the party, he delivered the keynote at the party's 1932 convention. His speech was a hit. The *Chicago Tribune* enthused, "He galloped over the Republicans like the Four Horsemen themselves and had the hall shrieking and yelling." As he galloped, he flayed the Republican Party, Herbert Hoover's party, for profligate spending and burgeoning bureaucracy. He denounced the Hoover Dam as a subsidy for western agriculture. He railed against tax moneys spent to "conduct researches upon the 'love life of the bullfrog' and the malformations of the doodle bug." The speech brimmed with an antigovernment populism that Manion would revive decades later to protest everything from the Tennessee Valley Authority to the Great Society. But in 1932 his populism was employed on behalf of soon-to-be New Deal Democrats.[24]

Manion came off his 1932 keynote certain he was on the cusp of something big. And his path seemed to run directly through the New Deal. As the Roosevelt administration launched its economic initiatives, Manion laid out a full-throated defense of the efforts. The man who in his keynote called for the "centrifugal forces of Democratic administration" now defended the growth of the state as a necessary response to the modern order. Traditional political arguments were no match for new political realities, Manion explained, arguing for a less literal interpretation of the Constitution. The government had to grapple with "circumstances vastly different from those which confronted either the government or the citizen in 1776 or 1789." So it had to regulate, not for the sake of regulating but to safeguard the individual. Those who would contend that new regulations impinged on individual freedom failed to understand modern America, Manion argued. "That conservatism is archaic, if not criminal, which would insist that government police the radio with those methods found adequate for the Pony Express." A bigger government in the face of the growing fiscal crisis would not "subordinate the individual" but "prevent the individual from being submerged. . . . It is to prevent Socialism, and not to establish it, that recovery measures have been adopted by national and state governments." Capitalism and individualism could only survive if the government extended its power and protection.[25]

This vigorous defense of the New Deal paid off, though not in the form of the Senate seat Manion wanted. In 1935 Governor Paul McNutt appointed him head of the state's National Recovery Administration. It was the perfect position for Manion, who was known for his speech-making abilities. Across the Hoosier state he stumped for Franklin Roosevelt's bold new vision of government, even defending the New Deal against the Supreme Court, which from 1935 on repeatedly struck down administration programs. Manion argued the Court continuously reversed laws without considering why government expanded into new areas. In the process, the justices were transforming the Constitution from safeguard to roadblock. "We talk about laws that regulate public utilities," he offered by way of example. "Those laws do not regulate public utilities; they protect consumers of light and power." Manion contended that all the New Deal's protective measures—workplace regulations, minimum wage, maximum hours, the elimination of sweatshops and child labor—were "literally commanded by the spirit of our American Government objective."[26]

In these New Deal defenses, Manion brought together his belief in individual liberty, natural rights, and antisocialism to forge an articulate, impassioned endorsement of liberal governance. Yet all this loyalty and effort failed to result in a spot on the Democratic slate. In 1938 he lobbied hard for a Senate nomination. He drew up a six-point prospectus outlining his electability, including his New Deal advocacy, his support among unions and within the party, and his status as a veteran. But the new governor, Clifford Townsend, blocked him, in part because of his Catholicism. After a decade's effort, it had become clear Manion would not replicate his father's career as an elected official.[27]

Regnery, too, found the 1930s an auspicious time to be a Democrat. He was twenty-four when he returned from Germany in 1936, ready to apply his youthful energy and nimble mind to the pressing problems facing Depression-era America. An enthusiastic Roosevelt backer, he found much support for his politics as a graduate student at Harvard. In his first year he read John Maynard Keynes's newly published *General Theory of Economics, Interest and Money*, which argued in favor of government intervention in the economy. Shortly thereafter, in the summer of 1937, he set off for Washington to work in the Resettlement Administration (RA), "full of illusions and anxious to have a small part in what seemed to me to be a great and promising program to give some of the people who had been left behind a better chance."[28]

That optimism wilted upon contact with the RA's bureaucracy. In his memoirs, he called it "badly administered and almost completely unrealistic," enumerating various failed projects, from a needlework community in New Jersey to a furniture factory in West Virginia. "My commitment to the New Deal, to the idea that the solution of the obvious economic and social ills of the country was to be found in Washington, was given its final blow by a summer spent there." He returned to Harvard a bit less idealistic, and when he left with his master's degree he sought to help impoverished communities not through government agencies but through a private religious organization, the American Friends Service Committee. There he met Eleanor Scattergood, whom he married, and the couple worked for a few years in a Pennsylvania coal-mining community before heading back to Chicago in June 1941.[29]

Manion and Regnery were not alone in their journey from New Dealers to conservative media activists. John Chamberlain, who would edit the influential right-wing magazine the *Freeman* before becoming a contributing editor at *National Review*, spent the 1930s at the *New York Times, Harper's,* and Henry Luce's *Fortune*. Before cofounding *Human Events*, Felix Morley worked as an editor for the *Washington Post*, where he won the paper its first Pulitzer Prize. A number of future writers for *National Review* were working with the Communist Party. Two of the magazine's most central figures—William F. Buckley Jr. and William Rusher—were not yet old enough to vote.

Which is not to suggest no one in media was protesting the New Deal. As historian Alan Brinkley showed, radio provided fertile ground for populist protests against the administration. Father Charles Coughlin and Huey Long drew massive audiences as they attacked Roosevelt from the right and the left. As newspaper columnists and radio commentators, George Sokolsky and Fulton Lewis Jr. kept up a steady drumbeat against the New Deal in the 1930s (and would play a role in the early conservative movement of the 1940s and 1950s).[30]

The real source of anti–New Deal sentiment, though, could be found in print. Tensions ran high between the Roosevelt administration and the men FDR dubbed the "press lords," newspaper publishers who made no secret of their Republican sympathies. Typical of these press lords was Frank Gannett, founder of the Gannett Corporation and owner of several New York newspapers, who helped found the National Committee to Uphold Constitutional Government in 1937. A short-lived organization meant to counter Roosevelt's Court-packing plan, the committee sought to convince "leaders of thought" that Roosevelt was a dictator-in-the-making, whose plans for a managed economy would send the United States down the totalitarian path paved by Italy and Germany. In addition to his work for the committee, Gannett sought to organize the anti–New Deal vote in the 1938 midterms and made his own quixotic presidential bid in 1940.[31]

Gannett was not the only press lord arrayed against the New Deal. Roy Howard of the Scripps-Howard newspaper chain, William Hearst of the Hearst conglomerate, and Robert McCormick of the *Chicago Tribune* were all outspoken supporters of the Republican Party. Indeed, McCormick shaped the editorial pages of his *Chicago Tribune* as one of the central sites of protest against the growing federal state. Because of the prominence of these publishers, the main media complaint of the era was not against liberals but against conservatives. Liberal commentator George Hamilton Combs, debating press bias with conservatives Fulton Lewis Jr. and Bill Buckley in 1955, complained that the main barrier to effective Democratic governance was "a preponderantly, in fact almost exclusively, Republican press." His was a common charge, not just in the New Deal era but for much of the twentieth century, until conservatives unseated it with their countercharge of "liberal media bias." By and large, though, these leaders of anti–New Deal media would not be central to conservative media activism after the war. Indeed, the forge that fashioned postwar media activism was not the New Deal but World War II and the anti-intervention movement.[32]

"This little publication represents the protest of two experienced American journalists against the loss of standards in contemporary American writing on current events," Felix Morley wrote in 1945, looking back at the first year of *Human Events*. "These standards have been a wartime casualty." So much had been lost in the run-up to war, Morley believed, losses exacerbated by the war itself. It wasn't just that reporting had sought to manipulate Americans' passions—Morley was not committed to dispassionate writing— but that it sought to do so on behalf of what he believed was an immoral war. Moreover, the open saber rattling of an earlier era had given way to something he found far more insidious, "a subtle regimentation of public opinion through official agencies of Public Enlightenment," a press-government alliance *Human Events* was founded to disrupt.[33]

For the founders of *Human Events*, as for many conservative media activists, World War II offered their first experience as political—and media—outsiders. As opponents of American intervention, they found themselves on the outs with both major parties and the mainstream press. It was not an inevitable outcome. The rise of Hitler and growing unrest in Europe did not, initially, lead to a push for interventionist policies. In the mid-1930s a commitment to neutrality, in both word and deed, united the two parties in a broad foreign policy consensus. Roosevelt signed a number of neutrality acts that constructed a rigid embargo meant to keep the United States from being drawn into hostilities. Yet while the language of neutrality continued to pervade politics in the late 1930s, anti-intervention forces quickly found themselves on the defensive. As war flared in Europe, Congress passed the 1939 Neutrality Act. Despite its name (and its later emergence as the conservative alternative to lend-lease), the act represented a defeat of anti-intervention forces by lifting the arms embargo and reestablishing the cash-and-carry policy, which allowed trade with warring countries so long as the United States did not provide credit or transport. Anti-interventionists feared the policy, though cloaked in impartiality, would drag America deeper into the affairs of Allied nations.[34]

The shift toward intervention in public sentiment and national policy roused intense opposition from those who believed the government was setting the country on an irreversible course toward war. These opponents hoped to take their case to the nation in the election of 1940. Their standard-bearer in the Republican Party was Robert Taft, elected to the Senate in the Republican sweep of 1938. The son of a president, Taft quickly emerged as a staunch opponent of the New Deal—and an even stauncher opponent of U.S. involvement in World War II. He believed the United States had no national interest in the European war and faced no direct threat given its distance from the warring powers. Though he voted in support of the 1939 Neutrality Act, he kept his eyes firmly fixed on nonintervention, arguing in May 1940 that the Nazi regime, then on the march in France, posed less a threat to the United States than the "infiltration of totalitarian ideas from the New Deal circle in Washington."[35]

A month later, the Republican convention pitted Taft against political neophyte Thomas Dewey (the mustachioed candidate who four years later would be mocked as "the little man on the wedding cake") and Wendell Willkie, a dark-horse candidate whose biggest backers seemed to be the pro-intervention press: the *Herald-Tribune*, *Time*, *Fortune*. Henry Luce, who would later call for an "American Century" in which the United States was more actively involved in world affairs, had his reporters stumping hard for the unknown Willkie, who in May was polling at only 3 percent. One of the correspondents for *Time*, a leading Luce magazine, cabled from the campaign train: "Take me off this train. All I can do is sit at the typewriter and write, 'Wendell Willkie is a wonderful man. Wendell Willkie is a wonderful man.'" Though Dewey led in the first round of balloting, his support faded as the fight emerged between Willkie and Taft. On the sixth ballot, polled well after midnight, Willkie won.[36]

For anti-interventionists, the GOP convention was a disaster. With Roosevelt and Willkie facing off, there was no voice in the national race opposing U.S. involvement. Bipartisan agreement on foreign policy, which worked in their favor in the mid-1930s, now shut them out of the mainstream debate. To keep the issue of nonintervention in the public eye, in September 1940 a group of devoted anti-interventionists founded the America First Committee (AFC). The AFC called for shoring up American defense preparedness to ward off attack while preserving American neutrality by barring aid to warring nations. Within three months, the organization boasted sixty thousand members (and would peak at eight hundred thousand), including famous pilot Charles Lindbergh and salt magnate Sterling

Morton. Anti-interventionism cut across political identities: pacifists and German American Bund devotees, Republicans and Democrats, left-wingers and right-wingers. The organization made strange bedfellows, garnering endorsements ranging from socialist Norman Thomas to anti-Semitic anti–New Dealer Charles Coughlin, from Progressive senator Robert La Follette to conservative Robert Taft.[37]

Anti-interventionists had a media voice as well. The *Chicago Tribune*, headed by Col. Robert McCormick, staked out a fixedly anti-interventionist stance. McCormick fired reporters he felt rattled their sabers too loudly, like his Paris bureau chief who cabled in 1939 that Hitler and Stalin were secretly plotting together, and hired those like Victor Lasky who gave interventionists grief. The *Tribune* dubbed the Lend-Lease Act "the Dictator Bill" and heaped praise upon the AFC. Though McCormick never joined, he did express his pleasure with the AFC to the organization's founders. Nor was McCormick alone. John T. Flynn, a slight, hot-tempered journalist whose weekly column in the *New Republic* made him one of the leading political commentators of the 1930s, began to turn on Roosevelt in the late 1930s because of the administration's softening position on neutrality. He soon emerged as one of the country's most vocal anti-interventionists, heading up the New York chapter of the AFC. But his political stance exacted a high price: his anti-Roosevelt turn cost him his column and access to most national publications.[38]

Though started by a group of Yale students, the AFC quickly became an organization centered in the Midwest, with most of its supporters located within three hundred miles of Chicago. At the center of that support was Robert E. Wood, a retired general and chairman of Sears Roebuck. Square-jawed with slicked-down gray hair, the sixty-one-year-old had earned his war stripes, first fighting in the Philippines at the start of the U.S. occupation and then in France during World War I. He went on to have a wildly successful career at Sears, where his interest in a stable economy led him to back New Deal reforms. He began to sour on the Roosevelt agenda by the late 1930s, believing policies like a national minimum wage and the implementation of the National Labor Relations Board threatened to stall economic recovery. Foreign policy, though, was the source of Wood's break with FDR, as it would be for Regnery, Manion, and a number of other future conservative leaders. Though Wood lobbied to be secretary of war, he was deeply troubled by the prospect of American intervention, which he believed would be an economic disaster for the United States. When AFC founder R. Douglas

Stuart asked him to support a committee against U.S. intervention, Wood readily agreed. No sooner had Wood agreed to chair the national organization than it found monetary support from a prominent Chicago businessman: William H. Regnery.[39]

While it's unclear whether Henry Regnery joined the AFC as well, by the late 1930s he had abandoned his support for Roosevelt's domestic and foreign policy. The thoroughness of the break was evident in Regnery's recollection of the 1930s. After noting Roosevelt and Hitler entered office just weeks apart in the midst of an economic crisis, he went on to comment, "Both Hitler and Roosevelt—each in his own way—were masters of the art of manipulating the masses, and by a strange quirk of fate they died within a few weeks of the other." It was but one example of how deeply disillusioning the war was for Regnery. Fifty years later in a letter to Pat Buchanan, who was toying with the idea of launching a new America First Committee, Regnery asserted that the majority of Americans opposed U.S. involvement but had been manipulated into supporting it by "the President and those who form public opinion."[40]

In making this claim, Regnery reflected the AFC's deep suspicion of the press. Promoting a minority view in a highly politicized and emotional atmosphere, the AFC drew a great deal of press notice and condemnation. Members of the organization "found segments of the press highly suspect" and took to monitoring radio programs to expose their interventionist leanings. In this critique were the seeds of Regnery's revolt: his belief that an elite group molded public opinion, sublimating the will of the majority for its own selfish ends. It did not yet make sense to call this "liberal bias" because liberalism was not the defining issue, but Regnery was convinced bias was at play. Frustrated that noninterventionist voices had been muffled, Regnery renounced mainstream parties and papers and began seeking ways to push back against these opinion shapers.[41]

Manion also found refuge in the AFC. Had he retained hope for a future in Democratic Party politics, the approaching war may have provoked a different response from him than it did. As things stood, however, Manion felt no obligation to back Roosevelt's foreign policy. In the late 1930s, Manion adopted a code of Americanism, a concept somewhere between a political philosophy and a mind-set that exulted the American form of government, venerated founding documents, and, in the postwar era, offered a positive alternative to communism. Americanism emphasized the differences between the United States and Europe; for America Firsters, American exceptionalism could not endure if the country allowed itself to be swept up in Old World problems.

In 1941, Manion, the newly appointed dean of the law school at Notre Dame, joined William Regnery as one of the AFC's national directors. An effective orator, he was part of the organization's communications efforts, which consisted primarily of public speakers and radio spots. He was slated to make his first appearance as a national director for America First on December 14, 1941. He would never make it to the podium. One week before the scheduled speech, the Japanese attacked Pearl Harbor. The attack, so devastating to the noninterventionist cause, would provoke skepticism from prominent conservatives in the 1950s and 1960s. Husband E. Kimmel, the admiral at Pearl Harbor during the attack, made the rounds of the conservative media circuit in the 1950s with claims that Roosevelt knew of the attacks in advance (a claim echoed by Robert A. Theobald, author of the Devin-Adair publication *The Final Secret of Pearl Harbor* [1954]). But in 1941, such claims sounded seditious. Even more so when, three days after the attack, Germany declared war on the United States. Under the pressure of these events, the AFC disbanded.[42]

With U.S. entry into the war, anti-interventionism scooted to the far fringes of American politics. The national unity forged by the war offered an opportunity to heal the rifts created by the battle over intervention. But rather than reconcile, conservative media activists planted themselves firmly outside the foreign policy consensus as they focused on the emerging postwar world. Regnery was the first to go, anxious about another victors' peace and retribution against Germany. Highly critical of the Treaty of Versailles that ended World War I and no happier with the peace outlines being floated in 1944, Regnery became an early and vocal advocate of revisionist histories of the war—histories critical of the Allies and more subdued in their criticisms of Germany—as well as calls for an easy peace for Germany. He considered the revisionists to be the only ones "who kept their heads" in the "mass insanity" of the closing days of the war. Because of their clear-eyed view of the world, "the means of communication were largely closed to them, more than we realized." Before the war ended, he would join efforts to reopen the means of communication for those outside the mainstream of American foreign policy thinking.[43]

For Manion, the break came later. The end of the war signaled a period of tremendous success for the new dean. He oversaw the founding of the Natural Law Institute at Notre Dame in 1947, which formalized the law school's dedication to Thomistic philosophy. In the political realm, the end of the war and debates about the postwar world created new opportunities for Manion. As talk turned to the development of an international security organization, Manion was well-placed to consider the constitutional questions such an organization raised. World peace sounded good, but what would it mean for American sovereignty? It was a question Manion began writing about as early as 1944. Ruminating on the question of sovereignty and postwar alliances, Manion wondered whether the federal government had the constitutional authority to enter such alliances, to create "a binding commitment to join in the forceful suppression of aggression all over the world." What worried Manion most was that such a commitment would expose American citizens to unconstitutional infringements on their rights. The federal government was bound by the Constitution, but international bodies were not. Manion concluded that entering into certain international treaties would effectively amend the Constitution with nothing more than a Senate vote. While Manion was not yet advocating a change to the treaty ratification process, his cautions signaled the transformation of his AFC noninterventionism into the anti-U.N. sentiment that would become a hallmark of postwar conservatism.[44]

The United States did join the United Nations, and by the end of the decade the Cold War had escalated. The Soviet Union broke America's nuclear monopoly, China underwent a communist revolution, war broke out in Korea. It was in this climate that Manion penned *The Key to Peace* (1950), a slender volume dedicated to "the perpetuation of real Americanism." The book argued America's strength lay in its tradition of godly morality, individual liberty, and limited government. Americans in the early space age, Manion worried, were being led astray by a host of intellectuals and experts who promised to "take off for the Mountains of the Moon in search of ways and means to pacify and unify mankind." But the answer to America's problems lay not in the Sea of Tranquility or on foreign shores. It lay instead in the foundations of America's republican government, a government dedicated not to state power but to individual liberties. "The need now is not for 'new concepts,' 'fresh approaches' and 'ingenious improvisations' in the cause of peace and unity. The need now is for rediscovery, and renewed understanding of the tried and true principle of Americanism."[45]

This call for a return to Americanism, which Manion understood as a return to the limited government and traditional morality of the past, struck a chord with the reading audience. Key to Peace clubs began popping up around America. Right-leaning newspapers heralded the work as "the finest politico-spiritual study of America," in the tradition of Tom Paine but with "roots [that] go deeper to moral obligation to God." The best-selling book fueled a lengthy speaking tour, during which Manion expounded on an Americanism rooted in the Constitution, the Declaration of Independence, and the Ten Commandments. His emphasis on the last of these laid the groundwork for his conservatism, which held that government could remain small so long as society remained moral. "Social justice, when it comes, will not proceed from legislative enactments aimed at the perimeter of society," he said in a 1951 speech at Cornell University, "it will rather be diffused through the community as a healthy contagion radiated from the contrite hearts of individual men." The message found so wide an audience that Manion tendered his resignation from Notre Dame in early 1952 and began to keep a full-time speaking schedule.[46]

The speaking tour, along with his work on the American Bar Association's Special Committee on Communist Tactics, Strategy, and Objectives, brought Manion to the attention of Robert Taft, who in 1952 was eyeing another presidential run. Taft persuaded Manion to join the Lawyers-for-Taft committee. When Taft lost the nomination to Dwight Eisenhower, Manion continued his public breach with the Democratic Party and filmed a Democrats-for-Eisenhower commercial. Never an Eisenhower enthusiast, he instead took the opportunity to attack Democratic candidate Adlai Stevenson. In phrasing that recalled his campaign speeches against Herbert Hoover twenty years earlier, he said, "In this campaign we are promised, both by the Democratic record and the Democratic candidate, not the limitation of governmental power, but the indefinite expansion and continued concentration of that power." The consequences of supporting such a platform, Manion warned, were dire indeed. "We are told we can defeat this despotism in Moscow only by establishing despotism in Washington. Consciously or unconsciously, we are thus attempting to defeat Communism abroad by surrendering to it at home."[47]

Manion's support bore fruit when Eisenhower won the election. As a sop to Taft supporters, Eisenhower appointed Manion chairman of the Commission on Intergovernmental Relations, considered at the time to be one of "the most important Eisenhower commissions." He approached the position with unbridled zeal, believing he'd been given the task "to restore the constitutional authority of the states." Framing the committee as a critical tool for limited government was his first priority as chairman.

He claimed "widespread, if not unanimous support" among commission members—largely conservative Republicans and Dixiecrats—for devolving federal power to the states. And he had support from outside the commission as well. J. Howard Pew, the former head of Sun Oil, applauded Manion's goals for the CIR. "You will have many heartaches," he told Manion, "and, of course, you will not accomplish many of the things which you hope for; but you will plant many seeds of a sound philosophy, which will some day help to bring to fruition your ideology."[48]

With such encouragements, what happened next was perhaps inevitable. With the spotlight trained on him—with his name appearing in high-profile publications like the *New York Times* and *New Republic*—Manion wanted to use his platform to do more than attack the federal bureaucracy. He wanted to promote his pet initiative: the Bricker Amendment. The Bricker Amendment applied a Tenth Amendment philosophy to foreign relations. Sponsored by Taft's fellow Ohio senator, John Bricker, the amendment proposed that no treaty or executive agreement that could be interpreted as contradicting or altering the Constitution could be signed without ratification by the states. It was meant to counter agreements like the U.N. Convention of the Prevention and Punishment of the Crime of Genocide. Bricker supporters argued the treaty, which outlawed acts that caused "serious . . . mental harm to members of [a national, ethnic, racial, or religious] group," impinged upon freedom of speech and thus altered the Constitution. By requiring states to ratify treaties, the Bricker Amendment would ensure that such end runs could not happen, making it a powerful statement against both executive-power creep and U.S. involvement in the United Nations.[49]

When Bricker first floated the bill, Eisenhower brushed it off as "silly." As it began to attract more attention and support from nationalists on the right, he came out publicly against the amendment, arguing that in waging the Cold War, the president needed some leeway on the international stage. Manion stepped up his campaign for the amendment at the same time Eisenhower's frustration with Bricker backers was intensifying. Manion promoted the amendment on Paul Harvey's national radio program and in speeches across the country. By February 1954 he had spoken in support of the amendment in all forty-eight states. That was enough for Eisenhower. After two weeks of resignation leaks in the press, and with Manion showing no intention of departing, Eisenhower requested his resignation.[50]

Booted from the Eisenhower administration, Manion was ready to wash his hands of the two major parties. They'd failed to keep the country out of war, failed to roll back the New Deal, failed to take an aggressive stance against communism. And mainstream politicians weren't the only ones Manion was ready to take on. Recalling his resignation fifteen years later, Manion detailed the forces aligning against him in the fight over the Bricker Amendment. He mentioned neither Eisenhower nor Ike's chief of staff, Sherman Adams, the two men who eventually asked Manion to resign. He instead focused on others: James Reston, Marquis Childs, Joseph and Stewart Alsop. These newspaper commentators—whom he referred to in his resignation letter as "certain left-wing columnists"—worked as a united front according to Manion, acting "on signal" to take him down for daring to defend conservative policy. Everywhere he looked, the media—newspapers, network radio and television news, magazines, and journals—all seemed locked in a liberal consensus. This, he decided, was a far greater barrier to conservative governance than the bipartisan blackout. If conservatives were going to claw their way back in from the outside, they were going to need to first find a way to impair and offset liberals in the media.[51]

The last holdout in mainstream politics was Bill Rusher. No doubt his longevity in mainstream politics came from his love of the political game. He was a party man through and through, a Republican from the start, and rather late to life as an ideologue. Anti-interventionism had no place in his northeastern Republicanism, so World War II proved no problem for him. A student at Princeton when the United States entered the war, he backed Willkie in 1940 like the vast majority of his fellow undergraduates. Indeed, if he was an outsider in his opinion on the war, it was because he was *too* keen on intervention, outstripping both Willkie and Roosevelt in his eagerness to join the fight. (His future colleague at *National Review*, Bill Buckley, two years younger than Rusher and still in high school, spent the prewar years printing up anti-interventionist newspapers with his siblings to hand out to neighbors. William F. Buckley Sr. was a member of America First.) Unable to fight because of poor eyesight, Rusher spent the war in Air Force administration in India.[52]

If Rusher was out of step with the anti-interventionism of many future conservative media activists, he was even more so in his advocacy of progressivism. In his 1943 senior thesis, "The Progressive Element in the Republican Party from 1936 to the Present," Rusher recommended the GOP adopt a more liberal set of policies. His was a pragmatic concern: the electorate was more progressive, so Republicans had to be as well if they had any hope of winning elections. His penchant for politics found an outlet in the

Young Republicans, where he not only learned the art of politicking but also imbibed a touch of pragmatism—or if not pragmatism, an understanding of how central a role the art of the possible played in partisan politics (as well as how much personal grudges, pettiness, and shortcomings shaped outcomes). He teamed up with two other Young Republicans, Charles McWhorter and F. Clifton White. They were all behind-the-scenes men, organizers rather than politicians. They knew how to fight, and fight they did.[53]

Only . . . what was it Rusher was fighting for? In the 1940s, his main political identity was Republican. Progressive Republican, if his senior thesis was any indication. For Rusher, it was neither the war nor national sovereignty that sparked his move to the outskirts of mainstream politics. It was communism. When Whittaker Chambers published *Witness* (1952), his memoir of life as a communist-turned-anticommunist, Rusher inhaled the eight-hundred-page tome. It gave Rusher a philosophical framework for the fight against communism. Philosophical frameworks weren't something Rusher had really ever had. He claimed "no coherent world view and no religious beliefs." The Republican Party was the repository of his passions, the thing he believed in. And in 1952, it took precedence over Chambers. As Taft and Eisenhower clashed, Rusher threw his weight behind Ike, the popular general who seemed destined to break the Democrats' twenty-year hold on the presidency.[54]

In 1953, with the election won and Eisenhower safely in office, Rusher turned his attention back to communism. His friend Robert Morris was working for the Senate Internal Security Subcommittee and constantly attempting to lure Rusher from his job at a Wall Street firm to join him. Rusher wasn't ready to give up his job just yet—junior associates couldn't take long leaves of absence—but between *Witness* and Morris, Rusher had converted to a hard-edged anticommunism that held internal subversion out as the greatest threat to America in those early Cold War years. It was that militant anticommunism that also led him, in 1954, to break with Eisenhower, who had until then been Rusher's white knight, the salvation of the Republican Party.

The issue was Joe McCarthy. The Wisconsin senator had spent the first few years of the 1950s aggressively seeking subversives in the federal government. Rusher saw the liberals line up against McCarthy, saw the press begin to take aim. In that atmosphere, he believed Eisenhower should have been the leading edge of McCarthy support rather than a participant in his downfall. Frustrated by Ike's anti-McCarthyism, Rusher took matters into his own hands, moving to Washington to serve as associate counsel of the Senate subcommittee. He had made a transformation. Though still a Republican, he identified now as a conservative. And pragmatism—the pragmatism that until then had chosen a Wall Street job over red-hunting in Washington, that chose Eisenhower over Taft—had given way to idealism. Debating the importance of electability with Rusher, Paul Lockwood, a former Dewey aide, held that since a person must first get elected in order to have any influence on policy, electability was the primary consideration for a candidate. Rusher strongly disagreed, arguing, in one spectator's recollection, "that politicians without principles were at best technicians and at worst susceptible to unprincipled positions if not corrupt temptations."[55]

Given this newfound ideological fervor, Rusher grew less and less interested in partisan politics. He still liked the machinations, and he would stay active in Young Republican circles in order to help pull that organization to the right, but national two-party politics was becoming corrosively unappealing. He even moved his voter registration to Washington, D.C., which at the time had no electoral votes, effectively disenfranchising himself from presidential elections. Politics, he had concluded, could "never really do what needed to be done." What was needed was something more revolutionary than quadrennial trips to the ballot box, more fundamental than writing laws and enacting policy. To topple the insiders, one had to stop being an insider. So Rusher, like Manion and Regnery, opted to become an outsider. Having started writing on politics and ideology, and having met a rakish young right-winger with a puckish little journal of opinion, he decided to quit the Senate subcommittee and Washington and move back to New York.[56]

Time to take up the battle of ideas.

Chapter 2

The Outlets

Henry Regnery flipped through his notes a final time as he waited for the rest of the group to arrive. In a few minutes Room 2233 in New York City's Lincoln Building would be packed with some of the brightest lights of the conservative movement, gathered together at his request. Writers, publishers, and editors made up most of the guest list, including William F. Buckley Jr., the enfant terrible of the right; Frank Hanighen, cofounder of *Human Events*; Raymond Moley, *Newsweek* columnist and author of the anti–New Deal book *After Seven Years* (1939); and John Chamberlain, former editor of the *Freeman* and an editorial writer for the *Wall Street Journal*.

When everyone was settled, Regnery explained why he had called the meeting. As 1953 came to a close, he observed, the men in Room 2233 were unquestionably on the losing side of politics. And that puzzled him. "The side we represent controls most of the wealth in this country," he told those gathered. "The ideas and traditions we believe in are those which most Americans instinctively believe in also." Why then was liberalism ascendant and conservatism relegated to the fringes? Because, Regnery argued, the left controlled institutions: the media, the universities, the foreign policy establishment. Until the right had a "counterintelligence unit" that could fight back, conservatives would remain a group of elites raging against a system that by all rights they should control.[1]

Regnery had rehearsed these arguments several months earlier when he described the upcoming meeting to Robert E. Wood, the driving force behind the America First Committee and *Human Events*. He explained to Wood that the upcoming meeting was an "attempt to coordinate the large number of people who are on our side, but whose effectiveness is limited by isolation and lack of communication." Isolation and lack of communication—formidable obstacles, to be sure, but not insurmountable ones. For while Regnery believed liberals manipulated public opinion, he also believed conservatives could do the same by eroding public faith in the mainstream press and providing their own alternatives. That belief propelled Regnery and his fellow media activists into action. Convinced that media were key to shaping public opinion and that public opinion was key to political power, they launched a number of new media outlets to overcome both liberal dominance and conservative isolation.[2]

As the meeting in Room 2233 suggests, from the start conservative media activism was a group effort. It emerged as a shared intellectual and political response to the new postwar world. The activists involved forged close (and often contentious) personal and professional relationships. Their ventures, which included *Human Events*, Regnery Publishing, the *Manion Forum*, and *National Review*, among many others, drew from the same pool of supporters and benefactors. The social and institutional networks they created thus set them apart from conservatives involved in media in earlier eras. Only with the creation of this postwar network did the concept of "conservative media" take its modern form.

The springboard for all this activism was the America First Committee, convened more than a decade before the meeting in Room 2233. Though the nonintervention movement collapsed when the nation went to war in 1941, its most conservative set of donors and organizers endured. Even before the war ended, they were looking for ways to push back against the emerging consensus that the twentieth century must be Henry Luce's "American Century," with the United States deeply involved in world affairs and international institutions. Concerned that foreign policy was veering off course as the war wound to an end, the men behind America First came together again to support a four-page foreign policy weekly.

And so, in a small apartment in Washington, postwar conservative media got its start.

To hear Felix Morley tell it, *Human Events* began with an article he wrote in 1942 for the *Saturday Evening Post*. Titled "For What Are We Fighting?" the provocative piece reflected a skeptical stance toward American involvement in World War II, one rarely seen post–Pearl Harbor.[3] But this was not merely Morley being a contrarian—he wrote from a stance of principled opposition to the war. An experienced journalist and Rhodes scholar, in 1933 Morley became editor of the *Washington Post*. From his perch at the *Post* he regularly skewered the Roosevelt administration in sharp-quilled editorials that won him the Pulitzer Prize in 1936.

Not exactly the profile of a political outsider.

Morley's eventual exile, to the extent that it existed, was self-imposed. In 1940 he resigned from the *Post* to become president of Haverford College, a Quaker school just outside Philadelphia. Haverford was in his blood: it was where his father taught mathematics, where Morley received his undergraduate degree, and where Morley and his two brothers were born, right on campus. The family's ties to Haverford were a reflection of how central the Quaker faith was to Morley's life. The pacifist tradition of the American Friends reinforced his belief before Pearl Harbor that the United States must stay out of the war and his belief after that the postwar world must be arranged to prevent future conflicts.[4]

The *Saturday Evening Post* article caught the eye of Frank Hanighen, a fellow Haverford graduate with solid nonintervention credentials of his own. In 1934 Hanighen coauthored with H. C. Engelbrecht *Merchants of Death*. An exposé of the armament industry, *Merchants of Death* became a best seller and a favorite in antiwar circles. Hanighen, a foreign correspondent for a number of newspapers including the *New York Times*, had been active in America First before heading to Europe to cover the war for *Reader's Digest*. When he came across Morley's article in 1942, he knew he had found a kindred spirit. While he appreciated Morley's continued opposition to the war, he was even more impressed with the plan for the postwar world that Morley described in the article. Back in the United States a year later, Hanighen headed to Haverford with a scheme to convince Morley to use his plan for the postwar world as the basis for a new publication.[5]

Morley needed little convincing. His skeptical stance on the war opened him to accusations of isolationism, a damaging epithet in the 1940s. It particularly irked Morley, whose politics hardly fit the isolationist mold. In the late 1920s he had served as director of the Geneva offices of the U.S. League of Nations Association, later writing a favorable study of the League called *The Society of Nations* (1932). Yet those credentials had not spared him accusations of isolationism. Which is why Hanighen's proposal intrigued him so: a newsletter focused on the postwar world could illustrate that pacifism was not simply an oppositional philosophy but one that could advance a positive plan for the future.

Inspired, Morley began working his connections with journalists and professors. Among these was William Henry Chamberlin. Chamberlin, also a graduate of Haverford, had marinated in the radicalism of Greenwich Village before alighting to the Soviet Union in 1922 as the foreign correspondent for the *Christian Science Monitor*. He arrived in Moscow an ardent advocate of communism. But as he observed the subjugation and violence upon which the Soviet government relied, Chamberlin changed. "Enthusiastic hope gave way first to detached disillusionment," he wrote, "and finally horrified repulsion." The god that had failed so many others failed Chamberlin as well.[6]

Their engagement in foreign policy debates and their broad experience as journalists made Morley, Hanighen, and Chamberlin ideally suited to launch a publication on world affairs. Their shared anti-interventionist stance and wariness toward communism ensured that publication would have a strong point of view. That point of view would not yet be called "conservatism"—"Americanism" was a more common term, a holdover from the days of nonintervention; "conservatism" would become more common in the mid-1950s—but in time *Human Events* would emerge as one of the leading sites of conservative media activism.

Human Events did not look like much when it launched in February 1944. A four-page essay by Chamberlin comprised the entire first issue, sent to 127 subscribers from the newsletter's headquarters (a.k.a. Frank Hanighen's D.C. apartment). The funds and subscriptions had been wrung from a handful of donors, most of whom had gathered in Chicago in early 1944 at Hanighen's invitation. Hosted by former AFC president Robert E. Wood, the meeting was a veritable reunion of America Firsters: Charles Lindbergh, Colonel McCormick, Sterling Morton, William H. Regnery. Their network, disbanded by the war, re-formed around *Human Events*.[7]

Though Hanighen and Morley were considered the founders of *Human Events*, Chamberlin joined them in signing a "Statement of Policy" a month after the publication of the first issue. The statement, largely written by Morley, laid out the purpose of *Human Events*. The philosophy he outlined was one of libertarian Americanism, rooted, as the newsweekly's name suggested, in the principles of the Declaration of Independence. The statement promised analysis "undertaken primarily from the viewpoint of the essential American tradition" and in defense of the "development of Man as an individual." In the field of international affairs, this meant a wholesale opposition to both communism and imperialism.[8]

While dedicated to foreign policy, *Human Events'* founders did not overlook the domestic scene. Indeed, their statement of policy warned that the postwar threat to American ideals was "more insidious because it comes to a large extent from within." Morley, who had once called promoters of a postwar alliance with Britain "Anglo-American Nazis," now pointed to "a domestic counterpart of National Socialism" that was "already affecting the freedom of the individual and the vitality of local self-government." Provocative language for a publication that also promised it would "never be classifiable as vindictive, misleading or deliberately propagandistic."[9]

In addition to expressing a philosophy of politics, the statement of policy also contained a critique of American journalism. In the 1940s, the founders of *Human Events* were less concerned with the liberalism of the media than with the blackout of their nonconformist ideas. They believed mainstream American journalists were shutting out alternative points of view, that they were "coloring, slanting, selecting and editing the news" in order to tamp down any criticisms of the war. Morley argued that in trumpeting the official line doled out by government agencies, journalists had played a role in the "subtle regimentation of public opinion." Never one to shy away from a Nazi comparison, he added, "While we have not yet carried these practices as far as did the unlamented Dr. Goebbels, the general direction of governmental propaganda has paid that Nazi leader the sincerest form of flattery."[10]

Dedication to "the reporting of facts that other newspapers overlook" thus inspired the founders of *Human Events*. But while touting this fact-based approach, they also promoted a distinct point of view. By the early 1960s, *Human Events* arrived at this articulation of its mission: "In reporting the news, *Human Events* is objective; it aims for accurate representation of the facts. But it is *not* impartial. It looks at events through the eyes that are biased in favor of limited constitutional government, local self-government, private enterprise, and individual freedom." Distinguishing between objectivity and impartiality, the editors of *Human Events* created a space where "bias" was an appropriate journalistic value.

The tension between those two ideas—between objectivity and ideology—would become a defining feature of conservative media, one evident fifty years later in Fox News's slogan "Fair and Balanced." On the one hand, the editors of *Human Events* insisted their work was objective. They understood the cultural and political power of objectivity and were unwilling to relinquish all claims to it. Yet theirs was also an ideological publication, dedicated to the propagation of conservative ideas. That contradiction was resolved—to the extent it was resolved—in two ways. *Human Events* pledged to report, in a factual way, the stories and angles other media missed because of their liberal biases. In such news stories selection, not content, would be biased. (*Human Events* also ran conservative columnists, opinion pieces, and analyses that made no pretense at content neutrality.) The editors also believed their ideological worldview was correct, and so believed they did not need to sacrifice accuracy in order to be ideologically consistent. In other words, there was no contradiction to resolve.

The editors of *Human Events* worked out this logic over the course of the 1950s. But Morley would not be there to help. By 1950, he had severed his ties with the publication he helped found.[11]

Change in the structure of *Human Events* happened first behind the scenes. Hanighen and Morley shared editorial responsibilities, with Hanighen taking the lion's share of the work until Morley stepped down as president of Haverford in 1945. Hanighen wrote and edited "Not Merely Gossip," which began as a mimeographed one-page supplement of news items and brief analysis. By the end of the first year it expanded to two pages, then to four, adding a newsy air to the analytical essay. Those weekly essays were Morley's turf. He edited and often wrote them, occasionally inviting contributors like former America Firsters Norman Thomas, a perennial Socialist Party candidate, and Oswald Garrison Villard, who resigned his editorship of the *Nation* over its support for intervention. The eclecticism of these contributors' politics reflected the publication's still-unsettled political identity at a time when modern conservatism had not yet fully solidified.[12]

As journalists, Hanighen and Morley had a handle on the editorial side of the venture. But the practical side of the business, from production to promotion to circulation, was beyond their ken. So they turned to a young man with a keen interest in publishing and strong ties to the noninterventionist community: Henry Regnery. Regnery came aboard with a vision of expanding *Human Events'* readership and production. He wanted to apply modern promotional techniques to boost circulation, while at the same time offering a broader range of products: reprints, pamphlets, perhaps even some books. He tackled the business end of the publication from his perch in Chicago, while Hanighen and Morley collaborated on editorial content in a new office in Washington. With a broader vision in mind, the three men incorporated *Human Events* in 1945. They split shares equally, a move that Morley would come to regret. But at the time, Hanighen's labor and Regnery's limitless funds made an even split seem like the logical arrangement.[13]

Tensions grew as the venture expanded. Regnery had some suc-

Figure 3. Henry Regnery at the
LaSalle Hotel, Chicago, October
3, 1964. Hoover Institution.
Abernathy Photo Company.

cess with his pamphlets, which included University of Chicago president
Robert Maynard Hutchins writing such essays as "The New Realism" and
"The Atomic Bomb Versus Civilization." He also published Karl Brandt's
"Germany Is Our Problem," the Stanford professor's response to Henry
Morgenthau's book of the same name. The modest success of these revision-
ist pieces, which pleaded for a more lenient peace with Germany, spawned
a monthly pamphlet series edited by Regnery and Morley.[14]

   In taking full responsibility for producing and financing the series,
Regnery found his calling. He dove in, removing himself from his family's textile business and setting up shop in an office south of the Loop. In
September 1946, he incorporated an affiliated nonprofit, Human Events
Associates, to handle the business side of the pamphlets. As he set up a
staff, he also forged ties with Frank Chodorov, publisher of a four-page
broadsheet called *analysis* that appeared every month or so—regularity was
not Chodorov's strong suit—from a shabby office near the Brooklyn Bridge.
analysis launched the same year as *Human Events* and attracted a similarly
small number of subscribers (between two and four thousand). Chodorov
also shared a similar history of antiwar activism, having lost his position at
the Henry George School of Social Science in New York in 1942 because

he continued to speak out against the war after Pearl Harbor. Regnery considered Chodorov "a born pamphleteer" and turned to him for promotional copy as well as pamphlets opposing the income tax. While his affection for Chodorov waned over time—Regnery would soon dismiss him as an "anarchist" and an "old bore"—the partnership was productive. In 1951, *Human Events* absorbed *analysis*, and Chodorov became an associate editor before joining the *Freeman* and *National Review* in the mid-1950s.[15]

Because of the staff and organizational structure required for the pamphlets, the editors decided to economize by moving the printing, mailing, and promotion of *Human Events* to Regnery's Chicago office. Regnery sought to bring more promotional verve to the newsweekly but met resistance from Hanighen and Morley. By 1946 *Human Events* had grown from its initial circulation of 127 to around 4,000 (about half of which were individual paid subscriptions). That increase, however, did not translate into profits, as the company ran a deficit of some $10,000 a year. Regnery pushed for punchy promotional letters to reel in new donations and subscriptions. But it was not to be. A publication like *Human Events*, Morley declared, would not stoop to anything so lowbrow as advertising. He insisted on editorial review of promotions to ensure they met the publication's exacting standards.[16]

The debate over promotional content revealed a much deeper division over the purpose of *Human Events*. In making his case, Regnery hurled a broader charge: that the editors feared gaining too many readers, lest *Human Events* be degraded by its popular appeal. "We have nothing to fear from 'mass' circulation," Regnery contended. "The only thing we have to fear is that the desire to obtain 'mass' circulation might have a bad effect on editorial content. In our case there is no danger of this, I am convinced." In Morley and Hanighen the publication had rigorous gatekeepers. The danger, Regnery argued, lay in the other direction. If the editors resisted efforts to increase circulation, *Human Events* was destined to end up like Albert Jay Nock's short-lived *Freeman*, an anti-intervention, libertarian magazine published in the 1920s that remained an inspiration to conservatives in the postwar era: respected among the Remnant but unlikely to last long enough to have a transformative effect on society.[17]

Hanighen and Morley disagreed. Morley conceded public opinion had a role to play in publishing. When subscribers kept canceling because they believed *Human Events* was too sympathetic toward Germany, the editors took greater care with their phrasing to ward off that criticism. Even in these early days, subscriber feedback and the associated economic considerations could influence content. But on the whole, Morley dismissed the idea of "catering to the mass opinion of ill-informed persons." "We did not start this enterprise for that purpose," Morley wrote Regnery, "and personally I would rather see it fail than to compromise our basic position." Hanighen put forward a separate theory of how media functioned, contending that publications like *Human Events* succeeded by "affecting public opinion indirectly." That is, they were read by a small number of elite opinion makers, who then circulated the ideas to the masses through policy, popular media, and public stances. "We do not 'fear mass circulation,'" Hanighen replied to Regnery with an edge of disdain. "We are simply not interested in mass circulation."[18]

The strained relationship between Regnery and the editors was exacerbated by Regnery's growing interest in book publishing and by the distance between D.C. and Chicago. After publishing a compilation of *Human Events* essays, Regnery organized publication of *Blueprint for World Conquest* (1946), a collection of documents from the Communist International, which had an initial run of five thousand copies. The success of these ventures spurred Regnery on, and in early 1947 he proposed a series of hardcover books "representing the best in contemporary thinking from all nations."[19]

The expansive nature of Regnery's interests worried the editors, who felt the Chicago office slipping from their control. They first asked to transfer all operations associated with the newsweekly back to Washington. They next insisted on preapproving everything Regnery published. After all, since he published under the *Human Events* name, his books would affect the reputation of the newsletter. "With that same distinctive name," Morley explained, "the effects of what is said cannot be divided." When Regnery pushed back, noting he had no advance notice of the contents of *Human Events*, Morley shrugged him off. Regnery was hired to deal with business, not content, and couldn't match Morley's and Hanighen's years of experience.

It was a clarifying moment for Regnery. After meeting in Indianapolis in the spring of 1947, he and the editors agreed to sever the book and pamphlet publication from the newsletter. The newsletter remained the domain of Human Events, Inc., and the publishing enterprise was allowed to briefly operate under the banner of Human Events Associates. Regnery retained his position as a director within Human Events, Inc., but would have to drop "Human Events" from the name of his new company. Thus in late 1947, Regnery Publishing was born, joining Devin-Adair and Caxton Printers in the tiny world of conservative publishing houses.[20]

The first few years of publishing were difficult. Regnery knew it would not be easy, focused as he was on issuing books that cut against "the reigning intellectual orthodoxy." As if to prove his oppositional chops, Regnery launched his operation with three revisionist works on Germany: Victor Gollancz's *Our Threatened Values* (1946) and *In Darkest Germany* (1947), and a translation of Max Picard's *Hitler in Our Selves* (1947). The books, which were critical of the Allied treatment of Germany and the postwar order, did not sell, but Regnery didn't mind. In a way, he was following Hanighen's model of indirect influence: read by the right people, books could have an impact far greater than their sales figures.[21]

Regnery established his press as a nonprofit, modeled after university presses. He made the decision, he later wrote, "not because I had any ideological objection to profits, but because, as it seemed to me then and does still, in matters of excellence the market is a poor judge. The books that are most needed are often precisely those that will have only a modest sale." Markets could tell what people liked but not what they needed. It was a much different philosophy than "the marketplace of ideas," which presumed that in an unrestricted system, the worthiness of ideas could be assessed by the number of adherents they attracted. As unprofitable as most early conservative media ventures were, Regnery's was a shared faith, though in tension with the free-market ideology to which most on the right adhered.[22]

Regnery may have believed he was operating as a nonprofit (and there were, to be sure, no profits to be found on his company's balance sheets), but the IRS disagreed. As publishers welcomed profits even if they did not always find them, the agency ruled Regnery Publishing was not entitled to tax-exempt status. In March 1948 the company was again reorganized, and Henry Regnery Company began its corporate existence in earnest.

The IRS had determined that the publishing house was not a nonprofit, "but that was not of much help in finding a way to operate profitably," Regnery noted ruefully. Mortimer Smith's *And Madly Teach* (1949), a "primer for parents" that denounced modern education philosophy for its lack of rigor and its emphasis on "collective virtues and collective ideals," was the best-selling book Regnery published in his first few years in business. It received a favorable write-up in *Time*, which immediately boosted sales, and went through several editions. While Regnery felt lasting gratitude toward Smith—"it was his book that really got me started," he wrote a friend—occasional modest successes would not keep the company afloat. For that, Regnery needed a more profit-oriented venture, a money-spinner to fund the publication of books that advanced his political and moral beliefs.[23]

For a brief time he found a way to satisfy both his political and pecuni-
ary interests with a contract from the Great Books series. The brainchild of
Robert Hutchins, the wunderkind president of the University of Chicago
(a post he assumed at age thirty), the Great Books series was established
as a sort of greatest hits of western civilization. It included works like
Plato's *Republic*, St. Augustine's *Confessions*, René Descartes's *Discourse
on Methods*, David Hume's *Enquiry Concerning Human Understanding*,
and John Stuart Mill's *Utilitarianism*. When the University of Chicago Press
passed on publishing it, Hutchins turned to Regnery. Regnery believed the
series could provide the core of his backlist, the steady sellers publishing
houses rely on for their baseline income. So he took on the project, operating
at a loss the first two years before beginning to make a profit on the series.
Yet no sooner had he begun to see returns on his investment than he made
a publishing decision that cost him his Great Books contract—and launched
the career of one of the right's brightest stars.[24]

Henry Regnery was not William F. Buckley Jr.'s first choice.
Buckley, along with his father, William F. Buckley Sr., had arranged a
lunch with Devin Garrity, the tall, bushy-browed publisher who took over
Devin-Adair Company from his father in 1939. With a strong backlist of
books on Ireland and on ecology, Garrity had the resources to publish
books that reflected his conservative politics, regardless of their profitability.
Like Regnery, Garrity kicked off his conservative publishing in the post-
war era with revisionist histories of the war, most notably George Edward
Morgenstern's *Pearl Harbor: The Story of the Secret War* (1947). He
attracted big-name authors, publishing a bevy of books by John Flynn, a New
Deal critic, cofounder of America First, and strident anticommunist. Garrity
also worked with Senator Joseph McCarthy on his 1951 and 1952 books,
America's Retreat from Victory and *McCarthyism, the Fight for America*.[25]
As the most well-connected conservative publisher, Garrity was naturally the first choice for Bill Buckley—and Buckley was used to getting
what he wanted. Son of a wealthy oilman, he was unusually eloquent and
quick-witted. He was also a bit of an outsider in Connecticut, where the
Buckley family made its home. The Buckley siblings, ten in all, were "politically combative," according to Buckley biographer John Judis, reflecting
the conservative convictions of their father. In 1939 they started their own
newspaper, *The Spectator*, to spread their support for U.S. neutrality. One
of Bill's sisters recalled weekly country club dances as sites of combat rather

than courtship: "Instead of everyone dancing to Frank Sinatra records, you'd find us in every corner surrounded by controversy because we were the only conservatives and America Firsters." Buckley established himself as a devoted contrarian during his undergraduate career at Yale. Whether sparring on the university's debate team alongside future brother-in-law Brent Bozell or sparking controversy as editor of the prestigious *Yale Daily News*, Buckley left a lasting impression on the university.[26]

And the university left a lasting impression on him. By his senior year Buckley had grown sharply critical of the institution's values. He first laid out his critique in a series of editorials urging Yale to advocate "free enterprise" rather than nurturing relativism and collectivism. He intended to extend that critique in an Alumni Day Speech in which he denounced Yale's devotion to the "laissez-faire theory of education," his term for the marketplace-of-ideas approach that held that "in the 'arena of public and conflicting opinion' . . . may the best thought, the best idea, the best concept win." Buckley, though a fan of the marketplace, believed it was a poor measure of the quality of ideas—an unsurprising stance given the minority status of many of his political beliefs in midcentury America. When the administration got wind of the speech, they pressed Buckley to rewrite it. He offered to step down instead, a proposal the university quickly accepted.[27]

Vexed by their acceptance—Buckley had assumed that on such short notice Yale would be forced to keep him on the program—he spent the year after his graduation teaching Spanish at Yale in the mornings and writing a book about the university in the afternoons. Having heard nothing from Garrity after their lunch, a silence Buckley took as a lack of interest, he approached Regnery with the finished manuscript in the spring of 1951. Regnery passed it along to Bill Strube, one of his sales and promotions associates, who responded with an enthusiastic evaluation. "I am tremendously impressed," he wrote, marveling at "the 'promise' of a vigorous young mind who might well develop into a writer and thinker of major stature."[28]

Regnery agreed. He offered to publish the book but warned Buckley, who was eager to take advantage of promotional opportunities presented by Yale's 250th anniversary in the fall of 1951, that the small publishing house couldn't do so quickly enough to meet that deadline. At least, not without some help. So Buckley, with financial assistance from his father, advanced Regnery $3,000 to speed publication. The Buckleys poured more money into promotion and production costs, contributing a total of $19,000 to the publication of *God and Man at Yale*. The mix of resources necessary to publish the book was an early model for conservative publishing, which would often rely on upfront sales or funds from the author before moving forward with publication. Right-wing books served a small, diffuse, niche audience; breaking even on a book (much less turning a profit) was no sure thing, and publishers seldom had the pockets or the penchant for taking risks on unproven authors.[29]

Buckley, however, quickly proved himself. The book made a splash not only at the Yale bookstore, where customers queued up early the day the book went on sale, but in bookstores throughout the Northeast. In the first six months, *God and Man at Yale* sold over 35,000 copies, landing it as high as #16 on the *New York Times* best-seller list. Yale's administration unwittingly boosted sales by lining up McGeorge Bundy to review the book for the *Atlantic*. As Buckley biographer John Judis revealed, a member of the Yale administration assured trustees, "We intend to take the offensive in this matter and not sit by waiting for complaints to roll in when the book is published." Bundy, a Harvard professor and Yale alumnus, was up to the task, admitting he experienced a "kind of savage pleasure" in writing the review.

That "savage pleasure" was evident in the published review. Bundy opened by calling the book "dishonest in its use of facts, false in its theory, and a discredit to its author." From there the review lurched from point-by-point rebuttals of Buckley's thesis to personal contempt for Buckley himself. (At one point Bundy called Buckley "a twisted and ignorant young man" with "views of a peculiar and extreme variety.") Nor was Bundy alone in his invectives. The book triggered such controversy that the *Saturday Review* published dual reviews, one a respectful disagreement, the other a full-throated denunciation. The latter, by Frank D. Ashburn, began by assuring readers Buckley "seems certain to have a profitably polemic future" and closed by comparing him to Stalin, Goebbels, and Torquemada. "The book is one which has the glow and appeal of a fiery cross on a hillside at night," Ashburn concluded. "There will undoubtedly be robed figures who gather to it, but the hoods will not be academic. They will cover the face."[30]

For Buckley and Regnery, such responses proved their point. Buckley had attacked the institutional orthodoxies of Yale and found himself impugned for daring to question them. Not that Buckley was opposed to orthodoxies; he just felt Yale should adopt different ones: namely, free-market economics and Christianity. For Regnery the reviewer response was doubly instructive. It not only demonstrated the bias in book reviewing, dominated as it was by East Coast reviewers, but also confirmed the need for right-wing publishing.

The book landed on the best-seller list despite the forces arrayed against it; surely that was evidence of the audience he was determined to cultivate.

So impressed with Buckley (and his sales) was Regnery that he immediately commissioned him for a second book. This time, Buckley teamed up with his old debate partner Brent Bozell to pen a defense of Joseph McCarthy. Again, his timing was spot-on. Published in early 1954, *McCarthy and His Enemies* hit shelves as the nation was absorbed by the McCarthy-Army hearings. The book landed Buckley and Bozell in the headlines and boosted sales for the Regnery Company. Ashburn's predictions of Buckley's "profitably polemic future" seemed to be coming into full flower.[31]

But Buckley had his sights set higher than the world of books. Like many others in the field of conservative ideas, he recognized the need for a right-wing journal of opinion. Conservative journals existed, of course, but each had its flaws. *American Mercury* had shown promise when William Bradford Huie bought it in 1950, turning it into a conservative journal with some fifty thousand readers. Writers like Buckley, Max Eastman, and James Burnham sharpened their quills there in the early 1950s. But in 1952 it fell into the hands of an anti-Semitic editor, driving away its more respectable contributors. Other journals like the *Freeman* (an attempt to resuscitate Albert Nock's work) and *analysis* served only narrow interests and tiny readerships. Buckley had written for several of those magazines but ultimately found them unsatisfying. As had other conservative leaders: John Chamberlain, who had been a journalism professor at Columbia and an editor at *Time* before leaving liberalism behind and joining the *Freeman* and the *Wall Street Journal*, argued in *Human Events* that the right needed more "supporting media." Regnery regularly lamented the "means of communication in this country are pretty well controlled by the left" and worked to promote Russell Kirk's proposal for a new journal that would "abjure the cant of yesterday's 'liberal' and 'humanitarian' and 'progressive' cliques." Conservative media outlets may have grown in the 1940s and early 1950s, but clearly they were not yet meeting the right's perceived needs.[32]

Buckley was committed to filling those needs. Committed and well-placed: he proved his editorial skills and ideological chops at the *Yale Daily News* and his nose for controversy with *God and Man at Yale*, and tapped into a world of financial and institutional support through his father and Henry Regnery. Others saw this potential as well. Regnery and Russell Kirk had been toying with the idea of a monthly magazine, possibly a redesign of the *Freeman*, which was in dire financial straits. In casting about for personnel, they kept coming back to Buckley. At the end of his reader report on *God and Man*, Bill Strube noted to Regnery: "I would also like to add that when and if we are prepared to go ahead with a magazine, Mr. Buckley should definitely be considered as a strong candidate for editor. He seems to me to be first-rate."[33]

Buckley, though, had his eye on a magazine of his own. According to Willi Schlamm, an Austrian refugee who worked alongside Henry Luce for several years in the 1940s, the idea originated in 1952, after Schlamm left *Fortune* and started editing the *Freeman*. Impressed with Buckley, Schlamm floated the idea of founding a new conservative journal. Buckley was intrigued by the suggestion. He grew even more interested in 1953, when the *Freeman* collapsed as a result of editorial differences and was refashioned into a monthly libertarian journal under Leonard Read and Frank Chodorov. Rounding up the *Freeman's* cast-offs, Buckley ventured forth.[34]

To raise money for the project, Buckley circulated a fifteen-page staple-bound memorandum, "Re: A New Magazine." There he laid out his plans, from the journal's ideological goals to its format to its organizational structure. *National Weekly*, as the magazine was tentatively titled, would "forthrightly oppose the prevailing trend of public opinion." But it would not be merely a voice of opposition wailing jeremiads from the wilderness: "Its purpose, indeed, is to *change* the nation's intellectual and political climate." Such a purpose contained an optimistic faith in the power of media to remake, rather than just reflect, public opinion.[35]

In the magazine's statement of intentions, Buckley not only laid out *National Weekly's* political perspective but further developed his view of American media and its effect on politics. Both sets of ideas were rooted in a disdain bordering on disgust with the general political consensus that dominated party politics and the press. "Middle-of-the-road, *qua* Middle of the Road, is politically, intellectually, and morally repugnant," the statement began. The press in particular drew Buckley's disdain for sustaining this morally malignant middle-of-the-roadism. In introducing his project, he acknowledged that *National Weekly* would enter the world as "a minority voice." Yet he ascribed the minority status of conservative politics to the willful practices of liberal media. "America's 'respectable' press has ordained that such voices as ours are of the past, and are not worth serious attention. But," he rallied, "events in the very recent past positively establish that there is a widening gulf between the 'respectable' press and the American people, that they look upon each other, increasingly, as strangers." Enter *National Weekly*, a pugnacious journal of conservative opinion.[36]

Buckley saw *National Weekly* as a way not only to strike back against liberalism in the press but also to uproot the "reprehensible journalistic trend toward a genteel uniformity of opinion." As a natural contrarian, Buckley had nothing but contempt for conformity. Derision dripped from his descriptions of "that decadent, lukewarm mood of indifference which permeates our Liberal press." Denouncing "sentimental uniformity," Buckley vowed his magazine would "never join that mutual-admiration society of complacent American journalism" but would instead preside over "the manly presentation of deeply felt conviction." Liberals might dominate the press, but Buckley felt certain that once the battle was joined, committed and virile conservatives would be well positioned for victory.[37]

Well positioned, in part, because of Buckley's belief in the political power of the published word. During a period of retrenchment and small government in the 1920s, left-leaning magazines like the *New Republic*, the *New Yorker*, and the *Nation* (older but refashioned in 1918 under editor Oswald Garrison Villard) began to appear. In these magazines Buckley saw the foundations of the New Deal. Indeed, "so total a revolution as Mr. Roosevelt's would have been inconceivable" without these serious journals of opinion. He was careful to point out that while such journals did not conceive revolutionary ideas, those ideas required journals in order to be "intellectually popularized and politically begotten." The time was ripe, he believed, for a new journal with new ideas. "New Deal journalism has degenerated into a jaded defense of the status quo," he argued. Time for a fresh start.[38]

Buckley's critique of 1950s politics and journalism was twofold: that they were both too moderate and too liberal. These seemingly contradictory complaints came together in the notion of a midcentury "liberal consensus"—the idea not only that Americans broadly agreed on the scope of the New Deal state but that political alternatives to that consensus were tainted, perhaps even illegitimate. The force of that consensus naturalized what conservatives saw as its radicalism: if so many Americans subscribed to the rapid expansion of state power and regulation, then how could it be extreme or un-American? Undoing that consensus was the new magazine's primary purpose.

National Weekly, renamed *National Review* in the buildup to the publication of its first issue, corralled a slew of new and established conservative voices. They represented a variety of conservatisms, a breadth Buckley insisted upon in hopes not only of fusing a broader conservative philosophy but also of preventing the sorts of divisions that had caused other right-wing publications to fold. That range was reflected both in the magazine's mast-head and its format: regular columns allowed writers with differing opinions to develop their own niche, whether it was Willmoore Kendall on "the liberal line" or Russell Kirk on the academy. To further cement the group, editors held weekly meetings that they playfully, and accurately, called "Agonies." Buckley meanwhile maintained final editorial say—he held all the magazine's voting stock—an arrangement meant to forestall any publication-ending factionalism.

Like other conservative media, *National Review* got off to a rocky start. Within a few years its circulation had reached about 16,500, not nearly enough to keep the magazine afloat. Indeed, it was bleeding funds "at a rate that suggested it was not long for this world," as Bill Rusher put it. It was this rather bleak business situation that greeted Rusher when he arrived at *National Review* in July 1957. Abandoning party politics in the mid-1950s, Rusher turned his attention to the movement and media. He began to devote his free time to writing, which is how he caught Buckley's eye. Buckley became a Rusher fan after reading "Cult of Doubt," an article he wrote in 1955 for the first issue of the *Harvard Times-Republican*. Buckley excerpted "Cult of Doubt" in his "Ivory Tower" column for *National Review*. After praising the appearance of "a dissenting weekly newspaper" at the Ivy League university, he quoted Rusher at length: "The great majority of the American people are now convinced that the struggle for survival must not be led, on behalf of the American society, by some doubt-ridden egghead exquisitely poised between Yea and Nay. The world will go—and perhaps rightly—to those who want it most." Buckley, who launched his magazine denouncing the "decadent, lukewarm mood of indifference which permeates our Liberal press," had found a kindred spirit.[39]

At Buckley's request, the two Bills met at the University Club in New York in early 1956 to discuss a role for Rusher at the magazine. Buckley thought the lawyer would be ideally suited to write on the Supreme Court, legal affairs, and conservative jurisprudence. But Rusher was positioned to join the Senate subcommittee in Washington. When he informed Buckley he was heading to D.C., Buckley responded, "Well, consider us thoroughly exploitable." The two stayed in touch, and when Rusher decided to leave the committee after Joe McCarthy's death in May 1957 (which he saw as a sign that the era of congressional anticommunism was at an end), Buckley was ready to extend him an offer. Only this time it wasn't a position as a writer; now, Buckley was asking him to be the magazine's publisher.[40]

As publisher, Rusher not only managed the business side of the magazine but also participated in the spirited editorial debates at the heart of the magazine. He would emerge as one of the magazine's leading voices for ideological consistency and movement fealty. He would vociferously argue on behalf of building a broad conservative base, one he believed the magazine should serve even at the expense of electoral success. Rusher had done his time in the Republican Party; he came to *National Review* to challenge the GOP, not become its handmaiden. Though brought on board to manage the business side of the magazine, he just as often served as the counterweight to Buckley's emerging political pragmatism.

Conservative media activists were not limited exclusively to the domain of the written word. As *National Review* approached its first anniversary, Buckley appeared on the *Manion Forum of Opinion* to repeat his well-honed denunciations of American apathy. "Half the world is in chains—the other half seems to be wallowing in a sort of air-conditioned indecision," he told Clarence Manion's audience. "In America we lust after peace and prosperity indiscriminately, and we demand that both political parties promise us access to our neighbor's goods. In a word, by our behavior we strengthen the impression that we are more closely related to the beasts than to the saints." Buckley's doomsday tone was well suited for the show, which often depicted an America corrupted by two decades of New Deal governance and on the verge of ruin.[41]

In their discussion of the 1956 party conventions, Buckley and Manion found little worth celebrating. But they did manage to heap accolades on a common object: each other. Listeners who tuned in to the radio broadcast heard Manion lavish praise on the "patriot extraordinaire," still in his first year of publishing. Buckley in turn offered "a sincere gesture of appreciation of the extraordinary qualities of this very extraordinary human being." What neither man mentioned during the broadcast was how closely connected their media outlets were. Buckley's father had been one of the founding donors for Manion's radio program, which began in the fall of 1954. Manion in turn was a founding director of National Weekly, the corporation that owned *National Review*. Months away from his sixtieth birthday when he hosted the young editor, Manion was already something of an elder statesman in a movement that was just getting started. He was not alone on the airwaves—he shared space with Dan Smoot and a number of anticommunist preachers—but he would become the most politically influential of the first generation of conservative radio hosts.[42]

Figure 4. WGBF billboard, Evansville, Indiana, 1964. Chicago History Museum.

The *Manion Forum of Opinion* went live on October 3, 1954. Those who tuned in to one of twenty-nine radio stations that carried the *Forum* heard Manion's grave, clipped voice announce, "I am here now, next week, and hereafter to tell you the simple truth as I see it." In his opening monologue, he spoke to them of sacrifice and redemption, of the long-ago battles for American independence and the current clashes with communism—a new War of Independence, in Manion's eyes, with every American's personal freedom at stake. "We need first to revive our American faith and then to defend it with determination," he declared. "To that revival and to that defense, these broadcasts are humbly and prayerfully dedicated. The truth that made us free will keep us free. *Let us face it*." Truth: that was the watchword of the *Forum*. Manion called upon his listeners to return to their radios week after week to hear hard truths, to face them, to fight for them.[43]

His was not the type of program conservatives in the 1990s and 2000s would tune in to, the three-hour-long daily jeremiads punctuated by listener calls, parody songs, and audio clips supplied by the twenty-four-hour news cycle. By the end of the millennium conservatives could listen to one host after another, wall-to-wall right-wing talk for nine or ten hours a day if they so desired. In the early 1950s, though, the idea of conservative talk radio (much less "conservative media") was an alien concept. There were, to be sure, a few political commentators who tilted right: Fulton Lewis Jr., Boake Carter, Sam Pettengill—men whose presence on air belied the claims of a total conservative blackout. But they were isolated commentators, lacking both off-air activism and a broader movement to support their work.

Despite the on-air presence of men like Lewis, who was derided by critics as "the voice with a snarl" and praised by supporters as "the Voice of American Conservatism," Manion, like his fellow activists, considered the media landscape of the early 1950s a decidedly unfriendly place. Manion could stump far and wide for the Bricker Amendment, but what was that compared to the combined power of all the columnists and magazine writers and newspaper editors who argued against it? Worse yet, who failed to even take it seriously, presenting the United States' involvement in the world as an indisputable good? Conservatives needed a way to get their message out, to transform a small and scattered band of malcontents into a movement. For Manion, that meant radio. With a weekly show, he could expound his philosophy week after week, respond to changing conditions, and reach a nationwide audience on a regular basis. Unlike the roundtable shows like *Meet the Press* on which he occasionally appeared, he would not have to vie with an opponent for airtime or cede control to an interviewer or analyst. It would be his philosophy, his ideas, his show.

It quickly became clear, however, that sponsorship, the traditional way of funding such programs, would not work for Manion's show. He was a controversial figure, and sponsors risked getting swept up in any backlash against him. Businessmen were a cautious lot, wary of losing customers by openly backing unpopular views. The show would have to rely instead on donors. In July 1954 Manion incorporated a trust to handle donations and legal issues and began meeting with conservative industrialists and advocates. A group of seventeen men, including Henry Regnery, contributed funds for the first thirteen shows. They also sent out a fund-raising telegram to 350 others, asking for $250 to $5,000 to support Manion's efforts "to alert millions to efforts of those who would perpetuate American involvement in foreign wars and entanglement, international schemes while our own country rots from within from one-worldism, socialism, and communism." The telegram promised that fund-raising letters would go out to 50,000 more businessmen once the show launched. Thus the *Manion Forum* fund-raising network was built.[44]

When Manion took to the microphone for that first broadcast, he had thirteen radio slots secured, three months to find the donors and listeners to keep the program going. His fifteen-minute speeches aired once a week over the Mutual Broadcasting System, one of the four major networks of the day. Because of the way the Mutual affiliate system worked, only 29 stations carried the first few *Forum* programs. Even with this relatively limited reach, Manion managed to tap a large number of donors—nearly 400 in 1954—to keep his program going. With a network of contributors in place, Manion told a supporter in early February 1955, "It now looks as if I will stay on air indefinitely." He was right. The first broadcast was followed by almost 1,300 others, twenty-five years of conservative broadcasting.[45]

By the mid-1950s, an informal network of conservative media had emerged, bound by a shared belief in media bias and a shared sense of exclusion. Whatever their disagreements—and there were many, both of substance and personality—right-wing media activists agreed that established media were under the control of liberals. For each of these media figures, this state of affairs required more than just the exposure of liberal bias. They felt called to fight back with their own institutions, creating small, interlocking fields: conservative book publishing, conservative magazines and journals, and conservative broadcasting. They might not always have appreciated being lumped together—"I do get very tired of constantly being bracketed with [the libertarian] Caxton printers and Devin-Adair," Regnery grumbled to a friend—but they saw the necessity of working together to pool resources, promote crusades, and assail established media. As such, in the mid-1950s, it began to be possible for the first time to speak about conservative media in a meaningful way.[46]

Chapter 3

The Obstacles

On October 20, 1957, Dan Hutchings twirled his radio dial to 570 AM and settled into his living room. It had been a cool, clear day in Alderwood Manor, the small town near Seattle where Hutchings made his home. His family joined him for his Sunday evening routine, listening to the *Manion Forum* over Seattle's KVI radio station, an affiliate of the Mutual Broadcasting System. At quarter to nine, Hutchings heard the announcer's familiar voice. But instead of introducing the program as he always did, the announcer informed listeners, *"The Manion Forum of Opinion* originally scheduled for this time will not be heard; instead, a musical transcription will be heard." With that, music poured out of the radio, and Hutchings's mind began to race.

The missed broadcast troubled Hutchings for the rest of the evening. When he woke the next day, he hurried to his typewriter. He'd been expecting something like this. He had written Manion before, offering to act as his ears-on-the-ground in case anything unexpected happened. Nothing ever had, but how long could a man rail against powerful forces without retribution? Quickly sketching out the fishy circumstances—"No reason such as technical difficulties over which we have no control, etc. mentioned"—he searched for a way to relay his fears of government intrusion. Finally, it came to him. "All of us were disturbed," he closed. "Since Little Rock, anything could happen."[1]

Hutchings wasn't the only one worried. Those who listened to the *Manion Forum* over the Mutual network were left to puzzle over its unexplained absence. The *Forum* had come across every week for three years. So why had the interview with Herbert Kohler, a Wisconsin industrialist locked in a bitter strike with the United Auto Workers (UAW), failed to air?

The answer was not, as Hutchings feared, a phalanx of government officials come to stamp out dissent. But the real story would convince Hutchings and others that sinister forces were working to silence conservative voices. In battles over labor and regulation in the 1950s, conservative media activists ran into real limits in their efforts to cover controversial topics. For broadcasters especially, the effects of government regulation made plain the restrictions on speech in midcentury America. But these media activists were well compensated for their struggles. Their anti-unionism fortified the ties between industry and conservative media while severing those with establishment media. Soon a more cohesive, better-funded network emerged. As that network emerged, media activists developed an increasingly sophisticated and effective critique of liberal media bias, both honing it into a weapon in the conservative ideological arsenal and turning it into a rallying point around which the wider population of conservative groups would organize.

In the late 1950s, fights over labor and the right to unionize defined the outsider experience for conservatives. Though labor unions were themselves under fire—the tide had turned against unions in 1947 with the passage of the Taft-Hartley Act, which limited the ability of unions to strike and outlawed closed shops—anti-unionism remained a controversial position. And controversial opinions faced real barriers in the consensus-dominated news media of midcentury America.

Though anti-intervention in foreign policy and anticommunism in domestic policy shaped much of the early material for conservative media, anti-unionism soon emerged as a central concern. Despite the ease with which conservatives could assail unions as havens for communists, by the mid-1950s anticommunism was seldom their principal line of attack. Instead, a far more populist critique dominated postwar conservative anti-unionism. This critique envisioned the unionized worker not as a foreign menace or wild-eyed radical but rather as the victim of manipulative union bosses who first forced workers to join and then grew fat off their dues. Framed as a matter of worker's choice, it was an argument that traced back to the open-shop movement of the 1920s, which enabled employers to hire both union and non-union workers (though in practice this meant that they almost always hired non-union workers). From that perspective, conservatives were defending neither large corporations nor unions but the workers to whom they were hoping to appeal.[2]

In line with this argument, media activists often framed their opposition to unions in terms of monopoly, a reflection of the anti-bigness populism that was part of their conservatism. Calling unions "dictatorships" and "anti-democratic," Manion held that the problem was not labor organization per se but rather that unions had grown so massive and had fallen under the control of a cabal less interested in the welfare of the worker than in the accrual of power and wealth. *National Review* echoed this sentiment, arguing, "For many years, the great bullies in America have been the big, tough, cocky labor unions; yet those who cry out against their excesses are yawned away, dismissed as cranks, pests." Bullies and dictators, with the little guy under their heel.[3]

The prickly comment about being "yawned away" for opposing union excesses reflected media activists' awareness that their anti-unionism cut against popular opinion. Their view of unions, and by extension government, as the enemy of private enterprise contradicted the consensus view, most famously articulated by John Kenneth Galbraith, of how American society should work. That idealized model envisioned Big Labor, Big Government, and Big Business operating as countervailing forces, balancing the major sources of power in society. In such a system, government and labor limited the power of business. But in stark contrast to the right's interpretation, these limitations were considered a positive social good.[4]

The populist framework, however, opened an avenue for conservatives to rail against the "bigness" component of consensus rather than simply the labor component. Leveraging the language of rights and liberty, conservatives argued that in order to secure the greatest amount of freedom for the worker, unions had to be brought under antitrust laws. Extending antitrust laws to unions would outlaw the union shop, in which workers had to either belong to a union prior to being hired or join at the start of employment. Conservatives tagged union shops "compulsory unionism," a popular label among the "right-to-work" crowd, the businessmen and conservative politicians who wanted to extend Taft-Hartley's ability to curb union power. The union shop, they argued, took away workers' freedom to choose whether to belong to a union, impinging on their freedom of association. "Right-to-work" was built on the same argument: that requiring union membership took away the right of non-union members to take up employment in a union shop.[5]

This anti-union philosophy forged a natural partnership between conservative media activists and certain industrialists, as a look at the *Manion Forum* illustrates. From its inception, the *Manion Forum* received support from industry. A fund-raising telegram sent out a few months before the *Forum*'s launch included signatories like Frank Buttram, an oilman from Oklahoma; Edwin Gallun, head of a tanning and leather company in Milwaukee; Al Hill, a Texas oilman and son-in-law of billionaire H. L. Hunt; and William O'Neil, founder of Akron's General Tire and Rubber. William J. Grede signed as well. Grede made his fortune in the iron and steel industry and became known as a voice of "conservative, specifically anti-union, sentiment," which shaped his tenure as president of the National Association of Manufacturers (NAM). His successor at NAM, Charles R. Sligh Jr., also signed.[6]

Grede and Sligh, as presidents of NAM, understood well the power of radio. NAM employed radio to sell the idea of free enterprise, which it used to fight both government regulation and labor unions. The organization's goal during the New Deal era was to "restore America's faith in business—not government—leadership." After World War II, NAM launched *It's Your Business*, a panel-style radio program, and *Industry on Parade*, a weekly television show. Meanwhile, industry-sponsored commentators like Fulton Lewis Jr. and Sam Pettengill offered pro-business opinion in their news reports. Choosing to support the *Manion Forum*, then, was not a radical break from tradition for industrialists.[7]

These industry sponsors did more than contribute money and lend their names to the *Forum*. In order to help raise money for the program, some sponsors sent letters to colleagues, stockholders, and suppliers promoting the *Forum* and offering their endorsement. Bill Grede crafted his message in terms of freedom and Americanism: "We businessmen do not need to be 'sold' on pro-American principles. But millions upon millions of rank-and-file men and women DO NEED to be 'sold' on the Constitutional freedom they are now about to lose." By stressing the ease with which businessmen understood this problem, Grede suggested a natural bond between industry and "pro-American principles." Others more forcefully addressed the need to spread positive messages about private enterprise beyond the boardroom, lauding Manion for having "warned of the danger of destroying free enterprise by continuing down the road to Socialism" and asking "whether this Nation is to be ruled by a labor government, or by a government representing all segments of our society." One sponsor even proposed the *Forum* could be the mouthpiece for industry, since businessmen "have no constant medium of communication with the public."[8]

What message compelled these sponsors to put up their time, money, and reputations on behalf of the *Forum*? It was more than just the general support of private enterprise the *Forum* contained. Specific broadcasts appealed to specific industries. For instance, a few months after the *Forum's* launch, Manion devoted a program to the Tennessee Valley Authority (TVA). A government-operated energy corporation, the TVA had been created during the New Deal to provide affordable energy to rural populations not served by private power companies. Manion called the TVA "the most spectacular and best advertised instance of government ownership and operation," the most visible symbol of "creeping socialism" in the United States. Comparing the issue to slavery, he wondered: could "the free enterprise system of the United States peacefully, prosperously and permanently co-exist and compete with the large segments of established Socialism in the form of numerous business enterprises now owned and operated by the United States Government?" For Manion, the idea was as preposterous as peaceful coexistence with communism abroad. The only solution? Sell the TVA, and get the government out of the power business.[9]

Power companies lit up at Manion's call to privatize the TVA. They quickly contacted the *Forum* to request bulk reprints of the broadcast. The Southern California Edison Company bought 90,000, Virginia Electric, 37,000, Gulf States Utilities, 21,000. In all, power companies ordered over 165,000 copies. It was a boon for both parties: the reprints gave companies an independent source calling for privatization, while their sales filled the *Forum's* coffers and ensured its message reached far beyond its broadcast range. Results like this incentivized a particular type of coverage from the *Forum*.[10]

The *Manion Forum* also got involved in specific union campaigns. In late 1956, Ohio voters faced a referendum concerning the guaranteed annual wage and state unemployment laws. The proposed change would allow unemployed workers to receive benefits from both the state and their previous employers. The referendum was part of an agreement between General Motors and the CIO-UAW that established a guaranteed wage for the company's workers. But the math only worked if the company could subsidize its contribution to the unemployment package with state benefits. In order for the agreement to go into effect, enough states had to change their laws to lock in a guaranteed annual wage for at least two-thirds of the company's workers. The Ohio vote, if successful, would put the CIO above the two-thirds threshold.

Manion attacked the proposed change—and guaranteed annual wage as a concept—by arguing that limited unemployment compensation had to be combined with low payments "to spur the incentive of the unemployed worker to seek permanent employment." If workers were paid a living wage whether they worked or not, what motivation would they have to seek jobs? He called the guaranteed annual wage "a gross deception," masked by "a bomb-proof good name." This "union plan for paid idleness" represented collusion between Big Business and Big Labor to reshape public policy, as business and labor pooled their influence to strong-arm legislators into ratifying their agreement.[11]

The CIO lost the Ohio vote, thanks in part to Manion's efforts. The *Forum* had a strong presence in Ohio, broadcasting over a number of stations including those in three of the state's major cities, Cincinnati, Cleveland, and Columbus. More than just regular *Forum* listeners heard the broadcast, though. Numerous Ohio stations rebroadcast the program opposing the guaranteed annual wage, and reprints flooded the state. Herschel C. Atkinson, executive vice president of the Ohio Chamber of Commerce, believed the broadcast "did much to crystallize thinking in Ohio," seeing Manion's views reflected in newspapers across the state. "You refreshed the faith, even, of those of us who were thick in the fight," Atkinson reported. "You gave us renewed courage and confidence in the eternal rightness of our cause against the clever schemes and calculations of the Moscow-trained socialist-minded [CIO president] Walter Reuther." Manion framed the proposal's defeat as a win for democracy. The people, when given a choice, soundly rejected union policies that tended toward socialism. Pointing to Ohio and to a recent election in Indiana in which workers rejected the CIO by a wide margin, Manion gloated, "Mr. Reuther has just had to eat some bitter crow."[12]

This ongoing vilification of Reuther and union aims did not go unnoticed by labor unions. In mid-1956 they began to fight back, urging unions and their members to pull their accounts from St. Joseph Bank and Trust Company. St. Joseph Bank was a well-chosen target. It handled the *Forum*'s accounts, and its president, B. K. Patterson, was the chairman of the *Manion Forum*'s board of trustees. By applying intense financial pressure, union leaders hoped the bank would have to dump the trust, which funded the *Forum*, in order to stay in business. The trust would then become too great a risk, they calculated, for other banks to accept. Manion fought back, writing major corporations and urging them to set up accounts with the bank to counter any loss it might incur from the union action. Within a month, Sears Roebuck (headed by Robert E. Wood, a *Forum* sponsor and a key financial backer of conservative causes) and other companies had deposited $55,000 with the bank, while the *Manion Forum* added another $5,000 to its holdings there. With companies like Sun Oil and Inland Container backing him, Manion easily circumvented the boycott.[13]

In addition to their financial support, industrialists occasionally took a more hands-on role in conservative media activism. For instance, the publication of *Labor Union Monopoly*, former New Dealer Donald Richberg's hard-nosed call for union antitrust laws, relied on the deep connections between conservative media and industry in the late 1950s. In concert with industrialists, media activists coordinated their efforts to construct a unified message about the proper role of unions in society.

The story of *Labor Union Monopoly* began not with Richberg, the author, or Regnery, the publisher, but with Roger Milliken. In 1947, the tall, bespectacled South Carolinian inherited his family's Spartanburg-based textile company, a business that would make him one of the richest men in America. Milliken eagerly invested these monies in conservative causes. He sunk tens of thousands of dollars into Regnery Publishing and gave *National Review* a substantial amount to facilitate the magazine's launch (and remained a major contributor, leading Buckley to label him *National Review*'s "most important asset"). This support was a function of Milliken's belief that in advancing conservatism, he helped create a political and economic environment in which his business could flourish. In praising Regnery's "courageous editorial policies" (and passing along a $10,000 check with "no condition or stipulation"), Milliken noted that while he did not agree with everything the house published, he was convinced its perspective "deserves continuing exposure."[14]

The idea for a book on labor unions originated with *Human Events'* Frank Hanighen, who in early 1953 sent a musing letter to Regnery. "Remember Josephson's *The Robber Barons?*" Hanighen asked, referring to economic historian Matthew Josephson's popular 1934 book. "Big seller circa 1933–4, when the capitalists were on the run." The time seemed right, he thought, for a new book: *The Robber Bosses.* Hanighen sensed the winds were shifting, that labor was falling out of favor. Seizing the moment, he suggested someone write a book that "would be anti-labor, written from the anti-trust, anti-monopoly and individualist standpoint." Left to Regnery and Hanighen, the idea went no further. A few years later, however, Regnery mentioned it to Milliken over lunch. Milliken, who took a hard-line stance against labor organizing (a year later, he would close his Darlington mill when workers voted to form a union), was quite taken with the idea. After the luncheon, he wrote Regnery to urge him to "make it a main point on your agenda to get somebody to write the book." In exchange, Milliken offered to finance its distribution. As Regnery found the world of ideological publishing something of a nonprofit affair, the promise of distribution money ensured he would pursue the idea more eagerly.[15]

The first task was to find an author. Regnery floated the idea of Victor Riesel, a syndicated labor columnist who a year later would be blinded in an acid attack during his investigations into racketeering. Riesel supported unions but regularly criticized them for corruption and communist influence. Milliken was troubled by the choice. "It scares me," he wrote Regnery, "when you write that such a book ought to take up the 'Right to Work' legislation because I read into that statement the fact that both sides of this proposition would be presented." It made no sense to Milliken that a publisher like Regnery would give space to ideas he felt were harmful. Books vilifying industrialists took up plenty of shelf space already. Milliken wanted something to balance those muckraking tomes, to "expose the abuses of power that union leaders had indulged in" just as *Robber Barons* had done to capitalists.[16]

Their disagreement highlighted the two competing media philosophies with which conservatives would grapple well beyond the 1950s. On the one hand, Regnery's preference for Riesel reflected a belief in the power of impartiality. He understood the strong hold objectivity had on midcentury America: an author perceived as impartial would be more effective because his point of view would appear rational, factual, and disinterested. In Milliken's eyes, however, Regnery misunderstood the fundamental nature of American media. Establishment media were arbiters of objectivity; conservatives could never compete on that terrain. To counter their bias required not an impartial book but a distinctly anti-union one, one so persuasive that it discredited not only unions but also the media that had supported them for so many years.

Since, in Milliken's opinion, Riesel couldn't do such a job, he countered with Westbrook Pegler. Pegler had impressive journalistic credentials (he had won a Pulitzer in 1941) and the right ideological groundings (the

Pulitzer was for his articles in the *New York World-Telegram* on abuses of power by Hollywood unions). A Roosevelt detractor and constant critic of unions and the government, the syndicated columnist marched ever-right-ward after World War II. Here, it seemed, was the perfect fit for the book Milliken had in mind. Despite Milliken's offer to fund his writing, Pegler never responded to their requests. (He was perhaps still smarting from a lost libel suit that cost him $175,001—at the time, one of the largest sums ever awarded in such a suit—and spurred the anti-Semitic turn that made him a political untouchable in the 1960s, when even the John Birch Society cut ties with him.) With no word from Pegler, Milliken and Regnery cast around for other possibilities.[17]

In mid-June Regnery wrote Donald Richberg, then in his mid-seventies and living in Charlottesville, Virginia. Richberg's biography made him seem an unlikely candidate for the book they had in mind. He got his start in labor law as counsel for railroad unions before moving on to become general counsel and executive director of the National Recovery Administration during the New Deal. In 1934 *Time* called him "an avowed Leftist." In the intervening decades, however, Richberg had a change of political heart. His path to anti-unionism wound through the thickets of conservative anticommunism (in 1954 Richberg joined For America, an organization Manion and Robert Wood cochaired). By the 1950s, Richberg had become an occasional contributor to *Human Events*, where Regnery learned of his anti-union stance. Given Richberg's politics and his familiarity with conservative media, Regnery expected a receptive audience for his pitch for *The Labor Barons*, a "serious study" of union power and "right-to-work" legislation.[18]

Little did Regnery know he was in competition for his author. The same day he wrote Richberg, in a coincidence that raises questions as to whether news of the offer escaped Regnery's offices, Devin Garrity of Devin-Adair contacted Richberg to press him to write a book on "the union situation" in America. Pointing to the impending AFL-CIO merger and union successes in Detroit, Garrity suggested the time was right for a conservative counter-punch. The title was in place: *The State of the Union*. Would Richberg be interested?[19]

The head-to-head competition was unusual for the two companies. In the early 1950s, Devin-Adair and Regnery dominated conservative publishing (with Caxton Printers in Idaho carving out a small niche for libertarian books). But they seldom competed over authors, as Devin-Adair tended to land more established names while Regnery provided a platform for

up-and-coming movement leaders. For instance, in 1951 Devin-Adair published Joseph McCarthy's book *America's Retreat from Victory*, followed
the next year by his *McCarthyism, the Fight for America*. Two years later,
in 1954, Regnery put out Buckley and Bozell's *McCarthy and His Enemies*,
a vigorous defense of the senator by the soon-to-be founder of *National
Review* and his brother-in-law. So competition between the two houses was
something new. Richberg, for his part, took the offers in stride, sending outlines to both publishers, each of whom thought he was working exclusively
with the author. On receipt of the outline, Garrity immediately offered to
publish the book on a royalty basis. Regnery also expressed hopes for the
manuscript and received assurances through Frank Hanighen that Richberg
held him in high esteem.[20]

At summer's end, the impending conflict between the publishers seemed
unlikely ever to come to a head. Richberg balked at the commitment. He
sent identical letters to both men, citing his age and various ailments that
made him unequal to the task. After seeing an effective piece by Richberg
in *Human Events* that same week, Regnery put extra effort into maintaining
the relationship. Despite the author's demurral, Regnery assured Richberg
they would like to publish such a book by him, should he ever write one. To
cement the relationship, he arranged meetings with Milliken and himself
at Richberg's home, so the project's principals could meet. This personal
handling did the trick. By the summer of 1956, Regnery had Richberg's
manuscript in hand—much to Garrity's chagrin.[21]

The book galleys were ready by early 1957, and Regnery quickly circulated them to possible sponsors who could help fund the publication and
distribution of the book. In addition to Milliken, Regnery turned to Walter
Harnischfeger and J. Howard Pew for help. Harnischfeger was president
of P&H Mining, a multimillion-dollar company founded by his father. The
boom in postwar industry filled the company's coffers, and Harnischfeger
devoted some of this new wealth to conservative causes, including the
Manion Forum, America's Future (a constitutionalist, free-enterprise organization), and *National Review*. Pew's fortune came from Sun Oil, the
company that had helped Manion sidestep the St. Joseph Bank boycott.
The Pews had a long history of working with emerging conservative media
enterprises; Joseph Pew, the founder of Sun Oil and J. Howard's father,
had provided the start-up funds for *Human Events* in the mid-1940s, and J.
Howard funded *Christianity Today*'s launch in 1956. Such donors were the
lifeblood of early conservative media enterprises.[22]

Regnery turned to these deep-pocketed patrons not to extract donations but to secure bulk sales of the book, which they could then distribute to government officials, business associates, and other well-connected people within their circles. Best sellers might be good for the bottom line, but when it came to making an impact, Regnery put his faith in the clout of people with political and institutional power. "It seems to me," Regnery wrote Harnischfeger, "that if this book could be gotten into the hands of influential people in all parts of the country that it could have great influence . . . it is the sort of book, I feel quite sure, many editorial writers would make great use of." But why bulk sales and mass distribution? Why not sell the book through the usual channels—bookstores and newsstands—and let it sink or swim on its own merits? Wouldn't that be the appropriate free-market model?[23]

Not at all. The problem, Regnery argued, was that the book market was not a free market. Rather, it had become a New York–centered, liberal-controlled industry in which books of a conservative bent could make little headway no matter how promising their sales. New York's lock on the market troubled the Chicago-based publisher. He lamented that "nearly all books are published in New York, and the means by which books are brought to the public are fairly much controlled from New York," and there, the industry was saturated with "left-wing intellectuals." It was an insidious sort of bias, Regnery reasoned. Liberals could never be expected to publish or promote conservative books, so how could such books ever gain public notice? And it wasn't just book sales at stake. It was the control over ideas—"and it is still ideas," Regnery told Harnischfeger, "that run the world." In this way, Regnery extended the conservative critique of liberal bias in the media to the stately world of book publishing. As long as liberals controlled the communication of ideas, conservatives would be handicapped.[24]

Such a perspective meant Regnery had low expectations for reviews of the book, and here he was not disappointed. The biggest threat for a new book was not bad reviews but no reviews at all, and most major papers overlooked *Labor Union Monopoly*. The two that did review it reflected their papers' editorial stances. The *Chicago Tribune* saluted Richberg for hoisting "storm flags for all to see." In addition to the positive review, *Tribune* columnist Chesly Manly used the book to frame a four-part series on the ongoing Kohler strike in Wisconsin. The *New York Times*, on the other hand, dismissed the book's "hysteria" and concluded that when it came to unions, "the fear-ridden Richberg . . . is a dubious guide." Academic reviews, which reached a small but influential group of readers, criticized the book sharply, calling the author and work "bitter," "biased," and "unfair." Regnery saw in these results evidence of "a most effective form of censorship of ideas in this country."[25]

His belief that the usual channels of promotion and sales were blocked for conservatives led Regnery to develop alternative networks for book distribution. He made efforts early on to build relationships with more amenable outlets, which accounted for the bulk of the book's sales. Regnery did not exaggerate when he told a prospective promoter, "We have had a good many orders from Industry." In addition to bulk orders from Harnischfeger, who bought 500 copies, a foundation offered to buy up to 1,200 books for college and university libraries, and NAM inquired into the price for 10,000 copies. Sterling Morton of the Chicago-based Morton Salt bought copies for the presidents of a number of independent colleges. Clearly industrialists understood Richberg's book could be a powerful tool for their war against unions.[26]

In his hunt for wider readership, Regnery also turned to his fellow conservative media activists. This promotional strategy relied on two qualities of conservative media: their authority and their audiences. An endorsement from someone like Clarence Manion, whose conservative credentials were impeccable, ratified Regnery's and Richberg's standing with the right. Ideological credibility, as media activists demonstrated time and again, was a transferable property. For Regnery, calling on Manion paid off: the radio host plumped the book during his broadcast "Dictatorship by Labor" and a few weeks later brought Richberg onto the show to discuss his work. Likewise, conservative publications were prime promotional markets, as their readers were self-selected consumers of conservative media. Regnery ran advertisements in *National Review* and *Human Events* and distributed circulars through the *Dan Smoot Report*, which included the fliers with its newsletter.[27]

The development and promotion of *Labor Union Monopoly* demonstrated how, by mid-1957, loosely connected conservative media operations were binding themselves more tightly to one another and to industry. Behind these strengthened connections lay a set of philosophical assumptions. Both conservatives and industrialists saw themselves as the big losers in the postwar political order. Liberalism, with its support for unions and expanded government power, was carrying the day. Conservatives and industrialists understood that in order to regain the influence they had wielded in the pre–New Deal era, they first had to win the battle of ideas. Before unions could be brought to heel, opinion makers had to be convinced that, in Richberg's words, "Labor unions are not weak, altruistic organizations or servants of the common good, but are strong, selfish, ambitious aggregations of men seeking to dominate the business and politics of the nation for private profit." But they faced a significant obstacle in that battle: the means of communication all seemed to be in the hands of their opponents. Believing these liberal gatekeepers had walled off established media, both sets of self-styled outsiders sought new ways of getting their ideas across. For that, they looked to the conservative media network erected in the wake of World War II, including Manion, Regnery, Buckley, and Hanighen, among others.[28]

This was a fundamental theory of the conservative movement: that alternative outlets for disseminating their ideas were necessary because they wouldn't receive fair hearing in the established media. Were they right? Did conservatives need alternate channels, alternate institutions in order to get their messages across? Were the barriers real?

The *Manion Forum* was about to find out.

The trouble began when Mutual Broadcasting System received a recording of Manion's 160th program. The reel contained a prerecorded talk by Herbert Kohler, president of the famed faucet and fixture company in Wisconsin. Kohler, a first-time guest on the *Manion Forum*, addressed the ongoing UAW strike at his plant in Sheboygan. When Mutual programmers listened to the broadcast, they quickly protested. They couldn't air this.

In the broadcast, Kohler spoke out against "compulsory unionism," arguing that it presented legal and moral issues. The right to strike was running roughshod over other, equally important rights, such as the right to work without joining a union. But Kohler did not come on the program to speak only about principles. He also took issue with the way the union was conducting the Sheboygan strike. Charges of union-sanctioned incitement, physical violence, and mob intimidation structured Kohler's defense of his refusal to negotiate. The union was not his only target; Kohler also accused police and politicians of bowing to union "force and coercion." All this would stop "only when employers make it clear that they will not buy peace by rewarding lawlessness," calling on other employers to "have the courage to resist coercive union monopoly."[29]

It was a fierce speech, filled with hard-nosed ultimatums and images of the UAW's "reign of terror" in Sheboygan. By itself, however, the talk was not beyond the pale. So why did Mutual decide the interview could not air?

The answer, in part, lay in context. The strike at Kohler's Sheboygan plant was no ordinary one. The site of significant labor unrest in 1934, when deadly rioting broke out during a nine-week American Federation of Labor strike, the Kohler plant pushed out the union, inciting picketers who remained for seven years. Management quelled labor agitation through the 1940s and early 1950s. On April 8, 1954, however, a group of 2,500 workers—over two-thirds of the plant's employees—walked out when negotiations stalled over the establishment of a union shop. The conflict pitted the industry's second largest company against the country's second largest union, and both dug in their heels. The strike would drag on for seven years, a run that would earn it the dubious distinction of "the longest strike in history" and cost both the UAW and the Kohler Company millions of dollars.[30]

But time and money were not the distinguishing features of the Kohler strike. Rather, its intransigence, vitriol, and violence set the strike apart. Herbert Kohler had little to say to union leaders, having decided early on that he would not budge on the union shop issue. But he traveled far and wide to protest union demands and union violence, which he often spoke about in the same breath. And there was an alarming amount of violence, prompting *Time* to declare Sheboygan "the most hate-ridden community in the U.S." Shotgun blasts and paint bombs damaged homes; beatings sent a few nonstrikers to the hospital for extended stays. The Kohler factory was stocked with weapons in anticipation of mob violence. When opposing sides weren't slugging it out in local bars, they were fighting in the courts and before the National Labor Relations Board (NLRB), appeals and costs mounting for both parties.[31]

From the start, conservative media offered positive coverage for Kohler management. In its very first issue, *National Review* lauded Kohler's resistance to calls for a union shop and continued to beat that drum throughout the strike. When the UAW launched a boycott against Kohler in 1956, the magazine encouraged readers to buy as many Kohler products as they could. "We don't need a new wash basin, Lord knows, but tomorrow we're going out to get one. . . . And if Kohler starts producing peanut butter, we'll eat Kohler Peanut Butter till it comes out of our ears. So help us God, we will." Readers wrote in to share stories of their Kohler-studded remodeling projects. "You can count me in as a charter member of the Buy Kohler Club," one enthusiastic supporter wrote. Kohler responded in turn by buying a slew of advertising pages. The relationship, it turned out, was mutually advantageous.[32]

Manion also used the Kohler strike as a touchstone for union corruption and "right-to-work" laws. As the strike stretched into its third year, Manion took up the Kohler cause, recasting it as an issue of civil rights akin to the desegregation of schools. "If the Federal Government must forcefully protect the right of a child to go to a certain school in Georgia," Manion maintained (and Manion did not believe that it must but knew many Americans did), "then, by the same token, it must protect the right of a strike-breaker to pass through a picket line in Detroit or Kohler, Wisconsin. The civil right of a child to go to school is no more important than the civil right of his father to work for a living." As the Kohler strike trudged on for another year, Manion offered his microphone to Herbert Kohler.[33]

Given the intensity of emotion surrounding the strike, and the evidence that both sides had litigious dispositions, Mutual balked. Should the broadcast air, they feared, the union would sue the network and its member stations for defamation. In an attempt to limit their liability, Mutual offered to run an edited version of Kohler's remarks. The proposal infuriated Kohler, who was stinging from a recent loss. (A week before, the NLRB charged the firm with unfair labor practices.) After wrangling with Mutual lawyers, Kohler made a counteroffer: he would "protect and indemnify" the network and its stations against losses *if* they allowed the program to air unaltered.[34]

Kohler's offer held no appeal for the network. Inserting Mutual into the middle of the Kohler-UAW battle, conducted thus far with no concern for the damage inflicted on either side, seemed like a particularly poor business decision. The network executives made their final determination the morning of the scheduled broadcast. Unwilling to risk union ire or Kohler's retribution for an edited broadcast, Mutual scratched the program entirely. The decision came too late for another tape to be played in its place; most Mutual stations substituted music and offered no explanation. This was the music Dan Hutchings had heard on his radio, triggering his fears of government interference.

Mutual no doubt hoped the controversy would remain contained between itself and the *Forum*. Perhaps a few listeners would wonder what had happened to their regularly scheduled broadcast, but the *Forum* would be back on the next week. True, the *Chicago Tribune* had caught wind of the dispute (likely through Manion, with whom the paper had close ties), running articles the day before and the day of the broadcast delving into the details of the negotiations between both sides. Still, how much damage could that really do?

Mutual underestimated Manion's listeners. Letters poured in to the *Forum*'s offices from across the country. Conspiracy underwrote the responses. Where Washington listener Hutchings heard echoes of Little Rock and the nearing footfalls of the National Guard, others imagined more sinister plots. C. B. Smith of Christian Political Action admitted to being "intrigued by the action of the Broadcast system but not surprised." After all, he observed, "Men like Reuther—a Jew—have tremendous power in America. Until their source of power is separated from them they will do almost irrepiarable [*sic*] damage to this nation." While the anti-Semitism was unusual for Manion's correspondents (Manion himself does not appear to have ever expressed anti-Semitic views), the fear of behind-the-scenes power was not. Many listeners found it plausible that the powerful centralized government they had heard about week after week, in collusion with communist-controlled unions, had pulled the plug on the *Forum*.[35]

Even those not invested in these conspiratorial interpretations grew interested in the controversy. Press coverage quickly escaped the confines of Chicago; articles about the scotched program cropped up in New York, North Carolina, Indiana, Arizona, California, and beyond. The *Tribune* kept up the drumbeat as well, with front-page coverage the day after the broadcast failed to air, plus an article and editorial the day after that. Meanwhile, requests for reprints of the broadcast deluged the *Forum*, which sent out sixty thousand copies in a week's time. The controversy was spreading.[36]

Clues to how Manion would frame the incident could be found in a *Chicago Tribune* article from the morning of the planned broadcast. After dismissing Mutual's concerns about defamation—the talk contained "nothing that is not factual"—Manion sketched out a broader agenda. Anyone, he claimed, could denounce Kohler's actions, but say one cross word about unions and up swell the accusations of slander. "In my judgment the network's action is evidence of the problems inherent in getting facts of the conservative side of questions before the public," he charged. In connecting the Kohler controversy to concerns about a conservative blackout, Manion tapped into a powerful indictment about liberal bias in the media, one to which media activists would return time and again and hone into a powerful critique.[37]

That established media suppressed conservative ideas was not a new theme. Indeed, overcoming the conservative blackout was the explicit purpose of most conservative media enterprises of the period. Regnery had trotted out the charge when positive reviews of *Labor Union Monopoly* failed to materialize. But Manion was doing something more: transforming liberal bias from a vague claim of exclusion into a powerful and effective ideological arrow in the conservative quiver. With the Kohler controversy, he had an event that played out in the public eye to brandish as proof.

Manion wasted no time in doing so. When he went on air the next week, he had the accusations ready to go, speaking under the title "Kohler Censoring—Omen of Peril to Free Speech." The opening salvo set up Manion's argument. Recalling that he had been on air for over three years, he maintained that "it is safe to say that every one of these [broadcasts] dealt directly or indirectly with a contentious and controversial public question" without ever drawing charges of personal defamation. The idea of controversy was key to Manion's point. A primary component of "enlightened and serviceable discussion, controversy is as essential as it is inevitable," he told his audience. Contrary to what proponents of the "vital center" believed, it posed no danger to the nation. "The danger to our country now," he said, "is not that liberty will destroy itself in honest, earnest controversial debate but that liberty will be allowed to suffocate in the prevailing atmosphere of complacency and conformity."[38]

Complacency and conformity: here were Manion's true targets, just as they had been Buckley's in the formation of *National Review*. In a political culture overlaid with the veneer of consensus, Manion believed controversy represented a real threat. Those who stirred the pot earned epithets of "alarmist" and "witch-hunter" and "crackpot." Hadn't that been the case with the "militantly patriotic" Senator McCarthy? As thanks for ringing the alarm bells, he was cast as a power-hungry crank, the victim, according to one conservative commentator, of "a journalistic lynching party." Stirring up controversy in such an atmosphere was a dangerous proposition.[39]

Such name-calling, though, posed less danger than the institutional power of consensus. It was to this topic that Manion turned for the remainder of the broadcast. His subject: the Federal Communications Commission (FCC) and "equal time." During the negotiations over the Kohler broadcast, Manion and Mutual bandied about the idea of giving Walter Reuther airtime to respond to Kohler's charges. This would satisfy the network's understanding of the FCC's equal-time requirement by ensuring both sides had a voice. But like Roger Milliken, Manion had no interest in spending money and time giving a platform to his opponents, as it would violate his long-held stance that men of Reuther's stripe received plenty of free airtime and support from other outlets. Equal time was always a one-way street, Manion complained, "an ingenious contrivance of the conformists which merely works against those who are proposing to upset the managed conformity." Should conservatives ever try to exercise it, Manion believed they would find themselves stymied at every turn.[40]

Equal time made sense, Manion granted, as a defense against slander. Certainly no broadcast station should have to shoulder the legal costs of slander; providing time to reply constituted an appropriate response should such an offense occur. But controversy was not defamation—it was an essential component of public debate. "The Controversialists—like the Manion Forum—are merely the merchants of ideas that would otherwise be suppressed in the marketplace of public discussion," he told his audience. To silence their voices was not a form of protection but of censorship. And a dangerous form of censorship it was, for it would "subject the public to a black-out of news and argument that is indispensable to people who are charged with responsibility for governing themselves." How could Americans govern wisely if they were not allowed to hear a multitude of opinions?

Manion noted the FCC claimed to have no issue with controversy, only defamation. Given these assurances, the responsibility fell back on the networks and the stations. Their fear was no doubt real—the FCC had the power to pull their licenses. It made sense that managers would wish to "cleave to the line of conformity," to play it safe. Courage, however, was called for. If the FCC had promised not to pull licenses for controversial broadcasts, then stations had the responsibility to carry such material. After all, they were the gatekeepers in a broadcasting age, an age when the truth's "revealing light can now find its way into your living-room and from that point into your understanding only if the press services—and your radio and television sets—will bring it in." Manion believed those station owners and networks executives who chose not to allow wide-ranging opinions on air, who disguised their desire to control content with a "professed fear of the Government," had to be exposed.

The way Manion approached his criticism of equal time reflected an underlying problem with FCC regulation in the 1950s. For starters, the equal-time rule had no bearing on the Kohler-UAW controversy. Equal time, codified during the creation of the FCC in 1934, applied only to political candidates and did not require stations to give free time, only to offer the same rate to every candidate. Manion conflated equal time with the Fairness Doctrine, a common but significant mistake. The Fairness Doctrine was not a statutory requirement but rather a regulatory standard first enunciated in

1949. It created (or acknowledged) an obligation for broadcasters to offer balanced coverage of ideas that were both controversial and of public importance. "Balance" did not translate to equal time—broadcasters controlled how balance was achieved—but it did create a potential free-time obligation. That is, if the opposition viewpoint lacked sponsorship, the station still had to present it.[41]

Manion was not the only one confused about the regulations. The FCC on a number of occasions sent out clarifying memos; Congress created a lengthy report on the Fairness Doctrine to try to determine its meaning. This confusion meant broadcasters were often uncertain what their obligations were. Further compounding the problem were FCC sanctions. As late as 1968, Congress still could not decide whether Fairness Doctrine violations were finable offenses; other than fines, the FCC's only disciplinary tool was license revocation. Since stations could not broadcast without a license, this sanction effectively put them out of business, a measure so drastic and disproportionate that the commission rarely exercised it. This uncertainty contributed to the doctrine's "chilling effect": with no clear rules or penalties, some broadcasters steered clear of controversial material, while others used the confusion over the rules to control their content. The decision not to air the Kohler broadcast was made, in part, in response to this confused atmosphere.[42]

Still, the censorship angle caught on. Headlines in editorially friendly papers echoed Manion's take on the controversy: "Network Censorship Is Scored," "Mustn't Say Anything Controversial," "Gagging of the Manion Forum." The role of censorship victim promised not just publicity but increased sales as well. At the end of the broadcast reprint, Manion trumpeted in telegraphic form: *"demand for suppressed Kohler speech nationwide and heavy. . . .* Our first printing was practically exhausted within 48 hours of cancellation. . . . During the last week, we have had a steady flow of orders from corporations for this outstanding address." Reprint sales were not the only new income source. After the broadcast, Kohler began appearing on the *Forum*'s list of contributors.[43]

Manion's cries of censorship drew the attention of politicians as well. John J. Flynt, a Georgia congressman, contacted Manion to offer his advice and aid. "Mutual Broadcasting Company has no right whatsoever to impose that type of restriction or censorship on you or any other program on air," Flynt maintained, even if they suspected the talk would trigger a Fairness Doctrine request. In the proper course of things, the program would air, the opposing party would make the request, and the network would allocate time as necessary. Censorship by prior restraint was not allowed. (Flynt was conflating government and business in his argument, as prior restraint applied only to censorship by the government.) "I don't know whether you care to pursue this further or not," Flynt wrote, "but if you do, I hope that you will call me for any assistance that I might be able to give you."[44]

Not everyone was impressed with the *Forum's* cries of censorship. In mid-November, Manion made the front page of *The Kohler Strike and Boycott Bulletin*, the UAW's circular for striking workers. "Two peas in a pod are now screaming 'discrimination' and 'censorship,' and slurring the Mutual Broadcasting System as part of the 'internationalist socialist' conspiracy for barring the speech," strikers wrote in their weekly bulletin. They saw an ulterior motive in the censorship shouts, something perverse in the two men working "to hustle contributions while yelling 'Socialism' at a conservative radio station network" (as some considered Mutual). The circular excoriated Manion as "America's closest thing to a fascist in the intellectual world; Kohler his counterpart in the industrial field." Rather than trying to frighten workers with depictions of these two men joining forces, the UAW article dismissed them out of hand. After all, they reasoned, "The distance between the lunatic fringe and the junk-yard where all cracked pots are eventually thrown is very short, indeed."[45]

The Kohler controversy, with its specter of censorship, raised serious concerns (or, for the strikers, high hopes) about the uncertain future of the *Manion Forum*. Would Manion and his guests always have to be on guard against controversial statements or risk being dropped from Mutual stations? What price would conservatives have to pay to be heard on network radio? These questions cut to the very heart of the *Forum*. Just two weeks before the Kohler interview was supposed to air, the *Forum* celebrated its third anniversary. On that occasion, it derided shows that served up opposing sides of an issue, "with listening audiences left to ferret out the truth." Manion, who believed it was immoral to balance truth with its opposite, had no intention of joining their ranks.[46]

With this threat hanging over his head, Manion acted. Just three days after the dropped broadcast, the *Manion Forum* moved to terminate its relationship with Mutual. The *Forum's* agency, Victor Advertising, cited "recent developments" as the reason it would not renew the current contract, set to expire in just a few days' time. Because the stations needed time to restructure their schedules, the *Forum* extended its contract for four weeks. And so it went. On November 24, 1957, the *Manion Forum* went out over the Mutual Broadcasting System for the final time.

Ending the contract with Mutual had mixed effects. Overnight, the *Forum* went from 113 stations to 72. Rebuilding lost coverage meant contracting with independent stations, a project that would cost more money and require more work—locating amenable stations, nurturing relationships, setting up contracts. But independence had its benefits. Individual contracts greatly reduced the risk of another widespread blackout. If one station decided not to air a program, that decision would affect only one listening area. Further, station owners would only be concerned with the reactions of local listeners, rather than having to ascertain whether the broadcasts would be palatable on a national level.

Despite the work involved in setting up new contracts, Manion was confident he could replace the lost Mutual stations by year's end. "I am sure that we can extend our coverage to an equal number of stations and get better coverage without Mutual than with it," he assured one sponsor. More important, "we will be free from the menace of centralized censorship." Manion wasted little time replacing Mutual with a network of his own. "Network" in this case did not share the same meaning as at NBC or CBS, where it referred to a group of stations contracted with one company that would provide the bulk of its programming. The Manion Forum provided only one program. But in the sense that he created a network of stations from coast to coast airing the *Manion Forum* on a weekly basis, Manion's use of the word is consistent. Even before the break with Mutual, Manion regularly referred to the "Manion Forum network," an independent conservative voice broadcast across the nation. By 1958 this network had replaced the forty-one Mutual stations with forty-three independent ones.[47]

What, ultimately, did independence mean? For one, it meant that there would be no mediator between the *Forum* and its stations. Manion flaunted this newfound freedom, redoubling his attention to labor issues—so much so that in the year following the Mutual break, a full quarter of the *Forum's* broadcasts attacked labor unions.

Perhaps more important, the struggle with Mutual meant exclusion would become an integral part of the *Forum's* message and meaning, built into its very purpose. Manion took from the controversy two critical lessons: first, that there were real barriers to aggressively promoting a conservative message; and second, that pointing to those barriers was a powerful ideological and promotional tool. Never before had the *Forum* received such wide

Where Weekend Programs Are Rated—

The Manion Forum Outranks Its Network Competition

	Rating (Pulse)	Share of Audience (Percentage)
Manion Forum	**1.6**	**11**
Average Network Competition	**1.55**	**10**

New York, N.Y.		
WINS (Forum)	**.8**	**9**
WABC (ABC)	.3	3
WCBS (CBS)	1.0	12
WNBC (NBC)	.3	3

Philadelphia, Pa.		
WIBG (Forum)	**1.3**	**8**
WFIL (ABC)	1.8	12
WCAU (CBS)	2.0	14
WRCV (NBC)	1.3	8

Cincinnati, Ohio		
WKRC (Forum)	**2.8**	**15**
WCKY (ABC)	2.0	11
WCPO (CBS)	3.0	16
WLW (NBC)	2.3	12

Figure 5. *Manion Forum* promotional materials, including audience share and ratings information for select markets, 1961. Chicago History Museum.

and extensive coverage; never before had its message reached so many. The *Manion Forum* now had compelling evidence to back its charges of exclusion, which reinforced its populist message. *See?* it suggested. *There really are powerful forces seeking to silence us.*

From this incident, the *Forum* extrapolated a now-familiar interpretation of the media landscape. Conservatives stood outside the institutions of power, liberals inside. From this privileged position, liberals slanted news and opinion in their favor and silenced conservative critics whenever they could. Facing these barriers to access and control, conservatives had to create new institutions, new conduits, new networks to get their message out. And—in a new twist for the *Forum*—these new institutions could not intertwine with established ones. Conservative media had to be entirely separate or lose control of their content. The war of ideas could be waged no other way.

Existing separately from established media enterprises meant conservatives in media turned to one another to expand audiences, spread publicity, and bolster content. These were mutually reinforcing relationships. To provide evidence for claims, conservatives would cite one another. To establish legitimacy, media activists would trade on the reputations of other recognized conservatives. These collaborations, as illustrated in the development of Richberg's *Labor Union Monopoly*, increased throughout the 1950s. Ads for the *Forum* ran regularly in *National Review*; the magazine stamped Manion "one of conservatism's most literate and responsible spokesmen." *Human Events* took to publishing occasional excerpts from Manion's broadcasts and, later, his syndicated column. Manion in turn continued to invite Regnery authors on the show to promote their books, and in his newsletter he regularly cited *National Review*, *Human Events*, and a host of smaller publications, like the Church League of America's *News and Views*, Thurmond Sensing's column "Sensing the News," and the *Dan Smoot Report*. The danger of this self-referential system was that it could become unmoored from reality, creating an echo chamber that rendered it unintelligible to outsiders. But in the 1950s, conservative media outlets were neither numerous nor powerful enough to create a robust alternate media ecosystem.[48]

These reciprocal acknowledgments provided one set of connections; shared campaigns created another. On the heels of the Mutual controversy, Herbert Kohler became something of a cause célèbre in conservative media circles. In addition to in-depth coverage of the strike, *Human Events* published a Kohler editorial in its pages. *National Review* kept up its steady coverage of the Mutual controversy, devoting space to it a good six weeks after the dropped broadcast. Even after moving on from its Mutual coverage, *National Review* continued to track Kohler's labor problems, castigating "flashy and sensationalized anti-Kohler tidbits" in the press and labeling the union's tactics "guerilla warfare." Kohler rewarded this coverage handsomely, increasing ad buys by 50 percent in 1959 and another 25 percent in 1960.[49]

Regnery rallied around Kohler as well. In 1961, he published two books that dealt substantially with the Kohler strike. In addition to *Check-Off*, a book on union monopoly by *Human Events* contributor Jameson Campaigne, Regnery put out Sylvester Petro's *The Kohler Strike: Union Violence and Administrative Law*. Petro, a law professor at New York University and a former *Manion Forum* guest, had written a number of books on union monopoly prior to *The Kohler Strike*. In this work, he extended his condemnation to include the NLRB, which he argued should be abolished and replaced with state courts because of its favoritism toward unions. While reviewers in academic journals found the book full of "extreme bias and prejudice" and lacking "serious, objective reflections" and the *New York Times* meted out a scathing review, conservative media coverage was far more favorable. *Human Events* ran an excerpt from *The Kohler Strike*, while *National Review* (for which Petro had previously written a few labor articles) served up a glowing review. The Kohler Company's approval was even greater. It bought one hundred thousand copies of a special-edition paperback to distribute far and wide. On the Kohler issue, conservative media were presenting a united front.[50]

As the 1950s came to a close, though, things were beginning change. For much of the decade, these media outlets had offered conservative interpretations of the news, thoughtful philosophical tracts, dire warnings about liberalism and communism. They sought to awaken their audiences and to let them know they were not alone. Perhaps they did their job too well, because their audiences were beginning to demand more than just messages. They wanted action, and they wanted it from the conservative leaders they knew best: the media community.

The messengers were about to build a movement.

Part II

Leaders

Chapter 4

The Movement

It was an unseasonably warm September day in San Luis Obispo, California, when Olive Marcom sat down to write to Clarence Manion. She hadn't known much about the *Manion Forum* when she tuned in to his television program a few days before. A friend encouraged her to watch, saying Manion delivered "the low-down on what's really happening behind the headlines and news reports." In September 1964, that low-down largely concerned communism. In the context of the coming presidential election, Manion had turned his attention to victory in the Cold War and threats of subversion at home. His warnings of communist conspiracy alarmed Marcom. After moving to California from Minnesota, she had raised three sons in a suburban community with her husband, Bill. Just a few years before writing Manion she had joined Grace Church, an independent fundamentalist congregation in downtown San Luis Obispo. The idea that the life she had built—her family, her church, her country—was under threat left her searching for some way to fight back. "You know, Mr. Manion," she wrote, "after hearing all these startling, shocking things, a question comes to mind: What can I, one housewife, do?"[1]

Marcom joined thousands of other conservatives in asking media activists "What can I do?" By 1964, the answer was: "Plenty." Petition drives, local and national organizations, and Barry Goldwater's presidential campaign all provided outlets for eager activists looking for some way to promote the cause. But these outlets did not emerge sui generis at the beginning of the 1960s. They were created by the men and women in conservative media who moved out from behind their microphones and writing desks to the front lines of the movement. They were reluctant leaders—as *National Review* publisher William Rusher scolded a nagging correspondent, "*National Review* is a magazine, not a political party"—but cajoled by their audiences and readers they began holding rallies and establishing organizations that channeled the passions they stirred into meaningful action.

As movement builders, media activists imbued conservative organizations with a distinct set of values and behaviors. They emphasized the importance of ideas and ideology, stressing education sometimes at the expense of other forms of activism like petition drives, voter registration, and lobbying. They made the consumption of right-wing media a core conservative behavior, offering discounts to organizations and forging partnerships that bound together the institutions of conservative media and politics. And they policed the boundaries of acceptable conservative belief as they promoted, protected, and proscribed the many organizations that comprised the movement by the early 1960s. In doing so, they became more than just messengers. They became leaders.

By the late 1950s, "conservative media" had emerged as a meaningful concept with a coherent set of key figures. Sharing national reach and overlapping coverage, enterprises like the *Manion Forum*, *National Review*, *Human Events*, and Regnery Publishing were for many people the center of conservatism in America. Listeners and subscribers regarded them as part of a single project dedicated to advancing conservative ideas. But audiences did more than just listen and read. They saw these broadcasters, editors, publishers, and writers as authorities on conservatism. When questions arose about how best to shape their own beliefs, readers and audiences turned to media activists for answers. What books should they read? What policies should they support? What colleges were safe enough to send their children to?

The most pressing question they asked, however, was this: "What can I do?" The four words popped up time and again, a steady call for action sent over the transom on a daily basis. At first, conservative media activists responded with suggestions for individual action. During his first year on air, Manion added action statements near the end of each broadcast. "Action," he maintained, "must begin with each of us personally." It would take "*personal* effort" and "*personal* sacrifice": working in political circles, writing representatives, alerting neighbors, getting—and staying—angry. Tom Anderson, editor of the mass-circulated *Farm and Ranch Magazine*, dedicated one of his popular "Straight Talk" columns to answering the oft-repeated question "What can I do?" His initial suggestions—eliminate the income tax, end peacetime debt, and ban trade with communist countries—were well outside the scope of his readers' abilities. But some were within reach: subscribing to *American Mercury*, *National Review*, *Human Events*, and the like; contributing to Manion, Dan Smoot, Fulton Lewis, and other commentators of a conservative stripe; and supporting the advertisers for both. In a similar vein, *Human Events* unveiled a new section in 1960 called "What You Can Do," a regular feature aimed at those "at the grass roots." Each "What You Can Do" segment focused on a different piece of legislation, detailing not only its substance and impact but the "arguments to use in writing your Congressman," "WHEN to do your letter-writing," and "whom to write to." But these were calls to individual action. A movement required more.[2]

An opening for action on a larger scale presented itself in 1959 when President Eisenhower announced Soviet premier Nikita Khrushchev's visit to the United States. Conservatives had little use for Eisenhower—they considered him a "me-too" Republican perfectly willing to maintain New Deal–style governance—but seldom had they been as opposed to the president as when he invited the communist leader to America. The possibility of Khrushchev setting foot on American soil outraged conservatives. Inviting him to the United States, they argued, gave an air of legitimacy to the "butcher of Budapest" (as Richard Nixon had named him after the Soviets crushed the 1956 Hungarian Revolution). It undermined the show of support the country had just given the Soviet Union's satellite states during Captive Nations Week. And it continued a policy of coexistence that conservatives felt reeked of appeasement, an unwillingness to stand up to the Soviet Union that could only lead to defeat. Eisenhower's stance baffled conservatives: hadn't Khrushchev promised to bury them? On top of that, the president implored Americans to greet Khrushchev civilly, to withhold raucous protest and jeers. The audacity of this request led one *National Review* writer to pen "A Visit from St. Nik":

> *If he's tough and gruff and otherwise dismays you,*
> *Just count to ten and do not start a fight:*
> *He's coming here to bury you, not praise you,*
> *And he'd like to do the job and do it right.*[3]

Outrage coursed through conservative media, which presented a united front of opposition to the impending visit. Manion hammered away at it in a series of four broadcasts, including one featuring Cardinal Richard Cushing, the archbishop of Boston, and another with Senators Barry Goldwater and Thomas Dodd. At *National Review*, editors excoriated the policy position such a visit advanced. "If our opposition to Communism is to mean anything," they insisted, "it must rest on the insistence that Communist rule is *illegitimate*," that Soviet regimes were "usurping tyrannies." In his earthier style, Tom Anderson attacked Khrushchev directly: "You bloody, conniving, double-dealing, atheistic butcher, I assume you have a mother. When you get home, do me a favor, please: unleash her and toss her a bone."[4]

The Khrushchev visit, however, required more than editorials and insults. Conservatives picked up on the example of the Scandinavians, who had faced their own Khrushchev visit in August. News of the visit roiled the press in Denmark, Sweden, and Norway, generating plans of mass protests in Sweden. In the face of this opposition, Khrushchev canceled his visit, citing the "anti-Soviet" environment. If protestors in Scandinavia could overturn their governments' invitations to the Soviet premier, conservatives argued, the same could be done in the United States. Surely Americans were no less freedom-loving than *Swedes*.[5]

The organizing began immediately. Manion and Buckley joined Goldwater, William Grede, and others in forming the Committee Against Summit Entanglements (CASE), an organization chaired by John Birch Society founder Robert Welch. The roster of officers and sponsors included a number of fellow conservative media figures, including Anderson, libertarian publisher J. H. Gipson, and *Independent American* publisher Kent Courtney, as well as major sponsors of conservative media enterprises like Roger Milliken and Fred Koch, the Wichita-based engineer and entrepreneur who founded Koch Industries. The organization ran an open letter to Eisenhower in major American newspapers, outlining ten reasons not to exchange visits with Khrushchev and urging the president to rescind his invitation. Ads included a petition for readers to circulate among their neighbors and then send to the White House, a way of encouraging active engagement with the issue while also showing the breadth of popular support for CASE.[6]

But CASE was just a first step. News of other activities spread through conservative media circles in the weeks that followed. Manion detailed planned actions in Chicago and across the country. At *Human Events*, an editor came up with the idea of skywriting a giant cross above Washington when Khrushchev's motorcade set out, turning the heavens themselves into a medium of protest. *National Review* promoted rallies on the East Coast and sold tens of thousands of "Khrushchev Not Welcome Here" bumper stickers. In Washington, D.C., Brent Bozell took time away from writing for *National Review* to direct efforts for the Committee for Freedom for All Peoples, including the distribution of black armbands for protestors to wear during the visit. A *Chicago Tribune* article later claimed demand for the armbands left D.C. facing a shortage of black cloth.[7]

Efforts didn't stop there. Sensing pockets of resistance to the visit in New York, Buckley, who had threatened to dye the Hudson red to greet the "bloody butcher," seized on the idea of holding an anti-Khrushchev rally. He gave the project to Rusher, insisting, Rusher recalled ruefully, that it would only take "a couple of phone calls." But the rally Buckley had in mind was a much grander affair than his workload promise suggested. Taking place in Carnegie Hall, the rally featured big-name conservative speakers: Manion, Buckley, Bozell, conservative columnist Ruth Alexander, and *Reader's Digest* senior editor Eugene Lyons. Tickets sold for a dollar and went on sale the morning of the rally. Over twenty-five hundred people snapped them up and packed into the hall.[8]

Conservatives had been looking forward to the rally, but their highest hopes for it had been dashed two days earlier when Khrushchev's plane touched down at Andrews Air Force Base. Many of the organizers had been convinced that with enough public dissent, the Khrushchev visit would be scotched. Manion, for instance, noted he had been "bombarded with frantic protests against this unfortunate exchange of visits" and had faith that if that message could get through, Khrushchev would reconsider as he had with the Scandinavians. "I am sure you agree with me," Manion telegraphed sympathetic senators, "that Communism is no less distasteful to the American people than it is to the people of the Scandinavian countries." But Khrushchev had come. In fact, as ticket holders crowded into Carnegie Hall that Thursday evening, the Soviet premier was just ten blocks away at the Waldorf-Astoria, calling for strengthened economic relations between the United States and the Soviet Union.[9]

The Carnegie rally may not have stopped Khrushchev from coming, but it still had a purpose. As Manion told those gathered, their numbers served "to underscore our continuing active open support and sympathy for the more than 20 captive nations." After a prayer and the singing of the national anthem, the evening progressed through a series of speeches decrying

Khrushchev's visit "as a blow to American moral leadership and the cause of peoples enslaved by communism." Audience members, supplied with black flags and armbands, cheered condemnations of Eisenhower's reception of Khrushchev. They nodded as a former assistant counsel for the McCarthy hearings warned, "There is a murderer at large in New York tonight." And they listened closely as Buckley criticized not the crimes of Khrushchev but "the damage we have done to ourselves" in assenting to the visit. "I mind that Khrushchev is here," Buckley declared to no one's surprise, "but I mind even more that Eisenhower invited him." And yet it bothered him even more that the press had so roundly defended Eisenhower's actions and that the American people had, with an all-too-familiar apathy (or worse, weak-mindedness), simply gone along with it. The great offense of the visit was not Khrushchev's blood-soaked hands, Buckley argued, but that America had reached out for a handshake and stained its own. It was a pivotal moment in the shift from conservative anti-interventionism to conservative hawkishness. While the ostensible goals of the anti-Khrushchev campaign meshed with the nationalism of the 1940s and early 1950s—the refusal to extend diplomatic ties, the focus on preserving America rather than rolling back the Soviet threat—after the Khrushchev rally the movement took a decidedly hawkish turn.[10]

The rally proved a great success: a packed house, memorable speeches, national press coverage. It had also taken a great deal of time and effort to pull off. Rather than a "couple of phone calls," Rusher reported, planning the event required "the entire junior staff of the magazine [to be] torn from their regular jobs and thrown into performing the innumerable tasks and errands that had to be performed." Likewise, Bozell's attentions were entirely dominated by Khrushchev. Though planning a major project with Manion and Goldwater, Bozell believed Khrushchev's visit was more pressing. "I feel obliged to see this Khrushchev thing through," he explained apologetically to Manion as he placed the project on the back burner. "I have never felt as strongly about anything in my life—and consider all other duties secondary to this one." Manion consented to the delay, as organizing against Khrushchev consumed much of his time as well. [11]

The time seemed well worth the effort. Judging from bumper sticker sales, rally attendance, and audience feedback, the anti-Khrushchev organizing had tapped into a vein of discontent, a group ready to mobilize. But the rally had been a one-off event. Could people be organized long term to push for a broader agenda? Rusher seemed to think so; in fact, he thought it necessary. "As things stand," he complained to a friend, "we (the magazine) are forever being called upon to do things that are really outside our scope—run forums, stage rallies against Khrushchev, sell Khrushchev Not Welcome stickers, run a Conservative Book Club, etc." Rusher responded to these calls for action with exasperation: "You, sir, are a good example of why publishers get gray!" he told a writer who suggested the magazine organize a demonstration supporting the House Un-American Activities Committee. "*National Review* is a magazine, not a political party."[12]

Still, something had to be done. It seemed as though more and more people were awakening to the dangers of liberal governance and communism. The *Manion Forum* detected "a distinct turn to the Right" in the country, and now those right-wing Americans were, according to Rusher, "casting about for a suitable form of political organization." What was needed, Rusher concluded, was "some sort of conservative movement—a movement, not a party—marching along beside *National Review*." Yet as Rusher had noted, and as Bozell's and Manion's experiences could confirm, organizing was a full-time job. To take it on might mean shortchanging or even giving up the media enterprises they had built. If not them, though, then who? As it turned out, despite Rusher's assertion that they should not be the leaders and organizers of a movement, media activists would take up the call.[13]

In 1961, M. Stanton Evans—known as Stan to friends—recounted his experience as a conservative Yale student in the early 1950s. The Intercollegiate Studies Institute, an on-campus organization for conservative students, had introduced him to conservative writers like Frank Chodorov and Frederic Bastiet, to *Human Events*, and to the existence of right-wing publishers Regnery and Devin-Adair. "This literature offered welcome information—but it was more than that," he wrote. "From the perspective of 1961, the slight quantity of materials then available to a conservative student may not seem impressive. But to me, it was a discovery beyond price; for it meant that I was no longer alone." And the spread of conservative books and magazines did more than dispel Evans's sense of isolation. "It was on such foundations that the semblance of a conservative movement was launched at Yale."[14]

So Evans introduced his first book, *Revolt on the Campus*, which Regnery published in 1961. The book appeared at a time when conservative organizing had achieved critical mass. On college campuses, students coordinated local chapters of Young Americans for Freedom, an organization backed by the *National Review*. Barry Goldwater's *Conscience of a Conservative* overtook John Kennedy's *Profiles in Courage* on the *New York Times* best-seller list. Circulation and audiences were up for the *Manion Forum*, *National Review*, and *Human Events*. "The conservative movement," author Russell Kirk crowed, "is going great guns right now." That Kirk could even talk about a "conservative movement" showed how much had changed in a few short years.[15]

What happened? Despite Rusher's protestations that media enterprises had no place organizing a movement, they did just that. Media figures oversaw the emergence of a mass political mobilization as they created, funded, promoted, and evaluated organizations in the early 1960s. That this was a *mass* movement mattered: though a number of organizations since World War II had promoted agendas aligned with facets of modern conservatism, the organizations of the late 1950s and early 1960s were something new. National in aim, avowedly conservative in philosophy, and purportedly grassroots in nature, these organizations attracted thousands of members and, through their activism, won conservatism a place on the national stage.

Postwar conservative organizing centered on young people, particularly those in colleges and universities. The campus was a natural site of expansion for media activists, given their arguments about the importance of ideas and consequences of bias. Bred in the academy, the first generation of media activists saw the future of the movement in the institutions in which they themselves had spent the most time: media and universities. Both institutions, conservatives believed, were riddled with liberal bias, which was redirecting the natural conservatism of the American people toward a sort of soft consensus around socialism. To combat those forces, media activists focused their organizational energies on the campus. And the effort paid off: the most vibrant, fastest-growing organizations on college campuses in the early 1960s were conservative groups like Young Americans for Freedom (YAF) and the Intercollegiate Studies Institute. (One measure: the three most popular speakers on college campuses in 1962, in order, were Barry Goldwater, Bill Buckley, and Martin Luther King Jr.)[16]

In many ways, YAF embodied Rusher's hope for "some sort of conservative movement—a movement, not a party—marching along beside *National Review*." Born at the Buckley estate in Sharon, Connecticut, YAF drew together young, conservative, politically engaged students. In its early years, it was largely organized by Douglas Caddy and David Franke, founders of the Student Committee for the Loyalty Oath, which in 1959 successfully lobbied Congress to retain the loyalty oath for recipients of federal student loans and fellowships. In his authoritative study of YAF, historian John A. Andrew named four men the "elder statesmen" of the organization: Buckley, Rusher, Evans, and Marvin Liebman. All had close ties to *National Review*. Just twenty-six years old in 1960, Evans had sketched out a broader career in conservative media. Evans's primary post was as editor of the *Indianapolis News*, a paper owned, along with the *Arizona Republic*, by the conservative Eugene Pulliam. In addition to his work at the *News*, Evans had served as an editor at *Human Events*, *National Review*, and the *Freeman*. This experience in conservative media allowed the young Evans to emerge as an "elder statesman," having spent nearly a decade with those people behind the nascent movement. YAF forged ties with other media activists as well, filling its advisory board with people like Manion, Devin Garrity, radio preacher Carl McIntire, and *Manchester Union-Leader* owner William Loeb.[17]

What did it mean that YAF was so closely connected to *National Review*? The relationship shaped the philosophical groundings of YAF along the magazine's editorial line. YAF's founding declaration, the Sharon Statement, reflected the fusionist politics promoted at *National Review* (for good reason: Evans wrote most of the statement). In years to come, YAF would align with *National Review* as a force of "responsible conservatism." But it wasn't just an intellectual partnership. *National Review* defined YAF as a central player in the conservative movement, lavishing it with praise. "A new organization was born last week," Buckley informed his readers, "and just possibly it will influence the political future of this country, as why should it not, considering that its membership is young, intelligent, articulate and determined, its principles enduring, its aims to translate these principles into political action in a world which has lost its moorings and is looking about for them desperately?" Despite Buckley's later demurral that his "midwifery of [YAF] was purely ceremonial," the association with *National Review* shaped the organization from its very beginnings.[18]

YAF became the face of the "revolt on campus," claiming more than 350 chapters and 30,000 members by 1964. But it was not the first conservative organization to take root at colleges and universities. That distinction belonged to the Intercollegiate Society of Individualists (ISI), a libertarian organization begun in 1953 by Frank Chodorov. Like YAF, ISI had a media midwife as well: *Human Events*. It was in the newsweekly's pages that Chodorov first floated the idea of a conservative student organization.

Soon a $1,000 check arrived in the mail courtesy of J. Howard Pew of Sun Oil, funds Chodorov dedicated to starting the organization he had written about. Buckley, ever-present, served as its first president. (Though he was soon demoted by way of a brief note from Chodorov: "Am removing you as president. Easier to raise money if a Jew is president. You can be V-P. Love, Frank.")[19]

Victor Milione succeeded Buckley and oversaw the organization's transformation to the Intercollegiate Studies Institute in 1960. Milione, a twenty-eight-year-old from Pennsylvania, revamped the organization, shifting it from a fundamentally libertarian group to a conservative one. As part of that process, he sought to change the organization's name, turning to conservative media leaders for advice. "I think there are overtones of crackpotism to the word individualist," Regnery explained to Milione, a frequent correspondent, "it reminds people, somehow or the other, of nudists, etc." Buckley joined Regnery's condemnation of the word, in which he heard "solipsistic overtones." Rusher had no problem with the term "individualist" but thought the organization's name was too long and suggested the College Conservative League (which as a bonus had a better acronym than YAF, which Rusher found "faintly ludicrous-sounding"). This search for a new name demonstrated how much young conservatives like Milione relied on media activists for guidance. By 1961, ISI claimed a membership of around 13,000 spread over 54 campuses.[20]

Groups such as YAF and ISI focused on college students because of their belief in the power of institutional bias. In an assessment that mirrored their critique of established media, conservatives believed higher education had fallen under the control of a coterie of leftists. This control of higher education, like that of media, had significant consequences: professors and administrators could indoctrinate unsuspecting students under the guise of educating them, generating the same air of objectivity in the classroom that they created in the news media. Compounding this effect: the number of Americans enrolled in college skyrocketed in the 1950s and 1960s, thanks to widespread affluence and the GI Bill's education provisions. Now, conservatives feared, an entire generation was at risk of liberal indoctrination.

Liberal professors received the bulk of the blame. "You know as well as I what happens to [students] when some 'fuzzy' brained socialist professor gets them in a captive classroom," wrote one of Manion's correspondents. Little prepared by society to resist liberal and leftist doctrine, students simply went along. Why should they protest? Hadn't the liberal-controlled media been delivering the same message for years? Conservatives argued that college administrators endorsed this practice by promoting liberal professors and stymieing the few conservative professors on campus. Rusher lamented the plight of these conservative scholars: "They face many tribulations. Advancement comes hard. They are victimized by their departments." Worse, colleges, foundations, and government agencies only financially backed the work of these academics' liberal colleagues, resulting in a "neglected generation of scholars" who could neither make a name in their profession nor influence large numbers of students with their teaching.[21]

This critique of liberal bias in the academy marked a subtle but significant shift from the previous decade, when the right's goal had been ferreting out professors with communist leanings. The changed focus was logically consistent with the broader conservative argument that liberalism opened the door for socialism and ultimately for communist takeover. But some conservatives had moved on from communism in the classroom. In his column on higher education in *National Review*, Russell Kirk dismissed concerns with communist professors. "People who think that the Academy is honeycombed with crypto-Communists are wide of the mark," he wrote. "At most, never more than 5 per cent of American college teachers were Communists." The real threat, Kirk maintained, came from "dogmatic Rationalism," which he argued sought to deny free will and spirituality. Those professors who opposed this "academic imperialism" were subjected to a "complete blackout," liable to lose their jobs. So was born the image of the embattled conservative professor, who could be defended in the same breath that demanded the firing of leftist professors.[22]

Postwar conservative media activists circulated the critique of liberal indoctrination in higher education from the beginning. Buckley struck early with the Regnery-published *God and Man at Yale*, his 1951 work that denounced the secularism of his alma mater. By the early 1960s, Clarence Manion was turning his attention to campuses for the same reason that groups such as YAF and ISI focused on college students. Manion invited Professor John N. Moore on his program in February 1962 to discuss "ultra-liberalism on campus." Moore, who taught natural science at Michigan State University, met Manion a year prior when Manion traveled to East Lansing to address the Conservative Club at Michigan State. Their on-air interview revealed Moore's belief that Michigan State lacked "an appropriate balance . . . in the presentation of ideas." Liberals from around the nation came to campus, funded by the university, to speak to students, yet no conservatives were invited to offer opposing views. Moore claimed he had no interest in stifling liberal ideas on campus but rather "that the Conservative point of view should be given equal time." Equal time—another import from the world of media (though this time, the media activists were supporting it).[23]

In addition to professorial and speaker imbalance, Moore pointed to another sign that conservative views were absent from campus: the lack of conservative publications in the library. Moore had a special attachment to conservative media. He traced his conversion to conservatism from the writings of Plato to the pages of *Human Events* to the *Manion Forum*. So when he investigated the offerings in the Honors College Lounge at Michigan State's library, he took issue with what he found. The *Nation*, the *New Republic*, even *International Teamsters* had been made available to students, yet *National Review*, *Christian Economics*, and the *Freeman* were nowhere to be found. How could students replicate his conversion experience without access to the tracts he relied on? Penetrating this presumably hostile environment meant getting conservative media onto campuses. Working with campus groups, conservative media organizations turned their expansion efforts to America's colleges and universities.[24]

In late 1961, the *Forum* launched a new effort to place Manion's program on campus radio stations. The "revolt on campus" entranced Manion, who had already forged close ties to campus organizing efforts. He joined the National Advisory Board for YAF at the organization's founding, and his daughter Marilyn soon enlisted, becoming a director shortly thereafter. In early 1962, Manion brought Evans—"one of the truly bright luminaries of the American Conservative movement"—onto his program to discuss *Revolt on the Campus*. After noting that college campuses housed the majority of Manion's Conservative Clubs, Manion applauded the role of college students in "the nation-wide revival of Conservatism."[25]

The interview coincided with Manion's announcement that his program was going to "invade" campuses. As he explained at the end of the broadcast's reprint, "Inculcation of sound American, anti-Communist principles in the minds of our young people must be advanced by every possible means." The framing Manion chose was important. He was not arguing against bias on campuses. He was arguing for the proper kind of bias. As such, the *Forum* would provide the programs free to campuses that requested them. The University of South Carolina became one of the first to sign up, a fact Manion eagerly shared with sponsor Roger Milliken, a native of the state. Within a year, the university was joined by seven others, including Brown,

Help Make Manion Forum Broadcasts The

NEW CAMPUS CRAZE

MANION FORUM

ALREADY THOUSANDS OF STUDENTS HEAR THESE PROVOCATIVE BROADCASTS OVER THEIR OWN CAMPUS RADIO STATIONS

Figure 6. Promotional materials for *Manion Forum* college radio program, 1963. Chicago History Museum.

Montana State, Fairleigh-Dickinson, and Yale. While such a small number could hardly serve to hearten Manion, as always, he put a positive spin on it: the institutions served over fifty thousand students. "These are boys and girls with pliable minds, susceptible to 'Liberal' and Communist propaganda," a *Forum* fund-raiser contended. "For years they have had drummed into their ears the Socialistic nostrums of misguided Fabian professors, dizzy Keynesian economists, deluded do-gooders whose hearts bleed for Africa, Asia, even parts of Europe." Salvation now blasted from their campus radio stations in the form of the *Manion Forum*.[26]

The project to secure a place on campus radio stations, though small, still ran into problems that confirmed for Manion the censorious atmosphere of higher education. A student at the University of Tampa requested tapes to air on his campus station. A few months after he began airing the *Forum*, however, the student wrote Manion again, canceling his request. "Since the tapes have been arriving, we have met much controversy from the school and faculty," he reported. "They believe them to be too radical." Manion had little respect for the student's shoulder-shrugging capitulation—"young patriots are usually not stymied so easily"—but he found the story of suppression useful, publicizing it in the *Forum*'s newsletter. The loss of Tampa did not hurt the campus station program; by early 1963, the *Forum* could be heard at more than twenty colleges.[27]

College students were a prized audience for other conservative media enterprises as well. Rusher estimated somewhere between 20 and 25 percent of *National Review*'s subscribers in 1957 currently taught or attended college. The staff took no issue with increasing that number, as their efforts in the following years showed. In addition to offering student and faculty subscription rates, *National Review* experimented with distributing free copies at Princeton, a project the on-campus coordinator deemed a vital tool for propagating "the all too often unexpressed conservative viewpoint." *Human Events* likewise offered reduced rates to college students, while Regnery worked to get his books distributed to college libraries.[28]

These relationships between media outlets and college organizations, though occasionally fraught (especially when money exchanged hands), increased the reach of both groups and drew both parts of the movement even closer together. In the early 1960s the *Forum* and YAF produced a joint advertising circular, touting the "combined effort of two great patriotic organizations" to provide "the ultimate in public service programming." Notably, "public service programming" combined the *Forum*'s media efforts with YAF's activism, symbolized by pictures of meeting cards, presentations, mail, and magazines (YAF published a monthly magazine, *The New Guard*). Together, the prospectus suggested, conservative media and organizations could spread conservatism much further than either endeavor alone.[29]

Publicity for conservative college organizations came free of charge in most cases, often incorporated in stories and reports rather than as separate advertisements. A parade of YAF members appeared on the *Manion Forum* in the 1960s, including National Chairman Robert Bauman, who read an extensive excerpt of the Sharon Statement before launching into his pitch. ISI received favorable coverage in *Human Events*, where Frank Chodorov had first proposed the organization in 1950; YAF events scored frequent mention in the weekly's pages. The same was true at *National Review*, which, for instance, promoted "The ISI Leadership Guide" (a manual for starting conservative organizations) and YAF's 1962 Madison Square Garden rally, which drew eighteen thousand attendees. The organizations got behind-the-scenes boosts as well: in response to a letter from a concerned mother inquiring into the political nature of Brown and Tufts, to which her son had applied, Rusher counseled her not to worry about the political climate but to put her son in contact with the conservative strongholds on campus, YAF and ISI.[30]

In addition to the publicity, YAF and ISI received discounts and free subscriptions from conservative media outlets. Regnery offered a 20 percent discount on the company's books to members of YAF, for which his son served as a board member. He also constantly scoured for donations to distribute free books to members of both ISI and YAF. The pages of *Human Events* carried appeals for funds so the weekly could send free subscriptions to ISI members. These efforts were not mere philanthropy. Getting students in the habit of reading conservative publications—and pairing that habit with the claim that other media sources carried a liberal taint—created the potential for paying subscriptions after college. By linking activism and media, these outlets were helping make the consumption of ideological media a fundamental act of conservative identity.[31]

ISI built another relationship with *National Review*, one that would be replicated with other organizations and other media outlets. Most conservative media enterprises, because of their overt political nature, lacked eligibility for tax-deductible donations, a major stumbling block for individuals, corporations, and foundations that wished to donate generously. Many corporations and foundations, in fact, had rules mandating donations could only go to tax-deductible ventures. To sidestep this problem, the media outlets created financial relationships with selected tax-deductible organizations, then informed their donors to give money to the organization with a note directing the donation back to the media outlet. So someone wishing to give money to *National Review* would instead send their donation to ISI, noting that the donation should be used to subsidize *National Review* subscriptions for college students and professors. The magazine thus reaped benefits not only in funds but in increased circulation. Forty thousand dollars a year changed hands this way. Introducing money into the relationship, however, had its drawbacks. ISI, which struck a similar deal with *Human Events*, mismanaged the process so badly that both publications were left with thousands of dollars in unpaid bills, putting an abrupt end to the arrangement.[32]

Despite occasional problems, the relationship between conservative media and campus organizations benefited both groups. College activists gained access to the guidance, resources, and publicity conservative media figures could provide, while those in conservative media gained audiences and readers. Moreover, Bill Rusher got his wish for a movement marching alongside conservative media to which they could confidently direct correspondents seeking action.

The campus movement was a natural ally of postwar conservative media, given the intellectual orientation of media activists. For all the populist rhetoric that coursed through conservative media, people like Rusher, Manion, and Regnery were far more at home on a college campus than just about anywhere else. The factory worker, the high-school-educated housewife, the white-collar employee who would rather watch Red Skelton than read Leo Strauss—they were potential conservatives, too, but ones much more difficult for the principal media activists to reach.

Other groups could reach them, though, groups whose tactics and reputations these media activists had far less control over. As the conservative movement grew, competition over the movement's leadership grew with it. These were battles with high stakes: who would define conservatism's meaning, its goals, its membership. Those stakes would grow even higher as the movement started to draw attention from mainstream media. Under the bright lights of press criticism, media activists found their leadership of the movement challenged and their once-cohesive networks shredded by divisions over one new group in particular: the John Birch Society.

Chapter 5

The Millstone

Writing to Gina Manion, Clarence's wife, in 1961, Peggy Cies recounted an inquiry she had sent to *Human Events* a few years earlier, after she and her husband, William, joined the John Birch Society. Cies had asked the editors what they thought of the organization's founder, Robert Welch. "What Bob Welch says, you can trust," they replied. Cies told Gina her experience confirmed this. She and William, who ran a successful real estate company in San Marino, California, had been poring over back issues of *American Opinion*, the society's magazine, and marveled how Welch had gotten it right, time and again. In fact, just the week before her congressman John Rousselot, also a member of the Birch Society, said, "It's amazing how it seems to work out as Bob Welch says."

And yet Cies was irate. Not with Welch—"we count ourselves fortunate to have such a man as Bob Welch to give us inspiration and guidance"—but with Barry Goldwater and all the other conservatives who seemed willing to turn on the Birch Society in its time of trial. Goldwater, speaking at a recent appearance in Southern California, strategically distanced himself from the Birch Society. "We are all at a loss as to why he would knife an organization which to a large extent has helped to build him up," Cies wrote. She felt this new reticence about the Birch Society, shared by a number of conservative outlets and organizations, revealed a weakness within the movement: "Every anti-communist should be supporting every other anti-communist in this crisis which is upon us. It is the most discouraging part—of this whole struggle—the inability of the conservatives to really work together despite differences."[1]

Cies was speaking from the heart of a battle over the borderlines of conservatism. In the late 1950s and early 1960s, modern conservatism attracted an ever-growing number of spokesmen, sponsors, and supporters. From within the movement, this trend was heartening. From without, it inspired both curiosity and concern. The bright spotlight of press attention illuminated the movement's roughest edges and threatened to discredit conservatism as a whole. Easily lampooned as a loony secret society that saw communists lurking in every shadow, the Birch Society became the brush that tarred every part of the burgeoning conservative movement. Almost overnight, it transformed from one of the most vibrant organizations on the right to the movement's millstone. Contentious debates about how to deal with the Birch Society consumed conservatives in the early 1960s. As the leaders of the movement, media activists were at the heart of these debates. Policing the boundaries of legitimate conservatism, a fairly easy task in the 1950s when it came to issues like anti-Semitism, proved far more difficult in the 1960s. The clashes over the Birch Society opened a schism in the conservative media world that persisted throughout the decade, with reverberations that continue into the present.

The developments in conservatism in the 1950s went largely unmentioned in popular media. Academics took note: in 1955 social scientist Daniel Bell collected a number of essays for *The New American Right* (later released under the more derisive title *The New Radical Right*). This book joined others like *The Radical Right: A Problem for American Democracy* (1954) and *Conservatism in America* (1955), the latter of which sought to rescue conservatism from its modern practitioners, to move it toward the "vital center" rather than the rightward fringe. Columbia historian Richard Hofstadter began publishing articles on the subject as well, like "The Pseudo-Conservative Revolt" in the 1954–1955 issue of the *American Scholar.* Senator Joseph McCarthy and his defenders prompted these works, whose authors found the senator and his followers a troubling expression of reactionary populist radicalism. Many Americans opposed McCarthy's crusade, but the larger concern shaping these books—that not just McCarthy but McCarthy*ites* posed a danger to America—failed to penetrate the national consciousness. So when McCarthy faded from the national stage, so too did concerns about conservatives.[2]

Not until 1961 did journalists discover the "radical right" and "ultraconservatives." Once they did, though, the right became a media obsession.

Soon just about every major newspaper and magazine was devoting column space to the problem of the "radical right." Why the sudden interest? Conservative media efforts had been growing for several years; Goldwater's *Conscience of a Conservative* was in wide circulation. Yet neither of these developments had triggered inky paroxysms from journalists. So what had?

The John Birch Society. Founded in 1958 by candy magnate Robert Welch, the semisecret society was at the forefront of grassroots anticommunist organizing. It quickly attracted major donors like the Millikens and Fred Koch of Koch Industries, as well as tens of thousands of individuals attracted to its message that the communist conspiracy, aided by liberal politicians, represented an existential threat to the United States. Though backed by a board of prominent conservatives (including Clarence Manion), decision making flowed directly from Welch, who considered the society's authoritarian structure essential to achieving its goals. In addition to local chapters, the society's basic organizational unit, the society also sponsored a magazine, *American Opinion*, and a number of associated bookstores that peddled conservative books.[3]

Prior to 1961, the Birch Society drew little notice from mainstream journalists, never appearing in the pages of *Time*, the *Nation*, or the *Saturday Evening Post*, nary a mention in a single major newspaper. That changed in March 1961 when *Time* published "The Americanists," an article that coincided with a similar series in the *Los Angeles Times*. These pieces, written as exposés, presented Birchers as part of a secret society under the "hard-boiled, dictatorial direction of one man." To demonstrate the group's extremism, *Time* pointed to *The Politician*, a 302-page book Welch dubiously maintained had been meant as a private letter. The book—which *Time* dubbed "Welch's *Mein Kampf*"—contained accusations that everyone from John Foster Dulles to Dwight Eisenhower were Communist agents. Seeing communist conspiracy everywhere, *Time* wrote, such a cloak-and-dagger group would normally be dismissed "as a tiresome, comic-opera joke." So why pay them any mind? Because the number of Birchers was growing—and fast. By the early 1960s membership peaked between 50,000 and 100,000.[4]

There was something titillating about the idea of a secret society promoting accusations of presidential conspiracy, and journalists pounced. Completely absent from news coverage the year before, in 1961 the John Birch Society became all anyone could talk about. *Time* kept up coverage throughout the year, with the *Nation* quick on its heels. The *Los Angeles Times* series triggered a state investigation into the organization, keeping the

Birch Society front and center; other papers joined the fray with coverage of their own.[5]

These stories brought the society to the attention of readers across the country, many for the first time. Politicians were quick to denounce either the organization as a whole or the accusations of Eisenhower's disloyalty. After censuring the society from the Senate floor, North Dakota senator Milton Young inserted the *Time* article into the *Congressional Record* as evidence of his claims against the Birchers. Other denunciations offered more measured criticism. In response to the front-page editorial in the *Los Angeles Times* that capped its five-day series, Richard Nixon condemned the society for attacking communists by applying "the same evil methods they employ." However, Nixon continued, the Birch Society appealed to so many people because it promised to do what so few organizations did: "to fight the great battle for preserving and extending American ideals." Attention from prominent politicians generated more press coverage, and the Birch Society remained in the spotlight throughout the spring.[6]

Eventually, though, Birch Society exposés reached the point of diminishing returns; there seemed to be no secrets left to extract from the presumably secret society. So journalists cast a wider net, and out came the articles and books on conservatives, labeled the "radical right," "ultra-conservatives," "superpatriots," "extremists," and, in time, just "the ultras." These articles extended to conservatives the criticisms of the Birch Society. Calling them "the Rampageous Right," Alan Barth outlined the distinguishing characteristics of these "aginners": uncomplicated, conspiracy minded, antidemocratic. Despite these qualities, though, Barth saw little to fear in an organized right: "The Right may make itself a nuisance, but it will not make itself into a government. It is not a wave of the future; it is a voice of frustration and despair, a wail from an irrecoverable past."[7]

Most journalists and authors failed to distinguish between various strains on the right, jumbling organizations and enterprises together with little concern for their differences. A freewheeling *New York Times* article careened from the Birch Society to the *Manion Forum* to the American Nazi Party to *National Review*, lumping them all together as "right-wing extremists." Even those that took the time to delineate between a "Respectable Right" and a "Radical Right" cautioned "that on many essential elements of creed the two are inseparable and indistinguishable." The sins of the radicals tainted them all, a forty-three-page article in the *Nation* maintained, for respectability and radicalism were inseparable for conservatives; one provided political cover, the other roused the grassroots. Thus to talk of one was to talk of the other.[8]

Not surprisingly, the rush of new literature on conservatism provoked responses from media activists. Manion dedicated a broadcast to "gaudy little books about so-called 'Right Wing extremists,'" calling them a "big comic-opera chorus of bad print and cheap paper" designed to destroy conservatism. The authors, he pointed out, all admitted that dissatisfaction with liberal governance stirred conservative agitation. Where he believed they went wrong was in assuming such dissatisfaction was irrational. These writers argued conservatism was a psychological problem, "some sort of mental illness that begins with a harmless twitch six inches to the right of Arthur Schlesinger, Jr., and merges into madness as you approach the political location of people like [conservative military hero] General Walker." Manion countered conservatism was instead "the logical reaction to the failure of liberal policies." After all, no matter how much power these writers assigned to the "Radical Right," it was not conservatives who controlled the government. The Yalta agreement, the fall of China, the Bay of Pigs—these could not be laid at conservatives' feet. Dan Smoot was likewise unimpressed. "'Superpatriot,' if it has any meaning at all, means *having too much patriotism*," he wrote incredulously. "Is that possible?"[9]

Conservatives also responded to specific attacks. Buckley fired off a letter to the *New York Times* after it ran an article bundling *National Review* together with the American Nazi Party, equating the remarks to someone calling the newspaper "the most notable daily of liberals and Communists." In 1961 *Look* magazine published a piece on Kent and Phoebe Courtney's *Independent American* and its associated organization, the Conservative Society for America. The New Orleans–based publication was far more willing to dabble in conspiracy than national conservative media like *Human Events* and the *Manion Forum*, and it was also much more closely tied to white southern resistance to the civil rights movement. As such, while locally important, the couple was almost entirely ignored by the rest of conservative media. After the *Look* magazine attack, Phoebe Courtney sent subscribers a report dissecting the article's content. Courtney saw the article as part of a concerted effort by "Liberal-Socialists" to "throw the full spotlight of publicity on the Right Wing, with the hope that careless statements, or intemperate actions by members of the Right Wing would discredit the entire Conservative movement." While she didn't mind the ideological characterization of their enterprise—they proudly claimed membership in the "Far Right," which they believed was preferable to the "Far Wrong"—she took issue with the article's statements about their finances. (She quickly assured readers—and donors—that the *Independent American* was quite poor.)[10]

Despite this bravado, conservative media activists sensed danger in the new journalistic perception of the "radical right." Yes, there were now alternative conservative media, but their reach was limited. They could not serve as an effective counterweight for established media, where most Americans got their news about the world. So it was not enough to simply close ranks, to fire back at the *New York Times* or the *Nation* when their writers tarred conservatives as crackpots and radicals. However unfair or biased one thought the attacks were, they were undoubtedly effective. As long as the established media served as gatekeepers, the right was going to have to work on its image. And when it came to remaking conservatism's image, all roads led back to the same place: the John Birch Society.

"The write-up *Time* gives the John Birch Society now makes it nationally known, rather than a parochial embarrassment," Neil McCaffrey, *National Review*'s promotional consultant, wrote Buckley in late 1961. "Naturally, nothing would please the left more than to be able to equate conservatism with this breed. I think the moment has come when the magazine must publicly disassociate itself from them." McCaffrey was an early advocate for a public split with the John Birch Society. But he represented only one in a diverse set of opinions. Indeed, while media activists seemed united in their denunciations of established media's coverage of the "radical right," that public uniformity belied a more troubled atmosphere within conservative media circles. They understood they were the voices of conservatism, leaders to whom audiences, organizations, and now journalists looked to define the movement. So what should they do? Those in Buckley's camp chose to heap ridicule on the society and read it out of the movement, while others—*National Review* publisher William Rusher chief among them—preferred to keep a cautious distance and allow events to set the course. Still others, like Manion, argued conservatives should quietly develop alternatives to the society while publicly continuing their assault on established media for its efforts to discredit conservatism.[11]

All this was complicated by the deep ties binding conservative media to the Birch Society. Welch owned substantial shares in Regnery Publishing, and Regnery had published Welch's 1952 pamphlet *May God Forgive Us*, distributing over one hundred thousand copies. Two years later Welch and Regnery worked together again, this time on the publication of *The Life of*

John Birch, the story of the Baptist missionary after whom Welch named his organization. In a letter laden with irony, Welch congratulated Regnery for publishing the sensible rather than the sensational. Doing so, Welch wrote, allowed him "to avoid becoming so easy a target for the smear artists as young Devin Garrity, whose Devin-Adair Company has also published many books to which the influential opinion-molders of the last few years have objected so violently, and who has therefore become labeled in the book world, however unfairly, as a propagandist rather than a publisher."[12]

It was through Regnery that Welch and Buckley met. (Buckley later tweaked Regnery for this role: "You, you scoundrel, introduced me to Bob!") Prior to 1961, *National Review* lauded Welch as "an amazing man" and "as conservative as they come." Buckley, who would later avoid appearances with Welch, shared a podium with him at the *Independent American* Forum in 1959 and served (along with Manion, Bozell, Goldwater, and others) on the Committee Against Summit Entanglements, which Welch chaired. While Buckley fervently contested many of Welch's beliefs, not the least that Eisenhower was a communist, he pronounced those disagreements out of public view. With the sudden spotlight on the society, however, Buckley began to wonder if the time had come to make a public break.[13]

In navigating this question, Buckley had to consider the opinions of Clarence Manion. Manion had in 1959 accepted a position on the National Council of the Birch Society, a leadership group designed to "show the caliber of men" supporting the organization. He also served as a founding board member of National Weekly, the corporate entity behind *National Review*, a place from which he could exercise some influence at the magazine. From his position at the fulcrum, Manion played a critical role in mitigating the developing rift between the two organizations.[14]

Like Buckley, Manion had concerns about the Birch Society in light of the negative attention it was receiving. So in the summer of 1961, he decided to offer an alternative: the Manion Forum Conservative Clubs. The rising conservative sentiment that had drawn established media's attention had been good for the *Manion Forum*. By the time Manion announced his Conservative Clubs, his program could be heard over 235 stations, more than double his 1958 coverage. The staff had grown to eight people, who worked to transcribe broadcasts, organize fund-raising efforts, run the *Forum*'s press, and answer the 100,000 pieces of mail that reached the office every year. Weekly costs ran well over $10,000, raised from corporate and individual donors; over 700 industrialists had written fund-raising letters

Figure 7. *Manion Forum* support staff operations, 1961. Chicago History Museum.

on behalf of the *Forum*. The extra staff and money made it possible for the *Forum* to print and distribute books, pamphlets, and, starting just prior to the club announcement, a biweekly newsletter.[15]

The newsletter served as an indication of the nature of the *Forum's* growth. Had Manion been interested only in growing his media coverage, broadcast reprints would have sufficed. But he had more in mind. The newsletters previewed upcoming guests, but they also announced news and activities, promoted conservative books, kept readers informed of Manion's in-person events, and carried reports of Conservative Club activism. Indeed, this last purpose was the catalyst behind the newsletter and explained the timing of the launch; Manion needed a way for local clubs to connect to the national project.

The newsletter became one of the most important tools for Conservative Clubs because of the clubs' decentralized nature. "Deliberately, we refrained from 'organizing' or attempting to control any of these groups," he wrote Welch, arguing that should "the clubs stay small and unaffiliated, they will provide effective outlets for outraged energy." Small and unaffiliated: these features made the clubs unusual, the antithesis of the authoritarian structure of the Birch Society (which was modeled after the Communist Party, which Welch believed was the most successful political organization of the era). So that clubs could respond to local issues, there was no central leadership guiding them. The *Forum* tracked paperwork, sent out missives, and wrote a constitution, but no governance structure existed; there was no president or chair to direct and coordinate activities. Individual clubs did not interact. Manion had a reason for wanting to keep clubs small. "For the purposes of political action," he explained to a friend, "100 clubs with a membership of 10 in each club is more potent than one club with a membership of 1,000." His experience in politics led Manion to believe smaller groups would have all the benefits of teamwork without the divisiveness larger groups tended to invite. To ensure clubs stayed small, their sole structural requirement pertained to size: five members could start a club, and membership was limited to twenty-five.[16]

Through the newsletter, Manion directed these clubs toward study, discussion, and political action. Some of these activities focused on turning club members into "well versed spokesmen for conservatism," conversant in both conservative philosophy and current events. Thus reading and discussion topped the priority list. Newsletters guided members on how to read ("with pencil in hand—to underline, take notes, to study what you're reading"), why to discuss ("it clears up your thinking on a subject and enables you to restate it in your own words"), and where to turn for help (enclosing booklists from Devin-Adair, a reading list by Phyllis Schlafly, and the address of Patriotic Education, Inc., a Florida company that peddled Constitution study kits). This reading project served two purposes: promoting conservative publishing enterprises and chipping away at established media sources.[17]

In a memo to club members, Manion attacked newspapers and magazines for publishing only liberal opinions. No doubt these periodicals would defend their right to publish such opinions, but what about conservatives? "What about the right to hear the *other* side?" Manion asked. To get this other side, Manion pointed club members to a list of "excellent periodicals," ones that offered "the truth": the *Manion Forum* (naturally), *National Review*, *Human Events*, the *Chicago Tribune*, the *Dan Smoot Report*, and *American Opinion*, the official publication of the John Birch Society. It was a savvy move. In combining attacks on liberal media outlets with promotion of conservative alternatives, Manion provided a rationale for relying on conservative media sources.[18]

Reading conservative publications kept club members informed and
served to counter their exposure to liberal opinions, but Manion had higher
aspirations for the organization. For clubs to make an impact, they had to do
more than speak just to one another—they had to influence their communities. One way of achieving this was through the "letters to the editor" section
of local newspapers. Though this seemed like a small step, Manion saw it as
part of a larger project, a way to add balance to newspapers and circulate
conservative ideas locally. Some may dismiss letter writing as "mere busy
work, a fruitless task at best," Manion wrote club members, but the "letters
to the editor" section "is probably the *most widely-read* section of your
paper!" Certainly readers could relate to Manion's hypothetical letters page,
in which "Mrs. A answers Mr. J's letter about the local PTA. And scores of
spirited letters suddenly appear about chuck holes in the city streets." What
if, Manion asked, the discussion swirled around something more meaningful
than chuckholes? What if PTA debates could be replaced with debates about
the role of government, about foreign aid or taxation?[19]

Enthusiasm for Manion's clubs came from all quarters. The *Knoxville
Journal* firmly supported Manion's plan, and though the editors wondered if
anyone could get Congress to take a more conservative line, they expressed
"hope that thousands of conservative clubs will spring up at Dean Manion's
call." It seemed as though the *Journal* would get its wish—the *Forum*
received over three thousand club applications within three months of the
announcement. "Responses are pouring in from all directions," he reported
eagerly to a friend. "Here is a chance for the little guy to be President of
something and in concert with his neighbors, to throw his weight around
effectively for Constitutional government." Based on the rate of replies,
Manion anticipated ten thousand clubs would be up and running by the
1962 midterm elections. (The number settled at a much more modest six
hundred.)[20]

From the outside, the Conservative Clubs seemed like just one of the
many organizations springing up all over the country. But within conservative media circles, the purpose was clear: to provide an alternative to the
Birch Society. Manion explained it in gentle terms to Welch: "I found that
many of my correspondents were not ready for the John Birch Society. They
would join the infantry, but not the commandoes." And Rusher, who called
the planned clubs "tremendously exciting," supported them for the same
reason. Rusher hoped the clubs would serve as "an alternative lightning rod
down which the accumulating static electricity of conservatism might run

safely to the ground, in preference (and perhaps in some artfully-contrived rivalry) to that constructed by Br'er Welch." Yet while his concerns about the Birch Society motivated him to offer an alternative, Manion firmly believed the society's members were still a vital part of the conservative movement. Infighting should be kept behind the scenes.[21]

Over at *National Review*, opinions were far more divided. Much of the debate centered on whether a public row with the Birch Society would undermine the magazine's effectiveness. In urging a break from the society, promotions consultant Neil McCaffrey acknowledged there would be repercussions—"some of the rank and file in this group probably read the magazine"—but felt it would have to be done for *National Review* to have any influence on the national scene. "I think it can be done tactfully. In any case, it will have to be done sooner or later; better sooner. It's an Ayn Rand situation all over again."

The Ayn Rand comment served as a reminder that this was not the first time *National Review*'s editors had acted as conservatism's border patrol. In 1957, following the publication of *Atlas Shrugged*, Rand's paean to Objectivism as a philosophy inimical to religious traditionalism, Buckley assigned Whittaker Chambers to pen a review. Chambers delivered a predictably devastating takedown of the book, based on what he believed was the inevitable result of Rand's amoral philosophy. He famously wrote, "From almost any page of *Atlas Shrugged*, a voice can be heard, from painful necessity, commanding: 'To the gas chamber—go!'" Buckley would later note, with some pride, that "Chambers did in fact read Miss Rand right out of the conservative movement." It was a process he was prepared to replicate with the Birchers, sending a group of editors off to draft a takedown of the society.[22]

The draft provoked Rusher, who responded with a thoughtful, lengthy memo dissecting the Welch problem. Setting aside the financial issue of the canceled subscriptions and donations such an editorial would surely provoke, Rusher tackled the question of "what an injudicious editorial will do to NR's position *as a leader of conservative opinion* in this country." Rumors were already swirling that the magazine would attack Welch, prompting a deluge of letters and phone calls that all seemed to say the same thing: as a conservative publication *National Review* would do much more harm to the movement than the established media had when they went after Welch.[23]

While these objections mattered to Rusher, he was far more concerned with what he saw as an underlying attitude behind the editorial: "Who cares what the simplistic Right thinks?" Rusher argued they should care a great deal. *National Review* did not exist just so its editors could be as correct as possible—"we can be right without even getting out of bed in the morning." In putting out a magazine, the staff hoped to sway public opinion. Distancing the magazine from Welch would help with "borderline conservatives" and therefore should be done; but gratuitously bashing Welch and the Birch Society would cripple the magazine in the eyes of the "organized Right," which Rusher maintained accounted for "the great bulk of our readership, of our support, and of the warm bodies available for us to lead in any desired direction."[24]

The problem with *National Review*, Rusher continued, was that the editors misunderstood their importance to this group of conservatives. Oh, the organized right delighted in the magazine's witty takedowns of liberals, but they were far less keen to anoint *National Review* "as a spokesman and leader of the Right." Rusher considered this a good thing—some distance allowed the magazine more independence. "But it is one thing for us to be independent of the organized Right," Rusher warned, "and quite another for us to incur its enmity." The Birch Society, at any rate, would no doubt wither and fade under the concerted attacks of others; there was no need for *National Review* to pile on.[25]

Rusher's memo revealed much about his understanding of the relationship between conservative media and the movement. It reflected his hopes for the journal's influence and his recognition of its limitations, arguing in one sentence that the organized right could be led "in any desired direction" and in the next asserting that they viewed *National Review* "only secondarily and far less readily" as a movement leader. Moreover, given the wide range of adherents attracted to the movement and the indispensable role they played in conservative activism, Rusher argued that to remain influential, the magazine would have to choose which compromise they would make: the one that satisfied the movement or the one that satisfied the liberal media. For his part, Rusher felt that just as it had been unwise for Robert Welch to accuse the president of treason, it would be impolitic for the magazine to attack Welch and his organization.

Manion joined Rusher in working to prevent Buckley from breaking publicly with Welch. Upon hearing rumors of the *National Review* editorial, Manion called Buckley and offered a compromise. If the magazine would curb its criticisms—if it would chide but not break with Welch—Manion would use his position on the National Council to rein in Welch. No one could undo Welch's accusation against Eisenhower, which even Welch now doubted ("Eisenhower," the Birch leader admitted, "may be too dumb to be a Communist"), but the Birch Society remained a font of conservative strength and should be protected. Buckley, despite his reservations, agreed.[26]

Thus in April the editorial, appropriately titled "The Uproar," appeared under Buckley's byline. Set in a question-answer format, the editorial dismissed the current tumult surrounding the society, arguing that it was an attempt on the part of the press "to anathematize the entire American right wing." While rejecting the charges that the society was totalitarian and secretive, Buckley admitted that the magazine disagreed with Welch's analytical framework. *National Review* agreed "the Communist conspiracy is a deadly serious matter" but did not hold that it was in control of the American government. The editorial stressed this was not just a difference of degree but a difference of kind: "The point has come, if Mr. Welch is right, to leave the typewriter, the lectern, and the radio microphone, and look instead to one's rifles." Buckley, of course, did not believe it had come to that. All the same, he expressed hope that, if it curbed some of its excesses, the Birch Society would flourish.[27]

The editorial did not provoke a mass defection from *National Review* or an uproar of its own. Manion, who had come out in defense of the society a few weeks earlier, provided cover for Buckley, telegramming as soon as the editorial appeared: "Congratulations on 'The Uproar,'" he wrote. "Impregnable logic intellectually honest entirely fair eminently constructive. Hurrah for *National Review*." The magazine staff used this telegram to fend off critics, publishing it in the next issue and including it in responses to angry letters. Welch pitched in as well, writing Buckley to commend the editorial as "both objectively fair and subjectively honorable. And I want you to know it is deeply appreciated." Not everyone was appeased—Phoebe Courtney wrote to Manion to voice her strenuous disagreement—but the crisis seemed averted.[28]

Buckley had kept his end of the deal. The editorial had not severed relations between *National Review* and the Birch Society. Now Manion had to fulfill his part of the bargain, a much harder task. Welch, after all, was not a man willing to be handled. With the help of other members of the National Council, Manion prevailed upon him to submit his writings to an executive council (on which Manion sat) for review. From that position, Manion could raise questions about potentially libelous statements before they went out, a useful way of keeping Welch from indulging in his habit of "naming names." Preventing Welch from naming *more* names, however, did little to heal the damage done by the Eisenhower accusation.[29]

As established media turned their attention from the Birch Society to conservatism in general, the reputation of the organization began to present a bigger problem. Tarred by association with Welch, now everyone was suffering from his excesses. Manion believed the Birch Society as an organization had become a powerful organizational tool, but Welch now hindered the effectiveness both of the society and of the wider movement. The answer seemed to be to remove Welch, a tricky proposition in any case but more so when the man in question was known for his near-dictatorial governing style.

In a carefully worded letter, Manion broached the subject. Pressure, he noted, had been mounting for "big defections and critical denunciations." The editorially conservative *Wall Street Journal* had just laid out a defense for "genuine conservative thinking," excising the society from such conservatism by dismissing "authoritarian secret societies" and "strident, indiscriminate accusations of Communism." Could the *Chicago Tribune* and Pulliam papers be far behind? And if the papers all turned on the society, would prominent conservatives follow suit? To prevent the society from crumbling under such desertions, Manion argued, the public face of the organization would have to change. They would have "to provide another public image to convince the public *and* our membership, present and prospective, that the John Birch Society is not a man but a movement, not a person but a principle." "I am sorry to say this, Bob," Manion continued, "but the Society cannot play this vital role unless and until you gracefully retire into the editorial room." Welch, however, had no intention of retiring, gracefully or otherwise, and the matter was dropped.[30]

Manion's lack of headway coincided with Buckley's increasing irritation with the Welch issue. Buckley had not gone after the Birch Society, but by year's end, he was back in a fighting mood. Manion had corralled but not unseated Welch, and as long as Welch represented the organization, Buckley believed it could do no good. So Buckley decided on another editorial, one praising the society but damning Welch. He understood that publishing the piece would mean breaking publicly with Welch. An editor raised this point when discussing the issue, drawing objections from Rusher. What did it mean, he asked, to develop a break? Break off official connections with Welch? Social ones? ("Not," Rusher quickly assured him, "that I have ever had any, or want any!") Did it mean ending contact, professionally and socially, with those on the National Council and their organizations? In raising these questions, Rusher hit upon the larger consequence of taking the Welch feud public. Conservatives—particularly media and organization leaders—were so tightly intertwined that it was nearly impossible to cut out one part without injuring others. And Rusher had no intention of taking part in "a widening war upon nationally-known conservative personalities for whom I have feelings of friendship and respect."[31]

Manion once again stepped—or rather, was invited—into the breach. Having made up his mind on the editorial, Buckley called Manion to Indianapolis in early January 1962. With Rusher and other *National Review* staffers at his side, Buckley announced he had reached the breaking point with Welch. They debated the issue for five hours, at the end of which Buckley told Manion he would wait for Manion to come up with another solution. Desperate to avoid a public battle, Manion hurried off a letter to Roger Milliken, who had poured funds into the *Manion Forum*, the Birch Society, and *National Review*. (The Milliken family donations, in fact, paid off about 40 percent of the magazine's yearly deficit.) Manion was at a loss for what to do. He had no counterproposal, but he firmly believed that should Buckley proceed "to exorcise Welch and all of his works through the columns of National Review, the damage to his magazine and to the conservative cause will be irreparable." Milliken had no suggestions; a month later, the editorial was published.[32]

Covering six pages, "The Question of Robert Welch" dissected Welch's writings and assumptions, pronouncing them "false counsels." The editors spared the society and its members but cautioned that chapters would be effective inasmuch as they were able to "dissipate the fog of confusion that issues from Mr. Welch's smoking typewriter." Unlike a year earlier, this editorial provoked a hailstorm of letters. A few, like one from Bozell, praised the magazine for its stance. "Bravo on the Welch blast. It makes one feel clean again." A more even-handed friend acknowledged the difficulty involved but thought on the whole that "if a truly effective conservative movement is to be developed, its leadership must be kept out of the hands of the Rabble Rousers who are most vulnerable to attack." These, however, were the exceptions; the bulk of response indicated that Rusher may well have gotten his unwanted "widening war." Milliken reproached the staff while chalking the editorial up to a fit of temper. Now that they had gotten it out of their system, he sought assurance that they would get on with more useful ventures. (To mitigate the damage done by the editorial, Milliken quadrupled his donation to the Birch Society.) Other donors were equally unimpressed, as was the National Weekly board, whom Buckley failed to inform beforehand. Manion, distressed over the decision to come out fighting, resigned his board position.[33]

Subscribers reacted angrily, resulting in a torrent of cancellations and admonitions. Surveying the letters, one editor described them as coming from "decent, earnest, committed people . . . in the warfare of ideas these are the peons, not the officers. But they are sturdy peons." Over a third of them "thought NR was playing into the hands of the Communists, or at least was unpatriotic or non-conservative." More important, the non–Birch members who wrote in response to the editorial—and non-Birchers comprised a large majority—echoed Manion's concerns about splintering the conservative movement. "I am aware that the few subscriptions you lose by your recent attack on another conservative group will gain you many subscriptions from northern liberals," wrote a South Carolinian reader upon canceling her subscription, "but I shall not enjoy reading wisecracks about how you so successfully turned the knife in Welch's back." Phyllis Schlafly, who had begun to make a name for herself as an anticommunist activist, canceled her subscription as well. "I cannot support a magazine which joins the pack of anti-anti-Communists in their organized campaign . . . to divide and destroy the anti-Communist effort in America."[34]

The consequences of the *National Review*–Welch conflict stretched beyond a few hundred cancellations and lost revenue. Whatever his intentions, Buckley had opened a breach in the movement. As Rusher pointed out, "The Welch editorial has never been a 'caper'. . . ; it has been a wrenching break with a simplistic segment of *National Review*'s, and your own personal, following." This break exposed the complications that their organizational leadership had caused for conservative media activists. With organization came greater attention, with greater attention, more pressure to mark off the boundaries of conservatism. With definitions being forced upon them from the outside, conservatives had to respond. Manion and Buckley represented two possible paths: tightening ranks or expelling troublemakers. But both choices came at a price. The Welch editorial frayed the connections that had built the closely knit worlds of postwar conservative media and the conservative movement and opened gaps that would only grow wider over time.[35]

Chapter 6

The Muzzle

When 2,500 Democrats gathered at the Hollywood Palladium in November 1961 to hear President Kennedy speak (a privilege for which they paid $100 apiece), they anticipated a rousing speech on behalf of Pat Brown. After a rocky first term, Brown was running for reelection as governor of California. He had shed fifteen pounds and embarked on a statewide speaking tour to prepare for battle against his most likely opponent: Richard Nixon, the man Kennedy had dispatched with in the presidential race a year earlier. The Brown portion of the speech, though, was campaign boilerplate. It was when Kennedy detoured "to say a word about the American spirit" that he made headlines.[1]

"In the most critical periods of our nation's history, there have always been those on the fringes of our society who have sought to escape their own responsibility by finding a simple solution, an appealing slogan or a convenient scapegoat," he began. "At times these fanatics have achieved a temporary success among those who lack the will or the wisdom to face unpleasant facts or unsolved problems. But in time the basic good sense and stability of the great American consensus has always prevailed." Kennedy hoped the same would hold true for America in the atomic age, now that "the discordant voices of extremism are once again heard in the land." Those voices, he warned, were operating far outside the American tradition, replacing a commitment to democracy with calls for dictatorship. "Men who are unwilling to face up to the danger without are convinced that the real danger is from within. They look suspiciously at their neighbors and their leaders. They call for 'a man on horseback' because they do not trust the people. They find treason in our churches, in our highest court, and even in the treatment of our water."[2]

Kennedy declined to name names, but journalists reporting on the speech readily supplied them. "President Kennedy chose Southern California tonight to launch a direct attack on Birchite, fringe political movements that have sprouted amidst the tensions of the cold war," David Wise wrote in the *Boston Globe*. At the *New York Times* Tom Wicker singled out the Birch Society and the Minutemen. "The President mentioned neither group by name," he noted, "but left no doubt whom he meant." Nor was Kennedy alone in voicing concerns about extremism. A week later Dwight Eisenhower, no stranger to Birch Society accusations, joined the attack. "I don't think the United States needs super-patriots," he said in an interview with CBS. "We need patriotism, honestly practiced by all of us, and we don't need these people that are more patriotic than you or anybody else that's a man of good intent and tries to be a good citizen. That's just rot, if you'll excuse the word."[3]

Despite the provocation, there was little reaction to the speech in conservative media circles. Believing established media and the administration walked in lockstep, media activists on the right were hardly surprised Kennedy was repeating the extremism line that journalists had been advancing for the better part of a year. But its transition from press to politician mattered: Kennedy wielded the power of the state, so his heightened attention to conservatives had substantial consequences. Hints of how these consequences might be made manifest came in August 1962, when the *Wall Street Journal* ran what the *Manion Forum*, in a histrionic mood, called "a little squib . . . which should cause every Manion Forum supporter to dash for the sleeping pills." The piece reported broadcasters' concerns that Kennedy would "pack" the FCC so its head administrator could enforce "tougher regulations." Having had their run-ins with FCC regulations, conservatives saw nothing to cheer in this news.[4]

The FCC and conservative broadcasters eventually locked horns over the Fairness Doctrine, the regulation requiring stations to air balanced coverage of controversial issues. The right believed the Kennedy administration was using the doctrine to silence conservatives. And indeed, the doctrine *was* deployed to stifle right-wing (as well as left-wing) broadcasters in the 1950s and 1960s. Its use had real consequences for conservative broadcasters like Manion, Dan Smoot, Billy James Hargis, and Carl McIntire, straining their relationships with station owners and with the FCC. But the doctrine also proved an effective foil that these broadcasters used to dramatize their narrative of a conservative vox populi muzzled by liberal government. As such, in the early 1960s the Fairness Doctrine became not only a popular fund-raising tool but a potent issue around which conservative media activists aligned, in the process refining the oppositional, populist identity central to their vision of modern conservatism. It was in this moment that the long-standing conservative distrust of liberal media sharpened into the powerful political critique of "media bias."

"Right-wing fanatics, casting doubt on the loyalty of every President of the United States since Herbert Hoover, are pounding the American people . . . with an unprecedented flood of radio and television propaganda," journalist Fred J. Cook wrote for the *Nation* in 1964. Not only were the "hate clubs of the air" blanketing the nation, these "major propagandists" were acting in concert with one another, amplifying their message. "Except for the Citizens' Council Forum, dedicated primarily to the race issues, the themes and viewpoints of the right-wing broadcasts are almost identical and interchangeable, and their leadership is closely linked in the blood brotherhood of fanaticism. Though the organizations are autonomous, each encourages and promotes the products of the others, and the crossties of their leadership dramatize their identity of interests." Those shared interests, Cook argued, were most clearly embodied in the John Birch Society.[5]

Yet all was not lost. Cook believed the FCC, through the Fairness Doctrine, could come to the rescue: "One recourse for liberal forces would appear to be to demand free time to counter some of the radical Right's wild-swinging charges. The Federal Communications Commission's 'primer on fairness' provides that, where such controversial programs are aired, the opposing point of view must be presented if offended parties demand equal time." The problem, though, was that conservative broadcasters didn't trigger Fairness Doctrine requirements. They were careful not to "name names," thus leaving no specific group with a claim for rebuttal. But no matter: if the FCC failed, Cook contended, the IRS could pick up the slack by revoking conservative organizations' tax-exempt status.[6]

By the time "Hate Clubs of the Air" came out in May 1964, the points Cook made had been thoroughly debated in conservative circles. Indeed, the article served only to validate the right's belief that media and government coordinated their attacks on conservatives. For those outside of conservative circles, though, Cook had uncovered evidence of a media world few

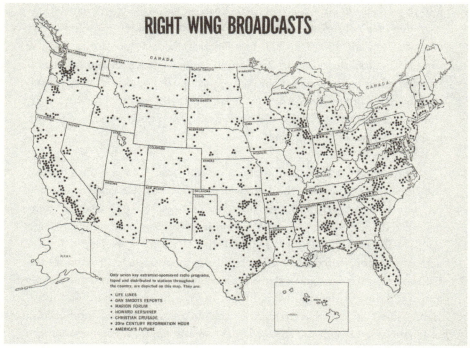

Figure 8. Map of conservative broadcasts developed by the National Council for Civic Responsibility, 1965. Chicago History Museum.

Americans knew existed. In particular, his taxonomy of conservative radio showed right-wing broadcasting had grown dramatically in a short amount of time. Charting nine programs, Cook counted at least 6,600 broadcasts a week, airing on 1,300 stations—about 20 percent of the nation's radio and television outlets—spread over 49 states (Maine was the only state beyond their reach). An accompanying map of the United States that marked these outlets was so cluttered with spots that Cook remarked it looked "as if the nation were seized with a virulent pox."[7]

By 1964, the pox had reached its peak, soon to enter a period of decline. But in the early 1960s, conservative broadcasters saw steadily rising incomes, which they used to expand their operations. The *Manion Forum, Dan Smoot Report*, and *Life Line* were the largest secular broadcasters. They grew significantly in the first few years of the decade, adding not only radio stations but new television programs as well. For instance, the *Manion Forum* could be heard on around 270 radio stations and, as of 1962, seen on nearly 50 television stations, primarily on the West Coast. It was an expensive expansion.

Television had much higher production costs than radio, and even when broadcasters scraped together enough money, airtime was hard to come by. The networks refused to buy right-wing programs because of their controversial nature, so time had to be secured through negotiations with local station managers. The combined costs of airtime, production, and personnel hours made television cost-prohibitive under the radio-broadcasting model.[8]

Enter the sponsors. H. L. Hunt, an idiosyncratic Texas oilman who was either the richest or second-richest man in the world, was the driving force behind the Life Line empire, a conservative print and broadcasting brand. Life Line was a peculiar case, structured in a way that kept it institutionally distinct from the rest of conservative media. Hunt founded the organization, ponied up the cash, and handpicked the talent. With virtually unlimited funds the show could air on hundreds of stations regardless of its popularity. Yet even with nearly inexhaustible funds, television proved a difficult format to master. While the *Life Line* radio show lasted from 1958 to 1979, the television program folded after only a year.[9]

Smoot and Manion pulled from a much broader, less wealthy pool of resources. More dependent on listener donations and subscriptions, they had to forge new relationships to secure sponsorship for their television programming. They found their salvation in dog food. D. B. Lewis, president of the Dr. Ross Pet Food Company, sponsored both shows on a number of West Coast stations. Smoot met Lewis in 1956, when the *Dan Smoot Report* was still only a print publication. Smoot had the ultimate bootstrapper biography: orphaned at eleven, a sharecropper until he left his uncle's home at fifteen, a rapacious reader who worked his way through high school, college, and into a Ph.D. program at Harvard University. He swapped Harvard for the FBI, where he hunted draft dodgers and communists throughout the 1940s. He was the voice of the *Facts Forum* for several years in the 1950s before starting his own outlet, the *Dan Smoot Report*, in 1955. The *Report* started out as a simple newsletter—Smoot lacked the funds for broadcasting—but that changed when he met Lewis, who liked reading Smoot's work but felt it needed a broader reach. "The socialists have practically all the big newspapers and magazines and they control practically all broadcasting," Lewis reportedly told Smoot. "And most of the public brainwashing which keeps the American people from realizing what's happening is financed by the advertising money of businessmen." Lewis wanted to counter that spending by sponsoring Smoot on radio and television, an offer Smoot happily accepted.[10]

But Lewis did more than just fork over some cash. According to Smoot's wife, Betty, Lewis not only offered sponsorship and a talent fee but "used all his native ability and economic strength to bully, threaten, tongue-lash, and otherwise badger milk-sop and left-wing television stations in his market area to accept the program." For those station owners who still refused to sell airtime, Lewis canceled advertising contracts with all their media holdings. Lewis did the same for Manion a few years later, helping expand the *Forum* to television in 1962. With a stable source of funding Smoot and Manion were able to set up regular production schedules. They attracted a few other local sponsors, and in some parts of the country sympathetic station owners aired their programs at no cost.[11]

The *Manion Forum*, *Dan Smoot Report*, and *Life Line* were the largest secular broadcasters, but they were not the only conservative voices on radio and television. Carl McIntire's *Twentieth Century Reformation Hour* and Billy James Hargis's *Christian Crusade* were the leading religious broadcasters. Fulton Lewis Jr. and Paul Harvey brought a conservative spin to the networks. A number of shows with a much more limited reach, like Kent and Phoebe Courtney's *Independent American* and Edgar C. Bundy's *Church League of America*, as well as shows on the margins of the conservative movement's orbit, like *America's Future* and Howard Kershner's *Commentary on the News*, comprised the panoply of syndicated right-wing radio in the early 1960s.

Sorting out the boundaries of conservative broadcasting was tricky business. Cook demonstrated an unusual level of care, for instance, in distinguishing between the *Citizens' Council Forum*, which in the early 1960s was still overtly segregationist and white supremacist, and national conservative programs that, while hardly paragons of racial progressivism, treated civil rights as a secondary issue during the 1950s and early 1960s. But neither he nor others in the established media delineated between religious and secular conservative media, bracketed together because of their shared politics. Like Cook, columnist Drew Pearson lumped together Manion, Smoot, Hargis, McIntire, and others as part of the same band of right-wing "hate-peddlers." In the minds of grassroots conservatives, too, these two universes were not distinct. The listening audience often grouped them together, constructing their own understanding of the conservative media world in their letters to broadcasters. In pleading for more coordination, one *Manion Forum* listener pointed to *Life Line*, the *Twentieth Century Reformation Hour*, and *Christian Crusade*, observing, "They all have the same objective as you have, and it would appear to me that you could further the cause of freedom if you could somehow work together." Another audience member listed McIntire, Smoot, and Fulton Lewis among his tally of "REAL, COURAGEOUS, TRUSTWORTHY, FARSIGHTED, FORTHRIGHT, AND UNDECEIVING DOWN-TO-EARTH AMERICANS."[12]

Yet in practical and political terms, McIntire and Hargis, as religious broadcasters who expounded on conservative themes like anticommunism, the United Nations, and creeping socialism, occupied a spot on the periphery of conservative media activism. They sought to win both votes and souls, but growing the church was generally more important than growing the movement. Institutionally, too, the religious broadcasters stood apart. Though they had ties to the secular activists, these ties were comparatively thin. Hargis and Manion, for instance, shared a sponsor, but Manion repeatedly declined to appear at Hargis's conventions. Likewise, Manion worried about stations where the *Manion Forum* was touted along with the *Twentieth Century Reformation Hour* and *Christian Crusade*, which his producer dismissed as "kook programs." Rusher went even further. Attempting to construct a policy group for "serious American conservatism," he justified it by noting, "This would give us a wonderful horn to blow whenever the Liberals try to insist that the Welch-Hargis crowd is the only, or at any rate the principal, spokesman for American conservatism." Neither McIntire nor Hargis wrote for *National Review* or *Human Events*, appeared on the *Manion Forum*, or published with Regnery or Devin-Adair. They largely self-published, Hargis through Christian Crusade and McIntire through Christian Beacon Press.[13]

Which is not to say the two groups never acted in concert. Nothing drew secular and religious conservative broadcasters closer than their shared sense of persecution and opposition to federal regulation. In the early 1960s, both groups found themselves locked in battle with the FCC over the Fairness Doctrine. Fueled by a belief that the doctrine was a regulatory tool used to silence conservatives, media activists worked first to expose the doctrine's inherent unfairness, then to force its repeal. Though their joint actions failed to lay the groundwork for a broader political alliance, they did reaffirm for both groups the dangers of regulation. Thanks to these Fairness Doctrine fights, by the mid-1960s conservative broadcasters of all stripes were convinced that media bias was a construct protected and promoted by liberal policymakers and a major threat to the right's ability to stay on air.

The Fairness Doctrine, generally given a birthdate of 1949, sprouted from a tangle of legislative and regulatory roots, a labyrinthine history that bedeviled broadcasters, Congress, and the FCC for the next four decades. Confusion over what the doctrine meant led the FCC to issue notice after notice in an attempt to clarify broadcasters' responsibilities. While no one quite knew how to execute or enforce the doctrine, its purpose could be sketched easily enough. Broadcasters had to cover controversial issues of "public importance," and in doing so, they were required to present "both sides" of those issues. These requirements reflected the doctrine's twofold purpose. First, it was meant to guarantee important issues were covered— that is, that broadcasters didn't simply fill the airwaves with entertainment and commercial programming. Second, the FCC intended to ensure radio stations didn't become propaganda outlets for a particular viewpoint. So there was an affirmative obligation to cover controversy, as well as to provide multiple perspectives.

These theoretical underpinnings, however, did not translate easily into practical guidelines. When Congress carried out a study of the doctrine in 1968 in the wake of its first Court challenge, members of the study committee discovered widespread confusion among broadcasters. As they traced the legislative history of the Fairness Doctrine, it became clear why: the doctrine had been cobbled together bit by bit—a phrase here, a revised section there—over decades. The Radio Act of 1927, which instituted the first radio regulations, obliged broadcasters to offer political candidates equal opportunities to voice their views. But the act included no language about fairness or controversial issues. In 1934 the FCC inched closer to the concept, affirming that it was "in the public interest for a licensee, so far as possible, to permit equal opportunity for the presentation of both sides of public questions." The legislation, however, insisted there was "no obligation" for stations to cover any public questions at all.[14]

As the country moved to a wartime footing in 1941 and worries about dissent and (nongovernment) propaganda mounted, the FCC abruptly shifted its position on the use of radio. In what became known as the Mayflower Doctrine, the agency made it clear on-air opinions were not allowed. "The public interest can never be served," the commissioners declared, "by a dedication of any broadcast facility to the support of its own partisan ends. Radio can serve as an instrument of democracy only when devoted to the communication of information and the exchange of ideas fairly and objectively presented. . . . In brief," they concluded, "the broadcaster cannot be an advocate." A strong statement against opinion broadcasting, and one widely understood to prohibit any on-air editorializing.[15]

When, in 1949, the agency reauthorized editorializing, it introduced the concept of fairness to ensure that opinion broadcasting did not devolve into propaganda. The new standard required licensees to use their stations to air "varying opinions on the paramount issues facing the American people." That mandate was strengthened ten years later with the addition of the Proxmire Amendment, which specified coverage of "public controversies" and insisted "the public has a chance to hear both sides." With the 1949 report and the 1959 amendment, what became widely known as the Fairness Doctrine was in place.[16]

Given the makeshift construction of the Fairness Doctrine, it should come as no surprise that when Congress combed through this legislative history, it found the doctrine "much less precise in both its definition and its application" than they had anticipated. Broadcasters constantly confused it with the equal-time rule, which stated that if licensees gave or sold time to one political candidate, they would have to give or sell the same amount of time at the same rate to the other candidates. But the Fairness Doctrine lacked such clear guidelines. The central concept, controversial issues, "has not been defined in the statute or in any FCC regulation." Further, enforcement of the doctrine was "ad hoc" rather than following any "general rule or regulation." What counted as legitimate controversy? What counted as deviant and therefore unworthy of discussion? There was no set answer.[17]

For conservative broadcasters, whose programs were by definition controversial, the uncertainty and vagueness surrounding the doctrine fed their suspicions that it was a nefarious instrument of government suppression. In a newspaper column about the doctrine, Manion warned that only messages "approved by the Federal Government" would be heard on air if the doctrine was fully implemented. "This is centralized censorship in its most reprehensible form." Those suspicions seemed to be confirmed when, on July 26, 1963, the FCC released a public notice concerning the Fairness Doctrine. The notice was meant to clarify licensees' responsibilities under the Fairness Doctrine when it came to controversial issues. It was not, the FCC insisted, new policy but rather a restatement of the obligations stations already carried. Yet for all the agency's assurances that it was simply reiterating existing protocols, the notice crystallized conservative concerns that government censorship was nigh.[18]

So what was it about the July 26 notice that raised conservative hackles? In two pages the notice outlined three broad categories of responsibility covered by the Fairness Doctrine. First, any time a person or organization was personally attacked in the course of a controversial program, the station had to track down those who had been attacked, send them the text of the broadcast, and offer the opportunity for "adequate response." The second category applied the same obligation to any partisan proclamations during election season. The third category involved balance on controversial topics of public importance, and here conservative broadcasters divined the FCC's true intent. The notice specifically pointed to "racial segregation, integration, or discrimination" and added: "In particular, the views of the leaders of the Negro and other community groups . . . must obviously be considered and reflected." So the FCC had its eye on the widespread practice among white southern broadcasters of blacking out news about the civil rights movement. The notice further clarified that in determining whether stations were in compliance with the Fairness Doctrine, the FCC "looks to substance rather than to label or form. It is immaterial whether a particular program is presented under the label of 'Americanism,' 'anti-communism' or 'states' rights.'"[19]

Conservative broadcasters skipped over the section on segregation and zeroed in on the language of "Americanism," "anti-communism," and "states' rights." Media activists saw these labels as code for "conservatism," a thinly veiled attack on their work. By removing the civil rights context, however, they made the FCC statement sound sharper than it was. "Americanism," "anti-communism," and "states' rights" were likely included because by 1963 segregationists were beginning to substitute these code words for openly racist appeals. Certainly within the South racism was still acceptable grounds for segregation, but those seeking to cultivate a national reputation relied increasingly on nonracist language. Thus the Citizens' Council, a white supremacist and segregationist organization, started to change its language as its radio program began to air outside the Jim Crow South. Nationally known conservative media activists, largely headquartered outside the South, had modified their language much earlier. When these activists discussed civil rights, almost to a person they opposed both the movement and any federal legislation to address discrimination. But they framed their opposition in the language of anticommunism and states' rights rather than racial superiority, at least by 1960. William F. Buckley Jr., for instance, famously penned a 1957 piece on segregation called "Why the South Must Prevail," arguing "the White community" should rule in the South because "it is the advanced race," but thereafter the magazine moved away from such explicitly racial justifications for segregation.[20]

And yet conservatives weren't entirely wrong to feel singled out by the FCC. The commission *did* have a bone to pick with them. For over a decade, conservative media activists had repeatedly challenged the central assumptions the FCC made about journalism. For much of the twentieth century, American journalists cleaved to the idea of objectivity: dispassionate "just-the-facts" reporting. Opinion and analysis had their place, but that place was distinct and separate from the news. News reports, whether in print or on air, were assumed to be bias free. Conservatives, however, saw "objectivity" as a mask concealing entrenched liberal bias. "Fairness and honesty are much to be desired in newspapers of any sort," conservative critic Russell Kirk wrote in his syndicated column, "but a Utopian 'objectivity' usually is a mask for concealed prejudices and partisanship." Kirk's view was broadly shared by conservatives, who saw signs of it everywhere. Dissecting a *Life* magazine article on the Kohler strike, *National Review* observed, "The pseudo-impartiality with which it pretends to weigh claims and facts 'on both sides' is only a cover for its UAW-tipped omissions of relevant evidence, its distorted version of known events, its loaded semantics." Given this reading of the media landscape, conservatives understood right-wing broadcasts not as controversial anomalies in need of balance but rather as answers to the slanted reporting that dominated every other sector of American media. For the right, fairness did not demand that liberals have a chance to respond to conservative broadcasters; conservative broadcasters *were* the response.[21]

The distance between the FCC and right-wing broadcasters widened even further thanks to another argument popular in conservative media: the values they broadcast were so widely shared and so fundamentally American that to give voice to "the other side" meant giving voice to America's enemies. So Clarence Manion attacked Khrushchev and Castro—did he now have to make his program available to them for rebuttal? Dan Smoot spoke out against communism—did stations have to offer airtime to communists? Billy James Hargis promoted Christianity and religious belief—did atheists thus deserve equal time?[22]

The FCC directly rebutted these interpretations in the July 26 notice and in a 1964 follow-up. First, the agency made it clear no station would have to give time to communists or atheists, as adherents to these views did not, in their judgment, meet the definition of "responsible groups" discussed in the July 26 notice. But neither could broadcasters hide behind labels of "anticommunism" and "Americanism" simply because the antitheses of these labels were "communism" and "anti-Americanism." There was, the agency held, significant room for disagreement on issues such as the best methods for fighting communism. Conservatives shot back with their contention that liberal anticommunism had more than enough spokespeople already.[23]

There were, then, core philosophical disagreements the public notice simply could not solve—in fact, that it highlighted in a way that antagonized conservatives and emboldened those who opposed them. There also remained considerable ambiguity that left ample room for confusion and conflict. Consider what happened after the *Manion Forum* created a series of broadcasts opposing the nuclear test-ban treaty under debate in Congress. The three broadcasts aired in August and September 1963 and included interviews with Congressman Craig Hosmer and retired admiral Chester Ward. Each broadcast contained vociferous opposition to the treaty, circulating under titles like "The Unlimited Dangers of a Limited Test Ban Treaty" and "The Test Ban Treaty: 'A Covenant with Death and an Agreement with Hell.'" The *Manion Forum* had no plans to air pro-treaty pieces; since his show began in 1954, Manion had guaranteed, "Every speaker over our network has been 100 per cent Right Wing. You may rest assured, no Left Winger, no International Socialist, no One-Worlder, no Communist will ever be heard." So no treaty proponents would be appearing on the *Forum*.[24]

Airing after the July 26 public notice, the *Forum's* antitreaty broadcasts sparked immediate challenges. The Citizens Committee for a Nuclear Test Ban, formed in mid-July 1963, filed complaints with the FCC and the three hundred stations carrying the *Manion Forum*, requesting free and equal time to reply. Manion believed that since he had not mentioned the group in his broadcast—indeed, he had never heard of them—there had been no personal attack and thus no grounds for complaint. But decisions about balance were not made by the *Forum*; they were made by individual stations. Station owners reacted in wide-ranging ways, exposing how unclear their understanding of their obligations was. In South Bend, Indiana, a station granted free time in response to the request. A Green Bay, Wisconsin, station initially denied the group free time to answer on the grounds it was not local, but the FCC held that absent a local group's request, the national organization must be accommodated. And a Birmingham, Alabama, station denied the Citizens Committee any time at all, arguing the station had aired plenty of news reports featuring President Kennedy and his supporters touting the treaty. Intriguingly, in a July 1964 report, the FCC declared this final argument valid, concluding, "If it was the licensee's good faith judgment that the public had had the opportunity fairly to hear contrasting views on the issue involved in his other programming, it appeared that the licensee's obligation pursuant to the fairness doctrine had been met." But that report was some time off, and in the meantime station owners airing the *Manion Forum* expressed concern that they would, in effect, end up giving half their airtime away for free in order to maintain their licenses.[25]

Such worries led licensees to consider dropping conservative programs like the *Manion Forum*. By the end of September, station cancellations began rolling in to right-wing broadcasters. Manion was alarmed to receive word that his program, as well as the *Dan Smoot Report*, had been dropped by KATU-TV in Portland, Oregon. When he canceled the program, the station owner directly referenced the July 26 notice. According to Manion, "The station stated that this new doctrine would cause unbearable expense and trouble for the station in providing equal time to answer controversial broadcasts." Manion also shared that he had received concerned calls from Portland noting that the cancellation of these shows "will completely silence the Conservative side of current events." Nor was the Portland station the only one. Within three months of the FCC notice, six other stations dropped the *Manion Forum*. A quick sampling of remaining stations revealed an uptick in requests for free time to respond to comments made on the *Forum*. Station owners voiced concern that if these requests kept coming, they would not be able to continue to run programs covering controversial issues. The administrative and airtime costs were simply too substantial. Whatever its original purpose, the July 26 notice had started to scale back the reach of conservative broadcasters. And revelations that surfaced a few months later would lead conservatives to suspect that had been the FCC's intent all along.[26]

"Freedom of speech is something precious to all Americans—liberals, conservatives, and the uncommitted alike—for the right to speak your mind without fear of government reprisal is almost as sacred in a free society as our faith in a living God." That conjoined civic and religious faith had long been part of Billy James Hargis's creed. He felt compelled to reiterate it in the September 1963 issue of his magazine *Christian Crusade*, not only because of the July 26 notice but also because of a memo sent to him by John Wesley Rhoads, a Philadelphia lawyer with connections in the attorney general's office. Written in December 1961 by labor leaders Victor and Walter Reuther at the request of John and Robert Kennedy, the twenty-four-page memo outlined ways the Kennedy administration could use the federal government to deal with the "radical right." In addition to suggestions involving the IRS and the attorney general's office, the Reuthers recommended using the FCC to investigate stations that offered free or discounted rates to conservative broadcasters and to encourage the administration and allied liberal groups to file Fairness Doctrine complaints against stations airing right-wing shows.[27]

"As any fair-minded American reads this secret document," Hargis wrote of the Reuther memo, "he becomes concerned over the intent of the liberals to use any means or go to any extremes to stop the 'grass-roots' conservative movement in America without regard to civil liberties or civil rights." Hargis explicitly linked the memo to the FCC notice. "It is clear to me that the Reuther Memorandum of December 1961 has been implemented in the communiqué from the Federal Communications Commission dated July 26, 1963." He then lit upon the passage from the public notice on Americanism, anticommunism, and states' rights to show how the FCC was targeting the right, using Manion's troubles over the test-ban treaty broadcasts to bolster his point.[28]

Hargis's interpretation immediately caught on. In a November editorial called "Coincidence or Not," *National Review* connected the dots for its readers. The first piece of evidence: the Reuther memo, which the editors described as an outline for the attorney general to "crack down on the Radical Right." The editorial spotlighted the memo's FCC recommendation, arguing the left was "aware that the Right has always depended heavily on the air waves to put forward its views, since most of the opinion-making channels are in effect closed by the Liberal orthodoxy in the academies, the major magazines, and the press." Second piece: the July 26 public notice. Like Hargis, the editors called attention to the clause emphasizing Americanism, anticommunism, and states' rights to underscore the dangers to the right.[29]

Because two points make a line, not a pattern, *National Review* added one more bit of evidence: a broadcast guide put out in August 1963 by the *Machinist*, a national union publication. The guide pointed to the July 26 notice, which the *Machinist* claimed "clarifies and strengthens the fairness principle" by mandating equal time for reply. (This was not technically correct; equal time was not required.) The *Machinist* then encouraged readers to listen to sixteen conservative radio and television programs (Manion's and Hargis's shows topped the list), note any attacks on labor, and send a detailed report to their local union. The union would then file a request for response time. *National Review* used this last piece of evidence to buttress the link between the Reuther memo and the July 26 notice: labor leaders called for the administration to use the FCC against conservatives, the FCC sent out a public notice singling out conservatives in a renewed call for fairness, and a major union publication used the notice to target right-wing broadcasters. The evidence may have been circumstantial, but for many on the right it was persuasive.[30]

The *Manion Forum*, too, echoed this connect-the-dots argument in a series of radio and television broadcasts dedicated to the FCC in October and November 1963. Manion had a personal interest in pushing back against the Fairness Doctrine, as it was costing him stations and threatened the continuation of his program. But when he turned to his microphone to make the case to his audience, he laid out a far more universal argument, one that again diverged from the FCC's vision of broadcasting.[31]

The Fairness Doctrine, like the FCC's other content regulations, was rooted in the idea that in broadcasting, public interest trumped private gain. That is, the profit motive could not be the sole driving force of a radio or television station; public interest had to be considered as well. Stations had limits on how much advertising they could run, as well as requirements for public-service broadcasting. The FCC could enact these constraints because the airwaves were a finite resource, owned by the public and licensed through the government. The government granted licensees the privilege to broadcast, but that privilege came with certain responsibilities.[32]

Manion, in contrast, made a market-based broadcasting argument in an October 1963 broadcast, "Do You Want Federal Censorship for Your Local Radio Station?" In it, he argued that "the most appropriate and effective censor of anything heard on the radio is the person who listens to it." In other words: Don't like it? Don't listen to it. "As soon as your objections are reflected in the radio ratings," he said, "the station obliges you with appropriate changes." The market would then determine which programs stayed and which went. He did not, however, point out that many stations carried his program for free to fulfill their public-service requirement, a contradiction that could not be reconciled with the free-market argument Manion was making. (Right-wing broadcasters defended this practice by arguing the radio market did not represent a truly free market, both because it was heavily regulated by the FCC and because conservative broadcasters had a difficult time convincing owners to sell them time.)[33]

Manion argued this market-based approach was fundamentally conservative. It amounted to "local self-government." And the alternative? For Manion, it was nothing less than "uniform Federal control of all radio and television programming." That, he told his audience, would be the result if the July 26 public notice went unchallenged. On his television program he broadened the argument, framing it as private enterprise versus government regulation. Who would Americans rather place their faith in when it came to determining fairness on radio? Would they trust the "honorable conduct of individual private business enterprises" or turn the project over to faceless bureaucrats? Manion trusted his audience knew the answer, but just in case, he pointed to the Reuther memo to make it clear the tools of government were not impartially or benevolently wielded.[34]

But Manion didn't stop there. He wanted not only to stoke public outrage but to change public policy. Since September he had been in contact with a number of senators and representatives, pushing for a congressional review of the Fairness Doctrine and the FCC's regulatory authority. He found a sympathetic audience in the conservative members of Congress. Kansas representative Bob Dole, who had appeared on the *Manion Forum* in early 1963, sided with the radio host against the agency and the administration. "As you indicate," he wrote to one of Manion's listeners, "this is a low-down method. Believe me, the Kennedy brothers are at their best when operating in this fashion." Senator John Tower promised a floor speech and a concerted effort to "cause the F.C.C. to pull in its horns, just a little if not a lot."[35]

In a late November broadcast, Manion brought on five members of Congress to rail against the Fairness Doctrine. Senator Strom Thurmond pointed to the Reuther memo and argued the doctrine was "another attempt to get our Nation to speak with one voice, the voice which preaches economic and social equality over personal liberty." Representative Craig Hosmer blasted the Kennedy administration for trying to manage the news and silence its critics. And Representative James B. Utt of Utah called the July 26 notice "the implementation of the Walter Reuther Memo . . . intended to strike a death blow at the Conservative broadcasts on the subject of religion, education and patriotism." Though this small contingent of opposition was not enough to change FCC policy, their support gave credence to the claims of right-wing broadcasters and journalists. It was one thing for defensive conservative media to complain and cry conspiracy; it was quite another for members of Congress to do so.[36]

In response to a flood of complaints from conservative and southern broadcasters, in 1964 FCC commissioners drew up a far more detailed Fairness Doctrine guide, popularly known as the Fairness Primer. When it released the document—which included twenty-eight case studies and two substantial appendices—the commissioners inadvertently demonstrated the persistent problem with the doctrine. Despite its length, the Fairness Primer still failed to define "fairness" or explain how to achieve it in any schematic and understandable way. Core concepts like "controversial issues" and "adequate response" remained undefined, left up to the discretion of the broadcasters. Philosophically, this seemed like an approach conservatives could get behind: individual broadcasters relying on their own judgments. Bureaucratically, it was a nightmare.[37]

The lack of clear guidelines made it difficult for broadcasters to know if they were meeting their fairness obligations. Moreover, there wasn't a graded punitive system for licensees who failed to meet the agency's standards. Fairness Doctrine complaints were reviewed at the time of license renewal. The FCC did not appear to have the power to levy fines for such violations (it was only in 1961 that the commission asserted the ability to fine, which it restricted to wattage violations), so its only recourse was to suspend or revoke a station's license. The combination of unpredictable and draconian penalties with an absence of clear rules created a chilling effect. Despite their ostensible obligation to do so, many broadcasters chose not to air controversial material rather than risk running afoul of the FCC.[38]

Conservative leaders were well aware of this problem. Asked by a Wisconsin listener why he didn't just file Fairness Doctrine complaints of his own, Manion explained that under such pressure "local stations would simply throw in the sponge and play records, or, which is worse, the Federal government would start approving all programs. This would be the end of free speech." *National Review* elaborated the point. Maybe, the editors mused, the Reuther memo and July 26 public notice and *Machinist* guide were all just a coincidence. After all, "the forces of repression do, everywhere, tend to rise spontaneously." The editors then set aside the question of coincidence or conspiracy to focus on the broader problem: "The truly mischievous aspect of the FCC's report is its hopeless ambiguity." Unsure what was permissible, broadcasters would tack toward the safest path, away from controversial issues.[39]

To conservatives, a trip down the safe path inevitably led to the silencing of right-wing voices. In midcentury America, modern conservatism was by definition controversial. It was out of the mainstream, not in step with the general political consensus. The continuation of Social Security was not controversial, but its elimination was. Containment of communism had largely become accepted policy, but rollback raised eyebrows. The strictures placed on controversial broadcasting, then, disproportionately affected conservatives. Yes, stations were *supposed* to cover controversial topics, but the FCC did not suspend licenses or entertain complaints for noncoverage (on issues other than civil rights). Play a few news pieces and some church broadcasts as a public service and the station was covered. But airing conservative programs meant airing controversy, and this inevitably meant licensees had to deal with the fuzzy fairness regulation. Better not to enter the fray, some broadcasters decided.

Adding to the right's sense of persecution was the nature of midcentury media. Though journalistic values were already beginning to shift as a growing number of journalists questioned the assumptions behind objectivity, in the 1950s and early 1960s reporting often echoed the administration line with little pushback. Administration claims were treated as fact, leading both the left and the right to criticize what they called "managed news." As all the postwar presidents governed, to some degree, to the left of modern conservatism, complaints about pro-administration news blended easily into complaints about liberal bias. From this vantage point, conservatives interpreted the Fairness Doctrine as a tool to black out their ideas and amplify their opponents', all done under the guise of objectivity and fairness. Little wonder the doctrine came to stand for much more than an attempt to impose broadcasting regulations.[40]

Legitimate grievance underwrote the right's opposition to the Fairness Doctrine and broadcast regulations. But conservatives soon discovered opposing the doctrine had a much broader utility. In time, it came to symbolize a host of right-wing grievances: onerous government regulations, limits on free speech, coordinated attacks on the right, systematic media bias. As such, opposition to the Fairness Doctrine transformed from a specific political complaint into a fundamental part of the conservative creed, helping construct and reinforce the right's oppositional identity.

In the process, conservatives fashioned a narrative not of a political faction attempting to change policy but of an epic, high-stakes struggle between the coordinated forces of oppression and the embattled, noble right. According to conservatives, the Fairness Doctrine was not just about broadcast regulations. It was a far more serious matter. The *Forum* made this clear in its fund-raising letters. Not only was the doctrine "the most dastardly collateral attack on freedom of speech in the history of the country," without direct intervention "programs that oppose Communist-Socialism, Internationalism, fiscal irresponsibility, appeasement of Moscow and of Communist stooges throughout the world could be snuffed out completely within the coming year." The doctrine was, according to Manion, a "dangerous blackout of the freedom of speech." Others later warned (less plausibly) that the Fairness Doctrine could soon be extended to print as well, leading to blanket censorship across all media forms.[41]

Undergirding these outsized allegations were claims that something nefarious was at hand, a coordinated effort to not only stop liberalism's political opponents in their tracks but abolish freedom itself. Calling the July 26 notice "the camel's head under the tent," the *Forum* lamented the show's "end may not be far away" thanks to "the dictatorial ambitions of Washington" to silence all conservative voices. In a fund-raising letter, the *Forum* charged that "the FCC notice was planned to cripple the amazing upsurge of Conservatism all over America" (a plan that could only be stopped with the help of check-writing donors). A *Forum* employee alleged that the Fairness Doctrine was part of "a diabolical plot to eliminate conservative broadcasts," which one right-wing station owner pegged as the "final all-out drive to silence all constitutional conservative, loyal opposition commentary." Southern columnist and radio host Tom Anderson blamed the Fairness Doctrine for shoring up "a rigged communications system which is brainwashing the American people" to weaken their resistance to communist conquest. Not just broadcasting licenses but all freedoms were at risk.[42]

Stakes this high required heroic opposition. "Fight the 'Fairness doctrine' with all your might and get others into the battle," one donor demanded. "We simply must not lose." A friend of the *Forum* painted the conservative position in dramatic historical terms when ruminating on "the utterly one-sided way" the FCC was acting. "When I think of Valley Forge," S. C. Lyons wrote Manion, "and of Calvary, and Nauvoo, I am again reminded that as long as there are people like you, George Patton, your sponsors, and similar Americans, there is still reason for us to have hope." In concocting this mythic narrative—heroes facing long odds, part of a centuries-long struggle against political and religious oppression—conservatives infused their opposition to the doctrine with historic significance. Such utility meant the doctrine would remain a powerful symbol of embattled conservatism long after it had been abolished.[43]

But as Manion's broadcast hinted, to change policy required more than an airing of grievances. It required political power. Conservatives could organize as pressure groups, but unless officeholders listened, activists were limited in the change they could effect. What the right needed was representation, which meant transforming the "little old ladies in tennis shoes" filling the ranks of conservative organizations across the country from neighborhood activists into a sizable voting bloc. And here, too, media activists would lead the way.

▶ # Part III

Elections

Chapter 7

The Purists

Bill Rusher was renouncing party politics.

Having dedicated the better part of his early life to the Republican Party, relishing in the battles his faction of the Young Republicans both started and won, the young lawyer expected to spend his life as a party operative. But all that changed in the backseat of a friend's car in the spring of 1954, as he listened to Vice President Richard Nixon denounce Senator Joe McCarthy's freewheeling hearings on government subversion. The betrayal was still palpable two decades later. Witness:

> I can remember the exact moment. The straw that broke the camel's back (not that it matters) was the speech (by Nixon, but Eisenhower had clearly put him up to it) about Joe McCarthy, to the effect that when you shoot at rats, you must make sure that you don't accidentally hit people. I listened to that speech, and divined its implication, in a car coming back to town from Westhampton. . . . Usually I was the life of the party on those long rides; but this time, after the speech, my friends couldn't rouse me from a silent lethargy. They could hardly have known that a whole young lifetime of uncomplicated devotion to the Republican Party was bleeding away, there in the back seat. I suddenly realized—and I would never wish such a realization on anybody—that my central premises had all been wrong; that all my political efforts up to that moment had been misdirected; that I had, in fact, to start all over again.

After that, Rusher dropped out of life as a party activist. He turned first to red-hunting for the Senate, then to working for *National Review*. Unlike politicians, ideas would never betray him.[1]

Despite Rusher's self-imposed exile from party politics, he remained keenly interested in political power. As did the media activists around him: ideas and rhetoric were central to their work, but they had dedicated themselves to media because they believed media work was key to organizing for political change, which inevitably led back to the ballot box and back to the party system.

The conservative media activists of the 1950s would not, generally speaking, run for office, write laws, or take government positions. In large part, this was because they believed those traditional routes to power were blocked by liberal gatekeepers. As with mainstream media and higher education, conservatives believed liberals controlled the party system and the federal government, with both Democrats and Republicans conspiring to keep conservatives out. In this argument, the conservative again became the outsider, the little guy facing entrenched power who had no voice except the one provided by conservative media. As the *Manion Forum* explained in the build-up to the 1964 election, "All tools of persuasion—radio, TV, literature, precinct work—must be used, because the Liberal-Socialist-Communists are IN THERE, and we Conservatives are OUT HERE."[2]

This charge—that conservatives lacked a presence in the political establishment—was not really true. A number of conservative congressmen held powerful positions in both parties, winning office as anti–New Deal Republicans or nestled in safe seats as Democrats from the Jim Crow South. But the platforms and leadership of the two major parties were well to the left of conservatism's ideological core, leaving media activists, their donors, and their supporters in an odd position. They had accumulated significant stores of social capital and economic resources. Their political connections had opened doors to federal appointments and congressional committees. Yet the real prize—control of a party, its nomination process, and, in time, the White House—seemed well beyond their reach. This sense of thwarted entitlement not only gave shape to media activists' particular brand of elite populism but also compelled them, even those who had forsworn party politics, to devote their energies to winning elections. As they did, media activists were transformed into political leaders.

▶ ▶ ▶

Before his backseat disillusionment, Rusher had been a committed Republican far more than a committed conservative. He backed Eisenhower in the 1952 Republican primary and stayed a loyalist until the McCarthy speech in March 1954. This set him apart from his future fellow travelers, many of whom toiled in the trenches for Taft and greeted Eisenhower's victory in the 1952 nomination race with suspicion. "The convention, needless to say, was a great disappointment," publisher Henry Regnery wrote *National Review*'s Buckley after Eisenhower nabbed the nomination. "Delegates, I understand, were bought or intimidated with Ford and General Motors dealerships, pressure from banks, insurance companies, and even, I am told, Ford Foundation grants." *National Review* echoed the charge. In the first issue, the editors blamed the machinations of eastern elites for Eisenhower's rise to power. "Early in 1951, a small band of Eastern financiers, international bankers and industrialists organized the Eisenhower boom and entrusted its inflation to a New York advertising firm. The rest is history." Manion saw it as a conspiracy of internationalists determined "to keep American foreign policy *foreign*," understanding that Taft, if elected, "would restore our capricious foreign policy to its proper confinement within the Constitution of the United States." Like Rusher, Manion didn't immediately jump ship. Despite identifying as a Democrat, he dutifully supported Eisenhower in the general election, snagged an appointment in the administration, and served as part of the "Eisenhower Team" until being forced out over the Bricker Amendment in 1954. Still, Manion considered his an early conversion. "I didn't wake up as early as Taft did," he admitted years later, "but I was up and out of bed before the sweet Conservative dreams of many of my good friends had begun to be disturbed."[3]

The "sweet Conservative dreams" of having one of their own in the White House went unfulfilled in 1952. But media activists were determined to see it through. What 1952 taught them was that the road to the White House might not run through either major party. As such, media activists in the 1950s cultivated third-party candidacies and half-baked electoral schemes as they attempted to pry their audiences away from longstanding party allegiances and toward an ideological approach to voting. These quixotic campaigns had little effect on the national political scene, but they were an important developmental stage for both conservative media and conservative electoral politics.

"We must have a political realignment in this country, and a new political party, to express the will of the millions of Americans who have been effectively disenfranchised by a system which asks them to choose between New Deal Democrats and New Deal Republicans," Chesly Manly, a reporter for the *Chicago Tribune*, wrote in the closing pages of *The Twenty-Year Revolution*. The 1954 book, written at Henry Regnery's urging, alleged New York bankers had stolen the nomination for Eisenhower. Manly envisioned that new party as a coalition between Taftite Republicans and southern Democrats, who had already showed their separatist impulse in the Dixiecrat revolt of 1948. This new party would call for limits to the "Marxist graduated income tax," withdrawal from the United Nations, new powers for congressional investigations into internal subversion, and a rollback of federal regulatory powers. Robert McCormick, Manly's long-faced, mustachioed boss and editor of the *Chicago Tribune*, supplied the name for this new venture: the American Party.[4]

McCormick was doing more in 1954 than whispering in Manly's ear about a new party. As a newspaper editor and publisher, McCormick believed strongly in media's power to shape electoral politics. An objective approach to reporting may have governed newspaper journalism in midcentury America, but the editorial pages of America's dailies continued a lively tradition of partisanship born in the eighteenth and nineteenth centuries. Politicos devotedly tracked the endorsements major papers made, and *N. W. Ayer & Son's Directory of Newspapers and Periodicals* included party affiliation as one of the descriptors of papers it catalogued. *Ayer's* had long listed the *Chicago Tribune* as "Republican," and the paper had a reputation as a citadel of midwestern conservatism. Indeed, the newspaper industry in general was believed to have a Republican bias, reflecting the business ties of owners and publishers. But in the mid-1950s McCormick instructed *Ayer's* to change the paper's affiliation from "Republican" to "independent."[5]

He did so because of events in 1952. At that year's GOP convention, McCormick, furious that Taft had been denied the nomination, bolted the party. Urging voters to reject both Eisenhower and Adlai Stevenson, he called for the American Party to replace the "international New Dealers" who controlled both the Democrats and Republicans. "A new party has to come," he insisted in a national radio address after his bolt, "because there are too many of our people not now represented by either the Republican or Democratic nominees. They have no place to go." Unable to organize a slate of candidates just two months before the election, McCormick and the

Tribune begrudgingly endorsed Eisenhower. "As we have said before and since his nomination, we do not believe the General is well-equipped for the Presidency," the editorial board wrote in its tepid, week-before-the-election endorsement. But even Ike was a better option than Adlai Stevenson. For now, anyway.[6]

With Eisenhower's victory, there was little hope the Republican Party would move in McCormick's direction. So in 1954, he launched a new Chicago-based organization called For America and appointed Clarence Manion and Robert E. Wood as cochairs. For America got off to an inauspicious start thanks to articles of incorporation that forbade political action. The decision was made so that For America could qualify for tax-exempt status, a valuable fund-raising asset. But some early recruits found it pointless, even bizarre, to build a new party organization that couldn't engage in political action. Hamilton Fish, a former New York representative *Time* magazine once dubbed "the Nation's No. 1 isolationist," resigned over this provision less than six months after the organization began. Calling For America "an utterly useless and futile effort and of no consequence politically whatsoever," Fish started his own "states' rights" political action committee to "carry out the original principles upon which For America was founded."[7]

Had he stuck around, Fish would have eventually gotten his way. Shortly after McCormick died in April 1955, the IRS denied For America tax-exempt status (as it did with most conservative organizations), and the group reorganized as a political action committee. During the reorganization Dan Smoot replaced Wood as For America's cochair. By 1955, then, For America had emerged as a central political action organization on the right, founded by a newspaper publisher and cochaired by two radio broadcasters. The ascendance of Manion and Smoot, coming not long after McCormick died, signaled a changing of the guard. Newspaper editors would continue to endorse politicians and shape political narratives, but for conservatives, a new generation of media activists was donning the mantle of political leadership. Housed not only at daily newspapers but at radio stations, magazines, and newsweeklies, these activists were more deeply rooted in ideology, more connected through shared networks, and far more active in organizations and electoral politics.[8]

Despite Fish's claim that For America was of "no consequence politically whatsoever," it developed into media activists' first conduit for political organization. It was not a mass organization—Manion later lamented that the group faltered because of an "overpopulation of distinguished 'Chiefs' and an underpopulation of working 'Indians'"—but it channeled the right's third-party energies in the 1950s. Manion, whose radio program launched a few months after For America began, promoted the organization every chance he got. And when the 1956 election rolled around, he and other media activists urged conservatives to reject the two major-party candidates and vote for a conservative: T. Coleman Andrews. Manion later claimed, with some accuracy, that For America "was almost solely responsible" for Andrews's independent candidacy. While it was a slapdash effort that failed to lay the groundwork for a lasting third party, the Andrews campaign eased conservatives into presidential politics and set the stage for much bigger campaigns in 1960 and 1964.[9]

T. Coleman Andrews, an accountant with a thick Virginia drawl and an easygoing charm, rose to national prominence in 1953 when Eisenhower appointed him to head what was then called the Internal Revenue Bureau. The appointment was a sop to the Byrd machine in Virginia, which had delivered the state to Eisenhower. In office, Andrews sought to rehabilitate the agency's reputation after a series of scandals during the Truman years. Changing the name to the Internal Revenue Service was part of that makeover. Yet like many other conservatives in the 1950s, Andrews, with his strong antistatist ideology and support for conservative causes célèbres (in Andrews's case, the McCarthy hearings), was ill suited for a role within the Eisenhower administration. In 1955 he resigned from the IRS, and soon afterward he began denouncing the federal income tax as "discriminatory, confiscatory and politically unsound." ("Now he tells us," groaned the *New York Times*.)[10]

The former tax chief's antitax stance made him a favorite in conservative circles, and soon his name started cropping up as the ideal 1956 candidate. Yet no one seemed to know how to make a third-party run happen. McCormick had floated the American Party idea, but no actual institution building occurred. When the colonel died, the most he had done to advance a third party was to shift the *Tribune*'s politics from Republican to independent. A smattering of independent parties across the country hewed to vaguely conservative principles, but none had the funding, structure, or personnel to launch a national campaign—certainly not on such short notice. While Manion continued to call for an "American Party" on his program, his language made an intriguing shift in late 1955. He began to argue the real threat to the "one-party system" was not a new party but "the emergence of a powerful new Presidential ticket" devoted to conservative ideas. A ticket, not a party.[11]

That was precisely what For America would deliver in 1956. The decision was a matter of strategy: no party had formally registered in time to appear on state ballots. Fourteen states, though, had "independent electors" up for grabs—electors For America's candidates could nab if they forwent a formal party affiliation. In August 1956, Kent Courtney, a conservative radio broadcaster and writer headquartered in New Orleans, organized a rally sponsored by For America, the Constitution Party, and the Federation for Constitutional Government in order to show the strength of conservative support for Andrews and his running mate, Thomas H. Werdel, a former representative from California. The pair was formally nominated at a "states rights-tax reform rally" in October, where Manion was the keynote speaker. It was a heavily top-down endeavor: no district work, just a convention to consider a slate of candidates. Andrews and Werdel accepted, though they announced they would be running a "week-end campaign," as they had business matters to attend to during the week.[12]

Conservative broadcasters dominated the campaign, but print-based activists had a role to play as well. The 1956 race marked the first election since the founding of *National Review*, and so was the first opportunity for its editors to chart their approach to electoral politics. They had reason to be wary. They had seen endorsement fights destroy earlier conservative publications. Battles over whether to endorse Eisenhower or Taft in 1952 played a role in the rift that led to the decline of the *Freeman* in 1953. Still, the editors of *National Review* were never going to abstain from electoral politics. While preparing to launch the magazine, Buckley, Willi Schlamm, and James Burnham went to Washington to meet with Senator William Knowland, the Senate minority leader and a favorite among conservatives. They urged him to run in 1956, offering to print a piece by him in *National Review*'s first issue to bolster his conservative credentials. Knowland toyed with the idea but decided not to challenge the popular president when Eisenhower decided to run for reelection. (Knowland instead embarked on a disastrous, career-ending campaign for California governor in 1958, losing to Pat Brown by 19 points.)[13]

Though Knowland declined to run, Buckley continued to publicly oppose Eisenhower's reelection. In April 1956, he lent his name to For America to support the registration of independent electors, signing a telegram urging conservatives to "defeat international Socialism which has captured both political parties." Soon after, though, Burnham—whom Buckley always held in the highest esteem—insisted *National Review* endorse Eisenhower in order to distinguish the magazine from the fringe right. Failure to do so would deny *National Review* the chance to be "a serious (whether or not minor) force in American life." It was a clever tactic: Burnham knew Buckley was preoccupied with respectability. Torn between his opposition to Eisenhower and his hunger for relevance, Buckley settled the matter by holding a debate in the magazine on the following question: "Should Conservatives Vote for Eisenhower-Nixon?" The magazine was flooded with letters that demonstrated how widely *National Review* readers diverged on tactical politics. On the eve of the election, Buckley made a statement that echoed McCormick's half-hearted endorsement four years earlier. Making clear he opposed the Republican platform ("essentially one of measured socialism"), he also admitted it was better than the unmeasured socialism of the Democrats. It was less an endorsement than a grant of permission: "Let those who prefer Eisenhower . . . vote for him, if they are convinced no other course of action holds out any practical hope." Buckley himself did not vote in the election.[14]

Buckley chose abstention over a vote for Andrews-Werdel (formally the Independent States' Rights Party), but the ticket did attract some support. The *Wall Street Journal* editorial board, which rightly labeled it a "party of protest," approvingly noted that it might pave the way for "displaced conservatives" to gain the attention of the two major parties. *National Review*'s Washington correspondent Sam M. Jones wrote an article strongly encouraging a vote for Andrews. Whereas the *Wall Street Journal* mainly concentrated on Andrews's economic positions, Jones focused on integration and civil rights. In its first few years the magazine, still finding its footing on presentations of civil rights, segregation, and racism, mostly relied on southern writers like Jones and James J. Kilpatrick to construct its pro-seg-regation defenses. The major exception was Buckley's editorial "Why the South Must Prevail," which concluded that "the White community" should predominate in the South "because, for the time being, it is the advanced race." Such overt racism largely disappeared from the magazine's pages by the late 1950s. (At least in terms of domestic policy: *National Review*'s defenses of colonialism and apartheid relied on both a Cold War framework and pronouncements of racial and cultural superiority.)[15]

Media activists did not put civil rights front and center in the 1956 third-party campaign. But they did use it strategically to attract white southern Democrats. At the October rally in Richmond to formally endorse the Andrews-Werdel ticket, Smoot appealed to the crowd by reading Adam Clayton Powell's statement that Eisenhower was willing to use federal force to ensure school integration in the South. Andrews acknowledged this dynamic as well when he said Eisenhower supporters were flocking to his ticket "in droves" after Powell's comments. Even without thunderous denunciations of integration, it was impossible to disaggregate the ticket from massive resistance. A thick-accented Virginian running on a states' rights ticket in 1956 could not be understood outside that context. Such a strong association with segregation limited the ticket's appeal outside the South.[16]

Andrews netted about 100,000 votes in 1956, with all of his support centered in the South (and almost all of that limited to Virginia). He had no impact on the race. His candidacy, however, was important for media activists. They had weathered their first election. Manion and Smoot had gained practical experience as organizers—Manion as chairman of a presidential campaign, however small—and the *Manion Forum* produced its first televised film. *It's Here—Forced Work Without Pay*, a "highly dramatized" piece, featured Manion and Andrews, as well as actors who portrayed factory workers lamenting the hardships caused by the income tax. *National Review* had its first Election Agony, gaining important insights into the tensions between ideological purity and electoral pragmatism, and the difficulty of providing direction to readers as voters when the most desirable candidate had no shot at victory.[17]

The Andrews campaign did something else, too. It completed For America's transformation into a political action group. As the 1960 election drew closer, Manion used the networks built in 1956 to revive the drive for a conservative nominee. In early 1959, Manion chaired a For America committee to form a new party. Ostensibly, anyway—Manion wasn't quite sold on the need for building from scratch what already existed. There were two national parties, both riven with ideological factions. The trick was to scrape the conservatives from one party, purge the liberals, and effect an ideological realignment—to create, in effect, a party of purists.

Manion saw potential for this particularly in the South, a Democratic stronghold that showed signs of weakening affection for the national party as leaders began to openly support black civil rights. In 1948 Strom Thurmond captured four southern states in his presidential bid under the States' Rights Democratic Party banner. As the civil rights movement gained momentum with the Montgomery bus boycott and the Little Rock desegregation standoff, white discontent with the Democratic Party continued to build in the late 1950s, creating an opening for conservatives. Could a new conservative majority emerge from an alliance of "hard-hitting Constitutional-minded men of the Southern states"—note the language, "Constitutional-minded" southerners, not segregationists—"and conscientious anti–Socialist Democrats and Republicans of the North"? Manion seemed to think so, stamping fund-raising envelopes with the message "Fusion of Conservatism—North and South—Sorely Needed Now."[18]

What candidate, though, could effect that fusion? It would have to be someone with national appeal, someone willing to take on the quixotic adventure of third-party politics in the United States. Upon formation of the committee to create a new party, Robert Wood of Sears Roebuck pointed out the biggest hurdle to realignment. "I think that a new Party is probably our best chance," he wrote a committee member, "but there is no use starting one unless we get the support of the Southern Conservatives." No doubt Wood's reservations played in Manion's mind when he read Judge Jim Johnson's treatise on the 1960 election. Johnson, a prominent member of the Citizens' Council and a justice on the Arkansas Supreme Court, knew well Manion's appetite for a conservative candidate; the two men first met while Manion was rallying support for the Andrews campaign. Heading into the 1960 campaign, Johnson had a new man for Manion to back: Arkansas governor Orval Faubus. "The basic domestic question facing the American people in 1960 will be the Federal-State controversy," Johnson explained. Writing from the heart of massive-resistance country, Johnson could attest to the grassroots fervor "the Federal-State controversy"—read: desegregation—could unleash. Who better to harness that energy than Faubus, whose armed refusal to desegregate schools led Eisenhower to send troops to Little Rock?[19]

Johnson located the heart of Faubus support in the white segregationist South. Yet he didn't frame his argument in explicitly racial terms. He instead opted for phrases like "states' rights" and "minority groups," language that could survive exportation to non-southern states. "States' Rights have become household words in Ohio as much as in Arkansas or Mississippi," Johnson argued. To further connect southern concerns with the broader conservative movement, Johnson argued the problems plaguing the South were the same ones plaguing the rest of the nation: liberal governance and communist infiltration. "Both major parties in their efforts to meet the demands of these minority groups have almost socialized America," he claimed.[20] By infiltrating civil rights groups, communists could thus control the course of American politics. For conservatives, it was a familiar portrait of an undemocratic trampling of the masses: split between two parties, "the people" had no voice in politics.

After his experience with Andrews, Manion had doubts about a southerner carrying a national ticket. As a work-around, Manion proposed that a southern conservative should fight for the Democratic nomination, while a northern conservative should vie for the Republican slot. Then at convention time, they could join ranks to form a new combined party, one that would deny any candidate enough electoral votes to win the election outright. In that scenario, the election would be handed to the House of Representatives, whose members would determine the next president. Manion was enamored of this electoral-college spoiler scheme, touting it as the only way to bypass two-party control. (He never figured out the mechanism that would cause legislators faced with such a vote to cast their lots with the conservative candidate, other than asserting, implausibly, that the unprecedented event would so unsettle them that they would suddenly embrace his vision of constitutional conservatism.)[21]

Faubus would do for the southern wing. But who to represent the non-southerners, the Taft Republicans? After reeling through several conservative Republicans, Manion lit upon Barry Goldwater. Tall and silver-haired, with broad, chiseled features set off by dark-rimmed glasses, Goldwater was a familiar face on the national stage by 1959, when he was well into his second term as U.S. senator from Arizona. In his first term he had risen to prominence as a leader of the Republican Right—not as a result of his anticommunism (which was intense but not unusual among Republican senators) but because of his opposition to labor unions. His calls for a more conservative Republican Party led the *Washington Post* to suggest in 1957 that Goldwater's version of the GOP would be "better symbolized by the extinct mastodon than by the live elephant." Yet as one of the few incumbents to survive the Republican rout in 1958, Goldwater seemed to point the way forward for conservatives. By the time he visited Manion's microphone for the third time in 1959 (he'd made his national radio debut on the show in 1957) he had become Manion's choice to become not only the Republican presidential nominee but the face of conservative politics.[22]

Goldwater took longer to make his mark on other conservative outlets, appearing only occasionally in the pages of *National Review* and *Human*

Events. National Review seemed particularly cool on Goldwater, showing a distinct preference for William Knowland in the 1950s. Only one article crowned him a conservative leader, and that was penned by Brent Bozell, Goldwater's speechwriter and the ghostwriter of *Conscience of a Conservative*. After Bozell's piece, Goldwater received no significant coverage in the magazine until the release of his best-selling book fifteen months later. *Human Events* offered more favorable reportage, embracing Goldwater for his opposition to modern Republicanism (an Eisenhower-style acceptance of New Deal programs). In 1958, publisher James Wick placed Goldwater on the Senate "Roll of Honor" based on his conservative voting record. And by 1959 the newsweekly occasionally ran articles by Goldwater about the state of the Republican Party and his support of Nixon's presidential candidacy.[23]

Goldwater's growing profile among conservatives encouraged Manion to meet with him in May 1959 to discuss a presidential bid. In that meeting, Goldwater made two things clear. First, no third-party bid was in the offing. Goldwater was a Republican through and through, and should the party choose Vice President Richard Nixon as its nominee, Goldwater would support him. Second, Goldwater agreed with Manion that only a conservative could gin up enough enthusiasm for a Republican win in 1960. Another me-too Republican, offering a watered-down version of the Democrats' liberal agenda, would be doomed to failure. Manion was sold. He shelved his third-party designs and got to work on the Republican nomination.[24]

Organizing for Goldwater consumed Manion's off-air time. He labored to put together a Goldwater Committee with one hundred big-name endorsers. But while many within Manion's conservative network supported the idea of Goldwater as the nominee, they balked at putting their names and reputations behind the drive. Some demurred for practical reasons. Robert Wood expressed "great admiration" for the senator but thought Nixon had the nomination sewn up. Newspaper publisher Eugene Pulliam voiced the same doubts—"I don't believe there's a Chinaman's chance to get him nominated in 1960"—though he signed on once Manion explained Goldwater had agreed to the efforts. Pulliam's reluctance highlighted the pragmatism of skepticism toward a Goldwater drive. While a principal supporter of Goldwater in Arizona politics, Pulliam understood what played well to the arid West's Republican parties was a far cry from what appealed to the party at the national level. Another group worried that Goldwater's political career would be ruined by an ill-fated quest for the presidency at a time when conservatism was still so far out of the mainstream. "I am not willing to be a party to having him sacrificed on the altar of protest," a Goldwater supporter explained when turning down the committee invitation. Goldwater himself got cold feet about the organizing going on around him, requiring Manion and Bozell to fly to Washington and assure the senator that they would not go public until he said the word.[25]

Others wanted assurances that Goldwater was a *real* conservative, as defined by their pet issues. Where did he stand on the income tax? On diplomatic recognition of the USSR? On court-ordered desegregation? In this vein, Buckley asked Manion for advice on whom the magazine should support in the upcoming primaries. The problem, he explained, was Goldwater's vocal support for Nixon. Given *National Review*'s anti-Nixon stance (Nixon was tied too closely to Eisenhower's modern Republicanism), Buckley was loath to support Goldwater, who he believed was "irrevocably entangled in the Nixon operations." In supporting Goldwater, Buckley argued, "we have contributed to the ascendancy of Nixon. And this I am not in the mood temperamentally to do." Even less temperamentally inclined to support Goldwater was Dan Smoot, who not only felt Goldwater was too closely allied with Nixon to do much good but also suspected that Goldwater "fails to comprehend the governmental principles that we are fighting for."[26]

Manion's challenge, then, was not only to rally support for Goldwater but to convince others on the right of Goldwater's conservatism. He aimed his persuasive efforts not at Buckley or Smoot or the Goldwater committee but at a much larger audience. To sell the right on a Goldwater candidacy, his supporters needed to make Goldwater synonymous with conservatism nationally. And who better, Manion thought, to spell out the senator's conservative principles than Goldwater himself?

The idea of a statement of belief, a Goldwater manifesto, appealed to Manion on several levels. First, it would marry a prominent politician with conservative ideals, advancing both together. Second, a Goldwater tract would popularize the senator nationally, getting his name in the news, on bookshelves, and on the lips of conservatives across the country. Finally, it would lay the groundwork for a Goldwater campaign without forcing the hesitant senator into a declaration of candidacy. The book could do the campaigning for Goldwater until he was ready to take up the call.[27]

The book, which would become *The Conscience of a Conservative*, came together through Manion's single-minded determination. When it became clear Goldwater would not have time to devote to the project, Manion brought aboard Bozell to do the writing. When a publishing company could not be found prior to manuscript production, Manion used Victor Publishing, a press he had created to publish pamphlets of his own. And when Bozell traipsed off to Spain for three weeks and then threw all his energies into protesting Nikita Khrushchev's visit to the United States, Manion hounded him about the manuscript until it was finished. Manion arranged for distribution as well, focusing on corporations that could use the purchase and dissemination of the book as a form of campaign contribution.[28]

Successful as Manion's efforts were, they carried no guarantee *Conscience of a Conservative* would find a sizable audience or even generate enough sales to recoup the senator's $1,000 advance. Buckley, in addition to being unenthusiastic about a Goldwater candidacy, saw little possibility for mass book sales. After all, Taft had not gotten very far with *A Foreign Policy for Americans*, timed to boost his name recognition and celebrity during the 1952 nomination drive. Nor would businessmen get behind Goldwater or his book, Buckley reasoned, because Nixon could easily win their favor with "a little old-time rhetoric about free enterprise." Without corporate bulk purchases or mass sales, the Goldwater manifesto would languish as Taft's had.[29]

A lot had changed since 1952, however. Where Taft had appeared to be the dying gasp of a Republican Old Guard, Goldwater stood at the base of a groundswell. He was already familiar to conservative audiences through his appearances on the *Manion Forum* and his favorable coverage in *Human Events*. And Buckley's doubts notwithstanding, Goldwater had credentials with conservative businessmen. During his first term, he had tried organized labor, particularly the progressive, politically active UAW, in the court of public opinion and before the Senate in hearings on corruption and racketeering in the trade union movement. By 1960, many knew Barry Goldwater as the senator who dared to call UAW president Walter Reuther "more dangerous to our country than Sputnik" and declared publicly that he would "rather have [Jimmy] Hoffa stealing my money than Reuther stealing my freedom." More important, though, unlike Goldwater, Taft had run at a time when there was no significant organizing on the right, whether at the grassroots or in the media. Taft had support from conservative leaders, but it turned out those leaders didn't have much in the way of followers.[30]

By the time *Conscience* appeared, however, media activists had remade the political landscape. As such, when *Conscience* launched in April 1960, it followed a trajectory quite different from Taft's lackluster sales. Within a few weeks, Manion's company had burned through over thirty thousand copies and had ordered fifty thousand more to meet demand. Well reviewed in the *Chicago Tribune*, *Washington Post*, and *Barron's*, chattered about on the *Forum* and other radio shows, covered in *National Review* and *Human Events*, the book built buzz. In the *Wall Street Journal*, John Chamberlain (a contributing editor to *National Review*) heaped praise on the conservatism espoused in the book, calling it "the creed of a fighter who has both a warm heart and a good mind." "There is more harsh fact and hard sense in this slight book," the *Tribune* declared, than in all the "vapidities" of Congress, electoral campaigns, and the associated commentary, while Goldwater himself "has the clarity of courage and the courage of clarity." At *National Review*, Frank S. Meyer concluded the book placed Goldwater "in the first rank of American statesmen." Meyer praised his willingness to stand on principle in "the present atmosphere of don't-rock-the-boat contentment with aggrandizing bureaucracy at home and complacent faith in coexistence abroad." *Human Events'* endorsement came in a four-page abridgment of Goldwater's book, complete with an order form and a plea to distribute as many copies as possible.[31]

Accolades and boosterism translated into sales. Through mail orders, in-store purchases, and, increasingly, campus bookstores, *Conscience of a Conservative* became a legitimate best seller, with one hundred thousand hardbacks and four hundred thousand paperbacks sold within six months of its release.[32] Goldwater's position with the Senate Republican Campaign Committee in the 1950s made him a nationally recognized figure; *Conscience of a Conservative* made him a nationally recognized *conservative* figure.

The book did better than the proto-campaign. With Nixon a prohibitive favorite, Goldwater declined to run. At the 1960 convention, where Republicans nominated Nixon and Henry Cabot Lodge, Goldwater admonished disappointed conservatives threatening to stay home in November to "grow up" and "get to work." The tough love appeared to work. Soon after the election, conservative media activists turned their attention to the next election cycle. And the combination of *Conscience* and Americans for Goldwater ensured Goldwater would remain the movement's best hope for the 1964 race.

"Dear Fellow-American on the Edge of a Precipice."

It was a typical opening for Leo Reardon's letters to *Manion Forum* sponsors and supporters. The journalist-turned-activist, who arrived at the *Manion Forum* after working for radio preacher Charles Coughlin and

Human Events, liked to play around with the salutation, adding a note of alarm ("Dear Fellow-American, Planning Your Bomb Shelter"), absurdity ("Dear Fellow-American on the Marxist Merry-Go-Round"), or poetry ("Dear Fellow-American, Wandering in a Forest of Uncertainty"). In April 1960, he opted for suspense. It was an election year, one in which the voters faced a "titanic task"—"to save the 'soul' of this Nation by electing a conservative Congress." Ratcheting up the stakes, Reardon warned, *"Unless a conservative Congress is elected, you will soon see in the sky the pall of Communism settling over this once glorious country."*[33]

The italicized dramatics were par for the course for *Manion Forum* fund-raising letters. There was, however, something odd about the emphasis on Congress. The letter was dated three days before the publication of Barry Goldwater's *Conscience of a Conservative*, a book Manion had commissioned, printed, and distributed in order to launch Goldwater's dark horse candidacy. For a year Manion had been working behind the scenes, organizing Americans for Goldwater to lay the groundwork for his chosen conservative candidate. So why did he have Reardon focusing all his arrows on Congress?

Goldwater was a long shot, to be sure, but in 1960 Manion, like his fellow media activists, also understood Congress represented their best hope for conservative governance. With neither party controlled by conservatives, they had little chance of snagging the presidential nomination. Getting conservatives into Congress was simply a far more practical goal. Representing smaller, more homogeneous groups of constituents, representatives could win elections without hewing to the political center. A bloc of conservative congressmen, cobbled together from Democrats from the South and Republicans from the far West and Midwest, could act as an impediment to liberal legislation.

Conservative media activists had good reason for favoring Congress as such a bulwark: the 80th Congress of 1946. Republicans swept the midterm elections that year, picking up majorities in both the Senate and House for the first time since 1932. The 80th congressional class included a number of anti–New Deal leaders, early expressions of modern conservatism. In addition to old hands like Robert Taft, young, strident opponents of Roosevelt-style governance took office. John Bricker, Taft's fellow senator from Ohio, made his mark with the noninterventionist Bricker Amendment. Joining Bricker in the Senate were freshmen Joseph McCarthy, William F. Knowland, and William Jenner. Knowland, a California conservative who would become Republican leader after Taft's death in 1953, attacked President Truman for a weak foreign policy, blaming the administration for the loss of China and the stalemate in Korea. Jenner of Indiana made a name for himself investigating internal communist subversion, branding President Truman a "saboteur" and General George Marshall "a front man for traitors." This made him a natural ally for fellow senator Joseph McCarthy of Wisconsin, whose insistence that communists had infiltrated the State Department defined conservative Republicanism in the 1950s.[34]

Investigating and grandstanding on communism characterized the conservative Republicans of the 80th Congress, but they also worked tirelessly to oppose the Fair Deal, the administration's liberal domestic policy program. Though these Republicans comprised only a small portion of the 1946 Congress, they worked with conservative southern Democrats to block Fair Deal legislation and pass bills removing wartime price controls, cutting taxes, and restricting unions. By relaxing economic regulations, lowering revenues, and restraining union power, the 80th Congress scaled back New Deal–style liberalism, hobbling the countervailing forces meant to contain business. While Truman derided them as the "Do Nothing Congress," conservatives in the 80th Congress learned that the right didn't need the presidency to shape the agenda. Obstruction could be a powerful force.[35]

So a conservative Congress was possible. But how to achieve it? With hundreds of local and state races across the country, and with party labels poor indications of ideology, how could voters divine which candidates for office were genuine conservatives? That question inspired the activism of Admiral Ben Moreell. In 1958 Moreell, a talented civil engineer who was newly retired from his position as chairman of the board for a steel company, founded Americans for Constitutional Action (ACA). The ACA was built around an explicitly electoral goal: to put more conservative senators and representatives in office. While it approached this objective from a number of angles, including fund-raising for targeted races and supplying staffers to conservative congressmen, the group's defining project was the ACA-Index. The index analyzed congressional votes to determine the conservatism of members of Congress. Vote for restrictions on unions, get a boost in the ACA ratings. Vote for federal aid to education, and down the number goes.[36]

The system was patterned after the Americans for Democratic Action's Annual Voting Records. The Americans for Democratic Action (ADA), founded in 1947 by a group of liberals including Eleanor Roosevelt, Walter Reuther, Arthur Schlesinger, John Kenneth Galbraith, and Reinhold

Niebuhr, was organized as a pressure group to support liberal initiatives and keep Democratic politicians true to FDR's New Deal vision. To support their efforts, the ADA rated members of Congress based on ten to twenty votes that the organization believed were the best barometers of liberalism. Before the ACA began its own index, *Human Events* publisher James Wick argued in the newsweekly that the best way to discern a member's conservatism was simply to reverse the ADA's rankings. Since the ADA "believes in Big Government, Big Labor, Big Spending and Big Taxing," Wick wrote, a low ADA ranking signaled the member's belief in "free enterprise, limited constitutional government and individual freedom." Developing its own ratings in 1960 allowed the ACA to move beyond defining conservatism as "anti-liberalism" and toward a positive definition shaped by the ACA's leaders. Conservative media activists latched on to the ACA rating system as shorthand for defining which representatives and senators hewed to their ideology. When Bill Rusher wanted to determine which members of Congress should receive gratis copies of the *National Review* (an attempt to grow the magazine's political influence), he settled on "the most conservative 50% of the two Houses, as rated by the ACA Index." Such a system gave the ACA influence over how conservatism would be defined by deciding which votes counted as conservative.[37]

But why would conservatives accept this new group's definition of conservatism? They did so in part because the organization's board boasted respected figures, from the president's older brother, Edgar Eisenhower, to former president Herbert Hoover, to movement fixtures like Robert Wood and Charles Edison, the former governor of New Jersey. Just as important, the group received regular endorsements from media activists at the *Manion Forum*, *National Review*, and *Human Events*. Promoting an ACA fund-raising drive in 1959, *National Review* explained the organization's position as "a chief rival and counterweight" to the ADA and the AFL-CIO's Committee on Political Education (COPE). "We wish ACA all the luck in the world," the editors wrote. In 1962 Manion hosted Moreell, an occasional guest on the program, to discuss the ACA's new voting index in advance of the midterm elections. Manion presented the ACA as a leader in the fight against the "irresponsible cult of international Socialists who call themselves 'liberals.'"[38]

Human Events emerged as the ACA's primary booster, thanks to a changing of the guard at the newsweekly. When James Wick came aboard as publisher in 1955, he revamped *Human Events*, dropping the esoteric essays of the paper's early years to concentrate on electoral politics and the

Washington scene. So when the ACA appeared with its goal to advance congressional conservatism, the newsweekly and the organization forged a natural alliance, built on their shared goal of electoral influence. And they shared more than just a common objective: the ACA worked out of the *Human Events* offices in D.C. until 1961. Personnel overlapped as well. Kenneth Ingwalson, the first executive director of the ACA, left at the end of 1960 to work as assistant publisher for *Human Events* (and later went to work for conservative publisher Crestwood Books).[39]

The arrangement conferred legitimacy on the ACA. *Human Events* regularly promoted the organization in its pages. Editor Frank Hanighen directed readers to use the ACA-Index, a guide to the ACA's ranking system printed and sold by *Human Events*, as a reliable measure of congressional conservatism: "You should, most emphatically, give special honor to those members of Congress who have earned an ACA-Index rating of 80 per cent or better." That announcement was paired with the article "How to Trap a Demagog" by John J. Synon, founder of the conservative Patrick Henry Club publishing house and an arch segregationist. "Nothing," Synon wrote, "unless it is a sloe-eyed woman, can be as deceptive as a practicing demagog." Synon had no advice for handling women, but he recommended the ACA-Index for dealing with demagogues. Demagogues relied on slick talk and emotionalism. By focusing on records instead of rhetoric, the ACA-Index countered demagoguery by offering voters "a deep-down analysis of the political character of each member in Congress." A few months later, *Human Events* published a blurb by Goldwater calling the ACA-Index "the finest work of its kind ever put between covers." Vouched for by these publications and politicians, the conservative reputation of the ACA-Index was secured.[40]

Synon did more than promote the ACA. Along with *Human Events*, he began to advocate the GOP as the natural home of conservatives. Synon urged fellow southern Democrats to replace their party loyalties with their ideological ones—a decision, he argued, that would lead them to the Republican Party. By studying the ACA-Index, he "learned, indisputably, that the Republican party—as a party—has lent little aid and comfort to the collectivists and is little to be damned for our plight. Republicans are not responsible; *IT IS THE LACK OF REPUBLICANS.*" Nor was Synon the only one making this argument. *National Review* used the ACA-Index to rank senators from most conservative to least, putting Democratic names in bold type so readers could see how densely they converged on the liberal end of the spectrum. Wrote the editors: "We believe the table speaks for itself." As the 1960s began, more and more media activists would edge away from the argument that there was no difference between the two parties, urging conservatives to look more favorably upon the GOP.[41]

The ACA and *Human Events* weren't the only ones looking to shape conservatives' electoral choices. At the *Forum*, Manion developed his own measure of congressional conservatism. The duplicative effort may seem odd in light of the ACA's comprehensive rating system. Certainly grassroots conservatives thought so—they were constantly urging media activists to coordinate more closely. In response to these calls, the ACA hosted a luncheon involving Manion, Rusher, Moreell, and representatives of other organizations and media outlets who met to discuss coordinating conservative groups for political action at the district level. While the proposed work was critical to the movement—helping conservative incumbents and recruiting opponents for liberal officeholders—those at the meeting concluded that the logistical obstacles were insurmountable. Better to build their individual organizations than work together on political campaigns.[42]

This go-it-alone attitude was typical of the early conservative movement. Time and again listeners wrote to Manion imploring him to combine his efforts with other conservative media and organizations, but Manion adopted a let-a-hundred-flowers-bloom philosophy. He understood such rating systems, if accepted as a standard, allowed their developers to control the definition of conservatism, punishing lawmakers for certain stances, rewarding them for others. So even though the ACA ratings were available and in common use, Manion opted to develop his own measure of congressional conservatism. The result was the Congressional Questionnaire. Intended to be filled out by candidates, the questionnaire read like the Nicene Creed of conservatism. Divided into twelve sections, each opened with a statement of belief and closed with the question "Do you agree?" For instance, question 5: "I believe that we should outlaw Communism and withdraw diplomatic recognition from the Communist governments, including the Soviet Union. Do you agree?" The miniscule space after each question made it clear that the questionnaire was not for explanations or clarifications but simple yes-or-no answers.[43]

As with the *Manion Forum* radio program, communism was the questionnaire's primary concern. The first seven questions addressed some aspect of conservative anticommunism, insisting that "'peaceful coexistence' with Communism is self-destruction." It showed how much at odds Manion and other conservatives were with reigning foreign policy consensus. In the party platforms of 1960, Republicans and Democrats agreed that fighting communism required foreign aid, continued diplomatic relations with the Soviet Union, increased international governance and law, and arms-control treaties. Manion's questionnaire set out a much different anticommunist vision and legislative agenda. It called for the United States to outlaw communism, revoke diplomatic recognition of communist governments, foment internal revolt in communist nations, and reject all arms-control agreements. Far outside the mainstream of either party, such measures would put the Cold War into a deep freeze. Yet for conservatives who believed coexistence was capitulation, these actions were seen as vital to victory over communism.

Only after dealing with communism did the questionnaire turn to issues like national sovereignty, financial solvency, and business protections. The policies Manion endorsed were solidly conservative, though not the most hard-line ones available. Thus the questionnaire did not call for the United States to withdraw from the United Nations but rather sought to limit the reach of international law by supporting the Connally Reservation, which would prevent the World Court from intervening in domestic affairs. Nor did the questionnaire ask legislators to support the repeal of the income tax, a pet project of *Forum* regulars J. Bracken Lee and Willis E. Stone. Instead it called for drastic cuts in federal spending, including the elimination of foreign aid and federal subsidies for everything from education to urban renewal.[44]

The questionnaire became a key component of the *Manion Forum's* 1960 election coverage, focusing attention on the conservative Congress that Leo Reardon had told his "fellow-Americans on the edge of a precipice" the country desperately needed. Declaring that the *Forum's* Congressional Questionnaire "is now famous," Reardon reported that over 100,000 copies had been distributed to listeners at no charge, with a goal of one to two million copies by Election Day. "Famous" was a questionable claim. The questionnaire may have landed in the hands of listeners and from there made it to congressional offices (one congressman reported receiving 148 copies), but the project operated below the radar. Newspapers and magazines failed to take note; even *National Review* was silent. But the questionnaire was not an outreach project focused on bringing people into the conservative fold. It was meant for voters already committed to the principles stated in the questionnaire. There was no need to explain the issues the questionnaire involved, because *Forum* listeners heard about them week after week. Moreover, the questionnaire did not simply state the issue and ask for the candidate's stance. Each point began with "I believe": by sending out the questionnaire, constituents signaled they agreed with its positions.[45]

At the end of July 1960, Manion spent a program discussing the impact of the questionnaires and explaining how listeners could best use them. Manion expressed delight that a number of candidates had earned perfect scores on the twelve questions—though, he advised, "don't demand or expect perfection. If your candidate answers nine or ten of these questions satisfactorily, he deserves your enthusiastic and energetic support." Manion encouraged his listeners to look at the ACA ratings (which he called "an excellent analytical index") and the questionnaire responses when considering which candidate to support. Combining these tools—one a measure of past behavior and the other of future intentions—would allow conservatives to uncover like-minded candidates.[46]

Learning where candidates stood was only the first step, however. "This informational effort will be useless," Manion cautioned, "unless you organize to elect the Congressional and Senatorial candidates who get passing grades on this comprehensive political examination." To this end, Manion presented the idea of "Voter Vigilantes." Introduced on his program several weeks earlier, Voter Vigilantes were neighborhood groups who, armed with information, would organize on behalf of conservative candidates. A member of Congress who agreed with eleven of the twelve principles on the questionnaire affirmed the potential of this two-step project: "If the people who are sending me this questionnaire would organize as minute men and women in their own neighborhoods and work earnestly to get out a big vote for these principles next November, my own election would be assured." Such organization, reproduced nationally, could turn Congress conservative.[47]

Human Events and the ACA likewise expanded their efforts to transform conservatives into an effective electoral force. After the 1960 election *Human Events* launched its "What You Can Do" section, structured to correspond with the congressional calendar. Published each week Congress was in session and modeled after the political guidance offered by labor unions, this section concentrated on fifteen key bills per year, providing a road map to constituent action. *Human Events* urged readers to purchase bulk subscriptions to this section so they could distribute it to neighbors, clubs, and friends: "You can MULTIPLY YOURSELF by sending Human Events to MILITANTS who are eager to wage a winning war against the 'giveaway liberals' who want to use other people's money to buy their way into power." And it had an effect: Congressman Henry C. Schadeberg, who scored a 100 percent rating from the ACA, credited *Human Events'* focus on electoral action with helping organize conservative voters in his district. "Human Events readers are ACTION people," he asserted in an ad for the newsweekly. "They get out and register voters; they bring them to the polls. A Conservative candidate for Congress can have a powerful sales force when a few thousand Human Events readers in his district start to act." (Given *Human Events* circulation—around fifty thousand—it's unlikely many districts housed "a few thousand Human Events readers.")[48]

The editors of *Human Events* had more in mind for these reader-activists. In January 1961, the newsweekly held the first Human Events Political Action Conference, a forerunner of the Conservative Political Action Conference (CPAC). In announcing the conference, *Human Events* framed it as a forum for grassroots activists. Members of Congress and conservative journalists would discuss the 1960 election results, then "tell you what *you can do back home* to promote sound legislation and defeat unsound legislation." Armed with that information, conservative activists could act as a counterweight to the "egghead Americans for Democratic Action and COPE" and their promises of "a Santa Claus government."[49]

Over the next three years, from 1961 to 1963, *Human Events* held six conferences in Washington, D.C., that brought together the politicians who topped the ACA-Index, the media activists who organized the movement, and the grassroots conservatives with the resources to sojourn to the nation's capital. Special discounts were offered to YAF and ISI members to boost the number of young activists who could attend. The conferences drew respectable levels of attendance—generally around four hundred to five hundred, plus dozens of officeholders. Soon *Human Events* was promoting the gathering as "a Homecoming for Conservatives of All Ages." And those who couldn't make it to D.C. could buy recordings of conference speeches, which the newsweekly presented as an important electioneering tool. "These recordings," one ad touted, "presented at public and private meetings, used on local radio stations, and loaned to other groups for their presentation, can spread the tremendous impact of this Conference among large numbers of people, and help to enlist their efforts and energies in the 1962 election campaigns."[50]

Other media activists saw these conferences as opportunities to mingle with politicians and to grow their audiences. None could match *Human Events'* influence with officeholders; its presence in D.C. and its inside-the-

Beltway focus ensured the newsweekly would have the edge on that front. But a gathering of conservative leaders and activists was fertile ground for growing their readership. Regnery and Devin Garrity saw it as a chance to boost book sales. Though a weekend's conference generally only yielded $500 to $600 in sales, Garrity believed it was a valuable "public relations venture." At the January 1963 conference, for instance, he showed a number of activists how to set up conservative bookstores. Regnery, while disappointed with book sales, praised the quality of people the conferences attracted. "They are a solid, substantial group of people," he wrote Wick, "and there is not a trace of the usual crack-pot element which seems to turn up at this sort of thing. I am sure that you will have a growing influence on American politics, and an influence for the better."[51]

While the publishers had nothing but praise for the *Human Events* conference, the newsweekly's competitors at *National Review* were a little less enthralled. After another successful conference in January 1963, Neil McCaffrey wrote to Buckley and Rusher to propose a National Review Political Action Workshop, "a series of nuts-and-bolts practical courses covering every level of political activity." McCaffrey, a promotions consultant for *National Review*, believed such a project would not only benefit the conservative movement but also boost the circulation of the magazine. "I am convinced there is a real hunger for this kind of information among NR readers, who are politically alert—and therefore frustrated, because so many of them lack the practical knowledge to translate their ideas into action," McCaffrey argued in his memo. "This explains in part why Human Events has nearly doubled the circulation of NR: Human Events at least gives its readers the illusion that they are coming to grips with practical politics." McCaffrey believed that just as *National Review* had responded to readers' calls for action with the formation of groups like Young Americans for Freedom, it now had to respond to its readers' growing hunger for electoral activism.[52]

As the 1964 presidential election loomed, media activists were poised to become full-fledged political leaders. The 1960 election had demonstrated their ability to promote and organize around a single candidate, even if they had been unable to secure that candidate the nomination. In the years that followed, they had given conservatives the tools for assessing candidates' ideologies and in the process cemented their reputations as the best judges of conservative policies and politicians. And through their political action conferences, they had begun the process of turning grassroots activists into organized voters—all under the leadership of those working in conservative media.

As much weight as media activists put on the *Human Events* conferences, however, they were not long-lived. In early 1963, Wick bemoaned the high cost of putting on the meetings two or three times a year. "It cost us, of course, far more money than we have ever spent to build up the attendance at the conference," he wrote Regnery. "Our cash inflow since the election has shown a serious drop. If it continues our circulation growth of the last 15 months may completely vanish." Indeed, the next conference in July would be the last one. A *New York Times* profile of the event focused almost exclusively on Goldwater, who spoke at a breakfast event. "No political endorsements are scheduled on the conference agenda," the newspaper noted. "But virtually every speaker had words of praise for the conservative Arizonan, words that provoked enthusiastic cheers each time." When the winter conference was postponed, the conservative Arizonan still loomed large. Announcing the event had been "postponed until the issues on which the 1964 election will be fought become clearer," *Human Events* instead urged readers to continue to write their representatives and work locally "for victory in 1964." The battle for Congress, the right's aim during the early 1960s, was being set aside for a much bigger prize.[53]

Chapter 8

The Partisans

In early 1963, Cletus Heibel of Dorr, Michigan, a forty-eight-year-old member of the UAW ("not by choice"), carefully cut two articles from the UAW newspaper *Solidarity*, then scrawled a handwritten letter to Clarence Manion. The articles were part of an in-depth investigation into what the UAW called "That Other Subversive Network"—the conservative movement. "I am enclosing the first two installments in which you have a very prominent part," Heibel wrote. "It seems that everyone to the right of Hubert Humphrey is a right wing extremist." The first part of the series covered the "financial 'angels' of the ultra-right." The second mapped out the network, linking funders to conservative media, organizations, and politicians. In particular, the union blasted three men who had emerged as political threats. The first, Roger Milliken, funneled millions of dollars into conservative organizations. The second, Manion, appeared weekly on a national radio program to promote conservative ideas. And the third, Barry Goldwater, had become the most recognizable conservative politician in the United States. Together they were the "the Donor, the Dealer, and the Darling" of the conservative movement.[1]

Manion had long been a UAW target, thanks to the role he played in defeating guaranteed annual wage bills in the Midwest. But he was not the only Dealer in the UAW's crosshairs. *National Review* and *Human Events*, "two of the 'bibles' of the Ultra-Right Wing movement," joined the Birch Society's *American Opinion* and ISI's *The Individualist* as "sheets that spew the same subversive philosophy."[2]

By 1963, such attacks were par for the course, especially in the labor press. What made "That Other Subversive Network" series different was the explicit link it drew between right-wing media and the political fortunes of Barry Goldwater. When Goldwater ran for president in 1964, media activists played a central role. For conservatives it was a genuinely media-driven campaign, one in which media activists definitively shaped the right's understanding of the issues, the candidates, and the parties. When Goldwater entered the race promising "a choice, not an echo," media activists took his message and infused it with new meaning for their audiences. That meaning reflected their distinct priorities: their belief in institutional biases against conservatives, their faith in the innate conservatism of the American people, and their preference for ideological integrity over political pragmatism.

The conservative media campaign took on heightened importance as Goldwater went from curiosity to contender. As front-runner and then nominee, Goldwater—and, by extension, conservatives—had a real shot at the presidency. For media activists, it was a moment of both opportunity and unexpected challenge. Established conservative outlets suddenly found themselves facing competition from upstarts who were able to leverage the attention and resources the presidential race provided to make a bid for readers and listeners. And right-wing media were no longer the primary group crafting Goldwater's message and image. When Goldwater won the nomination, conservatives had to contend with his Democratic opposition and mainstream journalists (which they often spoke of as one and the same). They also had to deal with the official—and decidedly unwelcoming—Goldwater campaign. For all these challenges, however, the campaign remained a rare opportunity to complete the process media activists had begun in the 1950s: to interact with their readers and listeners not just as audience members but as voters and partisan political organizers. By Election Day, conservative media activists would have a clear sense both of their power and of its limitations.

Clarence Manion was being replaced in the Goldwater movement, and it was due, in large part, to Bill Rusher's conversion. Rusher was the political strategist at *National Review*, having gained significant experience in the world of partisan politics during the 1950s. Even after growing disenchanted with the Republican Party and escaping to *National Review*, he remained an instinctively political animal. This did not mean, however, that he was willing to compromise basic principles. While he understood well the need for pragmatism in politics, he took that as politics' intrinsic flaw. As he explained it in

1969, "By 1956 I was rid—once and for all—of the idea that politics could ever really do what needed to be done. In my subsequent political activities, I have never forgotten or abandoned that conviction. I have, rather, merely considered it my personal duty to use that hard-won and otherwise wholly wasted expertise to press the conservative case in political terms whenever and wherever I could."

"To press the conservative case in political terms": for Rusher, this meant something different than a return to life as a party loyalist. His goal was no longer winning elections for winning's sake. Rather, it was to use electoral politics strategically to advance conservatism. Political pragmatism for Rusher was a tool for advancing his ideological commitments. He knew that what was best for the Republican Party and what was best for the conservative movement would not always be the same thing. When the two came into conflict, Rusher would always choose the movement. It was why he was willing to trim *National Review*'s sails when the magazine seemed to be drifting too far from the movement but adamantly opposed tacking toward the GOP to demonstrate the magazine's respectability or influence.[3]

This approach, which paired ideology with a sense of political timing and strategy, meant Rusher didn't have much interest in the Draft Goldwater campaign of 1960. He dismissed the effort as "premature, amateurish, and futile." It was a dispiriting year for him. Nixon had a lock on the Republican nomination, and no politician irked Rusher more than Dick Nixon: Nixon attacking McCarthy, Nixon meeting with Khrushchev, Nixon hedging every bet and pulling every punch. Rusher's irritation boiled over when Ross Hoffman, a traditionalist conservative and admirer of Edmund Burke who taught history at Fordham University, wrote *National Review* in 1960 to tout Nixon. Hoffman argued the vice president had "earned the right to be trusted" by *National Review* and, as a confirmed conservative, "should be allowed a little indulgence" if he veered to the center during the campaign. A cranky Rusher complained to Buckley, "Where and when did Nixon 'earn the right to be trusted' by conservatives?" He recounted Nixon's many apostasies, then added, "To say that a man with that record should be 'allowed a little indulgence' is to win the Understatement Award of 1960; he needs massive unilateral forgiveness." Rusher, who had attended every convention since 1944, stayed home in 1960. When Election Day rolled around, he cast a write-in vote for Barry Goldwater.[4]

After Nixon's loss, Rusher remained pessimistic about the Republican Party. Not just pessimistic: openly hostile. "Rusher's Razor" (as his favored dictum became known) maintained "No one, today, can be simultaneously honest, informed and successful in the Republican Party." Goldwater included: should the Arizona senator stay a Republican, Rusher believed, "he must either trim or fail; most probably he will try to compromise and wind up doing both." Party politics would inevitably do violence to conservative ideas. Yet Rusher was opposed to making that the magazine's public position. Grassroots conservatives championed Goldwater so *National Review* had to stand by him, lest it be perceived as "an impossibly perfectionist journal" too out of touch to deserve a hearing. Note Rusher's principal concern: the movement. He was not the least bit worried about seeming "impossibly perfectionist" to those on the outside of the movement but fretted regularly over whether the magazine seemed so to conservatives. That same impulse motivated him to argue against breaking with the Birch Society in the early 1960s. Sure, criticizing Welch may have been the right thing to do, but the magazine didn't exist to be right. It existed to be "a leader of conservative opinion." If it didn't attend to the desires of movement conservatives, he warned the editors, *National Review* would devolve "into a colorful, follow-erless eccentricity, or (almost as bad) into the only other thing left: bondage to the main line of the Republican Party."[5]

This attunement to the movement led Rusher to curb *National Review*'s criticism of Goldwater. In early 1961 the senator, serving his second stint as the chair of the National Republican Senatorial Committee, issued a twenty-nine-page manifesto called *The Forgotten American: A Statement of Proposed Republican Principles, Programs and Objectives*. If *Conscience of a Conservative* had been Goldwater's statement of conservative belief, *The Forgotten American* was his statement of conservative strategy. As such, the two documents demarcated the space between the dogmatic and the pragmatic. Some conservatives embraced this as good sense. *Human Events* reprinted the statement as a twenty-four-page pamphlet, offering bulk sales so readers could distribute it far and wide. In the *Wall Street Journal*, Robert Novak (who did not yet identify as a conservative writer) saw the manifesto as an attempt both to establish Goldwater as a contender for the 1964 nomination and to outline "a politically marketable brand of conservatism." Novak lauded Goldwater's search for a more palatable platform, approvingly cataloguing his many "departures from rigid conservatism."[6]

Those departures did not receive as warm a welcome at *National Review*, where Willmoore Kendall criticized them sharply in a column titled "Quo Vadis, Barry?" ("Where Are You Going, Barry?") Kendall suspected the answer was "to the center." Goldwater's watered-down opposition to federal welfare programs, for instance, was "a far cry, let us agree, from the welfarist views of Jacob Javits or even Richard Nixon; but they are also a far cry from those of the *Conscience*, where federal welfarism is opposed *per se* as incompatible with a healthy and free society." Where was the courage, the principle, in this moderated stance? Where was the uncompromising conservatism they had been promised? Kendall ultimately dismissed Goldwater's statement as "neo-Nixonism," a biting rebuke in conservative circles.[7]

What's most interesting about "Quo Vadis," though, is not Kendall's criticism but what happened when the page proofs landed on Rusher's desk shortly before publication. Reading the copy, Rusher's chest tightened as he realized it was too late to kill the piece and too ruinous to run it. How, he wondered, had such harsh criticism of Goldwater made it this far without any discussion? And why had Kendall of all people gone off the rails? Asking around, Rusher learned that although the column appeared under Kendall's byline, it had been written by Brent Bozell (the ghostwriter of *Conscience of a Conservative* and former Goldwater speechwriter). Bozell, living in Spain along with Kendall, had grown embittered toward Goldwater, whose endorsement of Nixon in 1960 he saw as a great betrayal. Rusher had little patience for Bozell's scorched-earth politics. After consulting with Priscilla Buckley and Frank Meyer, who had stopped by for cocktails, he prevailed on Jim Burnham to take the piece off the cover, soften the tone of the last few paragraphs, and add a statement clarifying that the opinions were Kendall's own.[8]

Writing to Buckley in Switzerland about the decision, Rusher groused that if the writers were to live in Spain, they had to give up their attempts to influence Goldwater through "long-distance shock therapy"—or at least do it "out of sight of *National Review*'s 37,000 readers." Not, he explained, because he had any stake in Goldwater's career. "As you know, my own personal optimism about the chances of doing anything through the GOP in general, let alone Goldwater in particular, makes Brent look like a positive optimist in comparison." He maintained, however, that such should not be the general position of the magazine. Failure to support Goldwater would leave readers "confused, and perhaps ultimately annoyed."[9]

Yet if Rusher was fatalistic about Goldwater in March 1961, by the fall he had experienced a change of heart. Surveying the potential 1964 field, he saw that the GOP's Taft and Dewey wings were gone. Nixon was off on a soon-to-fail mission to recover his electability by running for governor of California. There was an opening to be exploited by those who shared "a common conviction that it was time for the Republican Party to turn to the Right—away from the aggressive liberalism of Rockefeller, away from the calculated and empty platitudes of Nixon, and toward the conservative principles and personalities which had begun to make themselves felt on the national scene in the latter half of the 1950s." If timing and a lack of political skill had doomed the 1960 Goldwater drive, a year later Rusher discovered he had a measure of personal optimism about the senator's chances after all. He reached out to Clif White, a fellow veteran of the Young Republican wars, and the second drive for a conservative nominee was underway.[10]

Though Rusher and White were both based in New York, conservative organizing for 1964 began, as Americans for Goldwater had, in Chicago. This belied Rusher's attempt to distance the group from the party's Taft wing; Chicago-style conservatism still held powerful sway. But it was not solely a midwestern movement. The twenty-two attendees at the first meeting on October 8, 1961, came from sixteen states. They included wealthy conservative donors like Gerrish Milliken (brother of Roger), politicians like Ohio congressman John Ashbrook, and organizers like the chairmen of the Maine and South Carolina Republican parties. The group appointed White as their head. White and Rusher had fought together in the trenches as Young Republicans, driving the group to the right. They now sought to do the same for the Republican Party. Though the Rusher group gave Goldwater a heads-up, participants took care to note they were not meeting to draft Goldwater but rather to work for the nomination of a conservative candidate. Goldwater had proven reliably conservative and had a strong relationship with the movement, but he could also be capricious, vacillating between uncompromising conviction and an abundance of caution. And at any rate, as Rusher noted, "it was early, very early, to be talking about a specific candidate."[11]

Soon, though, the group grew indistinguishable from a proto-campaign for Goldwater. For good reason: the senator's star rose dramatically in the year that followed its first meeting. He won a 1962 AP poll of delegates from the 1960 convention, beating out Nelson Rockefeller, Richard Nixon, and George Romney. In a Texas poll that same year, he trounced Rockefeller 12–1. Yet despite the favorable tailwinds, efforts on Goldwater's behalf had to be kept under wraps. Rejecting names like Americans for Goldwater that would have tipped their hand, the Rusher group named itself Suite 3505 after the office White secured for the operation. Their concerns over secrecy were warranted. When word of the organization leaked to the press in December 1962, Goldwater met with White and repeatedly vowed he would not run. "It's my political neck," the senator growled, "and I intend to have something to say about what happens to it." When Suite 3505 learned of Goldwater's rebuke, they lapsed into despondency until one member blurted, "Let's *draft* the son of a gun!" Though Goldwater was still disinclined to undertake a presidential run, his supporters were determined to mount one for him. Suite 3505 kept working.[12]

While Rusher's group laid the political groundwork for a conservative nominee, other media activists began to work on a conservative campaign message. With Goldwater's rise in prominence, they sought to provide the justification for a conservative nominee within the Republican Party (rather than the third-party focus of earlier years). Promising to harness the power of "every mass publicity medium," the *Manion Forum* announced in 1963 that it was launching a new campaign for the next year's election. "On radio and television, through newspapers, direct mail and billboards we will appeal for a Conservative versus a liberal candidate for President in 1964," Manion declared. "We want a chance for a choice."[13]

The Chance for a Choice campaign structured the *Forum's* broadcasts over the next year. The campaign called for a conservative candidate to oppose a liberal candidate, turning the election into a referendum on the two competing ideologies. Manion developed a philosophical explanation for this focus on ideology, but it was born as much of necessity as anything else. Where Suite 3505 avoided identifying explicitly with Goldwater for strategic reasons, the *Forum* avoided it for regulatory ones. Openly endorsing a particular candidate could cost Manion his 501(c)(4) status, which at the time prohibited participation in campaigns on behalf of candidates for public office. Stumping for Goldwater on air could also trigger a flood of Fairness Doctrine complaints from the senator's opponents. "Because we are restricted against political action, we cannot plug for Goldwater by name," he told a friend, "but we will do everything short of that, of course." So Chance for a Choice remained framed as a battle of political ideas rather than candidates.[14]

There was a clear fiction to this distinction, given Manion's role in publishing and distributing *Conscience of a Conservative*. Victor Publishing, the *Forum's* private press that put out *Conscience*, played an important role in the Chance for a Choice campaign. As the sponsor for Manion's television program in the Midwest, Victor advertised not only *Conscience* but other Goldwater books it had acquired, such as *Too Grave a Risk* (1963) by Denison Kitchel (who would become Goldwater's campaign manager at the start of 1964) and Goldwater's second book, *Why Not Victory?* (1962). Later in the campaign Victor published and promoted two new Goldwater booklets, Stan Evans's *Goldwater or Johnson: Does It Really Matter?* (1964) and Frank Brophy's *Must Goldwater Be Destroyed?* (1964). "In other words," Manion explained, "there will be a full minute at the conclusion of the Manion Forum program during which the announcer will talk about what Goldwater has said and written and urge everybody to learn more about his views. I think that this will be a wonderful way to campaign for him without saying so." As a bonus, Victor would sell some books, covering the pricey bill for airtime.[15]

Though conditioned by the constraints of broadcast media, Manion's Chance for a Choice campaign was firmly rooted in media activists' constitutive concern with institutional bias. The argument for a conservative candidate was predicated on the belief that such an option had been denied voters as a result of the concerted efforts of a shadowy group—be they eastern elites, international financiers, or backroom bosses—that controlled the party structure, as well as the complicit liberal media that sustained and naturalized the bipartisan consensus. Taft supporters had rehearsed the argument, Americans for Goldwater had built upon it, but in 1964 media activists perfected it.

The argument against bipartisanship took on new importance with Goldwater's decision to run for the Republican nomination. To argue against bipartisanship was to cut against the prevailing viewpoint of the time, which celebrated centrist politics. In 1963 a puckish Walter Lippmann encouraged Republicans to nominate Goldwater so they might demonstrate to themselves the folly of tilting too far to the right. But once Goldwater won the nomination, Lippmann liked this scheme quite a bit less. In September 1964 he warned readers against voting for Goldwater, citing the candidate's "unworldly divorce from reality" and Lippmann's fear that his victory would "rupture that cohesiveness around the moderate center which is the special genius of the American party system." For conservatives, that rupture was the point. They saw bipartisanship as one of the fundamental flaws in postwar politics, particularly because it had congealed around nonconservative policies. While this opposition initially led them to advocate third-party candidacies, the Goldwater campaign transformed their goal into remaking the GOP.[16]

Likewise the media. Denunciations of bipartisan politics almost invariably came paired with criticisms of the media establishment that conservatives felt supported it. Goldwater himself grumbled about media unfairness. Stung by the coverage of his "extremism" line at the convention and subsequent depictions of him as a trigger-happy warmonger, Goldwater began striking a more moderate note but also sought to limit press influence in shaping the campaign narrative. In calling for televised debates (to which Johnson never agreed), Goldwater told reporters at a press conference that he would ask for one deviation from the 1960 Kennedy-Nixon debate: reporters would not be asking the questions. "You fellows are looking for news, but not necessarily for education," he lectured. "We are trying to educate." In a lighter but still pointed moment, his press secretary handed out gold pins to reporters on the press plane that read "Eastern Liberal Press."[17]

Goldwater supporters took an even stronger stand against what they saw as unfair attacks on their candidate. The National Economic Council, a conservative political group denounced by Arthur Schlesinger for "the fatuousness of confusing Keynes for Karl Marx," warned conservatives that the general election would consist of "the greatest propaganda battle ever staged in this country." James J. Kilpatrick at the *Richmond News-Leader* called mainstream journalists "assassins of the fourth estate" and criticized "the vicious bias of the press and the television networks against Barry Goldwater." Manion denounced the "slanderous propaganda being showered upon" voters. To a friend, he wrote resignedly about a recent *Saturday Evening Post* article: "It is only one of the many evidences that the establishment is determined to give Goldwater the 'works.'" "This has been the most disgusting campaign," a longtime supporter confirmed to Manion, "not only by the [D]emocrats, but by columnists, radio and TV commentators, and managers of companies have pulled out all the stops in trying to handicap Goldwater in every way. I do not see how some of them sleep nights." In these exchanges, conservatives built on a longstanding argument that established media were tilted in favor of liberals and that conservatives faced an uphill battle getting their message across. With an avowed conservative positioned to win the nation's highest office, they believed the press had jettisoned any pretense of objectivity and would stop at nothing to bring Goldwater down.[18]

Yet Goldwater's victory in the California primary, Manion believed, demonstrated that the press's power was not absolute. Goldwater didn't just defeat Nelson Rockefeller and the other moderate Republicans in the race;

he defeated what Manion, in a clumsy metaphor, called the "huge magazine and newspaper curtain which was systematically wrapped around the truth." This "paper curtain," Manion argued, attempted to "smother the Goldwater candidacy." "But, wonder of wonders, it didn't work. To the obvious shock and surprise of many of its fabricators, many more than a million California voters literally tore their way through the big paper curtain and registered their majority preference for Goldwater for President." According to Manion, they were able to tear through in part because Goldwater did not rely on the mainstream press to represent his positions. By 1964 he had laid out his views in two books and hundreds of syndicated newspaper columns. But more than that, he had an entire alternative media apparatus working to make his case to voters.[19]

The way media activists were making that case, however, became an issue when Goldwater won the nomination. The movement and campaign began to diverge, leaving media activists battling not only Goldwater's opponents but at times the Goldwater campaign itself. Suspicious of outsiders, the nominee surrounded himself with old friends, dumping the Suite 3505 team that had organized on his behalf for more than two years. The "Arizona mafia," which had started closing ranks around Goldwater in late 1963, took over the campaign, exiling Clif White in an attempt to distance Goldwater from the right-wing activists who engineered his nomination. Wary of the charges of extremism, Goldwater repudiated both the Ku Klux Klan and the Birch Society's Robert Welch—though echoing the *National Review* stance, he did not include the society's members in his denunciation, offering as tepid explanation, "they're not on the subversive list." He did, however, purge Birchers from his campaign. Having been "told right straight out that they don't want the cooperation of any official of the John Birch Society," Manion was left out in the cold, along with some of the most committed West Coasters who had won the California primary for Goldwater.[20]

Kept at arm's length, conservative media activists continued to openly support Goldwater. But behind the scenes discontent grew sharply. Nor was it just a fit of pique in response to their exile. There was a growing belief that Goldwater, the candidate they'd been promoting for so long, wasn't running a very effective campaign. Bill Rusher grumbled about "the really deplorable mismanagement, inefficiency and amateurism of [Goldwater's] jerry-built, Arizona-bred campaign staff (and to be entirely fair about it, Goldwater's rather amateurish underestimation of the problems and perils of a presidential candidate)." And he was the optimist on staff. Jim Burnham frequently bemoaned Goldwater's nomination and Buckley wrote in his column in 1964 "the Archangel Gabriel running on the Republican ticket probably couldn't win." After Rusher took him to task for persistent, public doomsaying, Buckley doubled down in a follow-up column. "Of course Goldwater could win. But the odds are as the odds are," he wrote. "It is not helpful to Goldwater or to the conservative cause to assert apodictically, and pridefully, that he *will* win."[21]

Disgruntled about their exclusion and concerned about Goldwater's chances, media activists found themselves in a bind. They understood the importance of Goldwater making the best possible showing—this was, after all, their chance for a choice—and so needed to keep grassroots conservatives on board and enthused. Doing so was no small task, however, especially after Goldwater met with fellow Republican leaders in August for what had been dubbed a "unity meeting." To help heal the divides in a party that never wanted him as its nominee, in August Goldwater met with Rockefeller and Nixon in Hershey, Pennsylvania.

The meeting signaled some reconciliation within the party—it swayed Eisenhower, who threw his full support behind Goldwater. But it did not win over the party's liberal wing. Senator Jacob Javits refused to support Goldwater, and Rockefeller rejected appeals to campaign for him, dimly praising his one-time opponent for joining the "mainstream" of American thinking. Rockefeller's backhanded compliment found plenty of counterparts in the press. "Sweet reasonableness flowed like chocolate at Hershey," the *New York Times* editors applauded. They doubted, though, that this reasonable Goldwater was the real one. Across the pond the *Guardian* wondered the same thing. Goldwater as a mainstream Republican, rubbing shoulders with Rockefeller and Nixon, hardly fit the image of the man who had defended extremism at the convention. A political cartoon in the *Washington Post* made the point more succinctly: "They decided in Hershey that the 'Goldwater Bar' is more palatable with fewer nuts!"[22]

For conservative activists, the new Goldwater did more than raise doubts—it raised tempers. Manion received a cavalcade of letters decrying Goldwater's capitulation, calling it the conservative Munich, the moment their leader abandoned his principles to appease the liberal wing of the Republican Party. (This was especially ironic, since four years earlier Goldwater had denounced Nixon's conciliatory meeting with Rockefeller as the "Munich of the Republican Party.") The letter writers begged Manion for some explanation, some way to make sense of what appeared to be a repudiation of all they had fought for. Maria Stille, a Birch Society member from California, captured their frustrations in her letter, declaring, "Senator Goldwater did not have to capitulate to the liberals who profess to be Republicans. Why did he do it? I would appreciate an answer if there is one. As an 'extremist' of the right," she continued, reclaiming the label Goldwater had tried to expunge at Hershey, "I cannot accept his statement that he does not seek our support—and I certainly cannot accept that Nixon is to now speak for us frequently from now until November. This is diametrically opposed to all we fought for and all we stood for in the San Francisco Convention." Manion tried to stanch the wound, calling the Hershey meeting "strictly 'pro forma'" and insisting that reports of the meeting were the work of liberal journalists who "will try their best to 'twist' the Senator out of the race."[23]

Yet discontent was hard to tamp down. Audiences continued to press media activists to do something about Goldwater's faltering campaign. Listeners like Esther Sheehan wrote Manion to complain about one of the campaign's bucolic but underwhelming thirty-minute television broadcasts: "People want to hear him make a fighting speech and looking at a man driving a truck, a farmer with his cows etc was a waste of money." The base didn't want a soft sell; they wanted Goldwater to come out swinging. "You are a man of great influence and ability," she told Manion. "Can't you do something to have him use the real issues he has?" Everyone, it seemed, had advice for the campaign. Jameson G. Campaigne, conservative editor of the *Indianapolis Star*, wrote Goldwater speechwriter Karl Hess to pass along one of his secretary's ideas: "Her suggestion was that you take the tune 'Hello Dolly' and fit some jingles to it 'Hello Barry' etc. The song is hot all over the country right now and it might be a heck of a good idea." (The campaign thought so, too; they tried to use "Hello, Barry" at the convention, but the musical's producer threatened the Republican Party with a $10 million lawsuit. The producer instead licensed it to the Democrats, whose convention opened to the tune of "Hello, Lyndon!")[24]

The campaign season was one in which media activists emerged as powerful political brokers, advisers, sloganeers, strategists, and intermediaries between the candidate and the base. As the Goldwater campaign took off, however, they found themselves in constant battle with other political factions: the liberal opposition, the Goldwater campaign, the grassroots right.

But outside factions weren't their only problem. In 1964, they were facing a new challenge from media upstarts who sensed opportunity in the right's rising political fortunes.

Henry Regnery planned to cash in on the 1964 election.

It wasn't a matter of changing his political stripes. True, Regnery had been slow to board the Goldwater for President train. In 1961, when Goldwater backed out of a ghostwritten labor union manuscript because he was "reconsidering his 'public image,'" Regnery called the idea of a Goldwater presidential run "absurd." "He is a fine man—honest, intelligent, and courageous," he wrote Felix Morley, "but he is no Robert Taft." Yet like Rusher, Regnery was won over by Goldwater's impressive rise in the early 1960s, and by 1964 he was a firm backer of the Goldwater campaign. No, this wasn't opportunism but rather a moment when pocketbook and politics aligned.[25]

As Goldwater marched toward the nomination, Regnery published three campaign-focused books: Edwin McDowell's biography of Barry Goldwater, Phil Crane's *The Democrat's Dilemma*, and G. R. Schreiber's exposé of the Bobby Baker affair. McDowell, an editorial writer for the Pulliam-owned *Arizona Republic*, cobbled together a traditional campaign biography, regaling readers with tales of Goldwater's backcountry adventures interspersed with approving summaries of his political creed. The McDowell book received a huge spread in *Human Events*, which printed a ten-thousand-word excerpt packaged as a pro-Goldwater handout, as well as a favorable review by Rusher in *National Review*. *The Democrat's Dilemma* received similar compliments from the magazine, and its author, Phil Crane, a young university professor, quickly became a conservative media darling.[26]

The book Regnery believed would make the biggest splash, however, was *The Bobby Baker Affair: How to Make Millions in Washington*. It explored the growing scandal around Baker, Lyndon Johnson's political adviser, who was accused of trading government contracts for cash and call girls. The scandal, which broke in the fall of 1963, resulted in Baker's resignation and a Senate hearing, but interest petered out after Kennedy's assassination. Regnery hoped to resurrect it, putting Johnson's character at the fore of the election. When Regnery was wrapping up publishing decisions on the Baker book, he had a feeling it would become a campaign phenomenon. Early sales numbers for the McDowell and Crane books were promising: the hardback of the McDowell book hit 17,000, prompting two paperback runs totaling

400,000 copies. Preorders for *The Democrat's Dilemma* topped 110,000. Regnery felt confident enough to order a first printing of 200,000 for the Bobby Baker book, which his distributor believed would sell out in a week.[27]

The plunge into low-priced paperbacks, which Regnery undertook with unusual alacrity, was a major shift for the publisher. Until 1964, Regnery approached the selection and publication of conservative books cautiously, favoring the timeless over the timely, lining up orders well in advance to cover any possible losses. He certainly desired profits and popularity but, in the absence of both, cultivated an air of speaking to an enlightened remnant in a benighted world. So what changed?

In the first half of 1964, as Regnery was planning his publication schedule for the year, three other paperbacks appeared that jolted the political and publishing world. By Election Day, more than 16 million copies of the books were in circulation, a number the Fair Campaign Practices Committee estimated at "about 60 times greater than last year's best-selling novel." "The standard book publishing world looks on in bewilderment," marveled the *Baltimore Sun*. The *Chicago Tribune* called it "one of the strangest publishing phenomena of American political history."[28]

Why all the fuss? Campaign books themselves were nothing new. By 1964 it was common for candidates to put out a statement of principle or glossy biography to introduce themselves to the nation. But these low-priced, mass-distributed paperbacks were different. They were self-published by unknown authors. They contained few mentions of Goldwater. And while they seldom appeared in traditional bookstores, each sold millions of copies, making tidy profits for their authors-cum-publishers.

Appearing in rapid succession, these "hatchets with soft cover sheaths," as the *Chicago Tribune* dubbed them, startled political observers with their dark and conspiratorial interpretation of American history. Yet readers burned through the books, all of which advanced the movement's case in 1964: liberal policies, put in place not by the people but by a few shady and corrupt elites, were destroying America at home and abroad. Though their subjects varied widely, these three books all reached the same conclusion: only a true conservative—that is, Goldwater—could stop the country's self-destructive slide. In *None Dare Call It Treason*, John Stormer spun a tale of internal subversion and weak-willed foreign policy that marked "America's retreat from victory" in the Cold War. Stormer, a Missouri Republican devoted to proselytizing conservative anticommunism, argued the United States was losing the Cold War through weak-willed foreign policy and internal subversion. Thirty years of liberal governance by both parties had given communists the upper hand. "Every communist country in the world literally has a 'Made in the USA' stamp on it," he wrote.[29]

Phyllis Schlafly, author of *A Choice Not an Echo*, accused "a small group of secret kingmakers" of denying conservatives opportunities in the Republican Party for the previous three decades. Playing off Vance Packard's best-selling 1957 book, *The Hidden Persuaders*, she argued that party elites had used the techniques of advertising to manipulate voters into picking the kingmakers' preferred candidate. To what end? So they could enact a "hidden policy of perpetuating the Red empire in order to perpetuate the high level of Federal spending and control" that would fill the kingmakers' coffers. With her book she intended to rally grassroots Republicans to keep these kingmakers from blocking the nomination of Barry Goldwater, the GOP's "one obvious, logical, deserving, winning candidate." A generous donor ensured that each of the delegates to the Cow Palace convention in July had a copy.[30]

After the convention, Texas rancher J. Evetts Haley joined them with *A Texan Looks at Lyndon*. Conservatives needed to look no further than the subtitle—*A Study in Illegitimate Power*—to get Haley's point, but those willing to delve further found two hundred pages of greased palms, stolen elections, and suspicious deaths. Haley's claims rivaled the darkest and most bizarre Clinton conspiracies, arguing President Johnson was better suited to the penitentiary than the presidency. The author called Johnson an "inordinately vain, egotistical, ambitious extrovert" and claimed Lady Bird Johnson mirrored "Lady Macbeth's consuming ambition for the growth of her husband's power." Of the presidential assassination that preceded Johnson's rise to the presidency, he hinted darkly, "What a strange coincidence."[31]

The books were instant successes. Self-published under the imprimatur Liberty Bell Press, *None Dare Call It Treason* sold its first printing of 100,000 books in a few months, then another 100,000 in the first half of April. Another 100,000 sold two weeks later. By the time of the Republican National Convention in June, the book was on its eighth printing. Before Election Day, Stormer had printed 6.8 million copies, the number of sales limited only by how many he could produce.

Schlafly's *A Choice Not an Echo* and Haley's *A Texan Looks at Lyndon* followed similar trajectories. Schlafly revealed her book to a group gathered in her suburban home in March, announcing that it would win the nomination for Goldwater. Manion, present at the meeting, confessed he was "hopeful merely" that the book could have such an impact. But when the book sold 600,000 copies in its first printing, he was cheered. Nearly a million copies were distributed by a single supporter in California before the election. In a letter to Fred Schlafly, Phyllis's husband, Manion divulged, "Everybody in California tells me that if Barry wins tomorrow, Phyllis'[s] book will be largely responsible." When Goldwater eked out a two-point victory over chief rival Nelson Rockefeller the next day, Manion became convinced that Schlafly's book had put Goldwater over the top. He was not alone in his perception of the book's power. One Orange County activist credited the book with dispelling the mystery and misinformation surrounding Goldwater. *Choice*, the activist explained, "made us familiar with this person and what he was about. . . . Then we identified with him." It was a telling claim for a book that said relatively little about Goldwater. The campaign books, though not explicitly about the candidate, were understood as an extension of his platform.[32]

How did these authors manage such massive sales figures? Bulk distribution. The seventy-five-cent paperback had been designed for mass propagation. The back page of the fifteenth edition of *None Dare Call It Treason* (one of three August runs) urged readers to "help awaken others!" by passing the book along to "friends, relatives, neighbors, clergymen, school teachers, libraries." Stormer offered bulk pricing to encourage multiple sales, giving a discount for as few as three copies (for $2.00 rather than $2.25) or as many as a thousand (at twenty cents apiece). Schlafly's book ended the same way, with an appeal for bulk purchases as a part of activists' "precinct work." Bulk distribution allowed conservative authors to bypass the publishers, bookstores, and reviewers that shaped the national book market. They instead relied on a network of conservative media sources and organizations to promote and distribute their books. They did this as much out of necessity as strategy. While a slew of conservative bookstores opened in the early 1960s, many under the auspices of local Birch Society branches, obtaining shelf space in regular bookstores remained difficult. Indeed, even getting the best-selling *None Dare Call It Treason* placed in stores often required red-baiting reluctant booksellers. As a consequence, despite the millions of copies in circulation, none of the campaign paperbacks made the *New York Times* best-seller list.[33]

Thanks to wealthy donors who financed this bulk distribution, these best sellers (*A Texan Looks at Lyndon* passed seven million copies in September) were treated like campaign paraphernalia: handed out at conventions and rallies, mailed to delegates and state party headquarters for free. In Dade County, Florida, campaign workers canvassed neighborhoods and in place of flyers and leaflets gave out nearly 200,000 copies of Stormer's book. All told, well over fifteen million copies of these three books were distributed before Election Day, doing far more to spread the conservative message during the campaign season than did Goldwater himself, who turned out to be a lackluster, unenthusiastic candidate.[34]

Sales were not the only unusual thing about the books. Though conservative publishing houses like Regnery and Devin-Adair were well established by 1964, each of these paperbacks was self-published. Stormer published under Liberty Bell Press, Schlafly under Pere Marquette, and Haley under Palo Duro. Schlafly chose to self-publish after the success of *Conscience of a Conservative* and *None Dare Call It Treason* convinced her that it was possible. So why, when successful publishing companies had been a mainstay of conservative writing for ten or fifteen years, were the most successful conservative books of the period—perhaps the most successful since modern conservatism emerged in the postwar era—self-published?

The likely suspects were costs, profits, and efficiency. The benefits conservative publishers offered were connections and funds. Conservative publishing houses were willing to take risks on ideological manuscripts, even those without potential for large sales, because they used their networks of mailing lists, sponsors, and organizations to identify and develop a market for conservative literature. Sometimes they were willing to take a loss on books they deemed important, as when Regnery published Russell Kirk's *The Conservative Mind* (1953), but in other cases they required authors to find the initial capital for publishing. For instance, when Manion wanted to publish his 1964 book *The Conservative American* as a paperback with Regnery, the publisher asked him to first line up preorders for fifty thousand copies. If the book caught on, Regnery would order a second printing using his own capital. To help stabilize their business models, conservative publishers relied on backlists and nonpolitical books, as Regnery had with the Great Books series and as Devin Garrity of Devin-Adair had with the Irish literature and poetry list upon which the company was founded in the early twentieth century.[35]

As Manion showed with *Conscience of a Conservative* in 1960, and as the campaign books of 1964 confirmed, when authors had networks and funds of their own, conservative publishing houses had less of a role to play. Certainly Pere Marquette and Palo Duro failed to carry the same cachet as Regnery, the house that had published *The Conservative Mind* and *God and Man at Yale*. But the conservative movement was growing quickly, with new adherents joining the ranks every day. Whatever authority Regnery or Devin-Adair may have had in more established conservative circles, there was little reason to think recent converts cared about a book's imprimatur. There were other ways to establish the conservative credentials of a book and its author. What was *Human Events* or *National Review* reporting? What did Dan Smoot or Clarence Manion have to say? Who introduced the book to the reader mattered as well. When the copy came from the local Republican Party or a fellow Bircher, credibility was conveyed as the book changed hands.

The three self-published authors were able to use their own resources and networks to capitalize the first printing. Subsequent success funneled funds back into the operations, fueling further production. The lack of an outside publisher carried certain benefits as well. Complete control resided with the author: control of content, of publication schedule, of distribution. Since printing and shipping happened elsewhere, authors did not have to worry about storing and organizing a half-million paperbacks in their living rooms. Suddenly, conservative publishing did not seem to be too difficult an endeavor.

For Regnery, the success of these authors was both inspiring and bedeviling. Having churned away in conservative publishing for more than fifteen years, he had never had books sell so well. Sure, a few of his books made the *New York Times* best-seller list, something none of the campaign paperbacks could claim because of their unusual distribution methods, but prestige and profits were not the same thing. So he adopted an "if-you-can't-beat-'em-join-'em" attitude and ordered hundreds of thousands of copies of his own campaign paperbacks. In the still-optimistic days of late summer, Regnery touted the new methods to a donor: "It seems to me this is the proper way to publish topical books. They can be brought out quickly, we can get nationwide distribution within a matter of weeks, and they are priced on a basis which makes it possible for people to buy them without having to make a large cash outlay." Sound reasoning, but it made a slight—and costly—logical error. It assumed because *some* conservative campaign paperbacks had become sensations, *all* of them would. But for Stormer, Schlafly, and Haley, bulk printing followed bulk orders. Regnery, tossing caution to the wind for once in the hopes of riding the campaign season wave, went all in on the expectation of orders.[36]

Regnery's books did not follow the remarkable arc of the famed paperbacks. Election Day came and went, but the piles of books went unsold. By March 1965 Regnery still sounded hopeful about the company's venture into mass-market paperbacks, touting the company's newfound ability to "reach a large market which hardback books rarely penetrate" and therefore "increase our volume, and strengthen our position [in] the business." Yet soon he was forced to admit that while conservatives had to find a way to reach out to new audiences, Regnery Publishing couldn't make the mass-market paperback work. He was certain newsstands would sell at least 30 percent of the Goldwater and Bobby Baker books, and privately thought they would sell as many as 60 percent. But the newsstands returned 85 percent of the books, which Regnery described as "a devastating blow." When Manion approached him again about bringing *The Conservative American* out in paperback, Regnery demurred. "One thing I have learned is that the market for such books is even more unpredictable than for hardbacks. In view of this, I feel that we should not go into any low priced paperback unless we have been able to pick up enough advance orders to cover us." The Regnery reticence was back with a vengeance.[37]

But perhaps Regnery's failures were a blessing in disguise. The best-selling paperbacks were circulating in the midst of a presidential election, and the peculiarities of this publishing phenomenon caught the attention of more than just conservatives. The Goldwater campaign revived media interest in the American right. In returning to the topic, journalists relied on the extremism framework erected during the Birch Society exposés. The election cycle overheated the rhetoric. In the *Chicago Defender*, a writer described the scene at the Cow Palace thusly: "This is Germany, 1933 and the Nazis are about to take over the country." Even absent invocations of the Third Reich, journalists painted the movement for Goldwater as sinister and un-American. The *Saturday Evening Post*, for instance, labeled Goldwater supporters "irrational," "fanatical," and "reckless." Columnist Drew Pearson reported the convention was rife with "whiffs of fascism" and "signs of intolerance and violence" that "resemble some of the telltale signs that developed in Europe after World War I. And they raise the question 'could it happen here?'"[38]

In this atmosphere, the paperbacks became a lightning rod for criticisms of the right. Commentators picked apart the books' claims, not only challenging their accuracy but using them to demonstrate the intellectual deficiencies of the American right. Critics found the books' numerous academic-style citations particularly incensing: "a parody of scholarship, subverted to the interests of smear," relying on "the scandalous use of seemingly scholarly footnotes." Liberal critics presented the books as evidence of conservatism's inherent anti-intellectualism. Writing for the *New Republic*, Bruce Galphin infused his survey of the "pop literature of the radical right" with some pop psychology. "It is no accident that the official campaign slogan, 'In your heart, you know he's right,' locates Senator Goldwater's appeal elsewhere than the mind," he began, before delving into the "emotional climate that prepares millions to be gullible converts." A review of the Stormer book in the *Guardian*, cleverly called "None Dare Call It Reason," noted the emotional appeal of the book and argued it was right-wing anti-intellectualism gussied up as scholarship. Conservatism, critics concluded, was an ideology of the heart rather than the head.[39]

Critics took the time to dissect the books' contents, but they were equally interested in exposing the apparatus behind their publication. They did not believe that the paperbacks' massive circulation resulted from the appeal of the authors' arguments but rather from the distribution networks of the conservative movement. The template for the Birch exposés came into play again as journalists portrayed a shadowy conservative underworld, both alluring and alarming for its ability to operate out of sight. Self-publication became a cudgel to discredit the paperbacks. The *Boston Globe* asserted Haley's book was "published under semi-clandestine circumstances by an ultra-right-wing Texas cowman." A *Newsday* review spun the self-publication as a necessity, calling the paperbacks the kind of books "that more often than not have to be printed privately since no recognized publisher would touch them." To further disparage the books, the review connected them to the political untouchables. "It is through splinter groups, and particularly the John Birch Society, that the hate literature gets its widest dissemination." The process of self-publication was particularly damning if there was something suspect about the "self" in question, so reviewers often lingered over the authors' backgrounds. Jack Anderson at the *Washington Post* described Haley's research aide as "a wealthy Texas rancher with close ties to the American Nazi Party," a detail meant to tie Haley and the book to the party. The *Chicago Tribune* felt the "whispering campaigns" against Haley had gotten so bad that it ran a lengthy report on his academic background, including his claim that the University of Texas did not renew his contract as punishment "by the university liberals because of his political views."[40]

Established conservative media activists responded to these attacks by enthusiastically endorsing all three books. At *National Review*, Stan Evans interpreted the books as evidence of how total the liberal control of media was. Calling the authors pamphleteers in the tradition of Tom Paine, he placed the paperbacks squarely in the American tradition. "If the tree of liberty has been watered by the blood of patriots and tyrants," he wrote, "it has also drawn nourishment from the ink of scribblers." Unlike the "unsavory one-man publications which have no beneficial effect"—the realm of crackpots—the pamphleteer demonstrated his worth by finding a vast audience. "The pamphleteer fills the gap between what the Establishment thinks people ought to read and what they in fact want to read." The massive circulation of the campaign paperbacks, then, was not only a testament to their worth but a condemnation of the system that sought to tamp them down. Self-publication became a virtue: "When the nation's best-sellers are produced in Alton, Ill., Florissant, Mo. and Canyon, Tex., rather than in the giant publishing houses of New York, the evidence is good that the communications gap has reached revolutionary dimensions." Even their over-the-top rhetoric and exaggerations recommended them. Pamphleteers, after all, did not exist "to administer even-handed justice, but to bring a suppressed side of the record to light." The very characteristics that critics used against the paperbacks Evans refashioned as virtues.[41]

The high passions on both sides transformed the paperbacks into symbols of incendiary politics and thus into a major issue in the campaign. The head of the Democratic National Committee, John Bailey, called on Goldwater, the Republican National Committee (RNC), and the chair of Citizens for Goldwater-Miller to publicly repudiate the books: "Never before has a president been attacked so viciously as in the flood of pocket books, none published by a company of recognized standing, as in the paperbacks which keep turning up at Goldwater rallies and in Goldwater headquarters." Dean Burch, head of the RNC, seized the occasion to return fire over the "Daisy" ad that had aired five weeks earlier. Television's first viral attack ad, the commercial apposed a little girl plucking flower petals with a nuclear countdown, insinuating a Goldwater victory would lead to atomic war. Calling Bailey's accusation the "most hypocritical statement of the campaign," Burch charged that it was in fact the Johnson campaign that relied on "slanted, biased and fraudulent propaganda which is unparalleled in American political history." Surveying the field, the head of the nonpartisan Fair Campaign Practices Committee declared the 1964 election "the bitterest and most vicious campaign that I've ever observed."[42]

On the local scene, the books generated even more discord. A Los

Angeles police officer was suspended after being accused of selling a copy of *A Texan Looks at Lyndon* to a local newspaper reporter. In New Hampshire, the state's Republican National Committeeman called for a ban on *None Dare Call It Treason* at all Republican functions in the state, where at least forty thousand copies had already been distributed among New Hampshire's six hundred thousand residents. The committeeman's actions were rooted in his opposition to the message of the book, which he believed "represents a radical extremist philosophy which is totally inconsistent with Republican Party principles." Sixty students picketed the home of Elmira College president J. Ralph Murray after he distributed nearly a thousand copies of the book to students, courtesy of an alumna who sent them "in the hope that students might choose to read it and be made aware of some of the dangers of creeping Communism in our Government, our education system, our churches, in fact all phases of our lives." Faculty joined in the protest, arranging a panel discussion and circulating a rebuttal to Stormer's argument. Nor were these conflicts limited to liberal attacks on conservatives. In Utah, the Republican secretary of state banned sales of the *Rocky Mountain Review* in the state capitol because it criticized *None Dare Call It Treason*. Though he admitted "it might be considered censorship," the secretary insisted, "I have a perfect right to do this."[43]

In the build-up to Election Day, the paperbacks were front and center. But did they ultimately make a difference? The Schlafly book was continuously credited with helping Goldwater win the nomination, but it's unlikely it was a determinative factor, given the political maneuvers Goldwater supporters had planned well in advance of the convention. The books certainly captured the energy and enthusiasm of conservative activists, giving them materials with which to proselytize that matched their own zeal and conviction. But the best sellers, which popped up so suddenly and received such biting press coverage, also helped solidify the impression that there was something unusual about the Goldwater drive, something excessive and even sinister about the passion behind it.

The campaign paperbacks found big-money donors because they were cheap, easy to circulate, and on message at a time when conservatives were willing to dish out big bucks in order to get their man in office. As a result the authors made tidy profits, to the surprise of many observers. One detractor called the profits "an unheard-of phenomenon in the field of undisguised political propaganda." Indeed, the election provided an infusion of cash to nearly every conservative media outlet, even those that didn't capture the imagination of legions of journalists. Conservatives across the country wanted as much material about Goldwater as possible to help them sell the candidate and his message. Reprints of *Forum* broadcasts and copies of *Human Events* passed from neighbor to neighbor. Suburban kaffeeklatsches in support of Goldwater took place at kitchen tables strewn with the latest issue of *National Review* and dog-eared copies of *None Dare Call It Treason*. The products of conservative media were the bibles of the Goldwater nomination drive.[44]

In such an atmosphere, there was little anxiety among conservative media activists about the rapid expansion of their field. Demand was high across the board. Budgets fattened as circulation soared at *National Review* and *Human Events*. A record number of stations were airing the Manion Forum. Regnery firmly believed *The Bobby Baker Affair* was going to take off—the *New York Times* had just declared that the controversy was "rapidly developing into *the* political scandal of the middle sixties"—and that the low-priced paperback model was the way forward in the future. All told, the Goldwater drive was a boon for conservative media. The question was, what would happen when it ended?[45]

Chapter 9

The Pivot

"Where does the Republican party go from here?" the *New York Times* asked the morning after the 1964 election. With Goldwater going down to "pulverizing, catastrophic defeat," the newspaper argued the election results had given the lie to the right's claim of a hidden conservative majority: "The candidacy of Senator Goldwater, who in recent years became the hero of these old-fashioned conservatives as well as of the neo-McCarthyites, Birchites and others on the fringes of the conservative position, put this long-discussed theory to the test. The results are now apparent to everyone." Conservatives had their chance for a choice. America chose liberalism.[1]

For the *New York Times*, the way forward was evident: the GOP had to recommit to being "a reasonable, responsible, modern-minded party." For conservative media activists, the next step was less clear. Most had reconciled themselves to a Goldwater loss well in advance, though the scale of Johnson's victory, along with a slew of down-ballot Republican losses, gave the results a particularly vicious sting. Those expecting despondency from right-wing media, however, would find themselves disappointed. After all, conservatives had been racking up losses for years; Goldwater's nomination had been a step forward. The challenge now was to figure out what went wrong and how to make a better showing next time.[2]

Goldwater's candidacy had come with a set of assumptions about the electorate, the Republican Party, and the power of the conservative message. His historic loss meant reassessing those beliefs. That reassessment began with an election postmortem that centered around two broad problems: outreach and image. Across the spectrum—from *National Review* to the

Manion Forum to *Human Events* to Regnery Publishing—media activists consciously pivoted from preaching to the converted to proselytizing to the apathetic. They believed that to win an election, they had to present themselves not as an oppositional minority but as an oppressed majority.

But they also knew their outreach would be continuously thwarted by the charges of extremism that had haunted the Goldwater campaign. True to form, conservative media activists invoked liberal bias as the source of these extremism claims but acknowledged such bias was unlikely to go away any time soon. So what to do about the wilder edges of the movement? And in particular, what to do about the Birch albatross? Such questions rekindled the pitched battles of the early 1960s, as media activists fought to define the boundaries of conservative thought and action. In their struggle to claim primacy in shaping the movement's direction, conservative media activists embedded their disagreements in institutional form, building a new but no less contentious conservative movement on the rubble of the Goldwater campaign.

When the dust cleared from the November landslide, most analysts concluded that the Goldwater campaign marked the collapse of the conservative movement. Perhaps it would twitch along for a bit, perhaps a few of the die-hards and true believers would try to carry on, but as a viable force in American politics, conservatism was done. The American people had been given a choice, as the *New York Times* argued, and they had resoundingly rejected Goldwater's philosophy. As James Reston put it, "Barry Goldwater not only lost the Presidential election yesterday but the conservative cause as well." Even many within the movement who didn't believe conservatism was finished saw the results as a major setback. "The election last Tuesday was a disaster," Regnery wrote to a friend a week after the loss. "I did not think that Goldwater would win, but I was convinced that he would make a much better showing than seemed to be the case."[3]

But while the defeat of conservatism seemed to be common consensus in the established press, conservative media activists saw cause for hope. No sooner had Regnery pronounced the election a disaster than he started to rally. "The liberals, of course, are calling the whole thing a defeat of conservatism which, I think, is only partly true," he mused, "and the fact remains that some 25 million people did vote for Goldwater either because, or in spite of, his conservative views. One can also argue that this demonstrates that there is a solidly based conservative movement which could conceivably grow in strength as time goes on." One could make that argument, and many conservatives did. Manion expressed similar thoughts to a friend the day after the election: "Our work is cut out for us now. Although the political roof fell [in] on the country yesterday, we must not forget that twenty-six million people voted Conservative for the first time in 30 years under terrific pressures from the whole Liberal establishment."[4]

The legend of the 26 million (sometimes 25, sometimes 27) emerged nearly as soon as the results were announced. Kent and Phoebe Courtney, publishers of the *Independent American*, marketed bumper stickers proclaiming, "26,000,000 Americans Can't Be Wrong!" (Though apparently the 43 million Americans who voted for Johnson could be.) Someone who worked on the campaign called the 26 million "the most dedicated, talented, purposeful group that has ever joined together in a political cause." The number came to stand not for votes for Goldwater but for an unshakable core of men and women committed to conservative ideas—as Manion put it, the "unreconstructed 'die hards'" and "hard core Conservatives." Others were more skeptical. *Look* magazine parsed the results and decided only three million of the votes cast for the Republican ticket represented "strong, hard-core support for Goldwater conservatism." But whether three million or 26, their numbers were clearly insufficient to win a national election.[5]

For over a decade, conservative media activists had worked to communicate with and coordinate people who saw the rise of liberalism as a great betrayal of the American creed. Yet that was not enough. As the radio preacher Billy James Hargis remarked to Manion, "The fault of the conservative movement is that we have talked to ourselves instead of to the uninformed." That strategy might have made sense when the movement was just getting underway, but to compete in national politics, conservatives had to reach beyond their base into the amorphous middle of American politics. And so, counting twenty-six million in hand and believing millions more could be won over to conservative principles, media activists targeted the uncommitted. "We're not interested in Conservatives," a 1965 pamphlet for the *Manion Forum* declared, "because the millions of Conservatives in America are *already* concerned about the facts we present on our radio and television programs." These listeners did not need to be awakened to the dangers of communism or expansive government. Bill Rusher concurred, concluding that "it is pretty clear that we have done all we can do in selling *National Review* to hard-line conservatives." It was time to enter new markets and build new audiences.[6]

Only . . . how? Expansion required money, and the campaign had exhausted the conservative base, leaving it thin on energy and resources. Compounding the problem were innovators in direct mail, who pooled the names of active Goldwater supporters and sold access to the address lists. These lists seemed like an easy way to raise funds from conservatives to pour into the expansion efforts. But because almost all conservative organizations and media institutions were attempting to expand after the election, direct mail tended to aggravate, not motivate, movement conservatives. Rusher fretted over the "truly alarming proliferation of conservative fund appeals that is going on these days," detailing to Buckley the mounds of fund-raising letters piled on his desk. Though at a loss for what to do about it, he grimly predicted that "it is almost certainly going to end by emptying the conservative purse and perhaps disillusioning the contributors as well." Right he was. An irate supporter of the *Forum* shot off a letter to Manion after receiving seventeen solicitations from conservative groups in ten days. "Each professed the urgent need of my sending money in order that they might remain solvent," he thundered. "None was interested in whether or not I remained solvent!"[7]

As a result, conservative media activists, who had seen their budgets fatten in the early 1960s, watched as funds shriveled in the post-Goldwater years. The *Manion Forum*'s income shrank 16 percent in the 1964–1965 fiscal year as it began losing stations and donors. *National Review*'s circulation dwindled. Regnery found himself sitting on piles of unsold paperbacks and in competition with the new start-up Arlington House. *Human Events* was reeling from editor Frank Hanighen's passing in early 1964 and the devastating death of publisher James Wick just days after the election.[8]

As revenue streams dried up, those in conservative media tried redirecting rather than expanding their reach. By creating contacts outside established conservative circles, changes in distribution helped enlarge the movement without significant outlays of cash. Manion, for instance, started up a short broadcast called the *Manion Forum Footnotes*, three- to five-minute pieces perfect for radio audiences increasingly likely to listen in the car rather than in the living room. The briefer time period forced Manion to be more colloquial and provocative, a welcome change from the occasionally stultifying weekly radio addresses. He relished pithy indictments of liberal issues, warning new safety regulations would only guarantee "the safety of universal unemployment" and denouncing Washington's "big tax-eating spendocracy."[9]

Television presented new opportunities as well. Manion and Smoot had been on television for a few years and believed it attracted a different audience than did their radio shows. Television drew a different set of guests, too, since the cachet of appearing on screen proved a powerful enticement for landing big-name interviews. "It has helped us immeasurably in getting important top-flight talent for both television and radio," Manion explained to a top advertiser. Buckley, who believed television was "an indispensable part of evangelization" in the modern age, took to the small screen as well. His long-running debate show *Firing Line* went live in 1966, giving the quick-witted editor a chance to spar with liberal guests while promoting a conservative point of view on a public broadcasting network.[10]

Television, however, was by far the most expensive medium, leaving activists dependent on big-money donors. This presented a particular problem for Manion, whose television program relied almost entirely on the sponsorship of dog-food manufacturer D. B. Lewis. Lewis drew a different lesson from Goldwater's loss than media activists did. Where the activists sought to broaden their reach, Lewis decided to narrow his, shifting priorities from the national to the local level. Better to build up conservatives' political power in a state like California, he determined, than to tackle the massive task of remaking the country. "I feel that California is one of the most critical states for our elections in the next couple of years," he explained when he pulled his television sponsorship. The money once used to sponsor the *Manion Forum* went to *Capitol Reporter*, a program out of Los Angeles hosted by Donald L. Jackson, a former Republican congressman who would go on to serve on the Interstate Commerce Commission during the Nixon administration. Manion lobbied hard to retain Lewis's sponsorship, but Lewis held firm. He would continue to support Manion's radio program, but the costly television sponsorship was done. The *Forum* went dark on most of the West Coast, leaving only a rump of second-tier stations in the Midwest. By the late 1960s, the *Forum* stopped all regular television production.[11]

One of the barriers to conservative programming, Lewis had long lamented, was the unwillingness of networks to syndicate right-wing shows. Vying for a national audience, the networks had little appetite for niche programming—and even less for controversial political spots that could alienate huge swaths of their potential viewership. Local station owners often felt the same way, refusing to sell Lewis time for Smoot's and Manion's programs. In the post-Goldwater years, the right's frustration over this television lockout led to the first attempt to establish a conservative television network. The project was the brainchild of David Dye, a businessman from Lubbock, Texas. Believing that "freedom and morality" would be lost "if the 'mass media' continues to be dominated by liberal and internationalist managements," Dye founded Medias Unlimited, a corporation whose main purpose was to organize conservative shareholders to take over a major network. He set his sights on CBS, arguing it was "the worst offender," with shows that glorified "violence, crime, brutality, sadism and sex." In his criticism of CBS, Dye blended social and political concerns in a pattern that would take on increasing importance to conservatives as fears of domestic communism lost political efficacy and fears of domestic disorder gained it.[12]

Dye became a momentary hero in conservative circles, appearing on Paul Harvey's and Clarence Manion's shows, winning plaudits from *Human Events*. *National Review*, however, kept its distance. Rusher told a reader that while "the objective is certainly worthwhile . . . we do not consider Mr. Dye's particular plan a very practical one, or feel that it is likely to succeed." For good reason: the Dye plan was a long shot, to put it mildly. He bought two hundred shares of CBS, then gave himself the goal of getting one thousand others to do the same. Each of those thousand then had to recruit twenty more share buyers in order for conservatives to have a controlling interest in CBS. CBS did gain thirteen thousand new shareholders in the first half of 1965—"We are confident that most of these are 'our' people," Dye told Paul Harvey—but conservatives never mustered enough shares to enact Dye's plan. The dream of a conservative network would have to wait.[13]

In the world of conservative print, innovations in distribution also yielded a wide range of results. Regnery worked tirelessly to get mass-circulation paperbacks onto newsstands and into bookstores but failed to produce a best seller on par with the self-published campaign paperbacks. Indeed, he had his hands full with remainders of his own campaign paperbacks. In 1965 he tried to unload one hundred thousand copies of *The Bobby Baker Affair* to Bob Welch at the Birch Society, who had been a shareholder in Regnery since its founding in the late 1940s. Welch, who had made his fortune in the candy business before starting the Birch Society, knew a bad deal when he saw one. He was reluctant to take the books on, even at six cents a copy. No matter how Regnery tried—and he tried endlessly—he couldn't stoke the interest of readers or donors. The low-priced paperback market continued to mystify him.[14]

While he toyed with mass paperbacks, Regnery continued to rely on a sponsorship model for most books. The publication of books like John

Davenport's *The U.S. Economy* (1964), a call to reduce the role of government in business, was subsidized by bulk sales to corporations like AT&T,
U.S. Steel, and General Electric. Yet even after returning to this more
cautious business model, Regnery found it increasingly difficult to keep
the company out of the red. He tried to secure a long-term loan from J.
Howard Pew, who had supported the company and other conservative
media endeavors for years. Pew considered the arrangement—a $200,000,
fifteen-year loan, contingent on Regnery raising an additional $200,000 from
other sources—but eventually decided the company was not a good risk. By
mid-1965, Regnery Publishing was on the brink. "I will have to work out
some sort of permanent financing," he hinted to a (wealthy) friend, "or else
sell the business."[15]

In addition to internal financial issues, Regnery was also facing new
competition. Witnessing a growing appetite for conservative books, in
1964 Neil McCaffrey launched two new endeavors: the Conservative Book
Club and Arlington House publishing company. McCaffrey, a Bronx-born
Catholic who was ambitious, talented, temperamental, and dogmatic in
equal measure, was an editor at Doubleday in 1957 when he wrote to
National Review, offering his skills in promotion to increase the magazine's
circulation (which at the time was around 17,000). Working alongside Jim
McFadden, McCaffrey set up a direct-mail program that helped boost circulation to 142,000 during the Goldwater campaign. McCaffrey, who liked
to mix self-promotion into his marketing work for the magazine, believed
the success of *National Review* came largely from his innovations. As he
explained to Rusher, "The content was just as good (some would say better)
at 17,000 as it was at 142,000. The difference was circulation promotion."
Here was someone not lacking in self-confidence.[16]

Redoubling his efforts to promote conservative politics, McCaffrey left
Macmillan, where he'd been an editor since 1961, to start his own publishing enterprises. The Conservative Book Club (CBC) was the first and most
successful of these efforts. Buoyed by secret access to *National Review*'s
closely guarded list of active subscribers, which he had to transcribe by
hand because the distinctive style of the labels would have revealed his
source, McCaffrey was able to quickly build the CBC's membership to thirty
thousand. Offering discounted prices on an array of right-wing books, the
book club provided a new way of marketing to conservative book buyers.
Both Regnery and Devin Garrity of Devin-Adair Publishing were cautiously
optimistic about this development, seeing it as a way to tap into their target

audiences. Contracts with the CBC came with a number of restrictions—publishers made less money and had to wait at least a year to issue paperback versions of their hardcover offerings—but the club seemed, potentially at least, like a good way to connect more easily with conservative readers.[17]

Regnery and Garrity lost enthusiasm for the CBC when it became clear a book club was not McCaffrey's only new project. In late 1964 he founded Arlington House, a publishing company developed, in McCaffrey's words, to "thoroughly, aggressively serve a largely untapped (and vitally important) market: responsible conservatives." "Most houses barely scratch the surface of this market—principally because they are unaware of it," he explained when he first proposed the company in 1963. And while he acknowledged houses like Regnery and Devin-Adair served conservative audiences, he didn't feel they did so very effectively. "For a variety of reasons, they are leaving most of the field untilled—and not merchandising to the limit such good books as they have," he told prospective investors. McCaffrey planned to use his direct-mail experience and book club to counter that trend.[18]

Garrity was the first to catch wind of the Arlington House development. "I am told that our friends in the Conservative Book Club intend to go into original publishing in a big way and that they are getting in touch with your authors and my authors offering good advances, etc for future books," he warned Regnery at the start of 1965. "Perhaps the only thing for you and me to do at this point is to consider forming a rival book club." Regnery was equally miffed, suspecting that this had been McCaffrey's and his partner's true purpose of the CBC all along—to cultivate buyers for Arlington books. "They may find that publishing is considerably more difficult than setting up a book club, and I don't think that either one knows much about it." With little appetite for sustained warfare, however, the publishers struck a cordial truce with McCaffrey.[19]

Regnery was right about the relationship between CBC and Arlington. When McCaffrey began reaching out to conservative authors in late 1964, he set his sights on Bill Rusher. He approached Rusher with the idea of writing a biography of Franklin Roosevelt. Buttering him up by calling him "one of the few real stylists on our side—and Lord, how tired we all are of hack conservative writing," McCaffrey noted Rusher could make quite a lot of money from the venture—$20,000 "at a bare minimum." "The market for a stylish and definitive anti-FDR biography is almost unlimited. It is a surefire bestseller." Ultimately the topic of the book didn't matter to McCaffrey; he believed strongly that he could profit off any conservative book now that the

CBC had taken off. "The Club is doing so well that we can assure a good sale on a conservative book, and this problem of distribution is three quarters of the battle in establishing a publishing house." While Rusher passed on the FDR book, he did pen an account of his years working for the Senate subcommittee as special counsel, published with Arlington in 1968.[20]

The CBC provided new means of distribution, but it aimed largely at committed conservatives (who else would sign up for the Conservative Book Club?). Other innovators sought to reach those not yet in the conservative orbit. The group Constructive Action, led by the sober young activist Ted Loeffler, focused on broadening the distribution of conservative reading material. Loeffler had been politically apathetic until Nikita Khrushchev's 1959 visit. "I realized this man stood for something I knew nothing about," he told a *New York Times* reporter in 1966. So he quit his job and devoted himself to an intensive study of communism, which eventually led him to found what the newspaper called "one of the nation's most aggressive, if little known, conservative organizations." After the Goldwater campaign, Constructive Action pledged to "split the atom of apathy!" by getting conservative reading materials into the hands of the uncommitted. Constructive Action partnered with Young Americans for Freedom to arrange an essay contest for college and high school students. In 1965 the contest centered on *None Dare Call It Treason,* putting 480,000 copies of the book into the hands of students over the course of a few months. The distribution project reignited the fiery debates of the campaign: attacked by Rowland Evans and Robert Novak as "a new scheme for peddling propaganda among American college youth," the book was banned from the Lubbock campus of Texas Tech and burned at Indiana University.[21]

None Dare Call It Treason was an easy call for Constructive Action—the book had been at the heart of the 1964 campaign and Constructive Action had no trouble raising funds from conservatives to further distribute it—but fund-raising for future essay-contest books required more effort. In 1965 Loeffler called Alf Regnery, Henry's son and an officer of Young Americans for Freedom, about the 1966 essay contest. Dave Jones, the executive director of YAF, believed Russell Kirk's *The American Cause*, published by Regnery in 1957, could become the next *Conscience of a Conservative.* But neither Alf nor Loeffler was sold. Despite his early successes, Kirk was hardly a household name. There was no guarantee the movement conservatives who readily donated to distribute *Treason* could be persuaded to contribute for Kirk's book.[22]

To better the odds, YAF determined that before any fund-raising appeals, donors should be primed through "a large and forceful advertising campaign" targeted at conservative periodicals like *Human Events*, *National Review*, and the Birch Society's *American Opinion*. Alf persuaded his father to carry out an ad blitz centered on the message that *The American Cause* was "the book which will revolutionize America, the book that will turn back socialism, and reclaim America for Americans . . . you know, the type of thing that appeals to the Birchers." In choosing this strategy, the Regnerys acknowledged the continuing importance of the Birch Society to conservative media activism. While YAF, *National Review*, and other institutions fought to marginalize the Birch Society, activists also understood that this sector of grassroots conservatism was critically important to supporting the work of conservative media and organizations.[23]

Selling the book to hard-line conservatives meant trumpeting the dangers of socialism and the revolutionary potential of the book. Selling the book to college students required something else entirely. Regnery understood this well. He advised Loeffler, who was writing an introduction to the new edition of *The American Cause*, to excise language about the "dangers and evils inherent in all forms of socialism" and "erosions of personal freedom." He assured Loeffler it was "not because I don't feel as you do about socialism and the welfare state, but because I think we will have a much better chance of getting students to read this book and think about it if we don't give the case away in advance. Students of this generation are skeptical and suspicious of being taken in; I think we must appeal to their sophistication and knowledge of the world, even if much of this is imaginary." The soft sell, in other words.[24]

In addition to the essay contest, which by the end of 1966 had been responsible for the distribution of over seven hundred thousand conservative books to over one thousand campuses, Constructive Action also developed a reception-room program aimed at professionals looking for reading material for their waiting areas. Citing lobbies as "an ideal location to bring our citizens into contact with publications giving basic truths and clear explanations of the positive values of Freedom and the Private Enterprise System," Constructive Action offered plans including *Human Events*, *Manion Forum* and *Dan Smoot Report* transcripts, *Reader's Digest*, and *National Review*. In addition, clients would receive a selection of conservative books, almost all of which were published or republished by conservative houses. Pitched to conservative professionals, the reception-room program offered an opportu-

Figure 9. 1965 "Dispel Apathy" calendar: "Now, for the first time, the steady day-by-day and year-by-year advance of Liberalism, Socialism, and Communism has been kaleidascoped and organized into a calendar. The result is stunning; the record speaks for itself." Chicago History Museum.

nity to reach a captive audience. With the right reading material on hand, the bored patient waiting for a teeth cleaning could become the newest convert to the conservative cause.[25]

Such efforts showed conservative media activists beginning to reorient their work in the post-Goldwater years, seeking to expand their base and reach new audiences while still appealing to the movement conservatives who had helped Goldwater capture the nomination. But they also recognized early on that pitching conservatism to new audiences wasn't enough, particularly when those audiences already had an opinion of conservatism. *Dr. Strangelove*, Birch Society exposés, and the image of a little girl juxtaposed over a nuclear explosion meant for many Americans, the prevailing image of conservatism was still that of a secretive, dangerous, fanatical horde. Before conservatives could win over the apathetic middle, they first had to work on their image problem. And that meant reckoning once again with the avatar for right-wing extremism: Bob Welch and the John Birch Society.

"Every conservative feels that Americans must be saved from themselves." The opening line from the *Manion Forum* ad ran next to a picture of a besuited businessman lounging atop a box of dynamite, a lit fuse zagging toward the explosives. The ad promoted the "Dispel Apathy" calendar, an annotated wall calendar with "the erosion of freedom graphically demonstrated." It marked anniversaries like December 2, 1963: "J. Robert Oppenheimer, security risk, awarded Enrico Fermi Award" and December 10, 1964: "Six more victims brought the number of whites tortured to death and cannibalized by Red Rebels in the Congo to at least 123."[26]

But more important than the anniversaries was the purpose of the project, which Manion saw as part of the post-Goldwater effort to win over "the vast majority of Americans": not conservatives or liberals but people who "couldn't care less about what is happening to their country—because they don't even know that anything is happening at all." It was this group the *Forum* wanted to bring into its audience, to introduce to the conservative creed. In a separate pamphlet, the *Forum* laid out its case for reaching out to the apathetic: "We know from eleven years' experience that, once Mr. Average American gets a chance to find out what is happening to his country, he becomes a dedicated Conservative." The materials laid out the logic behind the *Forum's* outreach campaign: a belief that all it took to transform the uncommitted into conservative foot soldiers was exposure to the conservative creed. It was a strange argument to make in 1965. Hadn't the Goldwater campaign been a referendum on liberalism and conservatism? Hadn't it thoroughly exposed the nation to the American right?[27]

Not at all, conservative media activists contended. They argued that the right's message failed to penetrate, that voters never knew what Goldwater stood for. To make their case, both Manion and *National Review* pointed to a blind poll conducted by Louis Harris. The poll asked not about candidates but about issues. On several subjects central to modern conservatism the majority of respondents agreed with Goldwater: on restoring school prayer, on curtailing federal power, on tightening security in government. After presenting the poll to readers, *National Review* editors wryly added, "Now if the American voter can only be brought to the point of agreeing to annihilate little girls who play with daisies, this country can have a conservative Administration."[28]

Both the poll results and *National Review's* sarcastic aside underscored a central conservative interpretation of the campaign results. During the election, opponents had successfully painted Goldwater as a dangerous madman leading a band of fanatics. Thanks to dishonest Democratic campaigners and their co-conspirators in the media, the right had been unable to control the image of the movement and its spokespeople. Even if conservative media could reach a larger audience, such efforts would be worth little if "Mr.

Average American" believed conservatives were nothing more than a band of extremists—or worse, a punch line.

At the heart of this problem was the John Birch Society. Conservative media leaders all acknowledged the Birch Society played a critical role in conservative organizing, providing the manpower for the Goldwater nomination drive in key states like California. Yet because of the negative national coverage of the group, the struggle to determine what to do about the Birch Society weighed heavily on their minds after Goldwater's loss. Manion stuck with the society, telling a listener that although he had been publicly denounced and slurred for his affiliation with the Birch Society, he "refused to run out on the selfless thousands who have found it a rallying point for 'right' thought and action when both are so badly needed."[29]

But not running out on was not the same as wholly supporting. Manion revealed an increasing discomfort with the society in the months after the 1964 election. In March 1965 he announced he would not appear at talks sponsored by the Impeach Earl Warren Committee, a group dedicated to one of the Birch Society's pet projects, the expulsion of the Supreme Court chief justice. Manion argued that while Warren's impeachment was ideologically desirable it was not politically possible. Political practicality, however, was seldom a yardstick for Manion's schemes. His insistence on it in this instance indicated uneasiness with the political cost of being associated with one of the society's more visible endeavors. A few months later Manion extended his sponsorship ban to include groups identifying as "'Local Chapters of the John Birch Society' or variations thereof." It was quite a statement coming from a board member of the Birch Society. His speech booker explained that "at the local level he wishes to make his appeal to Conservatives as broadly based as possible." The remark about "broadly based" appeal was telling. Manion clearly felt that appearing under the banner of the Birch Society limited his ability to reach a wider audience.[30]

Manion was not the only one distancing himself from the Birch Society in 1965. Bill Buckley had made the case against Welch in a 1962 column that ran in *National Review*. It was the sharpest anti-Birch piece the magazine had run, but even then Buckley had exempted society members from his rebuke, insisting that among their numbers were "some of the most morally energetic, self-sacrificing, and dedicated anti-Communists in America." After the Goldwater campaign, however, many of the magazine's editors felt Birch members no longer warranted exclusion from censure. The Birch

Society had become far too damaging to the conservative cause for these men and women to be excused for supporting the society. In 1962, Manion had helped mediate the Birch Society conflict, bringing Buckley back from the brink of a permanent rift with the Birchers. In 1965, their conflicting attitudes toward the society, rather than being mediated behind closed doors, became embedded in the institutions each man founded after the Goldwater loss.[31]

For Manion, the work began when he joined a group of conservative leaders hunkered down in the Marriott Hotel in Indianapolis on January 16, 1965, a day after a storm buried the city under ten inches of snow. Though some traveled halfway across the country to be there—Carl Wick of Californians for Goldwater and Hawley Bendixen from the Conservative Council in Syracuse, New York, both made the journey—the majority came from the Midwest. There was John L. Ryan, representing the Indiana branch of Americans for Constitutional Action; Oakley R. Bramble of the Conservative Federation of Michigan; and G. A. Buder from the Goldwater Committee of Missouri. Manion was the only national figure in attendance.[32]

All told, fourteen people gathered to oversee the creation of a conservative super-organization: the National Federation of Conservative Organizations (NFCO). The NFCO was part of a new push for coordinated action. True, for many years conservative media and organizations had been working together, promoting one another's activities and putting together events like the anti-Khrushchev rally. But in the wake of the Goldwater campaign, pressure grew for more purposeful, institutionalized coordination that would allow for better message control, more efficient use of resources, and stronger oversight of the movement. To achieve that end, the men gathered in Indianapolis created the NFCO as a "trade organization" that could unite "the grassroots, the experts and the financial supporters."[33]

The structure of the NFCO reflected, to its detriment, Manion's influence. As with Manion's Conservative Clubs, "individualism" was the overriding value upon which the NFCO was built. This was, after all, conservatives' basic nature; "to force them into a collectivist type of organization," a press release explained, "is to violate a basic tenet of conservatism." To aid coordination among groups, the NFCO named directors of operations, of intelligence and doctrines, and of information and support. Ultimately, the NFCO hoped to use these directors not only to feed information to conservative organizations but to barrage established media with news from the conservative viewpoint, believing "possibilities for exerting a conservative influence on opinion making media are unlimited." If journalists were genuinely committed to some semblance of balance, the constant influx of conservative material would make it impossible to ignore the right-wing point of view. Thus the NFCO directed its influences both inward on the movement and outward on the press.[34]

But as with For America, the NFCO was schizophrenic in nature. A national organization, the NFCO was hamstrung by its founders' decision to keep a low profile and allow local concerns to trump all others. With so little emphasis on actual coordination or maintenance of national priorities, the NFCO could hardly expect to effectively coordinate conservatives on a national level. It could act as a conduit but not as a leader. In this way, it reflected the weakness of both For America and the Conservative Clubs: focusing on ideological commitments over organizational practicalities, none of the groups could effectively influence politics on the national level.

Conservative activists without those ideological constraints were more successful. A month before the NFCO organizational meeting, another meeting of conservatives took place in Washington, D.C. In a confidential preliminary report, the Washington group sketched the background for its efforts. "With only a few short years of political and intellectual efforts behind them," the report began, "American conservatives achieved a success in 1964 which astonished them no less than it shocked their liberal antagonists: conservatives had nominated a conservative for the Presidency of the United States." No sooner had this success been achieved, however, than conservatives were hit with a "violent and vitriolic" response, a series of "deceits and distortions" that limited Goldwater's votes to the storied twenty-six million. The lopsided liberal victory raised a central question: "Why were the conservatives unable to carry their impressive successes to the culmination of victory?"[35]

This question troubled the group, which included Buckley, YAF chairman Robert S. Bauman, and Frank S. Meyer, a regular columnist for *National Review*. They looked to the success of Americans for Democratic Action (ADA), a liberal organization that wielded influence so broadly "that not even a president as powerful as Lyndon Baines Johnson dared ignore it." So they studied the ADA and found that it had "mobilized the intellectual and political resources of the liberal movement toward the single ultimate objective of achieving political power." The ADA paired existing organizations and media with new endeavors, uniting liberal leaders without running roughshod over other parts of the movement, particularly the grassroots activists. In the seventeen years since its founding, the ADA had seen members and former members rise to high office, from the solicitor general to the undersecretary of state to the vice president. The conservatives gathered in D.C. hoped to emulate the ADA's success. Thus was born the American Conservative Union (ACU).[36]

The ACU, though not an arm of *National Review*, was peopled with the magazine's staff and heavily influenced by its particular conservative philosophy. Frank Meyer took the treasurer position, and at least six of the ACU's thirteen directors were *National Review* editors, columnists, or staffers, including Buckley and Rusher. A conservative newspaper editor, Jameson G. Campaigne, also served as a director. Among the forty-five attendees of the Washington meeting, conservative media activists were well represented; Thomas S. Winter, the new editor of *Human Events*, was present, as were Regnery, Neil McCaffrey, a handful of conservative authors, and a sprinkling of additional *National Review* contributors. The political, organizational, and media endeavors of the conservative movement once again fused in the ACU.

The ACU today is best known for its yearly conference, the Conservative Political Action Conference (CPAC), which regularly makes headlines for the conservatives it banishes from the dais. Losing one's CPAC invite, as New Jersey governor Chris Christie did for embracing President Barack Obama after Hurricane Sandy, signals a person is on the outs with the movement. Drawing boundaries, though, is not a recent project of the ACU but one built into its very structure. As soon as the group was formed, it immediately faced a test of its conservative boundaries. Nowhere in the eight-page preliminary report had the ACU employed the phrase "responsible conservatism" or criticized the Birch Society. Had *National Review* and this new, closely allied organization decided to bury the disagreements of the past, to bond over their shared experience of election-season attacks and commitment to conservative principles?

Quite the opposite. Buckley felt the time had come to purge the movement of Birchers—or at least to draw sharp lines between responsible and irresponsible conservatives. Whatever distance he had tried to put between the two prior to the election had not been enough. Despite running Buckley's censure of Welch in 1962, *National Review* was tarred with the same brush of extremism and radicalism as the Birch Society. Buckley was not interested in seeing that pattern continue. To this end, the group decided that no member of the Birch Society would have a position within the ACU. This meant people like Manion and rising conservative star Phyllis Schlafly would have no role within the new group.

Nor was Buckley done denouncing the society. *National Review*'s editors had allowed Buckley to make his case against Welch in 1962, but he had spared the members of the organization. Post-Goldwater, though, the landscape had changed. The editors prepared to run a piece reading the whole society out of the movement, with Buckley dedicating three of his syndicated newspaper columns to the issue. In 1962, *National Review* editors had struck a conciliatory note toward the society. In 1965, they declared all-out war.[37]

In one of the weekly Agonies held at the magazine, in which editors worked over topics for future issues, the ACU became central to debate over a new Birch editorial. Several of the editors wanted the ACU to function as a safety valve, a place where displaced Birchers could go once their society had lost the last remnants of respectability. Rusher, always the voice of caution, had reservations. First, the editors had to weigh their responsibility to the men and women they had convinced to join the ACU—prestigious conservatives whose endorsements legitimized the organization. The original Advisory Assembly had won over these supporters with the "implicit assurance" that the ACU would be "a respectable vehicle for responsible conservatism." To use the ACU as a "homeopathic substitute" for former Birchers would not do. Unrepentant Birchers, Rusher implied, had no place among responsible conservatives.[38]

The use of the ACU in debates over the Birch editorial revealed the intent behind the piece. The editors were taking a final stand on the Birch Society—no committed Bircher had any place in the responsible (that is, the *real*) conservative movement. But they were also holding themselves out as the arbiters of true conservatism, dividing the movement between the Responsibles and the Irresponsibles. Rusher warned the editors the ACU would never be able to replicate the membership size and financial resources of the Birch Society—after all, "there are possibilities open to kookery that are simply not available to rational people." That noted, Rusher concluded the ACU could become "a substitute medium of effective action for the salvageable members of the John Birch Society." *Salvageable*. Only those who renounced the society and embraced the tenets of respectable conservatism would be counted among legitimate conservatives. A clear line was being drawn.[39]

The idea of salvageable Birchers infused Rusher's suggestions for the editorial as well. It would be a unique editorial, he maintained, because it would not be written for the magazine's "hard core" but for "the salvageable (and to a lesser extent even the unsalvageable) members of the John Birch Society," many of whom may not subscribe to the magazine but would certainly see this issue. Given this shift in audience, he implored the editors to use a soft touch, to avoid arguing in such a way that a Bircher would have to admit "that he was a fool to join the Society at all." Rusher understood the psychology of the situation: "If we insist upon surrounding and destroying them utterly, they have nothing to lose by fighting us to the end." As Rusher had always approached the *National Review*–Birch conflict as a necessary evil rather than a glorious crusade, he made an unheralded plea. He entreated the editorial staff to refrain from gleefully referring to the battle with the Birchers as the "Thirty Years' War" or a "knock-down drag-out fight." "Knock down, sí; drag out, no. I have better things to do with my next thirty years."[40]

Such was Rusher's position in late August. A month later, seeing little diffusion of the delight surrounding the impending editorial and fearing that such attitude would skew the tone of the piece toward outright nastiness, Rusher made a final appeal for reasonableness. He made his case in terms of the magazine's influence after the "forthcoming flap" with the Birch Society. Post-editorial, the magazine would lose some subscriptions and advertising—this, Rusher reasoned, could be both anticipated and endured. The editors could also expect the magazine's reputation to rise in the eyes of professional Republicans who, having also experienced the bitter Goldwater defeat, were equally eager to dispense of the "kook right."[41]

All well and good. But a third outcome lay in wait as well, one that could be avoided if only the tone of the piece could be moderated. "The American conservative movement," Rusher explained, "is getting to be a very large thing." As such, it was quite unlikely that the result would be a conservative movement with the Birch Society on one side and *National Review* on the other. A third group would no doubt arise, "a large number of responsible conservatives (or people who certainly *pass* for responsible conservatives)" who would stake out the middle or declare themselves above the partisan squabbling. That group, if given too much ground by any meanness of tone in the editorial, could stake out a moral ground above *National Review*, compromising the magazine's influence.[42]

Rusher predicted that when the dust from the Birch battle cleared, "we will look out on a new scene, as far as the American conservative movement is concerned." The "irresponsible right," he concluded, would be successfully segregated, cut off from the movement and effectively—perhaps permanently—incapacitated. *National Review* would have held onto, perhaps even increased, its status "as the intellectual fountain-head of conservatism." Yet Rusher also felt *National Review* would be diminished as a "vehicle for political leadership *per se*." And perhaps, he mused, that was for the best. "Writing a lively and heuristic journal of opinion is one thing; leading a political movement—even a conservative political movement—is quite another."[43]

Or was it? For nearly ten years, *National Review*, like the *Manion Forum* and others in conservative media, had concerned themselves with both media endeavors and movement building. The movement, though, was in good hands, according to Rusher. Political leadership for responsible conservatives could be channeled through YAF and the ACU. This hope gave the lie to Rusher's conclusion that the magazine could lose its role as a "vehicle for political leadership." Given *National Review*'s role in founding these organizations, and its continuing centrality in their activities, the magazine's political labors would continue unabated.[44]

Rusher proved prescient about the effects of the editorial. GOP denunciations of the society began in early September, starting with state-level politicians. By the end of the month, Senator Everett Dirksen, Congressman Gerald Ford, and former vice president Richard Nixon were grabbing front-page headlines by announcing Birchers were not welcome in the Republican Party. Barry Goldwater encouraged all society members to resign. And on October 19, 1965, the *National Review* editorial ran.[45]

As expected, subscriptions were canceled and sizable donations withdrawn. Phoebe Courtney of the *Independent American* pumped out a lengthy screed denouncing Buckley for trying "to arrogate unto himself the power to decide who is and who is not, in his phrase, 'a responsible Conservative.'" She defended Welch as "one of the most responsible leaders of the anti-Communist movement in this country today" and suggested other conservatives watch their backs: Buckley might be after them next. Others were even less charitable. A. J. Heinsohn, a longtime conservative activist and Birch Society member, accused Buckley of abetting "the Communist cause," using "the Communist technique of character assassination and falsification." "What a sad day it would be for America," Heinsohn concluded, "if dedicated, knowledgeable, anti-Communists were driven from the fray by a callow egocentric and his stable of former Communists."[46]

Manion, for his part, emerged as a member of Rusher's third group, the ones who sought moral high ground. Listeners deluged Manion with letters, uncertain what to make of this open feud between two parts of the movement that, until the Birch editorial, they had measured as brothers-in-arms in the battle for conservatism. The letter from Emil Herber, a listener from Fort Wayne, Indiana, was typical in its fretfulness. "Mr. Manion," she wrote, "there is so much talk and smear on the John Birch Society. In my mind you're the only one that can tell me just what do you think about the Society? Is it okay? I always thought it was. Anything I ever read and their thinking wasn't out of line, so could you please inform me. Some of my closest friends want me to join, so I would appreciate your guidance." Manion heaped praise upon the society in his response, insisting, "It is being smeared precisely because it is effective."[47]

Other letter writers turned to Manion for an evaluation of *National Review*. A Pensacola listener and longtime subscriber to the magazine confessed he had often donated small sums to keep *National Review* afloat and was in the process of sending forty or fifty subscriptions out to students. "Is this the wrong thing for me to be doing?" he asked. "These people seem to have a phobia, a hate complex." Why, he wondered, did they insist on tearing down members of the movement, when America had such powerful enemies arrayed against it? Manion's reply to another listener with similar concerns was pitch-perfect: "The main thing now is to avoid the temptation (a la Buckley) to fight among ourselves." The higher ground, just as Rusher had predicted.[48]

Another Rusher prediction came true as well. The Birch Society, under the combined pressure of attacks from outsiders and internal battles over the society's direction, had become effectively incapacitated. Over the remainder of the decade, its numbers declined dramatically and its prestige within the conservative movement dwindled. The Responsibles had managed to shrug off the Birch albatross and inoculate themselves, to some degree, from charges of extremism. The ACU, the institutional embodiment of responsible conservatism, quickly emerged as the leading political action organization on the American right, while the NFCO faded into oblivion. It seemed Buckley and the Responsibles had won.[49]

But the ground was shifting under their feet. Funds were drying up. Goldwater, stung by his loss, quickly endorsed Nixon for the 1968 nomination. Meanwhile the liberal coalition, strained to the point of breaking by civil rights, Vietnam, and an economic downturn, had begun to fracture, creating new opportunities for Republicans and the American right. How would conservative media activists adapt to the new financial and political realities? How much would they compromise in order to secure political power? And how would they deal with Rusher's worst-case scenario: the political resurrection of Richard Nixon?

Part IV

Adaptations

Chapter 10

The Compromise

The election of Richard Nixon marked the end of conservative politics in America.

That was the assessment of Brent Bozell, a long-faced, red-haired writer who knew a few things about conservative politics. Ghostwriter of *Conscience of a Conservative*, brother-in-law of Bill Buckley, founding member of Young Americans for Freedom: Bozell had the credentials to weigh in on the state of conservatism. And weigh in he did, in an open letter to movement conservatives in his magazine, *Triumph*: "Historians will differ as to the moment when the movement you lead ceased to be an important force in America. My own view is that the hour struck in 1964, with Goldwater's defeat, but there will be no one to doubt that it was all over by November 1968, with Nixon's victory." He concluded, "Nixon's resurrection, in a word, was your funeral, and all that has been missing is a suitable oration."[1]

By the time he penned his jeremiad in 1969, Bozell had expatriated to Spain. Having been let down by every institution in which he once believed, he was in exile not just from the United States but from modernity itself. He resigned from *National Review* in 1963, finding Buckley and his fellow editors insufficiently Catholic. He railed against the reforms of the Second Vatican Council, finding the Catholic Church insufficiently Catholic. And he believed the conservative movement had sold its birthright for a mess of pottage in the form of Richard Milhous Nixon.

Bozell's flight from modernity was unusual for his cohort of media activists, but his irritation at the Nixon backers in their ranks was not. Nixon's candidacy was divisive for the conservative movement in ways it was not for the Republican Party. Compared to the tumult in the Democratic ranks—Lyndon Johnson's stunning decision not to run for reelection, Robert Kennedy's assassination, clashes between police and protesters at the 1968 Chicago convention—the Republican nomination process was an orderly affair. Nixon emerged as an early front-runner and rarely ceded ground, deftly slipping into the role of the centrist candidate with George Romney and Nelson Rockefeller to his left and Ronald Reagan to his right. An orderly affair—unless you were a member of the conservative media. Then the nomination was far from a settled matter. Nixon was hardly the only choice for right-wing voters, not with Ronald Reagan and George Wallace in the hunt. Four years earlier, media activists had played a pivotal role in the nomination process, functioning not only as Goldwater's promotional team but as leading organizers of his early campaign. United behind a single candidate, their message was clear: back Goldwater. But with three potential standard-bearers in the 1968 race, right-wing media support failed to coalesce around one candidate. The absence of a clear choice further empowered these media activists. More than ever, grassroots conservatives needed Virgils to guide the way.

Nor did supporting Nixon spell the end of conservatism, as Bozell had predicted. Nixon may not have been the ideal candidate, but his presidency allowed right-wing media activists to try their hand at something new. It marked the first time since World War II that a candidate backed by conservative media had won the White House. Not only that, it marked the first time a candidate lobbied hard for the support of conservative media. Nixon wooed media activists throughout the campaign, making it clear that he understood they were the key to conservative support. Heady stuff for a group of political activists accustomed to being on the outside, looking in.

Proximity to power, however, had its own challenges. Media activists had spent some fifteen years mortaring opposition and oppression into the very foundations of the conservative identity. It was their lingua franca, their lodestar. How would they handle a president whose election they had supported, knowing full well he was at best a sometime-conservative? In the run-up to the convention, they sought to strike a balance between ideological integrity and political pragmatism. The Nixon administration would test how far they were willing to be led down the pragmatic path.

With Nixon as the early front-runner for the Republican nomination, the question of whom media activists should support in 1968 depended on two factors: how conservative they perceived Nixon to be, and how much they were willing to compromise to win. The first factor, Nixon's conservatism, was complicated. Red-hunting for the House Un-American Activities Committee (HUAC) won the young congressman conservatives' appreciation. Breaking the Alger Hiss case in the late 1940s elevated him to the anticommunist pantheon alongside Joe McCarthy. Then came the vice presidency. In hitching his star to Dwight Eisenhower, Nixon earned a reputation as a moderate Republican. Sure, he wagged his finger at Nikita Khrushchev in front of a set of cutting-edge kitchen appliances, but he also called the Soviet premier's stateside visit a few months later "justified and wise." The comment did not sit well with media activists who had feverishly protested the arrival of the "Butcher of Budapest" (an epithet Nixon himself coined in 1956). And at home, he stood by Ike on Earl Warren, on Little Rock, on the World Court—heresies all. So strong was the opposition to Nixon by the end of his vice presidency that no conservative media outlet endorsed his 1960 presidential bid.[2]

But absence—and a few years of the Great Society—makes the heart grow fonder. Both Nixon and the conservative movement underwent changes in the 1960s that, at least for some activists, healed the breach. Goldwater's loss had scarred media activists, leading many of them to reconsider the balance between pragmatic politics and ideological purity. The Goldwater nomination had changed Nixon as well. As his speechwriter Pat Buchanan explained, just as Nixon learned in 1960 that he couldn't win without the Rockefeller wing of the GOP, he understood that to win in 1968 "he had to make his peace with the Goldwater wing of the party."[3]

That peacemaking took the form not of rock-ribbed conservatism but of unshakable loyalty. In 1964 Nixon stumped for Goldwater when other prominent members of the party refused. George Romney and Nelson Rockefeller froze Goldwater out after the convention. Romney declined even to endorse the candidate, leaving Goldwater to wonder a few weeks post-election, "Where were you, George, when the chips were down and the going was hard?" Romney was in Michigan, distancing himself from the ticket. And Nixon? Nixon was everywhere: 36 states, over 150 appearances. When the election razed the GOP, cutting down not just Goldwater but most down-ticket Republicans outside of the South, Nixon stood his ground. The day after the shellacking, Rockefeller slammed Goldwater for abandoning "the mainstream of American thought" and attempted to read conservatives out of the party. In response, Nixon upbraided Rockefeller for being a "party divider" and a "spoilsport." Such loyalty left an impression.[4]

Nixon undid some of that goodwill in 1965, during Buckley's quixotic run for the mayoralty of New York City. Buckley believed the GOP needed to be scrubbed clean of Rockefeller Republicans, to be refashioned into a conservative party. That meant stopping liberal Republicans like John Lindsay from taking office. Nixon, a party loyalist, disagreed. With the Republicans still a minority party, it was not the time to cede winnable seats to Democrats. In that vein, columnists Robert Novak and Rowland Evans reported in the lead-up to the 1965 election that Nixon "described the Buckleyites as a threat to the Republican party even more menacing than the Birchers."[5]

As rather devoted Buckleyites, the crew at *National Review* had a few questions for Nixon about his comments. Rusher, who still harbored deep resentment toward Nixon for his anti-McCarthy statements in 1954, wrote several letters asking for clarification. Each went unanswered until well after the election, when it became clear Rusher would not drop the matter. Only then did Nixon respond, through his unimpeachably conservative assistant Pat Buchanan. By no means, Buchanan assured the Buckleyites, had Nixon ever meant to suggest they were like the Birchers. Quite the contrary. By distancing the magazine from extremism, Buckley made himself far more electable. And since Buckley ran as a Conservative Party candidate against the Republican Lindsay, Nixon believed he posed a far greater threat to the GOP than those half-cocked kooks at the Birch Society ever did. As Buchanan reaffirmed on behalf of Nixon, "It would be a tragedy for the nation if conservatives abandoned the GOP to form splinter parties. The result of such divisions would mean permanent minority status for both conservative ideas and the Republican Party." The editors cast a bit of side-eye at the response—why, after all, did it take six months and several public airings of grievance to wrest an explanation from an aide?—but in the end they let it go.[6]

They let it go because by 1966 a number of *National Review*'s editors were warming up to Nixon. Even as they expressed concern about the "calculating caution that has too often characterized Richard Nixon's public style," they found in his favor. "So all's well that ends well," an editorial responding to Buchanan's letter concluded. "And if Richard Nixon is willing to give personal leadership to the Republican conservatives, he will find them ready to follow him." The comment about "personal leadership" was an important one. Nixon was showing signs of interest in the conservative movement, and the editors of *National Review*, who were in search of a new standard-bearer to replace Goldwater, were willing to hear him out.[7]

One of the early signs of Nixon's attention to the right: his recruitment of Buchanan in January 1965. Buchanan was not at the time a leading light of the conservative movement. After graduating from Columbia in 1962, he went to work as an editorial assistant at the *St. Louis Globe-Democrat*, a paper with solidly conservative editorial pages. There he wrote "three to four editorials a day . . . on local, national, and foreign issues," he explained to Nixon when he met him in late 1964. Impressed by the young journalist, Nixon hired Buchanan as a speechwriter and liaison to the right, a role that took on new dimensions when Nixon began openly pursuing the conservative vote through their media. In 1966, Nixon invited media activists (most notably Rusher and Tom Winter of *Human Events*) and leaders of conservative organizations to meet with him at the Shoreham Hotel in Washington, D.C. Ostensibly it was just a chat; the *Washington Post* reported there was "no direct talk" of a 1968 run. In the hour-and-a-half meeting, Nixon ranged from Vietnam to inflation to the GOP's electoral prospects in the midterms. But the topics of conversation were hardly the point. The *fact* of the conversation, the display Nixon made of reaching out to the right: the courtship had begun. And thanks to Buchanan, this would be no secret affair. Immediately after the hotel rendezvous, Buchanan (whom Novak and Evans bemusedly described as a "young man, totally anonymous to national politicians") rushed to reporters to share the news. It made the front page of the *Washington Post* two days later.[8]

Having made his intentions widely known, Nixon dialed up the charm. January 1967 saw Buckley, Rusher, columnist Victor Lasky, and others gathered at Nixon's sprawling Fifth Avenue apartment (where future rival Nelson Rockefeller was a neighbor). There the former vice president did what he did best. Plunging into a discussion of foreign and domestic policy, Nixon exhibited his encyclopedic command of the political world. Rusher remained unmoved—Rusher would always remain unmoved when it came to Nixon—but Buckley? There was no more direct route to Buckley's heart than a vigorous exhibition of intellect and insight. As Neal Freeman, Buckley's personal aide, recalled, "I knew when we went down the elevator, early in the evening, that Bill Buckley was going to find some reason to support Richard Nixon." True, Nixon was no movement conservative, but the heart wants what it wants. And a smart, attentive, experienced, *electable* Republican was just what Buckley wanted in a 1968 candidate. More than a year before the election, he was recommending Nixon as the "wisest Republican choice."[9]

Buckley's infatuation drew sharp condemnation from other media activists. This occurred in part because they disagreed with Buckley on Nixon's conservatism and in part because Nixon overlooked them. In seeking to woo conservatives, Nixon focused on the print periodicals, particularly *National Review* and *Human Events*, and conservative columnists as the real source of influence within the movement. That focus reflected a belief, as E. J. Dionne put it in the classic *Why Americans Hate Politics*, that *National Review* was "the adjudicator of orthodoxy." It would have been more accurate to say it was "the adjudicator of respectability," a role the magazine wore with pride after its tussles with the Birch Society. Within the movement, other media activists contested *National Review*'s position as conservative standard-bearer. Outside of the movement, though, *National Review* was perceived as the source conservatives consulted to ascertain a candidate's bona fides. And thanks to Nixon's attentions to Buckley, by 1967 the pages of the journal reflected its founder's soft spot for Nixon.[10]

If the magazine could in fact adjudicate the movement's orthodoxy, that would have been that. But just as the magazine was riven with internal divisions over Nixon, so too were conservative media more generally. A sticking point for many media activists was Nixon's challenger from the right, Ronald Reagan. Given that Reagan would come to symbolize the ideal conservative politician, the reluctance of media activists to back him requires some explanation. The debate over Reagan versus Nixon was not a matter of the governor's ideology, which nearly everyone agreed was sound. Right-wing publishers strongly supported Reagan, who proved popular among conservatives in a way Nixon never did (a 1966 poll of YAF leaders' preferences for the 1968 race found 53 percent in favor of Reagan, 30 percent holding on to Goldwater, and a mere 15 percent for Nixon). Lee Edwards, a founding member of YAF and director of information for the Goldwater campaign, came out with *Reagan: A Political Biography* in 1967, a book heavily promoted by *Human Events*. Devin Garrity eagerly promoted the new governor, hoping for a new *Conscience of a Conservative* in Reagan's 1968 book *The Creative Society*. Garrity's support wasn't just about sales; he believed Reagan was "the only one of the candidates who really believes in old fashioned virtues." "The Reagan philosophy is basically my own," he told a friend.[11]

So Reagan had the goods. But then, Goldwater had had them, too, and a united, electrified base to back him up. In a post-1964 world, ideology wasn't enough to win broad-based support in conservative media. As Rusher pointed out in late 1967, "What high principles and valiant exertions can do for a Presidential campaign was done in 1964—and proved not enough." The ghosts of 1964 haunted them. For 1968, electability was the name of the game. "No sense running Mona Lisa in a beauty contest," Buckley said in 1967 before clarifying: "I'd be for the most right, viable candidate who could win." That dictum—later known as the Buckley Rule—turned on two requirements: "right" and "viable." Reagan met the first, but what about the second?[12]

Here Reagan failed to make his case. Everyone knew the governor wanted the nomination, but ultimately he positioned himself poorly. His plan resembled Lyndon Johnson's in 1960, when Johnson tried to stay above the fray during the primary season then swoop in at the convention as a compromise candidate. Reagan was banking, understandably enough, on the unlikability of Richard Nixon. According to Jeffrey Hart, a *National Review* contributor and one of Reagan's few campaign workers in 1968, Reagan saw Nixon as "the fellow who doesn't get the girl." There could be only one leading man, and a two-time loser like Nixon wasn't it. Hadn't Reagan already proven his superior skills? Nixon ran for the California governorship in 1962 and lost; in 1966, Reagan did the same, against the same candidate, and won.[13]

But Reagan underestimated how much his own inexperience diminished his standing as a would-be suitor. Perhaps someone from a different background could have made a go of it after two years as governor, but Reagan had been working as an actor just a few years earlier. While Barry Goldwater was mounting his presidential bid, Reagan was starring as a mob boss in a remake of Ernest Hemingway's *The Killers*. Buckley dismissed his potential as a candidate for that reason. "With a background spent out of politics," Buckley argued in his syndicated column in late 1966, "he cannot emerge as a credible candidate until his contributions to the art and/or practice of government become incandescent." As Reagan had not even been sworn into office yet, Buckley felt it was impossible for him to be viable in 1968. Even Reagan's fans had to balance this inexperience in making their case. "Essentially," Rusher claimed, trying to sell a friend on Reagan in early 1967, "there is no really good preparation for the Presidency." Indeed, Reagan's inexperience at age fifty-seven meant he "was mature but not sullied by the political process." With the movement thus divided on questions of ideological integrity and electoral viability, *National Review* split the difference. Up until the convention, the magazine stayed neutral on the Reagan/Nixon question, endorsing neither candidate during primary season.[14]

Once Nixon became the Republican candidate, *National Review* openly backed his candidacy. Yes, the editors admitted as the campaign went on, the middle road Nixon charted as a mainstream candidate was far from inspiring. As a practical matter, though, it was the right move. He would have to plot a careful course to stave off Wallace on his right and Hubert Humphrey on his left. *National Review* urged readers to keep the faith, "faith that when he gets the votes he needs, and no longer has to submit to that frightful wooing ritual mass democracy imposes on its leaders, he will speak with a clearer, firmer, less neutrally balanced voice." The lesson for the movement: when negotiating national politics, conservative candidates would have to moderate their message. Conservatives would have to trust that the candidates would govern further to the right than they ran—and would have to trust conservative media to divine the true intentions of the candidate in question.[15]

Neutral on Reagan, *National Review*'s editors were far more proactive in staving off the Wallace threat. For the conservative who didn't much care for Richard Nixon, George Wallace was a tempting option. Wallace, of course, came with some baggage. An arch segregationist, a blustering populist, the Alabama governor certainly didn't fit the "respectable conservatism" mold many in the conservative media had been trying to forge since Goldwater. But there was no clear consensus. Tom Anderson, host of *Straight Talk* and himself an ardent segregationist, dismissed Nixon as a "dedicated phony" and threw all in for Wallace. *Human Events* was cool on the candidate. At Regnery Publishing, Henry Regnery showed little love for Nixon but held Wallace in disdain.[16]

Meanwhile, despite pitched battles over Nixon and Reagan, the editors at *National Review* all agreed Wallace was a nonstarter. The magazine ran article after article on Wallace in the lead-up to the election, trying to convince readers he was no conservative. Frank Meyer called him a "demagogue" and a "populist." And populism, Meyer argued, was "the radical opposite of conservatism." Buckley accused Wallace of assuming "the full paraphernalia of conservatism, even though he is a welfare-populist." To cap off the argument, the magazine invited Congressman John Ashbrook and Senator Barry Goldwater, leading conservative politicians, to make the case against Wallace. Ashbrook dismissed him as a "big spender," while

Goldwater appealed to practicality: Wallace couldn't win, so why take votes from Nixon?[17]

Manion disagreed with this analysis of the Wallace vote. Where *National Review* saw in Wallace a threat to Nixon (and a threat to America, which would be governed by Hubert Humphrey if Nixon lost), Manion saw opportunity. Wallace, he argued, combined conservatism with the Democratic label. As such, he would not only peel off Humphrey voters but drag Nixon to the right. Win-win. It may not have been a popular interpretation—a 1967 *Human Events* poll showed the vast majority of conservative leaders believed a Wallace run helped the Democratic candidate—but Manion seldom concerned himself with popular opinion. Besides, Manion liked the Alabama governor. The two struck up a cordial relationship, culminating in Wallace's appearance on the *Forum* in the waning days of the 1968 campaign.[18]

The Wallace broadcast stemmed from Manion's effort to bring on presidential candidates to discuss their views on the Supreme Court, a pet issue for the former law school dean. He invited each candidate to "state his views on the prevailing unlawful disorder"—law and order! Right up Nixon's alley!—"and his proposals for the decentralization of government in the context." Wallace happily accepted the opportunity to speak to a national conservative audience. (Nixon and Humphrey declined.)[19]

Wallace, Nixon, Reagan—the debates over the Goldwater movement's legitimate heir flowed through conservative media. Listeners and readers turned to conservative media as guides, resources for determining which candidate would best advance their cause. A Texas listener asked Manion if the former star of the House Un-American Activities Committee was "genuinely anticommunist." In Idaho, another listener wanted Manion's opinion on how to rank Nixon, Reagan, and Wallace, particularly after reading some articles that questioned Reagan's conservatism. Once again, the leaders of conservative media were acting as guides for electoral politics.[20]

Razor-thin margins separated Nixon and Humphrey on election night, with Wallace poised as a potential spoiler. Strip away votes he did—nearly ten million of them, giving him five Deep South states—but when the final tallies were in, Nixon got his victory. For the former vice president, it meant vindication for 1960 and 1962. For conservative media, it meant unprecedented opportunity. Since the emergence of the modern conservative movement after World War II, no candidate backed by the movement had won the presidency. Nixon's election opened up a new world for the

movement and its messengers, one ripe with possibility and rife with obstacles. Whatever lay ahead, one thing was clear: the outsiders had made their
way in.

No sooner had Nixon won the White House than conservative media
figures began to worry. They backed Nixon believing—or rather, hoping—
campaign centrism would give way to governing conservatism. They were
savvy enough to know Nixon wouldn't go there on his own. A little pressure
was in order, a reminder that conservatives provided Nixon his narrow margin of victory and that he would need them in four years' time. Manion made
the point preemptively with his Wallace boosterism, arguing the threat of
facing Wallace in 1972 would keep Nixon "on a reasonably straight conservative path." To be sure, Wallace wasn't for everyone. His earthy populism
and full-throated defense of segregation put off people trying to make the
case for responsible conservatism. But others in conservative media agreed
with the underlying strategy to pressure Nixon from the right.[21]

Their first step? Claim credit for Nixon's victory. Not just on behalf of
conservatives but on behalf of conservative media. They were the gatekeepers, the kingmakers. Buckley, with characteristic modesty, reported
that "there are those who believe that but for *National Review*'s role in
the election, the slim lead of Richard Nixon would not have materialized."
At the *Manion Forum*, frequent guest Stan Evans agreed. Evans had substantial experience in conservative media: author of the Sharon Statement,
contributor to *National Review*, and editor of Eugene Pulliam's conservative newspaper *Indianapolis Star*. "I think we have to remember," he told
Manion's audience, "that Nixon's nomination was the work of Conservatives."
And that Wallace mattered: the millions who voted for the southern governor, he argued, signaled to the GOP that it would have to prove its
conservatism if it wanted the movement's backing. Govern from the right,
get the votes. Otherwise, support for Wallace would swell in 1972.[22]

Claiming credit, however, was not an end in itself. It was a proxy for
influence, and how that influence could best be wielded was a central debate
within conservative media. Should they behave as they had during the
campaign and paint Nixon as a friend, rooting out signs of his conservative
sensibilities to rally the movement and demonstrate their loyalty? Or should
they attack, early and often, to make it clear Nixon would not get a pass
simply because he wasn't Lyndon Johnson?

No one knew for sure. Manion called for keeping the heat on Nixon, advice he shared with Philip Crane at the American Conservative Union. Crane turned to Manion for counsel after a recent ACU board meeting uncovered "universal concern . . . over the possibility that once Nixon is elected, conservative Republicans in considerable numbers may rest on the oars or feel reluctant to speak out forcefully against the administration." Crane pointed to the 1952 election and the punch-pulling Ike's presidency had inspired. A Nixon administration could easily lead to the same, with dreadful consequences for conservative legislators who acted against principle to support the president. Based on these concerns, Crane suggested a sort of "Nixon score card," a way of assessing whether the president was keeping the faith or listing left. What he wanted from Manion were concrete moves by the administration that would let conservatives know which direction Nixon was breaking. Cabinet choices and foreign policy topped the radio host's list of concerns, and he urged Crane to "get in a few 'kicks'" on the subjects.[23]

Right-wing media figures weren't the only ones urging conservatives to get in their kicks. A few fellow travelers had made it into the administration—most notably Pat Buchanan and Tom Huston, a former YAF president-turned-White House aide—and they turned to media activists to pressure their boss. At *National Review* Rusher (never one to shy away from Nixon-bashing) took a call from Huston, who asked that Buckley and columnist James J. Kilpatrick go hard on "the disastrous series of liberal appointments" that followed Nixon's inauguration. Rusher pressed for a full-boil attack, but the resultant editorial barely reached a simmer, downplaying the appointments as "mostly of non-ideological types" that reflected the lack of hard-drawn policy lines in the administration. Yes, Nixon should pay more attention to the right, the editors said, but the real test of his conservative steel would not be appointments but his response to foreign crises. "Then we shall see what stuff Nixon is made of," they held, "then and not before."[24]

So temperate, so patient—and so out of line with the bold bluster that made the magazine the "vigorous and incorruptible journal of conservative opinion" it proclaimed to be in its first issue. The even-handed tone toward Nixon led *Human Events* publisher Robert Kephart to blast Rusher. *Human Events* had adopted a "rake-'em-over-the-coals" approach to the administration, and Kephart burned at the thought that *National Review* was positioning itself—and responsible conservatism—to the left of *Human Events*. On one occasion in early 1969, aggrieved by a perceived slap at Reagan supporters, Kephart mocked Rusher for seeking "The Secret

Conservatism of Richard Nixon." "I'm afraid if all you formerly solid types hop on the Administration bandwagon in this way," he wrote Rusher, "it will make it difficult for 'legitimate' conservatism to flourish." Then taking a shot at the magazine's pet phrase "responsible conservatism," Kephart offered his own taxonomy of the right. "Henceforth I shall answer to the appel[l]ation 'legitimate conservative,'" he declared, "leaving, I suppose, an unfortunate, but appropriate, antonym for those on my left."[25]

Rusher being Rusher, he couldn't let this attack go unanswered. Call him illegitimate, fine, but don't ever call him a Nixon supporter. *He* had never backed Nixon ("that tired, tergiversating tramp") and even now awaited the president's disappointments with "a sort of gloomy relish." But a magazine didn't always reflect its publisher's point of view, he explained. A journal of opinion housed many opinions, many divisions. At the end of the day *National Review* was Buckley's ward, and Buckley had thrown in with Nixon more than two years earlier. For all that, however, Rusher seemed cynically confident that Nixon would soon prove unworthy of Buckley's support, and the magazine could then return to its oppositional labors. Within a month of taking office, Nixon obliged.[26]

To the wider world, it was a minor incident, warranting only a four-paragraph story in the back of the *New York Times*. The secretary of state refused to restore a federal employee named Otto Otepka to his post in the State Department. A conservative cause célèbre, Otepka had been fired from State in the early 1960s for informing the Senate about the department's poor security conditions. What clearer sign did the right need that the Kennedy administration didn't take communist subversion seriously? As part of his outreach to conservatives in 1968, Nixon promised justice for Otepka and a shake-up at State.

Conservatives interpreted this as a pledge to reinstate Otepka. When that didn't happen, they charged Nixon with betrayal. "My disappointment with Nixon is approaching disgust," Manion wrote a friend upon hearing the news. "At home and abroad, we are sitting ducks for our enemies. The Otepka decision is the last straw." Nixon quickly course-corrected, nominating Otepka to head the Subversive Activities Control Board. When Manion covered the issue a few weeks later, he did so under the banner "Perseverance Pays off for Otto Otepka." (*Human Events* opted for the briefer "Otepka Vindicated.")[27]

Other issues would not be so readily resolved. What balm was there for conservatives in policies like the Family Assistance Plan (which would establish a guaranteed annual income) and the Philadelphia Plan (which instituted affirmative-action guidelines for federal contracts)? Yet it was foreign policy, not domestic, that turned media activists solidly against Nixon. Manion, while assuring listeners Nixon was a genuine anticommunist, worried the president would forgo attempts to roll back communists and instead try to "'mellow' them." He'd hoped Nixon would throw conservatives a bone, maybe by coming out against the "self-defeating embargo against the friendly anti-Communist governments of South Africa and Rhodesia." But no—even a year into his presidency Nixon said nothing about softening toward those apartheid regimes. Manion still counseled patience. He agreed with a correspondent that Nixon straddled the fence but assured him all was not lost. After all, as a straddler, Nixon "has one leg on the 'right' side of the fence. That is one leg more than we had under Johnson and Kennedy." He was, in other words, conservative enough. And with a bit of pressure, Manion believed he could be pushed all the way over.[28]

Then came China. The decision to open relations with a communist country, part of Nixon's strategy of realpolitik and multilateralism, signaled to conservatives Nixon wasn't straddling the fence anymore: he'd jumped over to the wrong side. No rollback, no containment—now it was all handshakes and agreements and thaw. Call it détente or "normalizing relations," but the right saw it as the gravest of capitulations, the worst of treasons. It was the bridge they couldn't cross.

When Nixon announced on July 15, 1971, that he would be traveling to Peking, even his most enthusiastic supporters in conservative media recoiled. A group of a dozen conservative leaders—the majority representing media—gathered at Buckley's home on the Upper East Side. There were four representatives from *National Review*, two from *Human Events*, two from the ACU. Stan Evans, popular conservative author and editor of the *Indianapolis Star*, showed up, along with Neil McCaffrey of Arlington House and the Conservative Book Club. They were joined by representatives from YAF and the New York State Conservative Party. Elected officials were purposefully excluded: this was to be a principled, not partisan, stand.[29]

Evans, who had written the Sharon Statement eleven years earlier at Buckley's Connecticut home, now took up the task of drafting an anti-Nixon statement. Much debate ensued as Buckley, one of the least willing to break with the president, tempered the language and softened the blows. By day's end, they had not a repudiation but a rebuke: a suspension of support. They would complain but not formally oppose. The statement ended with a reaffirmation of "our personal admiration" for Nixon (how Rusher must have hated that!) and a declaration that "our defection is an act of loyalty to the Nixon we supported in 1968."[30]

Suspending support did not mean formally opposing Nixon, at least not in 1971, but it did mean actively working to oppose the administration's foreign policy. Media activists tackled that project with relish in the early 1970s. During the last half of 1971, Manion dedicated roughly half of his broadcasts to foreign policy. A week after the Manhattan Twelve statement, the *Forum* interrupted a series of interviews on the Pentagon Papers to focus on China. Manion turned his microphone over to Henry Mooberry, the publicity director for the precisely named Committee of One Million Against the Admission of Communist China to the United Nations. Mooberry conducted a two-part interview with British businessman George Watt, imprisoned in China for nearly three years on espionage charges. The aim of the program was clear in the program's title: "Please, Mr. President: Read About One Man's Trip to Peking." Manion kept up the drumbeat for months, bringing on *National Review* columnist Erik Von Kuehnelt-Leddihn and journalist Stan Evans to expand on their anti-administration writings.[31]

The Nixon administration, knowing it had to keep conservatives on board, rushed to bring the media back into the fold in the wake of the Manhattan Twelve meeting. Nixon sent Buchanan to take care of the *Human Events* crowd and brought Buckley to Washington to meet with his national security advisor Henry Kissinger. After the meeting, Buckley brought Kissinger to talk with the Manhattan Twelve, but there was little either man could say to counteract the administration's actions in the fall of 1971: wage and price controls, arms control, the U.N. vote to admit China. Vice President Spiro Agnew went to make peace but to no avail. The truth was Nixon simply wasn't conservative enough anymore.[32]

Though the Manhattan Twelve had pledged not to formally oppose Nixon in 1972, they did include a caveat: "We propose to keep all options open in the light of political developments over the next few months." But the group was clearly not holding its breath. One of the Manhattan Twelve told conservative columnist Holmes Alexander that given the state of things, a Democrat would be preferable to Nixon. "He's doing things only a Republican can get away with," the signer fumed, disclosing the group was scrambling to find a Nixon alternative for the Republican primaries. They found that alternative in John Ashbrook. The Ohio congressman had extensive ties with the conservative movement reaching back to the 1950s: an anti-Eisenhower Young Republican, an early member of the Goldwater for President team, a member of HUAC, chairman of the ACU, a Conservative Book Club sponsor. Soon after Ashbrook's election to the House in 1960, Manion praised his soon-to-be-frequent guest as part of "an outstanding group of militant young Conservatives" who entered Congress that year. When he learned the congressman was thinking of challenging Nixon in 1972, Manion hopped on board. "At long last," he wrote Ashbrook, "I will have the happiness of supporting a conservative anti-Communist for President with no reservations." Shortly thereafter, Manion received a telegram urging him to join the advisory committee of Ashbrook for President.[33]

That committee came about thanks to the effort of two other media activists, Rusher and Tom Winter of *Human Events*. Along with the chair of YAF, they approached Ashbrook to challenge Nixon. As a sign of how thoroughly Nixon's overtures to China had flipped conservative support, *National Review* openly backed the Ashbrook drive, declaring in December that should the Ohioan run, the magazine would "of course endorse him." Endorse him they did a few weeks later. "No vote for John Ashbrook will be wasted," the editors concluded. *Human Events* offered a front-page endorsement and a glowing four-page review of the congressman's career and philosophy. Praise rolled in from the *Indianapolis News* and the *Manchester Union-Leader*. All a far cry from the Nixon glow of 1968.[34]

Manion, too, lobbied hard to gin up conservative support for Ashbrook. Letters poured in once Ashbrook declared his candidacy, and Manion stood firmly behind the congressman despite his long odds. When a director of Americans for Constitutional Action expressed concern over Ashbrook's obscurity, Manion staked out a principled stand. "I personally believe that it is not how well a new candidate is known but what he is known 'for' that should determine our support or rejection of him," Manion held. Showing little evidence of having lived through 1964, he argued that as long as the candidate had good conservative principles, the rest would fall into place. Rusher echoed these sentiments. Regardless of how the congressman might actually perform, he said, "I am profoundly glad that Ashbrook is in these primaries. By his action, he has preserved the conservative position—not in good health, to be sure, but at least alive and capable of being fought for."[35]

Conservative media may have gotten behind Ashbrook, but Republican officeholders wanted nothing to do with his candidacy. While stumping for Nixon, Reagan batted away claims that Nixon had sold out his conservative principles. Nixon's policies, he argued, were adjusted to the realities of the time. Goldwater opted (as usual) for a more apocalyptic tone. He warned the anti-Nixon insurgency endangered "the entire party, the entire country, the entire free world and freedom itself." Nixon, both Reagan and Goldwater argued, was far better than a Democrat and far more electable than Ashbrook. Ideological purity was fine for intellectuals, but in the world of practical politics, it had no place. As politicians, they were far more attuned to viability than the media activists turned out to be. Primary results bore them out: Ashbrook garnered around 10 percent of the vote in a few early races then quietly folded his campaign.[36]

So much for overthrowing Nixon. Facing another four years of the man Ashbrook slammed for offering "liberal policies in the verbal trappings of conservatism," the messengers redoubled their efforts to force the administration to the right. Just as they had in 1968, they followed the 1972 election with discussions of how best to influence Nixon. In an appearance on the *Forum* a few weeks after the election, Stan Evans started by translating Nixon's resounding victory into a win for the movement. "In an indirect way," he spun, "the election was a landslide for conservatism, in that it was a repudiation of the extreme liberalism of George McGovern." Resuming the hunt for "The Secret Conservatism of Richard Nixon," he found reason to hope in Nixon's return to conservative rhetoric. The chief lesson Evans drew, though, was the most profound. Conservatives should never have thrown in with Nixon in the first place. Principle had to take precedence over pragmatism. Evans denounced conservative leaders for deciding that, with Nixon in office, "we had to fudge, we had to compromise, we had to change our spots in order to be practical and to mesh with the necessities of political survival." At their feet Evans laid the blame for the administration's "leftward drift." With Nixon back in office, the time was ripe for even greater opposition.[37]

For all his failings, Nixon advanced the conservative cause considerably in his first term. He may have let conservatives down with his foreign and economic policy, but when it came to conservative efforts to reshape the media, he was a godsend. As the head of the executive branch, Nixon had the ability to orient the bureaucracy in a more conservative direction—a power he was eager to wield.

Topping the conservative wish list: changes at the FCC. Here the president did not disappoint. When a spot opened on the FCC in the fall of 1969, he appointed Dean Burch as the new chairman. Burch was an inspired choice. He played a central role in the 1964 Goldwater campaign, then served as the chair of the Republican National Committee before being forced out by the party's more liberal wing. During Burch's brief chairman-ship, Manion had urged him to "come out swinging" against the Fairness Doctrine. At the time Burch could do little more than inveigh against the doctrine, but as FCC chair he would set the tone for how the agency's policies would be carried out. The Reuther Memo had long ago convinced conservative broadcasters that Democratic administrations used the FCC to silence them. The installation of Burch as chair changed that dynamic. The jury may have been out on Nixon's conservatism, but Burch proved his met-tle five years earlier on the conservative movement's first major battleground. *Human Events* approvingly noted the appointment "angered at least one Republican senator, an Eastern liberal." Anything that irritated the liberal wing of the GOP easily won praise from the right.[38]

Of course, Nixon rarely made a move based solely on conservative approval. The administration had its own plans for Burch, none of them particularly aboveboard. Not long after the inauguration, Nixon's special assistant, Jeb Stuart Magruder, under direction from White House chief of staff H. R. Haldeman, outlined a broad plan of attack against the admin-istration's opponents on television and radio. The Magruder memo, as his recommendations became known, outlined a number of tactics to turn media coverage in favor of the administration. He proposed, for instance, using the FCC to monitor networks for signs of media bias, a project that could start as soon as Burch was "officially on board as chairman." Magruder's plans also included directing outside groups to use the Fairness Doctrine and requir-ing licenses not just for stations but individual newscasters. Other members of the administration planned to use Burch's appointment as well. White House special counsel Charles Colson pressured him to exempt presiden-tial addresses from the commission's calculations of balanced broadcasting. Essentially: if the administration was saying it, it was politically neutral.[39]

Later FCC appointments shored up conservative strength within the agency. In 1971 Nixon appointed Charlotte Reid, a representative from Illinois, as the first woman to serve on the FCC. Reid had close ties to Phyllis Schlafly, who had delivered several campaign speeches on her behalf. Her husband, Fred Schlafly, encouraged Clarence Manion to start filing Fairness Doctrine requests against liberal speakers once Reid was installed, adding that "the stations should be informed that the renewals of the licenses will be strenuously resisted." Two years later, *Human Events* gleefully reported that Nixon would not renew the five-year term of "far-out liberal" Nicholas Johnson on the FCC and would fill the Democratic seat with David Bradshaw, whose father-in-law had donated millions to the Nixon campaign. The focus on FCC staffing revealed how conservative interpretations of institutional bias would play out. Believing all institutions were ideological, conservatives sough not to strip out the ideology but to change it. Institutional conservatism, not neutrality, was their goal.[40]

Friends in high places bought conservative broadcasters breathing room. But proximity to power proved even more valuable on an elemental level. Nixon may not have been a conservative, but he understood the mood of the country was shifting in ways that aligned with fundamental conservative ideas. Concepts long central to the right's worldview—"silent majority" and "liberal media bias"—became subjects of national debate under Nixon, thanks to the legitimacy they gained from White House sanction.

Liberal media bias was an article of faith for media activists, the foundational assumption upon which they staked their legitimacy. Established media, the argument went, reflected the biases of their creators. They existed to perpetuate liberal ideas and persuade the public to accept liberal policies. While the movement embraced this argument, most Americans still believed in journalistic objectivity. They viewed Walter Cronkite as the most trusted man in America, not the mouthpiece of liberal propaganda.

Then came Nixon.

Nixon's evaluation of established media was not quite the same as that of conservatives. Anti-Republican? Maybe. Anti-conservative? Probably. Anti-Nixon? Most definitely. His antipathy toward the press wasn't abstract theory or conservative cosmology. It was personal. From the moment he growled "you won't have Nixon to kick around anymore" at reporters in 1962, the lines were drawn.

And yet the opening shots of the administration's campaign against media bias came not from Nixon but from his vice president, the avuncular Spiro Agnew. Greeted at the 1968 convention with a collective "Spiro who?" Agnew raised no hopes for the right with his nomination. (Nor for himself; he quipped about his ascension to the vice presidency, "I moved from a potential unknown to an actual unknown.") But within a year of taking office, Agnew was acting as the administration's pit bull. What's more, the former Maryland governor, once known as a moderate Republican because of his support for civil rights, soon became a saving grace for conservatives.

It began with the Moratorium to End the War in Vietnam, a worldwide protest held on October 15, 1969. At a GOP fund-raiser four days later in New Orleans, Agnew laid into the demonstrators. He denounced the moratorium as "an emotional purgative for those who feel the need to cleanse themselves of their lack of ability to offer a constructive solution to the problem." Targeting the establishment elite (a favorite target of conservatives as well as the administration), Agnew lambasted the "effete corps of impudent snobs" encouraging the unrest. Not everyone was impressed: Nixon distanced himself from the remarks and commentators pounced on Agnew for "raw demagoguery" and "truly monumental insensitivity." But conservatives were thrilled. And despite the mixed reaction, Agnew began to develop a sense of how he could steer national debate through punchy, pointed language. True, it drew condemnation from some quarters, but it drew attention, too. "If you can get your thought through to people," he mused, "it can be worth the risk." His willingness to take that risk in service of conservative ideas made Agnew an unexpected boon to the right.[41]

How much of a boon became clear a month later. On November 13, Agnew traveled to Iowa to deliver another barn burner, this time focused on television news and public opinion. It began as an attack on instant analysis, the relatively new practice where newscasters, editorialists, and experts responded to speeches immediately after they occurred. Nixon loathed it. He believed instant analysis undermined his ability to control the administration's message. Two weeks before sending Agnew to Iowa, the president delivered a televised address on Vietnam and raged when stations cut to their studios afterward to question his claims and interview his critics. Fortunately, he now had someone willing to hit back.

Agnew easily stepped into the role of administration bad cop, going after not just instant analysis but the entire news industry. A democratic society, he argued, could not function without an informed populace. A *well*-informed populace, not one misled by half-truths, obfuscation, and spin. Given that, Agnew questioned the wisdom of handing over so much influence to "a closed fraternity of privileged men, elected by no one." This select set of men, he argued, "perhaps no more than a dozen," determined the content of nightly news. In choosing the stories and writing the commentary, these anchors, producers, and pundits served up not objective analysis but the liberal pap of the New York–Washington echo chamber. And every night, forty million Americans tuned in, imbibing bias and mistaking it for neutrality.[42]

Like his moratorium speech, Agnew's Iowa diatribe grabbed headlines. Suddenly the question of media objectivity and liberal bias was part of the national conversation. Some in the media worried it was the opening gambit in a crackdown on free speech. "My feeling is that the White House is out to get us," one CBS commentator fretted. "We're in for dangerous times." Others, though, cosigned Agnew's concerns. The editors at the *Washington Post* saw no signs of liberal conspiracy in news coverage, but they agreed that editorial news needed reevaluation. Tom Wicker, a reporter for the *New York Times*, responded to Agnew's criticism in a 1971 address at the Massachusetts Historical Society. Though he dismissed Agnew as a "polyloquent pipsqueak," he agreed nonetheless that press values were problematic. "If I had been in Mr. Agnew's place and had been trying to make an intelligent, useful criticism of the American press, I would have said that its biggest weakness is its reliance on and its acceptance of official sources—precisely its 'objectivity' in presenting the news." Wicker called instead for journalists to take up the task of "journalistic muckraking," to "dedicate ourselves to the search for the meaning of things, and turn ourselves loose to be the true storytellers our time, novelists of the age, rather than professional recorders of accumulated facts and authorized views."[43]

Support came from other unexpected quarters as well. Antiwar protesters, no great friends of Agnew, heartily approved of the view that the news was too controlled by establishment forces. Indeed, from the New Left would come a media critique to rival conservatives', finding a mainstream voice in works like Edward S. Herman and Noam Chomsky's *Manufacturing Consent*, their 1988 book on the political economy of mass media. They were part of a long tradition of left-wing press criticism that, while important, never became part of the liberal identity in the United States (in large part because the left defined itself as much in opposition to liberalism as to conservatism).[44]

Instead, it was conservative media activists who made the most of the liberal bias charges. They didn't just laud Agnew—they loved him. They turned him into a touchstone, proof that theirs was a legitimate grievance. Six weeks after the speech, James J. Finnegan, chief editor for the *Manchester Union-Leader*, appeared on the *Manion Forum* to back up Agnew's claims. Conservative media, he argued, were "the only force standing between the liberal news media and the total monopolization of all news information available to the American people." A few months later, *Parade* magazine publisher Red Motley joined Manion to praise Agnew's indictment as "timely, and proper." And when it came time for the *Forum* to fund-raise in 1970, Agnew was front and center, symbolizing the call to balance established media's liberal tilt.[45]

Accolades for Agnew echoed through conservative media. Rusher, who would become friends with the vice president, described him as "a thoughtful, decent man" whose conservatism continued to develop while in office. (Agnew ordered a half-dozen subscriptions to the magazine so he could hand out copies to friends.) His speeches provided regular content for *Human Events*, and his portrait graced the newsweekly's ads next to the question "How Much News Is Being Withheld from You?" So popular was the vice president in their offices that *Human Events* released five of his recordings as part of their Audio-Forum. (Audio-Forum recordings were classed by topic: conservative classics, politics, communism, foreign policy, economics—and Spiro Agnew, who rated his own category as a conservative field of study.) Less than a year after Agnew caught the right's attention with his Iowa speech, conservative publisher Arlington House released *The Enemies He Has Made: The Media vs. Spiro Agnew* (a book destined to reside on bookshelves next to a *Human Events* promotional offering, *Agnew: Profile in Conflict*).[46]

When it came to media bias, Agnew made the charge, but it was up to conservative media to make the case. At first they offered only anecdotal evidence, like the eleven-item list of liberal media infractions James Finnegan offered *Manion Forum* listeners. But soon they developed a more systematic approach. Hard numbers, rigorous tallying, percentages, and tables and charts: how better to prove liberal bias was not a figment of the paranoid conservative mind but an irrefutable fact? It was a development that demonstrated, perhaps unwittingly, conservatives' continued reliance on the appearance of objectivity. Data, with its promise of neutrality, had an appeal that openly ideological arguments couldn't match—a tension media activists left unresolved.

One of the earliest efforts to provide support came from the Committee to Combat Bias in Broadcasting, an offshoot of the American Conservative Union. Inspired by Agnew, the committee set up a program designed to monitor television broadcasts for bias. In an effort to bring grassroots conservatives into their efforts (a way of keeping activists active in between elections), the committee sent out letters from *Human Events* publisher Tom Winter along with Media Watch Monitoring cards. Want to expose liberal bias? Just rate the listed news commentators as "presents news accurately and objectively," "tends to be liberal in his presentation," or "goes all out to distort facts and to discredit conservatives." (Note the committee didn't expect their watchmen to find conservative bias in the nightly news broadcasts.)[47]

The heavy lifting, though, fell to Edith Efron, a writer for *TV Guide*. Efron had caught media activists' attention in 1964 with an article criticizing the Fairness Doctrine. A former student of John Chamberlain at Columbia University's School of Journalism, she leaped into the media bias fight soon after Agnew's speech. Her article "There *Is* a Network News Bias" first ran in *TV Guide* and then *Human Events* two weeks later. For the piece, she interviewed Howard K. Smith, the self-proclaimed "left-of-center" ABC News anchor. Smith turned out to be the perfect subject. Though far across the political spectrum from Efron, he, too, believed journalists wore liberal shades that blinded them to improvements in the South, military successes in Vietnam, and the appeal of conservatives and Middle America. If even a leftist could see it, Efron reasoned, liberal bias must be real.[48]

Even before the Smith interview, Efron had determined to make a more systematic study of media bias. In 1968, she set about analyzing election coverage from September 16 through Election Day. Armed with thousands of hours of videotape and a grant from the Historical Research Fund (of which Buckley happened to be the projects chair), she plucked out a hundred thousand words on Nixon and Humphrey from each of the Big Three's nightly newscasts.

Then she started counting.

For and against: tick, tick, tick, until Efron had tallied every favorable and unfavorable word spoken about the candidates. Crunching the numbers, she found about half of all words spoken about Humphrey were positive. For Nixon? A paltry 8.7 percent. No wonder she concluded network news followed "the elitist-liberal-left line in all controversies."[49]

In the lead-up to the book's publication, Efron turned to Buckley and the network of right-wing media to get out the word about her work. She laid out a seven-item plan to use *National Review* and its stable of writers to advertise *The News Twisters*. For the magazine: "some splendid outburst" in September. For Buckley himself: a syndicated column, a book blurb, and an episode of his television show, *Firing Line*. For Rusher: a debate on *his* television show, *The Advocates*. For the Conservative Book Club: selection of the month. Even James Buckley, then the Conservative Party senator for New York, got a request: "Would you ask your brother-of-the-exquisite-dimples to walk around Washington . . . ostentatiously clutching a copy of my book?" Buckley happily forwarded the letter along to his colleagues, encouraging them to add their ideas. *National Review* would, of course, make "a special splash" when the book came out. "But," he added, "this is too good to preempt just for ourselves."[50]

Conservative media weren't the only ones interested in making sure

Efron's book made a splash. The White House instantly understood the importance of a book that broke down, in hard numbers, the extent to which the media were biased against the administration. After all, as John Chamberlain wrote in *National Review*, the book was science, not art. The charges of liberal bias were more than just "Mrs. Efron's say-so"—her quantitative tabulation proved her point. Such evidence (no matter how problematic the methodology might have been) appealed powerfully to Nixon. So he ordered Special Counsel Charles Colson to get the book on the *New York Times* best-seller list. Not an easy feat, but Colson, who had a nose for gaming the system, figured it out. He ferreted out which stores' sales were used to determine the list and bought up every copy they had. For years Nixon staffers stumbled upon boxes crammed full of *The News Twisters*. But it worked: Efron's book became an official *New York Times* best seller.[51]

So there were benefits to being close to power. And they extended beyond book buying. In the wake of Agnew's speech, conservatives sensed a climate change in American media. Manion pointed to the 1971 launch of "Spectrum," a sort of op-ed page for *CBS Morning News*. Debuting first on radio, the show trotted out commentators, many of them conservative, to offer news analysis. With the right-wing viewpoint now prominently featured on national television, "Spectrum" constituted "the greatest boon to our cause that has ever happened on 'air.'" And it wasn't the only place conservatives were popping up. Elsewhere on CBS, *60 Minutes* pitted conservative columnist James J. Kilpatrick against liberal Nicholas von Hoffman in a regular segment called "Point/Counterpoint." These joined Buckley's *Firing Line*, which first went on air in 1966 and Rusher's debate show *The Advocates*, conservative-centered programs that highlighted and legitimated the conservative perspective.[52]

Kilpatrick traced these developments back to Agnew, saying that after the vice president's speech "a sea change came over my friends in New York. . . . All of a sudden they began to think, my gracious, there is another point of view in this country after all." Even the publisher of *Human Events*, in the midst of selling his paper as an alternative to liberal media, had to admit that conservatives were popping up all over established media outlets—even the editorial pages of "that holy house organ of Liberalism—the New York Times." Though it would take a few decades to flower fully, by the early 1970s conservatives were taking the first steps toward one of the greatest victories: shifting the meaning of objectivity from factuality to balanced reporting.[53]

That victory required more than just placing conservatives in media. It required policing mainstream media outlets in order both to provide evidence of bias and to "play the refs," to convince media outlets that they were unfairly excluding conservative viewpoints. In 1969, Reed Irvine founded Accuracy in Media (AIM) for just this purpose. Outraged at media coverage of the 1968 Democratic convention that he felt favored the protesters, Irvine, an economist with the Federal Reserve, established AIM as a watchdog organization that would "investigate complaints, take proven cases to top media officials, seek corrections and mobilize public pressure to bring about remedial action" on behalf of "the consumers of the journalistic product and not the producers." The name was important: Accuracy in Media. It betrayed no ideological bent, reflecting instead a core value of objective journalism. As Irvine told Manion, "We felt that since the journalists all profess devotion to accuracy, we would be able to work wonders by simply pointing out to them cases in which they were inaccurate." But soon AIM was filing Fairness Doctrine complaints against programs they felt were "one-sided and biased."[54]

The use of Fairness Doctrine complaints was relatively new for conservative media activists, who during the 1950s and 1960s had their hearts set on repealing the doctrine. AIM advocated conservatives instead use it against nonconservative broadcasters. In his appearance on the *Manion Forum* in 1975, Irvine explained how to register a complaint, including the address of the FCC. He also updated *Forum* listeners on a Fairness Doctrine complaint the group had leveled against ABC, in which the FCC had agreed that the doctrine had been violated before being overturned by an appeals court. This use of the Fairness Doctrine reflected an understanding that the FCC was an ideological institution, one that, with Nixon in the White House, could be used effectively by conservatives. At the time, that was their only option. The Nixon administration strongly opposed the repeal of the Fairness Doctrine, seeing in it a powerful tool for managing the press.[55]

Initially Irvine used direct mail, letters to the editor, and Fairness Doctrine complaints to call attention to what he saw as biased reporting. As its budget grew, exploding to $1.1 million in 1981 from $5,000 a decade earlier, AIM would be able to engage in major campaigns. But even on a shoestring budget it had an impact. In 1971 it organized against *The Selling of the Pentagon*, a CBS documentary on the military's public relations tactics that led to conflict between the White House and the network. Agnew delivered a lengthy diatribe against the documentary, denouncing it as "a

subtle but vicious broadside against the nation's defense establishment."
Meanwhile Chuck Colson pushed for an equal-time response from the
administration to combat the documentary (which led to heated battles in
the FCC between Dean Burch and Nicholas Johnson). Irvine joined that
battle, detailing the documentary's inaccuracies in a seven-page report and
explaining the controversy to conservatives in *National Review*.[56]

AIM and the Nixon administration were ideologically aligned on issues
of media bias, but their ties did not end there. As historian Chad Raphael
detailed in his book *Investigated Reporting*, "The White House helped
expand the group's funding and coordinated many attacks on media bias with
AIM." Colson in particular saw AIM as a helpmate for the administration's
media-bias battle. When the Nixon administration put together a plan to
scale back PBS, Colson urged the use of AIM to generate FCC complaints
about the public broadcaster. Colson worked behind the scenes to get big-
name board members, advertisers, and funding for the organization. The
appeal of AIM was, as one Nixon aide put it, its usefulness as "a mechanism
under which private non-governmental pressures can be brought to bear on
the three networks."[57]

AIM also found a champion in Clarence Manion, who hosted Reed Irvine
on the show and regularly touted the "AIM Report," the group's newsletter,
and its investigations. In a 1975 *Footnote* (one of the *Forum*'s five-minute
radio snippets), Manion displayed how effective the many organizations and
activists working on media bias could be in creating a self-referential realm
of information and authority. Edith Efron, writing for *TV Guide*, penned an
article on the anti-American biases of TV news. The "AIM Report" publi-
cized Efron's conclusions, then added its own evidence of TV news bias. All
of which Manion presented to his audience. Three centers of authority—
Efron, AIM, and Manion—worked together to disseminate and legitimize
a conservative interpretation of biased news. Manion continued to burnish
Irvine's reputation as a defender of "true, accurate and unbiased reporting"
throughout the 1970s.[58]

AIM was not the only media-watchdog organization of the 1970s. The
National News Council (NNC), founded in 1973, was a mainstream organization intended to investigate complaints against the media (and forestall
greater government regulation). Populated mostly by liberals, the NNC
board invited Rusher to join in order to provide some ideological balance.
The existence of the NNC came, Executive Director William B. Arthur
said, at a time the country was undergoing "a degree of self-examination

and self-criticism on the part of the media without precedent in our nation's history." Wary of government interference with the press, Arthur argued that American journalism needed an independent body that could shore up public confidence in the news without inviting government regulatory bodies into the debate. Yet a number of outlets, most notably the *New York Times*, refused to deal with the NNC, limiting its effectiveness and ultimately leading it to shutter operations in the early 1980s.[59]

Nonideological watchdogs like the NNC were the exception. Much more common were groups like the Foundation for Objective News Reporting (FONR), established in 1975. Tom Winter of *Human Events* served as the chair; Stan Evans and *Human Events* editor Allan Ryskind sat on the board. Like AIM, FONR was an ideological organization that emphasized objectivity in reporting, acting as the guardians of fairness. Both groups did so not because they believed conservatives should be objective but because they believed mainstream media, having proclaimed itself to be objective, had to be held to that standard—or else be exposed for the liberal media conservatives were convinced they were.[60]

Their fixation on liberal bias shaped how media activists viewed the end of Nixon's presidency. The emerging Watergate scandal absorbed the administration soon after Nixon's second term began. Whereas a generation of mainstream journalists celebrated the role of the press in exposing the crimes of the Nixon White House, breathing new life into the profession and reinvigorating the field of investigative journalism, conservatives understood the scandal, and the press's role, very differently. Media activists immediately saw the hand of liberal malfeasance in the breaking scandal. A month after the Senate hearings began, *Forum* guest Dan Lyons, an anticommunist Catholic writer, argued the danger Watergate exposed was not a too-powerful executive but a too-powerful press. Nixon could organize a bumbling burglary, Lyons argued, but the press could bring down a president. In the interview, Manion called freedom of the press "a mask" disguising a formidable force in American society. "The result," he concluded, "is that a gullible public is caught in the talons of a power that ironically describes itself as freedom."[61]

The Watergate-as-liberal-conspiracy angle ricocheted through conservative media. Inspired by the Lyons interview, Paul Harvey repeated the attack in his nationally syndicated television commentary. How could the American people accept the ability of the "'centralized' mass media to turn a prosecution into a persecution"? When the conservative editors at the

Chicago Tribune joined the call for more press protections, an enraged Henry Regnery fired off a letter calling the press "utterly irresponsible," "a public menace," and "the spoiled child of American society." Jesse Helms's appearance on the *Forum* gave the senator a chance to rail against "the television networks" and "the incredible New York Times–Washington Post syndicate, which controls to a large degree what the American people will read and learn." All those media-bias charges the administration helped support were bearing fruit. "Nattering nabobs of negativity," indeed.[62]

Behind these charges of bias and conspiracy lay a shared belief about Nixon's connection to the movement. Though they had spent the previous few years denouncing Nixon for welfare-statism at home and capitulation abroad, the right believed he was being brought down for his conservatism, that liberals were using Watergate as a pretense to reverse the results of the 1972 election. "Indeed," the editors at *National Review* wrote, "the target is really not Nixon himself or this or that aide, but, rather, the 'new majority'" threatening to break the liberal hold on political power. The liberals seemed to be succeeding. While the editors argued Watergate wouldn't "change the fundamental political equations in the country," they joined their media cohort in fretting over the short-term effect. They laid the return of the Family Assistance Plan, several spending bills, and new arms-control agreements on the scandal's diminishment of the president's "political sinew, his moral authority, and his credibility." They weren't alone. Manion and *Human Events* feared Watergate would strip Nixon of his mandate and move him even further left. In many ways, Watergate granted Nixon a reprieve from his conservative critics. When Nixon pushed the same policies in his first term, the messengers heaped scorn upon him. Now liberals and their "mock horror over Watergate" bore the brunt of the blame.[63]

Then, Agnew. The one comfort in the mounting scandal had been the Agnew bulwark. If Nixon resigned, the vice president–turned–conservative darling would take his place. So when news broke that the vice president was under investigation for accepting bribes while governor of Maryland, the right-wing press reacted with confusion and conspiracies. *Human Events* drafted a dizzying array of suspects, from Archibald Cox and his "Kennedyites" to liberal Republican Nelson Rockefeller. Buckley, no longer as much a Nixon devotee as before, believed the president was advocating Agnew's resignation, in part to help purge himself of scandal and in part to do tidily away with "the most conspicuous conservative hardliner in the United States." More detailed analysis of the forces at work had no time to emerge. Soon after the first whispered rumors, Agnew resigned. Conservatives were despondent. They had lost a prominent spokesman and a favorite son for the 1976 election. Nixon's appointment of Gerald Ford raised no great cheer; whatever constraints conservatives had placed on the president prior to 1973 dissolved with Watergate and Agnew's resignation.[64]

Nixon's resignation a year later added a new argument to conservative media's response to Watergate. His abuse of power proved the federal government needed to be constrained. Prior to the resignation the argument found little purchase among people like Manion and Buckley and Regnery, all of whom held that neither the original break-in and bugging nor the attempts at cover-up amounted to anything outside ordinary political dealings. Once the White House tapes revealed the depth of Nixon's involvement and his resignation made shoring him up unnecessary, they dropped all pretenses. This, they argued, was what happened when government grew too big. Manion's first post-resignation program on Watergate focused on Nixon's Executive Order 11490, which gave the president broad powers in the event of a national emergency. Manion warned that the order empowered the president to "rule by decree." And as *National Review* did a final rundown of Watergate after the resignation, Rusher drew two lessons from the episode: the danger of "relentless liberal bias" and, far more important, the excessive power of the presidency. Watergate, he argued, was not an expression of Nixonian corruption but the result of forty years of federal expansion.[65]

Watergate may have provided rhetorical gains, but it was politically disastrous. Gerald Ford found few friends among conservatives and cemented their opposition when he named as vice president Nelson Rockefeller, the bane of conservative Republicans in the 1960s. So dissatisfied was Rusher with Ford that less than a year into his presidency the publisher declared, "I have made up my mind that, if there are no other choices in 1976 but Ford and some Democrat, I will vote for Wallace." Thus it was that after having "their president" in office, conservatives found themselves once again outside the Republican mainstream, throwing their energies into third-party protest politics.[66]

The outsiders-turned-insiders were back in the wilderness.

Chapter 11

The Contraction

"There was a time in America—not very long ago—when only liberal voices were to be heard on the nation's communications networks, and most national debates were limited to options which often seemed to offer little choice," Phil Crane reminisced. It was the end of 1973, nearly a decade after Crane had written *The Democrat's Dilemma* for Regnery during the Goldwater campaign. The square-jawed, well-coiffed Crane, now a congressman, had wended his way through conservative media, organizations, and politics. Now, sitting before the *Manion Forum* microphone, he recalled how different the landscape had appeared twenty years earlier: "Few indeed were the voices calling for national strength, limited government and fiscal integrity. Fewer still were the media outlets through which conservative spokesmen might reach a national audience and make available to that audience a viewpoint which not only represented a real choice but which, as we have seen, more recently represented the real views of the majority of Americans."[1]

Crane joined other conservative luminaries to celebrate the *Manion Forum's* one-thousandth broadcast. The next year brought even more festivities: 1974 was the *Forum's* twentieth anniversary, marked by a testimonial dinner that brought together so many top conservatives that Devin Garrity later remarked, "A well placed bomb could have done great damage to the conservative movement that evening." Phyllis Schlafly and Jesse Helms cochaired the dinner. Schlafly, a longtime friend of Manion's, had risen to national fame as the antifeminist organizer of the STOP-ERA movement, aimed at preventing the ratification of the Equal Rights Amendment.

Helms, elected to the Senate in 1972, was the face of the new Republican ascendancy in North Carolina, making a name for himself in both media and politics thanks to his popular radio editorials.[2]

Though the dinner celebrated Manion's media activism, it abounded with signs the movement had moved on. Media activists had been the architects of the early conservative movement, the main source of activism and political organization. While both Schlafly and Helms had media bona fides, neither was primarily a media activist. Schlafly was now an organizer, her writing an adjunct of her political work rather than the central mode of it. Same for Helms: he owned a radio station and used that platform to tremendous effect, but party politics was the senator's home turf. Much of media activists' early work—the *Manion Forum*, *Human Events*, Regnery, For America, Draft Goldwater—had sprung from the Midwest. The Manion dinner, though, was held in Washington, D.C., to serve the growing cadre of conservative journalists, think tankers, and politicians housed there. Media activism still mattered, but it increasingly vied with other centers of power. Struggling to retain audiences, short on both cash and credibility in the last years of the Nixon era, the first generation of conservative media activists lost their primacy in the 1970s. They would not regain it until the arrival of the second generation twenty years later.

Two events back in 1964 set in motion the dissolution of Regnery Publishing. The first: in June, Henry Regnery hired Harvey Plotnick. Plotnick, the grandson of Jewish émigrés from Eastern Europe, pursued a literature degree at the University of Chicago under the mentorship of Richard Weaver, author of the influential conservative book *Ideas Have Consequences* (1948). As an undergraduate, he became editor of the *Chicago Review*, a distinguished literary journal published by the university, then went on to work for Russell Kirk's *Modern Age* before being hired by Regnery. Then in August, two months after he joined the firm, the second event: Plotnick married Henry's daughter, Susan.[3]

Regnery had reservations about both developments. When it came to work, Plotnick was skilled and driven, assets the company desperately needed. He did not, however, strike Regnery as a particularly principled character. Regnery's doubts deepened when someone acquainted with Plotnick confided to him, "Harvey is not immoral, he is amoral. He has no morals at all." Not exactly the right fit for an ideological publishing house. "I went ahead anyway," Regnery later explained, "with the hope that Harvey might bring us what the firm needed to put it on a profitable basis—how right I was, and unaware of the price—and overcame my reservations with the guilty feeling that they probably arose from Harvey's Jewishness." Those same concerns about Plotnick's character and religion contributed to Regnery's misgivings about the wedding: "A wedding, my wife remarked, should be a happy occasion; at this one, we were both on the verge of tears."[4]

The tears were warranted. According to Regnery, over the next dozen years Plotnick took over the company, forced Regnery out, and institutionalized, then divorced, Susan. The takeover came first. The company's financial problems were critical by 1966. Because the firm was constantly operating at a loss, it was unable to service its loans in a timely manner, which had repercussions for the entire Regnery family. The $800,000 loan keeping Regnery Publishing afloat came from Central National Bank, where the family held a great deal of stock and where Regnery's brother Fred was a director. In May 1966 the Regnery siblings hunkered down and hashed out a plan. Henry's brother and sister bought enough stock to protect the bank. To get the publishing company on better business footing, Plotnick, who at that point had made a number of "spectacular and profitable" deals for the company, was made president, with Regnery retitled chairman of the board.[5]

But there was a catch. The new bylaws stated that the chairman would be responsible for duties "as determined by the president." Regnery balked at the ambiguity but felt he had little standing to complain, given how poorly the company had performed under his management. "I was not happy about this arrangement," he recollected some years later, time having done little to diminish his bitterness, "but felt that I had no choice, and deluded myself into believing that since Harvey was my son-in-law and a member of the family I would be able to continue to exert some influence over editorial policy and, therefore, that the basic character of the firm would remain unchanged." Regnery, however, was increasingly excluded from editorial decisions, and by 1969 he had effectively lost control of the company.[6]

The transfer of power from Regnery to Plotnick had real consequences. Plotnick put the company on sound financial footing, but he did so by intentionally shedding the firm's "conservative image." This meant more than just publishing nonpolitical books aimed at popular audiences; it meant actively avoiding books that might draw attention to the company's ideological origins. As Regnery put it, "His policy is to publish the books people want, rather than those they *should* want, as was my policy." Regnery soon learned his recommendation to publish guaranteed Plotnick would pass. When

Russell Kirk, whose 1953 book *The Conservative Mind* solidified Regnery's reputation as the foremost conservative publisher, offered *The Roots of American Order* to the firm in the early 1970s, Plotnick passed without even reviewing the manuscript. The final blow came in 1974, when Plotnick moved the firm from its original location in a building Regnery owned to a new space where he assigned Regnery to a windowless office. With that, Regnery was ready to break all connections with the firm and with Plotnick.[7]

Only there was still the matter of Susan, his daughter. By the early 1970s she and Harvey had two young children and a miserable marriage. Susan visited a succession of psychiatrists to treat her deepening depression. The first doctor told Plotnick he was the problem. This prompted the search for a second doctor, who confined Susan to Forest Hospital, where, Regnery reported, "their chief reliance seemed to be on drugs." By 1975, Regnery and his wife, Eleanor, overcame their aversion to conflict and demanded Susan be released. Over both Plotnick's and the doctor's objections, the Regnerys brought their daughter home with them. Within a few months, Plotnick "openly began to live with his secretary," and a year later the couple divorced, leaving Susan with the children and Plotnick with the company.[8]

The personal drama behind the collapse of Regnery Publishing distinguished it from other conservative media, but it was not the only company struggling in the 1970s. The money problems of the post-Goldwater era worsened as the movement diversified and the American economy declined. Paid circulation at *Human Events* tumbled from 110,000 to 62,000 between 1966 and 1974, a 44 percent loss at a time when the paper's political influence had never been greater. Publisher Tom Winter grumbled about the lack of advertising, particularly given the newsweekly's business-friendly politics. Businessmen no doubt worried about openly identifying with one of the foremost publications of movement conservatism, given how controversial right-wing politics could be. So they passed along their advertising dollars to the big national magazines like *Harper's* and *Newsweek*, even though, as Winter noted, those magazines "often take positions completely opposite to those of the businessmen."[9]

Low ad revenue wasn't the only problem. The onset of high inflation sent production costs soaring. Paper and ink costs climbed substantially, as did the cost of associated distribution services. At the same time, the massive restructuring of the postal service under the 1970 Postal Reorganization Act meant rates for second-class mail (that is, periodicals) increased annually, sometimes two to three times in a year, throughout the 1970s. Postage costs for *National Review*, for instance, doubled between 1977 and 1979, at a time when paid circulation actually decreased (meaning fewer magazines were being sent out). Without advertising to offset these costs, subscription prices climbed steadily, making it difficult to attract new subscribers.[10]

In 1975, things had gotten so bad at *Human Events* that, for the first time since the mid-1950s, they were forced to ask for contributions in order to stay afloat. The need to ask for money grated on the *Human Events* staff, which prided itself on the magazine's self-sufficiency (a rarity in the ideological publishing field). "We have diligently tried to practice the free enterprise principles we preach," Winter wrote potential donors, but the newsweekly had lost $168,000 in 1974 and was on track to lose even more in the current year. Inflation, postage increases, and direct-mail competition all conspired to push *Human Events* to the edge of insolvency. Winter believed free-market principles *could* save the publication but at the cost of its soul. *Human Events* was valuable enough to the hard core of the movement that the newsweekly could charge exorbitant rates to a small group of subscribers and end up in the black. But profitability wasn't *Human Events'* purpose. Its purpose was "to influence the policies of the government and, ultimately, the course of the nation." And to do that, they needed readers.[11]

Winter also had to stave off an attempted takeover. Richard Viguerie, who had risen to prominence as a leader of the New Right and direct-mail expert, had his eye on *Human Events* as well the ACU. Viguerie wanted to absorb whole cloth existing conservative institutions, convinced he could better lead the movement. When he proved unable to acquire either organization, he founded alternatives: the *Conservative Digest* and the Conservative Caucus. Viguerie's megalomania created friction with Washington conservatives, but not everyone was as displeased with him as Winter. Rusher found himself cheering it on. He had little affection for the *Human Events* crowd, whom he dismissed as a "rather inbred group of conservatives on Capitol Hill," and arrogance aside, he appreciated the energy and talent Viguerie brought to the cause—especially once Viguerie hired Neal Freeman, a former aide to Buckley and a future Washington editor for *National Review*.[12]

National Review faced similar economic challenges. It did better than *Human Events* at attracting advertisers. A 1971 subscriber survey provided ample evidence that advertising with the magazine was a good bet. Overwhelmingly male and married, some 44 percent of subscribers held a postgraduate degree, and another 21 percent had graduated from college. Over half of the subscribers were between the ages of 25 and 49, making them a relatively young cohort, and more than half were middle class. This survey data helped *National Review* steadily increase its advertising in the early 1970s. In 1974 alone its ad revenue grew 12.4 percent. But in the same year, the cost of printing went up 10 percent, paper 30 percent, and postage 25 percent. Advertising may have brought in around $35,000 more than the year before, but costs shot up by $84,000.[13]

While those both sound like small sums in light of the magazine's annual expenses, which amounted to more than $2 million, it meant that *National Review* was falling further and further behind every year and that ad sales weren't closing the gap. Nor were subscriptions. From a high of 128,154 in the first half of 1969, paid subscriptions steadily eroded, bottoming out at 85,894 at the end of the 1970s, a loss of 33 percent. Buckley calculated that were the magazine to raise its annual subscription rate from $12 to $18, *National Review* could dig itself out of the red. But not only did that risk the loss of more subscriptions, it would put the magazine out of reach of the people Buckley most wanted to reach: the curious but unconverted. By raising the price, "we would lose the student, the mildly inquisitive professor, the slightly disturbed minister; who begin to wonder whether, after all, there is a case to be made for the ancient traditions, for the old values" but who were not ready to invest so much in "a magazine whose political faith they are interested to learn something about but which they do not wish to iden-tify themselves with. Yet." Keeping them meant keeping rates competitive, which meant hefty annual losses. It was a tough time to run a lively little journal of opinion.[14]

National Review also suffered from a vision problem. In the early 1970s longtime devotees were letting their subscriptions lapse. One, Robert T. Jones, wrote to explain that in addition to delivery problems, the magazine simply wasn't up to its old standards. Jones admitted it might just be his own changing tastes, but he had come to feel that "the content of *National Review*, which had once seemed to me to be fresh, superb, and wholly right, often now seems a bit querulous and puerile, not to say tired."[15] Rusher took these comments to heart, in no small part because he agreed. The magazine had lost its spark. One only needed to look at circulation and newsstand sales to see something was off. Maybe it wasn't the editors' fault. Maybe, Rusher mused, "*National Review's* present condition is simply a synecdo-che of the present condition of American conservatism as a whole. In the late 1950's conservatism had just about all the aspects of a Cause Militant. Today, thanks to events in the intervening years, it can scarcely define, let along organize, itself; its leaders, almost to a man, are compromised by their own faltering performances; and the future does not, to put it mildly, look especially inspiriting."[16]

But he couldn't let it go at that because he believed there *was* an editorial problem. The editors had lapsed into a mode of languid irony, getting their thrills from being contrarian rather than conservative: "We get our kicks, and give our readers many of *their* kicks . . . by publishing articles in support of marijuana, abortion, the 'New York Times', etc." "'Man Bites Dog,' while a notoriously good headline," he wrote, "can hardly serve as a policy—and would cease, even if it were one, to be much of a headline." What worried Rusher more was the sense that the magazine's contrarian turn came from a general satisfaction with the direction of the country in the Nixon years. If there was nothing left to criticize, then *National Review* could no longer be the disgruntled Remnant, standing athwart history yelling stop. It would have to shrug, step aside, and politely allow history to continue on its way. And that would mean it would have to become something new: "a *gruntled* journal of opinion."[17]

There was only one problem with that: conservatives in the early 1970s were decidedly *not* gruntled. They were angry and motivated. But *National Review* wasn't tapping into that populist passion. It was cut off from what Rusher called "the Washington Conservative Establishment" as well as the grassroots right. As a result, it was no longer leading. "On what subjects, in the last four years, has *National Review* clearly been the bellwether of the American conservative movement?" Rusher asked the editors in 1973. "Where does the average conservative look, today, to find out what the conservative leadership is thinking and saying and worrying about?" Not *National Review*. Then he reiterated his concerns about the magazine's direction. "We find ourselves increasingly in the position of a man looking for a dog to bite. Meanwhile, the conservative troops increasingly march off to the tunes drummed out by latecomers." If *National Review* were going to reclaim its leadership mantle, it would have to not only iron out its financial problems but regain its focus.[18]

Broadcasters faced similar challenges to bottom lines and core values. In FY 1968 the *Manion Forum* raked in $364,416 in contributions. Then the bottom fell out. FY 1969 was $100,000 lower. Three years later, unmitigated disaster: contributions came in at only $136,678. One-third the revenue, one-third the stations. And as the *Forum's* reach withered, so did its ability to draw marquee names. Far fewer members of Congress stopped by the

Forum's microphone, replaced, interestingly enough, with members of anti-communist regimes unhappy with U.S. policy and press coverage. Among them were officials from the Republic of China and the apartheid states of Namibia, South Africa, and Rhodesia, who were looking for friendly outlets in the face of growing human rights protests. Yet these international guests did not generate the same enthusiasm or sense of political influence that leading national lawmakers did.[19]

The show was in danger. The *Forum's* manager, Emmett Mellenthin, commissioned a report from Salem Kirban, a direct-mail fund-raiser who moonlighted as a popular end-times prophet. (Author of books like *666* and *I Predict*, in 1981 Kirban would launch the nation's "first toll-free prophecy hotline.") Mellenthin combed over the report, combined it with his own observations, and gave Manion a frank accounting of the problems facing the *Forum*. First there were the supporters, the wealthy businessmen and the "plain folks on pensions." Depicted as "old faithfuls" and "dyed-in-the-wool conservatives since Roosevelt," they shared a common quality: they were old—very old. "We calculate their average span to be well into the sixties with a surprising percentage in their eighties and nineties." Retirements, company mergers, and above all death were thinning their ranks.[20]

Replacing them, though, was no easy task. Times had changed, and the old fund-raising methods weren't working. Companies once helmed by a single owner were now controlled by boards staffed with a new generation of businessmen. These new board members, Mellenthin lamented, "just don't 'dig' the Conservative slogans, clichés and code words that we are all prone to use." What did convince them were numbers. And not the sort of numbers the *Forum* liked to throw around—number of stations, number of supporters, number of years on air. They wanted the kind of media data that had come into common use: the size of the audience, their demographic makeup, and "concrete proof that we're getting our money's worth in reaching the unwashed"—that is, making converts rather than simply preaching to the committed. But the *Forum* didn't collect those kinds of numbers, and even if it did, the data would almost certainly work against the program's interest in retaining corporate donations.[21]

So corporate donations were not going to keep the *Forum* afloat. What they needed was a new generation of individual contributors to replace the rapidly diminishing number of pensioners. Here Mellenthin believed the *Forum* could successfully harness innovations in direct mail. For fifteen years the *Forum* had relied on internal mailing lists, pieced together by

Leo Reardon when he came over to the *Forum* from *Human Events*. No longer—"brokers now have millions of Conservative-oriented individuals cross-indexed every which-way on computers." Convincing those cross-indexed conservatives to support the *Forum* would require more than simply touting its on-air presence (the general boast the *Forum* used to sell itself to donors). "What we need then is a POSITIVE, exciting story to sell." And not just one story. With social issues increasingly provoking evangelicals, who were still a decade out from effective organization in the Moral Majority and Christian Voice, Mellenthin agreed with Kirban that the *Forum* had to develop both secular and religious appeals. This targeted approach reflected his understanding that the conservative movement was not an integrated whole but rather the fusion of two still-disparate strains. "The church-tax issue," he noted, "provides an emotional gimmick to comb suitable available lists for new support," but he added parenthetically that it would appeal little to their supporters in business and industry.[22]

All this analysis of audience and donors was just a prelude to what both Kirban and Mellenthin saw as the real problem with the *Forum*. Punchy sales pitches, gimmicky pamphlets, vervy language—none of it mattered if people turned on the *Forum* and then turned it back off five minutes later because they were bored. The *Forum* wasn't losing stations and listeners just because of an aging supporter base. It was losing them because, one, "some of the programs can only be described as 'dull,'" and, two, "WE ARE FOLLOWING, NOT LEADING." The tone of the memo suggests these tensions had been brewing behind the scenes for some time and that the staff, bolstered by Kirban's analysis, had finally summoned the courage to confront the issue. Mellenthin even confessed that the staff brainstormed guest ideas every day for two weeks, generating an excellent list, but they were too reticent to pass it to Manion. Now that they were willing to deliver it, the message was clear: we can't afford to have any more boring guests. "The damage to our image is too great and we can no longer tolerate loss of stations." He hastened to assure Manion this didn't mean getting rid of all the "old 'war horses,'" but it did mean delving into the right's rapidly expanding talent pool. It meant, in other words, adapting to a conservative movement that was very different from the one Manion had helped build in the early 1950s.[23]

Retooling the program would take some time, and in the interim, addressing the *Forum*'s financial problems required some creative thinking. One problem facing the *Forum*: while Manion had the support of a number of businessmen, it was increasingly difficult to attract corporate donations because the *Forum* lacked tax deductibility. Enter the Sino-American Amity Fund. The scheme worked like this. The fund loaned the *Forum* $25,000. Donors would send the *Forum* contributions made out to the Sino-American Amity Fund, which the *Forum* would use to pay back the loan. Donors would get tax-deductibility—something boards increasingly required for corporate donations—and Manion would get the money. Manion laid this out in personal letters to donors who inquired, noting, "For obvious reasons, we cannot put this information in a general letter." Tax shelters, after all, were best handled on the sly.[24]

This funding scheme, started in the late 1960s, wasn't enough to save the *Forum* from its financial freefall. In the mid-1970s, Manion turned to Eberle & Associates, the direct-mail firm that made its name fund-raising for Reagan in 1976. Dan Manion (Clarence's son) and Bruce Eberle were friends, making it a natural partnership. And a necessary one: by the time Manion hired Eberle, the *Forum* was in triage mode. Only 120 stations carried the program (with only 17 airing the shorter *Footnotes*). A contributor file of 3,500 donors supported the program, and the Eberle audit showed that 90 percent of those were over sixty years old. The steady march of time meant the file was "rapidly diminishing in number." But this information did little to turn things around. Soon the *Forum* was falling behind on its payments to Eberle & Associates, and in early 1979 Eberle terminated the relationship, gently suggesting that a smaller firm would better suit the *Forum's* needs. By the end of the 1970s the first generation of media activists was failing, unmoored from their clear ideological vision and unable to stay afloat financially.[25]

In 1975, Rusher was adrift. Nixon had resigned, Ford was a placeholder. Scanning the horizon, he saw no reason to hope the GOP would nominate a conservative. Indeed, it seemed likely they would nominate the man who had chosen Nelson Rockefeller for his vice president. So frustrated was Rusher with the Nixon compromise and the coming Ford compromise that he shot off a peeved letter to Bill Rickenbacker declaring that if forced to choose between Ford and a liberal Democrat, he would vote for George Wallace.[26]

The letter signaled a sharp break from Rusher's previous position—he had opposed Wallace as a spoiler in the past—but time had changed him. Seeing the post-Goldwater GOP take up with Nixon then Ford, with Rockefeller waiting in the wings. . . . It was too much. "I am through compromising with liberals, even in their Republican guises," he wrote Rickenbacker. And so Wallace. "He isn't my ideal candidate; in a sense he isn't my candidate at all; but he *is* the candidate of the social conservatives and conservative Democrats of this country." If the GOP couldn't come up with someone better, then a vote for Wallace it would be. Although there was another option, one the right had toyed with before. What if instead of Wallace conservatives put together their own ticket? What if they left the Republicans and Democrats behind once and for all? That was the scenario Rusher explored in 1975 when he organized a third-party ticket for the 1976 election.[27]

In the 1970s, Rusher came into his own, developing an identity distinct from *National Review*'s. His syndicated column, television show, and frequent appearances on CBS news programs gave him a fame that, while not equal to Buckley's, went far beyond what he had experienced in the 1950s and 1960s. With that freer rein, Rusher threw himself into a new effort: *The Making of the New Majority Party*. The book, a lean 162 pages of closely set type, first detailed America's party history (including "Nixon's betrayal of conservatives") and then laid out the strategy for building a new national party. He drafted the manuscript in the last two and half months of 1974, quickly revising it on a trip to Asia in January. It was at the printers by the first of March 1975. Rusher was in a hurry. The 1976 elections were looming, and he wanted to ensure he would be a major player in any third-party discussions. The normally fastidious Rusher told Tom Winter at *Human Events* that he would rather the book be a bit rough and on the shelves by May than be polished and delayed until September. His thoughts on subjects like abortion and tax reform could, he admitted, be hashed out more, but "the sheer existence of the book, and its availability to the conservative movement at the earliest possible date, is far more important." As a media activist he still clung fast to the belief that publishing preceded party politics.[28]

In the buildup to the book's publication, Rusher began organizing conservatives around his new party hopes. In February 1975, at the third annual CPAC organized by the ACU and YAF, Rusher led the formation of the Committee for Conservative Alternatives. Headed by Senator Jesse Helms, the committee also included Republican representatives John Ashbrook and Robert Bauman, as well as Rusher, Stan Evans, Phyllis Schlafly, and Tom Winter. The resolution that formed the committee charged both parties with failing to represent the country's conservative majority: "The question of our allegiance to those political parties is a matter of increasing doubt to conservatives." Which is not to say everyone was on board with the new party idea. Bauman was explicitly against it, and Reagan urged the conference to unite behind the Republican Party. Helms offered more of a middle road: conservatives should call a convention, and if neither party backed the right's political platform, then the framework for a new conservative party would be ready to go. (Helms's support was short-lived: at the Republican Convention a few months later he openly rejected the idea of a third party.)[29]

Rusher and Evans both had their eye on Ronald Reagan, with whom they met several times in 1975. After a meeting that did not go their way, Evans typed up a detailed, five-page argument in favor of Reagan's third-party candidacy. Look, he explained to the former governor, unseating Ford, weak as he is, is a nonstarter. You're lagging 15 to 20 points in the polls and are even further behind in key midwestern states. And say you win the nomination—what's it even worth? The Republican brand has been blighted by Watergate, Vietnam, and inflation. Run as a Republican and you run as "the heir-apparent of both Nixon and Ford." Some prize. But imagine instead running on an independent conservative ticket. Rather than being co-opted by the tainted pragmatists of the GOP, the Reagan name would stand in opposition to the bankrupt politics of both parties. Imagine: teaming up with George Wallace on a stick-it-to-the-man ticket. Or, Evans quickly offered, sensing Reagan did not share his preference for the former Alabama governor, just getting Wallace's endorsement. "He could very plausibly say that his health does not permit him to run"—Wallace was wheelchair bound following a 1972 assassination attempt—"that the emergence of a new party under your leadership is a vindication of what he has been saying for years about the two major parties, and that his followers should vote for you." What it boils down to, Evans concluded, is that your base is conservative. Why not run on the ticket of a conservative party?[30]

Wallace, too, was an option if Reagan was unwilling to run. Rusher, who liked Wallace's strategic (rather than ideological) pragmatism, had no qualms with the governor as a candidate. Nor did a Wallace nomination bother Bill Loeb of the *Manchester Union-Leader*, who heartily endorsed the project. While Loeb admitted he was opposed to third parties in principle (his father had warned Teddy Roosevelt against splitting the GOP in 1912), he did not consider Rusher's new party to be a third party but rather a replacement for a defunct Republican Party. For his part, Loeb believed Reagan lacked the fire to lead conservatives away from the existing parties: "He's a great salesman and a great talker but the one who goes to Washington has to be a tough S.O.B." And who was a tougher S.O.B. than George Wallace?[31]

Rusher understood the limitations of each man as a movement leader: "Reagan and Wallace probably both represent, in their respective ways, political dead ends for the expression of American conservative thought: the one too soft and genial, and the other too Southern, parochial, etc." After seeing both of them stumble year after year, he predicted that "this will be the last year for both of them on the national political scene." Yet there was something exciting about that as well. Someone new would rise up to replace them, and if that new someone hailed from the Sunbelt and appeared "young, good-looking, and articulate," well, watch out. He could be "the new master of us all." And when he appeared, Rusher wanted to be ready for him.[32]

The CPAC meeting fed into work Rusher was already doing to try to get his third party on the ballot in a number of states as part of his Committee for the New Majority. The problem was that getting a new party onto state ballots was a cumbersome, expensive affair. (In 1968 George Wallace shelled out $1.3 million just to get on the California ballot.) But Rusher cared more about a new majority than a new party, and there were plenty of extant third parties that the conservative majority could pour itself into. In particular, both the American Party and the American Independent Party had strong conservative bona fides and, more important, had already secured ballot placement.

The American Party was formed in 1956 under the guidance of Clarence Manion, intended to be a vehicle for former taxman T. Coleman Andrews. It had since come under the control of Tom Anderson, the proudly segregationist media personality who penned the "Straight Talk" column and voiced its associated radio show. Anderson ran as vice president on the party's 1972 ticket, pulling about a million votes along with his running mate, John G. Schmitz. But Anderson presented a real problem for Rusher, who worried about the party being perceived as the storehouse for crackpots and kooks. Anderson effectively blocked Wallace's hopes for an American Party nomination by moving the convention to June, a month before the Democratic National Convention. Wallace couldn't make a play for the American Party nomination because he needed to stay in the Democrats' good graces in order to play a role at *their* convention. In thwarting Wallace, Anderson won the open support of Willis Carto, the editor and publisher who had turned the *American Mercury* from a conservative magazine into an anti-Semitic rag. By the 1970s Carto was running Noontide Press, a leading publisher of anti-Semitic and Holocaust denial literature. Anderson and Carto, then, had become the face of the American Party. These were not the sorts of people Rusher wanted to be involved with.[33]

Fortunately a good chunk of the American Party didn't want to be involved with them either. In mid-January 1976, a majority of the American Party's state organizations seceded. They signaled their support of Wallace and his American Independent Party by naming their offshoot the American Independence Party. This, in Rusher's estimation, "largely (I would not say entirely) sanitized them on the subject of kookery," and he believed the remaining stains could be removed by pledging to support the American Independent Party nominee and allying with Rusher's Committee for the New Majority. To sell the splinter group on this plan, Rusher flew to Chicago to persuade them that he was, in fact, "a true-blue conservative." It was a somewhat distasteful task, he explained to Buckley: "I found myself in the unfamiliar and not terribly appealing position of having to 'prove' my own conservatism and 'justify' my association with you and other dangerous left-ists." But this he did, and the two AIPs came into alignment.[34]

Buckley was skeptical of the whole project. Not the book—he had read a draft of it and was generally favorable toward it. While he seemed unpersuaded of the feasibility of the actual party—"I think [the book] lacks a sense of having annihilated the Republican Party, and lacks also a description of the catalyst that could bring the new party into being"—he nonetheless approved of the effort. But he was concerned Rusher was falling in with a bad crowd. When planning his new majority party, Rusher understood the dangers of a takeover by conservatives well to his right, those Buckley had classified as "the irresponsible right." His concerns shaped his tactical approach to running a third-party candidate in 1976. Rather than rely exclusively on state parties, he recommended the designation of inde- pendent electors in any state where "extremists" could take over the state party organization. This, he explained in an attempt to assuage Buckley's concerns, would ensure the movement was a legitimate force for respon- sible conservatism. Yet as Rusher became more involved in the effort and started consorting with activists to the right of Buckley's sharply defined Responsibles, the relationship started to strain.[35]

Nor was the new party effort the only thing estranging the two Bills. Buckley and Rusher were also at loggerheads over George Will, who had been hired on as *National Review*'s Washington editor at the same time that he became the conservative columnist for the *Washington Post*. The issue: Rusher had serious doubts about Will's conservatism. Nor was he the only one. Stan Evans met Will in 1972 on a television panel show and quickly concluded he was not a conservative—in fact, he was something far more insidious. "What I recollect most vividly," he told a friend a few years later, "was his penchant for dressing up liberal policy stands in conservative-sounding rhetoric." Little wonder the folks at the *Washington Post* liked him. *National Review's* fascination with Will, however, Evans found "considerably more puzzling."[36]

Rusher was unrelenting on the subject. He considered Will's attacks on Agnew to be beyond the pale. He allowed that Will could, of course, criticize the vice president. "But the kind of tendentious and absolutely unnecessary savaging that he has been giving Agnew in his recent columns, both in National Review and in the 'Washington Post', is something else again." Even his attempts to compliment Will were immediately corrupted by his dislike for the writer. "I acknowledge that much of his writing is sinewy and provocative," he told the editors, before immediately switching back: "(Much of it is all rather bitchy and, as just noted, not a little shrill; but we all have our idiosyncrasies.)" His antipathy even led him to defend Nixon. After Will penned a particularly aggressive column about the president, Rusher warned the editors that Will "is taking us into war with Nixon just as surely as Johnson took us into war with North Vietnam—in both cases, without the benefit of an official declaration by those empowered to do the official declaring." By the end of 1974, Rusher was formally asking the editors to consider Will "be asked to seek his fortune elsewhere."[37]

Both his new party activism and anti-Will lobbying made clear the differences between Rusher and Buckley. If Buckley was obsessed with respectability, Rusher was obsessed with authenticity. Just as he had insisted that *National Review* attend to the "simplistic right" during the Birch Society dust-up in the mid-1960s, in the mid-1970s he located the movement's heart not in Washington or the establishment but in populist activists. Rusher's divergent understanding of the movement strained his bond with Buckley, cooling a relationship that had never been particularly warm. (Buckley and Rusher genuinely respected one another, but they never developed an intimate friendship.)

The developing breach was healed thanks to a bit of personal pragmatism on Rusher's end. In March 1976 he stepped down as head of the Committee for the New Majority. His weekly column was an important source of influence and income, and his syndicate had begun to grow nervous over his joint role as journalist and political organizer. While he remained involved behind the scenes, hoping to steer the party's selection of a nominee, his association with the party faded. As did the party itself—it had no impact on the 1976 campaign. Nor did Reagan. His attempt to snatch the Republican nomination away from Ford failed, and Ford went on to lose the general election. The entire episode left Rusher frustrated with the former governor. After Reagan lost, albeit narrowly, primaries in New Hampshire and Florida, Rusher called his bid for the nomination "a serious mistake." Moreover, he felt it had been "a near-fatal drain" on the new party effort.[38]

Once his initial frustrations with the 1976 race burned off, Rusher came to see the election in a more favorable light. In the summer of 1977, he penned a column looking back at the failed campaign for a new majority party. "America's conservative majority had—and blew—a spectacular chance," Rusher began sourly. They blew it because conservatives rededicated themselves to the two major parties: Reagan made a run for the Republican nomination, and Jimmy Carter—understood (rightly) in the 1970s as a centrist rather than a liberal—made Democratic conservatives more comfortable with their party than McGovern had. Yet all this led Rusher to hold out hope. Conservatives controlled the GOP, and they now had a chance to win over the Democrats: "Carter in particular, while not as conservative as (say) Reagan, is clearly open to conservative influence and has among his closest friends and highest appointees men who are conservative by any fair definition." Indeed, Carter's election demonstrated that the right had to change, not by giving up its principles but by abandoning a reflexive opposition to the Democratic Party. If conservatives understood Democrats only as "the Enemy," they would miss a vital opportunity. "If Democratic administrations of the Carter type are inevitable, and for the foreseeable future they seem to be, then at least a portion of America's conservative activists ought to be on the inside, looking out, instead of on the outside, looking in."[39]

"On the outside, looking in." No phrase better described Regnery in the 1970s. While Rusher was experimenting with third-party politics Henry Regnery was desperately seeking a way back into the book business. Throughout the mid-1970s he deluged former supporters with business plans and fund-raising letters, detailing his scheme to start a new conservative publishing house to replace the company that bore his name. It was a tough sell. In its first iteration the firm took twelve years to turn a profit and even then never very much of one. Meanwhile, conservative media everywhere were struggling. And Regnery was asking for a lot of money. He estimated it would take half a million dollars to relaunch the company. Regnery planned to kick in $300,000 of his own money but would need to raise the rest from investors.[40]

Another complication for fund-raising was Regnery's age. It was one thing to invest in the Regnery of 1947, a young man in his mid-thirties with the time to build and cultivate a new company. It was quite another to fund the project thirty years later, when Regnery was sixty-five and, despite his considerable skills, had already lost the business once. Aware of this dynamic, Regnery brought aboard Bruce Fingerhut. Not only did Fingerhut have experience in the industry—he worked as an editor at Notre Dame Press—but he also had the right ideological bona fides: he received a Weaver Fellowship from ISI and was a graduate student of Gerhart Niemeyer, the anticommunist and traditionalist conservative who had served as Barry Goldwater's foreign policy adviser during the 1964 campaign. In proposing the new company, Regnery assured his backers that Fingerhut had the "experience, talent and energy to do the work." Regnery would assume the position of president, while Fingerhut would serve as vice president and editor in chief.[41]

So much for practical matters. Regnery also had a philosophical argument to make for his new company. "What Eliseo Vivas calls 'the sustaining intellectual and moral structures of civilization' must be interpreted anew to each generation and were never in greater danger than now," he wrote in his 1976 proposal for his new publishing firm. Liberals, he argued, still controlled the institutions that disseminated ideas and shaped public opinion: the schools, the media, the publishing industry. And the people who controlled those institutions controlled the culture. For Regnery, the liberal domination of cultural institutions—especially the media—explained so much: the corruption of Watergate, the unchecked growth of government, the permissive court decisions on issues like integration, criminal rights, and pornography. If conservatives wanted a better America, they would have to invest in better media. And not just any media. "However great the influence of mass newspapers, of TV and radio may be," he wrote, "it is still ideas that run the world, and it is finally books, and not necessarily the most popular, that put ideas into circulation." Regnery had once wielded that influence; he was desperate to wield it again.[42]

"The destruction of my old firm and all that I tried to make it stand for was a difficult and disheartening experience for me," Regnery confided to Robert Welch in 1978. But publishing was in his blood—it was all he had ever known—and so he began again. This time, he reasoned, it would be easier. He had his old backlist of conservative books, as well as name recognition and years of experience. What he didn't have, at least not at first, was the right to use the name Regnery. After extensive negotiations, Regnery and Plotnick struck a deal. Plotnick would publish as Contemporary Books, and Regnery would take back the Regnery name.[43]

Regnery also wrangled from Plotnick publishing rights to the Gateway series, a set of paperback classics marketed to colleges and universities, and to many of the conservative books initially published by Regnery in the 1950s and 1960s. This was quite a get: the Gateway books would provide a steady income (about $95,000 a year) and the conservative books would reaffirm the new company's ideological identity. Regnery planned to republish now classic books like Buckley's *God and Man at Yale* and Kirk's *The Conservative Mind*, introducing a new generation of conservatives to these foundational texts. But the first purpose of the reborn Regnery was to publish new conservative books. Kirk had a new manuscript ready to go, as did Ephraim Sevela, a Russian filmmaker looking to publish his controversial critique of Israel. The first big splash from the new firm, though, echoed back to the early days when Regnery was just starting out. In 1978, Regnery released *Harvard Hates America* by John LeBoutillier, a sharp-tongued, charismatic New Yorker fresh out of Harvard undergrad. LeBoutillier was on the Buckley track: well moneyed, politically engaged, irreverent and rebellious. (Buckley was unimpressed with the book, which he found "badly written and pompous.") *Harvard* did relatively well, selling some 14,000 copies in the first year. It seemed possible that the second incarnation of Regnery Publishing might just make it.[44]

First, though, there would need to be some staffing changes. Hiring Fingerhut proved to be a miscalculation. As good as he looked on paper, he was, in Regnery's words, "utterly irresponsible." Regnery fired him at the end of 1978 and replaced him with Henry F. Regnery, his second son. Henry had joined the company when it relaunched and quickly demonstrated both the pragmatism and passion the firm needed. He threw himself into the work, hiring a young, committed staff and dedicating himself to learning the ins and outs of the industry.[45]

Then: tragedy. Six months after Fingerhut's dismissal, Henry and Dennis

Connell, the company's sales manager, boarded a flight to Los Angeles for the American Book Sellers Convention. As the DC-10 reached takeoff speed, the left engine-pylon assembly failed, smashing into the wing slats before landing on the runway. The plane mounted three hundred feet before rolling sideways and slamming into a nearby field. Its full fuel tanks ignited on impact. All 271 people aboard, as well as two on the ground, were killed instantly. It was the deadliest airline accident in American history.[46]

The Regnerys were devastated. The personal tragedy overshadowed everything else, but after a few months it became clear that Henry's death had serious consequences for the business as well. His passion had reenergized the staff, and his death, Regnery reported, "left the firm in a completely demoralized state." Suffering from heart problems, Regnery couldn't take over the business. The succession of young men he brought in to run it foundered as Fingerhut had. As conservatism flourished in the 1980s, Regnery Publishing struggled to capitalize on an opportune moment to expand the right-wing book market.[47]

As did his competitors. In the late 1960s Arlington was acquired by Computer Applications, which then sold it to Starr Broadcasting, a company chaired by Buckley. It continued to publish conservative books throughout the 1970s, though its founder, Neil McCaffrey, became increasingly interested in books devoted to music and film. By the end of the decade Arlington had mostly ceased to publish right-wing books. In 1979 it was acquired by Shamrock Broadcasting, and in 1982 it was sold again, this time to Outlet Books. Buckley generously attributed the company's failure to the movement's success. Arlington, he wrote, "suffered finally from the success of the fight it waged: conservatism became increasingly acceptable and other publishers, better capitalized, were willing to take on authors up until then tolerated only by Arlington House and of course, pre-eminently, the Regnery Company."[48]

Notably absent from Buckley's recollection was Devin-Adair, Devin Garrity's company that had been the premier publisher of conservative books in the 1950s. Devin-Adair continued to put out important right-wing books in the 1960s, including Stan Evans's *The Liberal Establishment* and Ronald Reagan's *The Creative Society*. Buckley's omission of Garrity was a matter of both personality and politics. Garrity lacked Regnery's gentleness and generosity; like McCaffrey he perceived slights readily and clung to the grudges they generated. There was also a whiff of bad business dealings around him. When Regnery floated to Bill Rickenbacker the idea of merging with Devin-

Adair in 1979, Rickenbacker warned, "Be careful with Devin Garrity. I've heard he drives a hard bargain."[49]

Garrity toyed with a number of ideas to shore up his company during the 1970s. In 1971, he started the Veritas Book Club to compete with the Conservative Book Club. Having turned sixty-five in 1970, Garrity also began looking for his successor. He intended to train his son-in-law Alan Cross in the business, knowing that he "shared my political and economic views." Cross joined the company in 1976 as general manager, following an attempted takeover of the firm (a "palace revolution," Garrity called it) by parties who wanted to "change the image" of the publisher. Cross, however, struggled with alcoholism and within a year had left the business to pursue treatment. When Devin Garrity died in 1981, Cross returned as general manager. The company, though, was not on solid footing, and appeals to keep it running found no takers.[50]

For the *Manion Forum*, the next generation seemed well in hand. Two of Manion's children, Dan and Marilyn, had been involved in the movement as officers in Young Americans for Freedom (Marilyn as secretary and Dan as a director). They also labored for the *Forum*. For years Marilyn provided administrative services, coordinated the Conservative Clubs, and penned the *Forum*'s monthly newsletter. She occasionally advised Manion on responses to letter writers, as when one anxious listener asked advice on Goldwater in 1964, concerned that the senator was a "Trojan Horse" and secret liberal. "Daddy," she wrote in the margins of the listener's letter, "I would say to him that Goldwater most nearly represents the philosophy you hold—that he is not of course perfect—that besides, no two Conservatives think exactly alike and therefore you could never please all of us 100%." She even occasionally conducted on-air interviews, functioning as the *Forum*'s "youth voice." After postponing her wedding for a year in order to work for her father's program, she finally left in mid-1966 to join her new husband in Chicago. From there she continued to write Manion's newspaper column and the *Forum*'s newsletter.[51]

In 1972 Dan joined the board of trustees, overseeing the *Forum*'s fund-raising efforts, particularly its forays into direct mail. Like his sister, he also conducted a number of on-air interviews. He left in 1978 to run for state senate, a seat he held until 1982. Dan Manion would make national headlines in 1986 with his contentious nomination to the federal bench. He was pilloried in the press as incompetent and intemperate, a mediocre lawyer and a hot-headed ideologue. As proof, Democrats pointed to error-ridden court briefs and to his request that schools post the Ten Commandments after the Supreme Court had ruled such displays unconstitutional. He became a lightning-rod for liberal opposition to Reagan. "Our highest courts deserve first-rate judges," one anti-Manion advertisement declared, "not second-rate extremists." It was a trial run for the Robert Bork nomination battle the next year, with one major difference—Dan Manion won appointment to the federal bench.[52]

The Manion children—including Chris, a younger son—were not the only ones supplying interviews for the *Forum*. Clarence Manion, who turned eighty in 1976, increasingly turned his microphone over to others throughout the 1970s, most notably Fr. Daniel Lyons and Captain Frank A. Manson. A Jesuit priest, Lyons made frequent appearances on the *Forum* and had a close professional relationship with Manion. And then the scandal. In 1975, Lyons left the priesthood in order to marry Mary Cooney, a twenty-three-year-old Irish singer. The decision ended Lyons's value to the conservative cause, Fred Schlafly told Manion. "I think his usefulness has been destroyed," Schlafly wrote, before musing, "but maybe in this liberal era he is more acceptable to audiences than if he were still a Jesuit Priest." Discarded by the more mainstream conservative media outlets, Lyons became the editor of Billy James Hargis's *Christian Crusade*. Manson then took on a much larger role. A navy captain and historian who served as a speechwriter for a number of admirals, Manson had a way with words. He was also a committed conservative, emerging in the late 1970s as a leading opponent of the drive to return the Panama Canal to Panamanian control. Manson conducted his first interview for the *Forum* in August 1977 and over the next two years appeared forty-eight times. He was on the program as much as Manion himself, a clear signal that the show was beginning to morph into something new.[53]

The sudden death of a key *Forum* staffer in mid-1979 threw the program into chaos. Emmett Mellenthin had been with the *Forum* for its entire twenty-five-year run. As managing director, he had been vital to keeping the show on air. Bookkeeping, talent booking, sound engineering, donor relations: Mellenthin did it all. When he died, the *Forum* went dark. For three weeks, no new programs aired as the team scrambled to find someone to replace him. When Manion returned to the air in July, he was in a nostalgic mood. Rather than discuss current events, he retold the story of the *Forum*:

how, a quarter-century earlier, he had been appointed to the Eisenhower administration, how he had fought with Ike over the Bricker Amendment, how he had chosen principles over power. It was a well-rehearsed narrative, the founding mythology of the program. The occasion of Mellenthin's death led Manion to ruminate on first things, not only for the program but for the nation (two events tightly intertwined in Manion's mind). He told of Washington crossing the Delaware, of the "long painful" fight for independence that the *Forum* continued to wage. "From the time of its inception, the basic purpose of the Manion Forum has been to promote a popular, activated understanding of what the immortal language of our Declaration of Independence means." That was a cause to which he continued to dedicate himself. "You will hear more of my reasons why," he said as the program ended, "in future Manion Forum broadcasts."[54]

It was his last broadcast. On July 14, six days after the Mellenthin broadcast aired, Manion suffered a stroke. He died two weeks later.

Manion's funeral took place at his parish church in South Bend, Indiana, which he and his wife, Gina, an Arabian horse breeder, had attended for forty years. The hot July day was punctuated with strains of "America the Beautiful" and "God Bless America," a blending of the religion and nationalism that were the warp and woof of Manion's conservatism. In the closing line of his final *Footnote* broadcast he had reiterated just that point: "Regardless of its civil code of laws, a society that is not held together consciously by its teaching and observance of the laws of Almighty God is unfit for human habitation and doomed to destroy itself." In a year when the Moral Majority and the Christian Voice were emerging as major political players, it was an argument both modern in sentiment and quaint in expression.[55]

The decision of whether to continue the *Forum* fell to the Manion children. Dan and his younger brother Chris brainstormed ways to keep it going, but money proved to be the sticking point. One major donor made his funds contingent on Chris devoting himself full-time to the *Forum*, which the family discouraged. Finally they decided to end the program. Dan explained the decision in a final address, which aired on August 19, 1979. "Sometimes shoes are hard to fill, and often footsteps are tough to follow. But fingerprints are never duplicated," Dan told the audience. "The Manion Forum is Dad's fingerprint. It is a vast legacy through which he touched us all. The other members of the family and I choose to leave it that way—never duplicated, never smeared, but unmistakenly Dean Clarence Manion."[56]

Not every conservative media outlet was shuttering operations at the end of the 1970s. But as the New Right, the religious right, and the Reaganites were gathering steam, conservative media were losing it—crippled by shrinking budgets, tragic losses, and a sense of aimlessness. A conservative resurgence was coming, but they would not be at its helm. For the generation of conservative media activists who had built the movement, it seemed the time for media leadership was over.

Chapter 12

The Comeback

"Let me now simply and briefly do what I came here to do tonight, and that is, as President of the United States, to salute the editors, associates, and friends of *National Review*."

Ronald Reagan, bedecked in black tie, stood before one of the friendliest crowds he would encounter in his eight years in office. It was *National Review*'s thirtieth anniversary, and Reagan was eager to fete the magazine that had been so important to his own rise to power. "The man standing before you was a Democrat when he picked up his first issue in a plain brown wrapper," Reagan reminisced, joking about the magazine's risqué nature in an era of liberal dominance.[1]

But oh, how times had changed. "*National Review* is to the offices of the West Wing of the White House what *People* magazine is to your dentist's waiting room," he told the crowd. Nor was *National Review* the only new reading material in the West Wing since Reagan took office. Twenty-four copies of *Human Events*—"the President's favorite newspaper"—were delivered to the White House every week. During the 1980 campaign, Reagan had made clear the paper's influential role: "Not a week goes by during my campaign that I don't make time to read *Human Events* from cover to cover."[2]

Everywhere one looked in the 1980s, conservatism was on the rise. Reagan won back-to-back landslides and Republicans retained control of the Senate three elections in a row, something they hadn't done since Herbert Hoover was in the White House. It was a boon for conservative media, too— sort of. The Reagan Revolution brought fifteen thousand new subscribers to

National Review ("obviously because a number of the opportunists in that Establishment crowd think it advisable to have *National Review* on their coffee tables now," Bill Rusher observed). It was not nearly enough to make the magazine profitable, but it was a reversal of the steady decline of the 1970s. Regnery was selling more books—also not enough, but more. Yet it was all a far cry from the early days, when conservative media activism was vital to conservative electoral success, when the two seemed to rise and fall together.[3]

Which leaves us with an unresolved and vitally important question: Why did the political movement attain its greatest success at the very moment conservative media was in decline? As Ronald Reagan entered the White House, *Human Events* and *National Review* were struggling to stay afloat, Devin-Adair and Regnery were on the verge of dissolution, and the *Manion Forum* and *Dan Smoot Report* were permanently off-air. The next generation of media activists would not appear until Reagan's final days in office. So what did it mean that media activism was at its nadir while Reagan governed? And when the next generation finally emerged, what effect would it have on conservative politics in the post-Reagan era?

"We are coming, particularly if Reagan is elected, to a time when it will be appropriate to look back on and sum up some of the real and important accomplishments of modern American conservatism," Jameson C. Campaigne, the conservative editor of the *New York Daily News*, wrote a few months before the 1980 election. There was a tinge of nostalgia to his words even then, on the eve of the movement's most important political victory. Bill Rusher's sentimentality about Reagan's election was even more pronounced eight years later when the Reagan administration—and Rusher's tenure at *National Review*—was coming to a close: "With Ronald Reagan's election as president I felt that the curtain had come down on a long and extremely successful play in which I had been privileged to have a modest part."[4]

Throughout the movement, activists greeted the 1980 election as both a victory and a valedictory. A week before Election Day Robert Heckman, the executive director of YAF, declared conservatives were entering "the 'post Reagan' phase of our movement." Reagan had joined the YAF board in 1962, and in the years that followed—from his "Time for Choosing" speech in 1964 to his years as governor of California to his presidential campaign in 1976—he was "our chief spokesman and most prominent political personality." But no more. However the election turned out, Reagan would no longer represent the movement's future.[5]

These responses to Reagan's coming victory indicated just how tightly linked he was to the conservative movement—and why he was less dependent on media activism in 1980 than Goldwater had been in 1964. Reagan had proven his bona fides over the preceding twenty years, winning support from a range of conservative media, organizations, and institutions. Throughout the 1960s and 1970s, media activists had held him up as their political beau ideal. Though they may have wavered at times on the question of his electability—witness Bill Buckley during his Nixon phase in the late 1960s—his ideological credentials were never in doubt.

As president, Reagan instead had to prove himself to a new set of conservative leaders. In the absence of media leadership, other groups vied for control of the movement. The most successful of these was the New Right, represented by activists like Richard Viguerie, the direct-mail guru, Terry Dolan of the National Conservative PAC, Howard Phillips of the Conservative Caucus, and Jerry Falwell of the Moral Majority. These leaders of the New Right claimed to command millions of conservative grassroots activists in the United States, particularly the newly organized religious right.[6]

The New Right had a penchant for political purity, turning social issues like abortion and gun control into litmus tests for candidates. They specialized in the politics of opposition, which quickly put them in a tough spot vis-à-vis Reagan. Reagan was tied to the old conservative movement, the one the New Right had little control over, and as such Viguerie and his compatriots sought to mark their territory by outflanking Reagan from the right. In the 1980 Republican primaries, the New Right backed not Reagan but Republican congressman Phil Crane, then former Texas governor John Connally, before finally coming into the Reagan camp for the general election.

Reagan's election seemed to provide little succor to New Right leaders. They constantly lashed his right flank, landing their first blows before he was even sworn into office. No sooner had Reagan won the presidency than New Right leaders began engaging in displays of public hand-wringing over his appointments. And it was Viguerie who, three weeks after Inauguration Day, lamented to the press: "Most of us expected to be disappointed and get the short end of the stick. But I didn't know it would be this short."[7]

Reliable Reagan critics, the New Right gained plenty of attention from the mainstream press. They found fewer friends in conservative media. In a column reprinted in *Human Events*, Rusher delivered what amounted to an eight-hundred-word eye-roll over the New Right. Though reluctant to turn a family feud into a public squabble, Rusher wrote, he nonetheless had to object "to a handful of dissident conservatives making a cottage industry out of criticizing Ronald Reagan and then peddling their work-product to avid buyers in the liberal media." How easy they made it for the mainstream press to bash Reagan! With both left-wing and right-wing dissenters lined up to criticize the administration, the media could regularly attack the president while still maintaining the appearance of even-handedness. Meanwhile, Rusher lamented, pro-Reagan conservatives went unrepresented.[8]

Much of the *National Review* staff viewed the New Right leaders as Johnnies-come-lately to the movement, demanding rigorous fealty to social issues that had only recently become the drivers of politics. Thus while the New Right and fellow travelers like Pat Buchanan threw a spectacular fit over the nomination of Sandra Day O'Connor (whom they believed was insufficiently anti-abortion), *National Review* provided cover for the Reagan administration. The debate revolved around a handful of abortion-related votes O'Connor cast in the early 1970s. For the New Right, these were deal breakers. Viguerie saw no room for debate: "Mrs. O'Connor's record on abortion is unequivocal: She has actively favored it." Buchanan called the nomination "a political tragedy of the first order," leaving the anti-abortion movement "no choice but to depart, temporarily and perhaps permanently, from the President's coalition."[9]

The tone was quite different at *National Review*. Observing that "abortion was not a sundering issue in the early 1970s" when O'Connor handed down her rulings, the editors shrugged that people were known to change their minds, and at any rate "the conservative movement is not synonymous with the anti-abortion movement." All told, "we see nothing to move us into the opposition." After O'Connor's first year on the Court, they felt vindicated in their judgment, praising her support of the death penalty and noting she "is also emerging as the states' rights champion on the Supreme Court."[10]

Reagan's impeccable credentials made it difficult for even these new conservative leaders to open up lines of attack against administration apostasies. In pushing back against the O'Connor nomination, the New Right and anti-abortion activists were careful not to aim their arrows directly at the president. Buchanan's response was typical (and ironic for a former presidential aide): blame the staff. The snubbing of social conservatives was "so alien to what is known of Ronald Reagan," Buchanan wrote, "the question must be raised. Was the President misled about Ms. O'Connor's record? Misled by the Department of Justice, by the White House Staff, or by Judge O'Connor herself?" Viguerie echoed the charge: "The President has been poorly served by members of his staff responsible for the appointment."[11]

Ultimately foreign policy would unite the New Right and conservative media activists, while demonstrating the limits of both. With the rise to power of Mikhail Gorbachev, the Cold War abruptly switched from deep freeze to rapid thaw. In response, the Reagan administration shifted from the hard-line "evil empire" posturing of the first term to the politics of détente. Conservative hawks, who had seen their numbers swell with the rise of neoconservatism in the 1970s, were stunned by Reagan's about-face. Now recognized by most historians as a pivotal policy choice that helped draw the Cold War to a peaceful end, at the time conservatives saw Reagan's moderation as a mystifying betrayal.[12]

In 1987, a proposed arms-control treaty became a lightning rod for conservative anger over the Cold War thaw. In response, Reagan suggested that the right opposed the treaty because they believed Soviet-American relations could only be resolved through armed conflict, not negotiations. Stung by the accusation that they were warmongers, conservative leaders struck back with a mix of disbelief, anger, and sorrow: Suddenly being a hawk was a *bad* thing? *National Review* accused Reagan of dropping "a political neutron bomb, leaving the structure of the conservative movement intact but devastating its members." The New Right had even harsher words in store. "Reagan is a useful idiot for Soviet propagandists," Howard Phillips snarled. Viguerie called him "an apologist for Gorbachev." Buchanan lamented that "the Great Communicator who preached Peace Through Strength today preaches peace through parchment." Conservatives were distraught.[13]

And yet, what did their opposition amount to? They neither changed Reagan's mind nor broke with the administration. There would be no document to rival the Nixon-era suspension of support over China, no denunciation as profound as Buckley's post-Beijing declaration that "we have lost—irretrievably—any remaining sense of moral mission in the world." As the Reagan years wound to a close, conservative media had been unable to reassert leadership of the movement, and the New Right had largely lost its leading role. Far more quickly than media activists had, the New Right leaders saw funds dry up, organizations collapse, and influence wane. In the year after Reagan's reelection, Viguerie's business dropped off by 40 percent. His magazine *Conservative Digest* was no longer making a profit and would be shuttered a year later. The National Conservative PAC dissolved as well; the Moral Majority closed up shop in 1989. Only versed in the language of opposition, the New Right failed to find a way to navigate conservative success.[14]

Reagan may have governed in an era of limited media activism, but his administration helped ensure future presidents would face far different conditions. During Reagan's years in office, charges of media bias continued to gain institutional strength on the right, particularly in the proliferation of media-watchdog organizations. In 1987, Brent Bozell III founded the Media Research Center (MRC), an organization similar to Reed Irvine's Accuracy in Media, in order to "document, expose, and neutralize the liberal media." Son of first-generation media activist Brent Bozell Jr., he had been a standard-bearer for the New Right, taking over the National Conservative PAC after the death of its founder, Terry Dolan. But Bozell did not stay put for long. Resigning after less than a year at the helm of both the National Conservative PAC and the National Conservative Foundation, he quickly found success with the MRC. By 1991 the organization had 25,000 newsletter subscribers and an operating budget of $1.8 million. The red-bearded Bozell, an avid promoter of the center's work, began popping up on so many programs that one journalist dubbed him "a soundbite in search of a microphone." As he promoted the center, he also promoted balance. "There's no such thing as an objective press," he argued, echoing Fulton Lewis Jr.'s remarks a half century earlier. "You can't fault a reporter for being biased conservative or liberal. You can however fault a reporter or a media institution for not being balanced and that is the problem."[15]

Shortly after starting the MRC, Bozell reached out to Bill Rusher, asking the soon-to-retire publisher to join the organization's board. Rusher happily accepted. His decision to join the MRC coincided with his immersion in media-bias research. In 1988 he published *The Coming Battle for the Media*, which advanced the (by then unsurprising) thesis that mainstream media churned out "a steady diet of tendentious 'news' stories carefully designed to serve the political purposes of American liberalism." He argued that while journalists did not intentionally tilt the news, they inevitably brought a framework to bear on their reporting, a situation that required strong editors to rein in personal biases and ensure a "reasonably well-balanced" assortment of stories. Building on the style of conservative media criticism found in books like *The News Twisters* (1971) and *The Left-Leaning Antenna* (1971), Rusher relied on studies of media as well as anecdotal evidence of liberal bias. (Two years later, the MRC published a book in the same vein,

And That's the Way It Is(n't): A Reference Guide to Media Bias.) Widely reviewed, Rusher's book won plaudits for its seriousness and tone, but few reviewers concurred with his conclusions. Most agreed with the *St. Louis Post-Dispatch* reviewer who determined Rusher was "a calm, well-lettered ideologue . . . [whose] ideological, theoretical framework collapses upon close inspection."[16]

In the book, Rusher did more than decry media bias—he called for regulation. As a supporter of the Fairness Doctrine, he joined an eclectic group: Phyllis Schlafly, Accuracy in Media, the ACLU, the NAACP. But that group—all activists who had figured out how to use the Fairness Doctrine to their advantage—was on the losing side of a battle that consumed the FCC in the 1980s, ending finally in the repeal of the doctrine and the rise of national talk radio.

Long a thorn in the side of conservative broadcasters, the Fairness Doctrine had been declared constitutional by the Supreme Court in the 1969 decision *Red Lion v. FCC*, which cited the scarcity of airwaves as a central justification for fairness regulation. In the face of that ruling, the conservative push against the doctrine largely went dark in the 1970s. The Nixon administration, eager to wield the FCC against political enemies, opposed the doctrine's repeal, and conservative broadcasters had more pressing budgetary matters to attend to. But with Reagan's election, the possibility of repeal reemerged. Within months of taking office, Reagan appointed Mark Fowler as chair of the FCC. Fowler, a thirty-nine-year-old communications lawyer who served as counsel on Reagan's 1976 and 1980 campaigns, spearheaded the deregulation of the telecommunications industry. Fowler was philosophically opposed to regulation, believing it interfered with the healthy functioning of the free market. Four years into his seven-year term he claimed the vitality of the industry in the wake of deregulation was "'Exhibit A' for Adam Smith." "Who are we in Government to dictate which program is good and socially desirable and which is bad and socially undesirable?" the FCC chair asked. "We should let the marketplace decide." "I take it as an article of faith," he said elsewhere, "that any successful businessman is meeting a public need." Music to a Reaganite's ears.[17]

The Fairness Doctrine was in Fowler's sights from the start. Soon after he became FCC chair, he asked Congress to eliminate it. The nature of his request helps explain why the Fairness Doctrine took another six years to eliminate. Because its origins were so murky, no one was quite sure who had the power to dispose of it. Did the FCC have the authority to do away with it on its own accord? Did Congress have to amend the Communications Act? Did the Supreme Court have to declare it unconstitutional? Fowler wanted to clarify the lines of authority so that when the Fairness Doctrine was killed, it stayed dead. So he took his time. He held a series of hearings on the Fairness Doctrine, which led to a 1985 report—110 pages long—in which the commissioners declared they "no longer believe that the fairness doctrine, as a matter of policy, serves the public interest." They also declared the doctrine "constitutionally infirm," arguing that there was compelling evidence to indicate, contra *Red Lion*, that not only were airwaves no longer scarce but the Fairness Doctrine had a measurable "chilling effect," impairing the "journalistic freedom of broadcasters." Yet the commission argued it could not do away with the Fairness Doctrine on its own. The courts had jurisdiction over questions of constitutionality, and Congress . . . well, they wouldn't go so far as to say Congress had sole authority, but they indicated they would prefer Congress repeal the doctrine and take the issue out of their hands.[18]

Congress, however, was not inclined to do so. A hefty majority of lawmakers preferred the Fairness Doctrine—including conservative Republicans like Newt Gingrich and Trent Lott. Once the District Court of Appeals in D.C. ruled the doctrine was a regulatory standard rather than a law (a 2–1 ruling with Justices Antonin Scalia and Robert Bork comprising the majority), Congress sought to protect the Fairness Doctrine by making it law, thus removing it from the FCC's authority. In 1987, the Senate voted 59–31 on a Fairness Doctrine bill; the House affirmed it in a 302–102 vote. Then Reagan vetoed it. Absent congressional intervention, authority remained with the FCC. The Supreme Court ordered the commissioners to rule on the doctrine's constitutionality, and in August 1987, they did just that. "The fairness doctrine chills free speech," the new chair of the FCC declared, "and contravenes the 1st Amendment and the public interest." In a 4–0 vote, the commissioners eliminated the Fairness Doctrine. Congress tried in 1989 and 1993 to reinstate it but to no avail.[19]

The politics of the Fairness Doctrine battle illustrate how sharply the history and myth-making surrounding it have diverged. In 1987 and 1989, the Fairness Doctrine had significant support from conservative politicians and media activists who believed it could be used to counter the influence of mainstream media. In the late 1980s, there was no influential conservative broadcasting to silence, no reason to see the Fairness Doctrine as a threat. Only in 1993, with a Democrat in the White House and Rush Limbaugh taking over the airwaves, did conservatives return to an earlier view of the doctrine as a tool of liberal censorship. (The 1993 version of the Fairness Doctrine legislation was dubbed the "Hush Rush" bill, a clear sign of the changing political atmosphere.) While the doctrine would have a long after-life as the specter of government regulation, after 1987 it was only as a useful bogeyman, nothing more.[20]

The changing politics of the Fairness Doctrine stemmed from a major disruption in the media landscape: the *Rush Limbaugh Show*. Limbaugh's radio program, which started as a local show in Sacramento in 1984, went national in 1988, a year after the doctrine's repeal. The timing suggested that regulation had been the sole force constraining conservative broadcasting. But Limbaugh's success rested on a number of parallel developments: dereg-ulation, technological change, broadcast innovation, and shifting patterns of conservative leadership. Combined, these conditions ushered in a second generation of conservative media activism—one significantly different from the first.

Rush Limbaugh did not have the polished pedigree of his predecessors in conservative media. He did not get his start in the hallowed halls of Yale or amid the marbled columns of the Capitol. He was a radio kid, a college dropout, a vinyl-spinning disc jockey. Entertainment, not politics, was his mother tongue. Only after Reagan took office and Limbaugh resettled in California did his shtick evolve from rock jock to shock jock. The "shock" came not only from Limbaugh's politics but from the way he presented his point of view: ribald and profane, meant to provoke as much as proselytize.

The pompous and provocative persona he adopted for his show drew not from national radio figures like Clarence Manion and Paul Harvey but from local radio hosts like Joe Pyne, Barry Gray, and Bob Grant. Joe Pyne's syndicated show was not strictly conservative—his program was touted as "fist-in-the-mouth" radio—but he understood the power of playing to emo-tions. In stark contrast to Buckley's *Firing Line*, which relied on trenchant intellectual sparring and formalized debates, Pyne insisted, "The subject must be visceral. We want emotion, not mental involvement." Likewise Bob Grant, who got his start filling in for Pyne before becoming a mainstay on New York radio from 1970 into the twenty-first century, played the role of political shock jock, particularly on issues of race. (In addition to frequently hosting David Duke, a white supremacist, in the 1970s, he lamented the lack of attention to "white rights," saying the country was being overrun by "millions of subhumanoids, savages, who really would feel more at home careening along the sands of the Kalahari or the dry deserts of eastern Kenya.") Limbaugh credited Grant with paving the way for him at WABC in New York, where both men worked. "He was the trailblazer," Limbaugh said after Grant's death in 2013. "He was the pioneer who took the arrows."[21]

Had Limbaugh stayed local, he likely would have faded into history like Pyne and Gray. But technological and regulatory changes opened the way for Limbaugh to experiment with a new, interactive national format. In addition to the Fairness Doctrine repeal, there were a series of technological shifts that explain why the talk-radio format Limbaugh pioneered emerged when it did, and how it did. The opening of the FM spectrum, which was less susceptible to static and interference, led music stations to abandon the AM dial. AM station owners thus had space to innovate as they searched for alternative broadcast formats that would draw listeners. To take a chance on a three-hour block of provocative political talk required at least a touch of desperation on behalf of station owners.[22]

Telephone technology had to change as well if a simulcast national call-in show were to be feasible. The ability to make free nationwide phone calls on a toll-free line was a relatively recent innovation in the 1980s. Expensive, cumbersome, and limited, the Zenith system introduced in the 1950s required operators to manually connect toll-free calls. The first automated systems appeared in the late 1960s, and while they were sufficient for high-volume national companies like hotel chains and airlines, they were prohibitively expensive for something like a three-hour daily radio show. It was not until 1982 that AT&T introduced the modern direct-dial toll-free calling system that national call-in shows use. Talk radio could have emerged without this technology, but it would most likely have lacked the interactivity that gave the genre its populist and participatory qualities.[23]

These technological and regulatory changes helped make the *Limbaugh Show* a hit. A year after going national, Limbaugh was pulling in about nine hundred thousand listeners in an average quarter hour. (Radio ratings are based on two metrics: the number of listeners per quarter hour, and the aggregate number of listeners per week.) He was also making major money from his "Rush to Excellence" stage show. Americans—and the media—started tuning in en masse in the 1990s. At the end of 1990, the *New York Times* magazine offered a profile of Limbaugh that spilled out over six pages. Limbaugh-mania had commenced.[24]

Limbaugh became a multimedia sensation in 1992 when he crossed over from radio into television and print. After lengthy courting by an editor at

Pocket Books, he agreed to write *The Way Things Ought to Be*. Limbaugh was a reluctant author. An unusual talent behind the microphone, he had never been drawn to the written word. While in Sacramento, he bylined a column that an assistant cobbled together from bits of the radio show. Limbaugh traded up to a more professional cobbler for *The Way Things Ought to Be*, working with *Wall Street Journal* writer John Fund. The book was far from a literary masterpiece, but that did little to dint its rapid sales. *The Way Things Ought to Be* catapulted to the top of the *New York Times* best-seller list in 1992, where it stayed for most of that summer. Pocket quickly optioned a second book. *See, I Told You So* netted him a $2.5 million advance and sold well when it was released in 1993. Limbaugh, though, was done with the trade—twenty years passed before he wrote another book.[25]

Limbaugh followed this foray into writing with the debut of his new television show. Television was a better fit for the broadcaster: not only was it a more natural extension of his talents, but he also had connections with a skilled producer who was determined to make conservative television a success. Limbaugh met Roger Ailes in 1990. Like Limbaugh, Ailes—talented, paranoid, ambitious—built a career in entertainment long before getting involved in politics, working as the executive producer of the *Mike Douglas Show* before a stint as a communications consultant for Nixon. In the 1980s, he doled out media advice to Reagan, George H. W. Bush, and Rudy Guiliani before returning to television in 1993 to run CNBC. While there he moonlighted as Limbaugh's producer.[26]

The Limbaugh-Ailes partnership was one of those pairings that seems like it should have revolutionized the industry: the man who built talk radio teamed with the man who would build Fox News. Early indicators suggested the show would be a hit on par with the radio program. A syndicated program (as opposed to a network show), the *Rush Limbaugh Show* had to be sold to individual stations. Multimedia Entertainment, the boutique syndicator responsible for the profit-churning talk shows *Donahue* and *Sally Jesse Raphael*, placed the program with 185 stations by the time it aired in September 1992. It was Multimedia's biggest launch. And it meant that when Limbaugh went to air that first night, 95 percent of the country could see him. (They hadn't yet succeeded in finding a Washington, D.C., station, leading Limbaugh to quip, half jokingly, "Could it be that they don't want Congress to see this show?") So it was that by the fall of 1992, Limbaugh had a best-selling book, a successful television show, and a national radio program with a listenership of nearly fourteen million people each week.[27]

And yet he had something even more important than those millions of listeners and readers and viewers—in the fall of 1992, he had the ear of George H. W. Bush.

The president of the United States was carrying Rush Limbaugh's bag.

They were making their way into the White House—Limbaugh, George H. W. Bush, and Roger Ailes—for a brief visit, and Bush had insisted. Limbaugh told the story frequently afterward, confessing embarrassment, but not quite enough of it to keep him from emphasizing that part. *The president of the United States carried his bag.*[28]

It was 1992, and things were not looking good for Bush. A year earlier he had scored record-breaking approval ratings, thanks to the lightning fast war in the Persian Gulf. But the positive feelings toward the president lasted about as long as the war itself. An economic recession had settled in—never a good backdrop for an election—and now Bush faced a three-way race against a charismatic southern Democrat and a reedy-voiced Texas independent. Bush knew Ross Perot, the third-party candidate, was a major threat to his reelection. Perot's cranky populism wasn't going to win the presidency, but it could easily skim off votes from conservatives who were disappointed that the patrician president not only failed to connect with them but had also gone back on his no-new-taxes pledge.

The man whose bag Bush carried was having a much better year—best-selling book, new television show, and a four-year-old radio program that was making him millions. He had been called "the most dangerous man in America" and wore the title proudly. And just a few months earlier he had gone on air with a number of very nice things to say about the Perot insurgency. No one knew for sure what impact the radio host might have—Limbaugh had not been a cultural or political force the first time Bush ran for the presidency—but Bush didn't want to take any chances. So he brought Limbaugh to the White House, put him up in the Lincoln Bedroom, and reaped the rewards. Limbaugh's on-air tone changed afterward. It was another base covered.

The scene on the White House lawn illustrated just how different the second generation of conservative media activists was from the first: they were profitable, popular, and powerful, wielding influence that reached far beyond the conservative movement. But their influence raised important new questions: *Should* media activists lead a political movement? What happened when their priorities as billion-dollar businesses diverged from the interests of the conservative movement and the Republican Party? And what were the consequences of a movement coming to see liberal media bias as so pervasive that it became difficult to differentiate between spin and reality?

To understand the relationship between Republican politicians and the second generation of conservative media activists first requires a better understanding of the contours of the second generation. Popular, accessible, and so *relevant* in a way the preceding generation had not been, the radio and television talk hosts made big money—something the first generation had never managed to achieve. Set against the backdrop of rising conservative political power, that combination of popularity and economic success meant the second generation was treated far more seriously by politicians and journalists.

Context accounts for some of the difference. The first generation turned to communications because they believed it was the only way to fight the inexorable tide of liberalism. By the 1980s and 1990s, there were innumerable institutions dedicated to the conservative cause—what Sidney Blumenthal called the "counterestablishment"—and politicians with the power to enact conservative policies, however imperfectly. Intellectuals took up residence in think tanks, politicians in statehouses and Congress, organizers in groups like the American Conservative Union or Young Americans for Freedom. In this atmosphere, conservative media drew from a distinctly different reservoir of talent. The second generation of media activists were entertainers first, conservatives second. Limbaugh, the radio pioneer, started as a disc jockey. Radio host Glenn Beck got his start as a morning-zoo shock jock. The cornerstone personalities of the new conservative cable network Fox News, founded in 1996, were also pulled from the ranks of entertainers. Bill O'Reilly came up through network news, working on the tabloidy *Inside Edition* before moving to Fox News. Fellow Fox News personality Steve Doocy started out as host of *House Party with Steve Doocy* on NBC as well as the children's show *Not Just News*.[29]

This entertainment background often came at the expense of formal education. For the first generation of conservative media activists, education was key. Buckley went to Yale, Regnery to MIT and Harvard, Rusher to Princeton and Harvard Law, Manion to Catholic University and Notre Dame. O'Reilly banked impressive credentials from Marist College, Boston University, and Harvard's Kennedy School, but Beck, Limbaugh, and Sean Hannity, the top conservative radio hosts of the 2000s, all lacked college degrees. None of which is to suggest the second generation of media activists lacked intelligence but rather that their backgrounds reflected a different type of training, one that allowed them to construct a more authentic-seeming populism than did the ivy-draped educations of their predecessors.

But this large cast of characters was still off-stage during the first Bush administration. For the better part of a decade, from his national syndication in 1988 to the launch of Fox News in 1996, conservative media *was* Limbaugh. Print publications abounded but continued to struggle economically. And television remained a puzzle. Limbaugh's show, which ran for four years, was moderately successful. Yet while the sets got sleeker and the production more professional, the medium never gave Limbaugh the sort of thrill he got from radio. In mid-1996, he announced that, despite his promise to stay on air until the nation had converted to conservatism, he was ending the show.

The announcement immediately sparked rumors that Limbaugh wasn't really retiring from television but rather readying himself for a move to Roger Ailes's new venture. Ailes was on his way out at America's Talking, the two-year-old NBC cable channel devoted to talk television. The channel, which provided a platform for cable news mainstays Steve Doocy and Chris Matthews, was being replaced by a new joint venture between NBC and Microsoft. The new channel, MSNBC, was envisioned as a competitor to CNN, which since 1980 had been the only all-news channel on cable.[30]

But Ailes would not be heading that new network. His tenure at America's Talking had been divisive, so much so that he had nearly been forced to resign. The network offered him an opportunity to stay on, but not as a driving force at MSNBC. So Ailes left, heading straight from the offices at 30 Rock to the waiting embrace of Rupert Murdoch.

Murdoch, an Australian media mogul who for decades had been angling to expand his television holdings in the United States, quickly ascertained Ailes's value when the two met in 1995 to discuss collaborating. A failed attempt to buy CNN left Murdoch, who was irritated by Ted Turner's refusal to sell and eager to exact revenge, intent on starting a news channel of his own. He believed Ailes was the ideal person to run it. It was a decision with important consequences, for while Murdoch saw the channel as an alternative to what he saw as biased reporting in news, it was Ailes who brought a fierce and unrelenting partisanship to the table. Both had axes to grind: Murdoch against Turner at CNN and Ailes against his former team at MSNBC. When Fox News Channel launched on October 7, 1996, its founders had clear objectives and ample resolve.[31]

Fox News represented the culmination of a half century of conservative hopes. Conservatives had fostered the dream of their own network for
decades, circulating schemes that generated enthusiasm but not results. So
long as there were just a handful of major networks, both cost and institutional inertia forestalled an ideological takeover. It simply required too
much money to buy out shareholders at NBC or CBS, who at any rate were
not interested in selling. The introduction of cable TV services broke that
monopoly, while introducing another. It took more than a year, for instance,
for Fox News to become available in New York City, where Time Warner's
control of Manhattan and Brooklyn cable blocked distribution. Not until
the rise of digital cable could multiple cable news channels compete in the
same markets.[32]

And compete Fox did. Even before the September 11 attacks and the
Iraq War stimulated the American appetite for round-the-clock news, Fox
News's programming was breaking through. By early 2001 *The O'Reilly
Factor*, an opinion show hosted by Bill O'Reilly, topped the ranks of cable-
news programming. The channel's top-rated show, *The O'Reilly Factor*
captured the differences between CNN and Fox News. CNN, tying its
reputation to reportage and interviews, relied heavily on network-style
news packages. Fox News, at least in its prime-time opinion programming,
borrowed heavily from the world of talk radio: personality driven, overtly
partisan, and laced with a thin edge of vitriol. After the September 11 attacks,
MSNBC, Fox News, and CNN went toe-to-toe-to-toe for a share of the
rapidly growing audience, and Fox News came out on top. Even six months
after the attacks, when CNN's and MSNBC's audiences plummeted from
their September highs, Fox News remained relatively steady—and surpassed
CNN in the monthly ratings for the first time. CNN retained the edge in
advertising revenue for a while, but Fox eventually caught up there, too.[33]

On the heels of Fox News's launch came a surge of right-wing talk-radio
shows. Lagging more than a decade behind Limbaugh, the sudden spate
of conservative shows could be traced to a second wave of deregulation.
The deregulation of the communications industry, from the repeal of the
Fairness Doctrine to changes in ownership limits to the sweeping 1996
Telecommunications Act, did not cause the second generation to emerge but
did guide and ease its entry into the world. By enabling consolidation, these
regulatory changes allowed Murdoch to expand his media holdings (laying
the groundwork not only for Fox News but the 2007 acquisition of the *Wall
Street Journal*) and enabled the rise of Clear Channel Communications. By

2000, Clear Channel owned one in every ten radio stations in the United States. Clear Channel and its subsidiary Jacor, in addition to profoundly restructuring the music industry, were the driving forces behind the conservative talk channels that soon saturated the nation.[34]

As a result of deregulation, the three hours a day of Rush Limbaugh had become, by the 2000s, wall-to-wall right-wing talk. A slew of new hosts gained national syndication between 2000 and 2002: Sean Hannity, Michael Savage, Laura Ingraham, Bill O'Reilly, Glenn Beck, Mark Levin, Monica Crowley. The combination of easy syndication and the hunger for political talk after the September 11 attacks remade the radio landscape, almost exclusively along conservative lines. A 2007 study of 257 news/talk stations by the progressive Center for American Progress found 91 percent of the programming was conservative, an imbalance they concluded was not market driven but a result of "multiple structural problems in the U.S. regulatory system."[35]

While broadcasting was the heart of the conservative media renaissance, the gains quickly spilled over into the publishing industry. Regnery reemerged as a central player in 1986 when Alf Regnery, Henry's eldest son, took the reins. Books such as Pat Buchanan's *Right from the Beginning* (1988), the memoir that marked him as a leading voice of populist conservatism, and *Senatorial Privilege: The Chappaquiddick Cover-Up* (1988), a big-selling exposé of Ted Kennedy's deadly 1969 automobile accident, made the company a major player in both publishing and politics. Investors took note: in 1993 Eagle Publishing, a venture in conservative writing undertaken by Thomas L. Phillips, acquired both *Human Events* and Regnery Publishing (and a 50 percent share in the Conservative Book Club). After forty-five years apart, Regnery and *Human Events* were back together and, at least for a while, turning a profit.[36]

Under Alf Regnery and Eagle Publishing, Regnery revived. With a thriving conservative counterestablishment setting up shop in Washington and in broadcasting studios across the country, the atmosphere was ripe for conservative best sellers. Nearly a dozen Regnery books topped the *New York Times* best-seller list between 1996 and 2014, including Bernie Goldberg's *Bias* (2001), Laura Ingraham's *Power to the People* (2007), and Michelle Malkin's *Culture of Corruption* (2009). Inevitably, success drew competition. At the Free Press, editor Erwin Glikes cultivated conservative writers like George Will, Robert Bork, and Dinesh D'Souza. After Glikes's sudden death, Adam Bellow continued his work. Bellow had a keen understanding of the changes that were happening in conservative book publishing, observing in 1994, "The liberal monopoly on public debate has weakened. I'm always being asked, 'What manipulative magic did you use to create this audience for conservative books?' But the audience has always been there. It's just that before, conservative ideas were walled off in a ghetto."[37]

In 2010 Bellow left Free Press for HarperCollins, where he helmed the conservative imprint Broadside Books. In founding Broadside, Bellow was at the tail end of a publishing trend stretching back into the late 1990s. For decades the right, particularly Henry Regnery, had railed against liberal control of the book publishing industry. It was the raison d'être behind firms like Regnery and Devin-Adair: they published conservative books because no one else would. Yet when Pocket Books hit the Limbaugh gusher with *The Way Things Ought to Be* and *See, I Told You So*, publishers took note. Soon the nation's largest publishing companies were establishing conservative imprints: Random House launched Crown Forum, Simon and Schuster started Threshold Editions, and Penguin founded Sentinel. These publishers pumped out best sellers by Ann Coulter, Glenn Beck, and Mike Huckabee, authors who in an earlier era would likely have turned to Regnery and Devin-Adair but now had the option of working with prestige presses.[38]

The riches flowed even toward the ever-struggling *National Review*. The Republican Revolution spiked circulation from 150,000 in 1992 to 250,000 in 1994—a much bigger boost than Reagan's election had delivered, a sign of how seriously conservative media were starting to be taken. Its ledgers showed black for the first—and only—time that year, a remarkable moment for a forty-year-old magazine that had never been self-sustaining. It continued to rely on fund drives to make up the shortfall in its operating budget, but the rising tide of profitable conservatism lifted even the leakiest boats. The journal's adventures in profitability, however, did not take place with Buckley and Rusher at the helm. Rusher retired to San Francisco in 1988, and Buckley stepped down as editor a year later. He named as his replacement John O'Sullivan, a British journalist who served as an adviser to Margaret Thatcher in the 1980s. In 1997, O'Sullivan handed over the editorship to twenty-nine-year-old Rich Lowry. The new generation had arrived at *National Review*.[39]

Within a year of Lowry's ascent to the editorship, the magazine that once stood athwart history leaped across the digital divide with National Review Online. It heralded a new era for conservative media activism, when the barriers to entry plummeted and innovation flourished. But something unexpected happened. Conservative media activists, who had been at the forefront of the movement, were not making nearly as much headway as liberal media activists. Sites like MoveOn.org were revolutionizing the organizational process on the left. Democratic candidates like Howard Dean were remaking the electoral process through data analysis, online organizing, and microtargeting strategies. Where were the conservatives?

Stuck. Or if not exactly stuck, at least boxed in by the inertia of power. By the end of the 1990s, conservatives no longer had any legitimate claims to outsider status. Think tanks, political groups, and lobbying firms sprung up across the capital, centers of conservative political influence. Fox News and talk radio were remaking the media landscape, making conservative voices not only accessible but nearly inescapable. The right still leveraged its outsider attitude, reveling in its Washington rebeldom, but the movement had accrued some of the trappings of institutional power: reticence and replication. It was difficult to convince activists to change tactics when the movement seemed to be doing so well. Political scientist David Karpf called this the "outparty innovation incentive." Liberals, who had limited pull in the Clinton administration and even less in the Reagan-Bush-Bush years, had every reason to try something new. And they did. They used new technologies to build networks, fund-raise, and lay the groundwork for offline activism. Meanwhile, the right used the new media to duplicate their work in the old media: to communicate with like-minded audiences and air grievances about liberal control of institutions. Even innovators like Matt Drudge, whose Drudge Report web aggregator drove news coverage in the 1990s and led to a short-lived show on Fox News, focused his media efforts on information and messaging, not organizing.[40]

The second generation of conservative media had done something the first generation had repeatedly failed to do. They found a way to make their work profitable and popular, ensuring that the conservative message reached every pocket of the country. Manion may have boasted about a national radio network, but he was largely hosted on second-tier stations and always in danger of losing coverage. He and other broadcasters relied on free and discounted airtime, hefty donations, and one or two wealthy sponsors. Thanks to Rush Limbaugh, Fox News, Clear Channel, and the phalanx of right-wing broadcasters who appeared in the 1990s and 2000s, conservative radio and television had become a mainstay of American life, not only reaching an audience of millions but driving the shape and focus of the rest of the news media—and reworking the definition of objectivity in the process.

Just as their predecessors had, the second generation of media activists made the issue of liberal media bias central to their mission. Unlike their predecessors, however, they emphasized balance as a primary component of objective reporting. The first generation of media activists couldn't abide balance, because they believed not only that they were rickety rafts of truth barely staying afloat in an ocean of liberal bias but also that "the other side" represented an existential threat to America. Airing the liberal point of view wasn't just unwise, it was immoral.[41] But times had changed. With the rise of political debate shows in the 1970s, many conservatives increasingly understood "balance" as a route to influence. Bill Rusher, Phyllis Schlafly, and James Kilpatrick all gained access to national audiences through these types of shows, and Buckley routinely invited liberals onto *Firing Line* for on-air sparring. And balance wasn't just a path to power—it carried with it the moral virtue of fairness and the promise of objectivity.

Nowhere was this embrace of balance more evident than at Fox News. The channel carried the tagline "Fair and Balanced," a phrase capacious enough to contain the ambiguities still unresolved after decades of conservative media activism. It was a promise and an indictment. We'll give you both sides, Fox News pledged, unlike the supposedly objective news teams on other outlets. The channel thus proclaimed a devotion to some of objectivity's central values: fairness and even-handedness. "We report, you decide," as another Fox News slogan declared. Yet there was a second, contradictory meaning behind "fair and balanced": as an explicitly conservative network, Fox News balanced the liberal bias of established media. Like *Human Events* before it, Fox News thus carved out a space to be both objective and biased, arguing it should be trusted because it was right, and because it was right-wing. Even as other media outlets scoffed at Fox News's claims to balance, they quietly folded the concept into their idea of objective reporting, relying increasingly on "on the one hand, on the other" coverage to ward off accusations of bias. By spurring these changes in the meaning of "objective," conservative media activists had remade American journalism. And journalism wasn't the only place their efforts were being felt. By the 1990s, media activists were fundamentally transforming party politics as well.

When George H. W. Bush lost the 1992 election, Ronald Reagan sent a letter to Rush Limbaugh. "Dear Rush," the former president wrote, "thanks for all you're doing to promote Republican and conservative principles. Now that I've retired from active politics, I don't mind that you've become the number one voice for conservatism in our country." Beaming with pride, Limbaugh read the letter on his television show. The Limbaugh era of Republican politics had arrived.[42]

Reagan was not the only one taking note of Limbaugh's relationship to the Republican Party. In 1993 *National Review* put him on the cover, touting him as "The Leader of the Opposition." But it was the 1994 congressional elections that made Limbaugh's reputation. That year's Republican landslide, spearheaded by Newt Gingrich and the Contract with America, had a number of causes. But Limbaugh reaped most of the credit. Calling the campaign "Operation Restore Democracy," he regularly advocated a Republican victory on his program. In advance of the election he urged his audience to ignore talk of a Democratic surge: "This is not the time to be depressed. This is the time to remember the weapon that you have, and that is the vote." The *New York Times* called it "a big moment in the world of talk radio," suggesting Limbaugh "may be a kind of national precinct captain for the Republican insurgency of 1994." There was an antigovernment mood that hung over the country, which fit well with the spirit of conservative talk radio. The problem was no one could quite figure out whether talk radio was driving, reflecting, or amplifying it. How much, in other words, did Republicans need to attend to the voices on air?[43]

Quite a lot, if their victory celebrations were any indication. At the Georgia party where Newt Gingrich celebrated his reelection, a local talk-radio personality named Sean Hannity played host. And when the new Republican members of the House met to celebrate their "revolution," they put Limbaugh front and center. "The Majority Maker" read the button one representative slipped onto Limbaugh's lapel. The lawmakers made him an honorary member of their caucus, placing the popular pundit at the forefront of their victory march. "Rush is as responsible for what happened here as much as anyone," proclaimed Vin Weber, a former congressman turned Republican strategist. Pollster Frank Luntz showed that people who imbibed ten or more hours of talk radio per week voted 3–1 Republican. Such a poll couldn't discern the causal relationship (did they listen because they were already conservative activists? Was the listening part of a conversion process?), but the correlation was enough to make Republican lawmakers pay attention.[44]

As conservative media proliferated, they gained more cachet with politicians. In 1992 and 1994, Rush Limbaugh had been just about the only game in town. He received plenty of praise from Republican lawmakers—but there was no doubt that the Republican Revolution of 1994 was engineered by the politicians. Rush may have provided air support, but mobilizing the ground troops had been the work of Newt Gingrich, the Contract with America, and an energized Republican Party. By the 2000s, however, there were many more conservative media outlets and an even greater sense that they could make or break Republican politicians.

While Republican politicians had been currying the support of media activists for a generation, the balance of power had shifted by the 2000s. The first generation of conservative media may have snuck one of their own past the GOP's gatekeepers in 1964, but the second generation *were* the gatekeepers. When Nixon, for instance, blasted the Buckleyites as a bigger threat than the Birchers, it took months for the candidate to respond to repeated entreaties from Bill Rusher over the issue. Even then the reply was handled by Nixon's emissary to the conservative movement, Pat Buchanan, who was the only person on staff interested in responding. Those days were long past. When Michael Steele, the chairman of the Republican National Committee, dismissed Limbaugh in 2009 as an "entertainer" who indulged in "ugly" and "incendiary" rhetoric, the blowback was so fierce that Steele quickly apologized.[45]

But if 2009 looked like it would once again be the Year of Limbaugh—in a June Gallup poll asking respondents to name the person who speaks for the GOP, he came in second, right behind "no one"—by year's end it was clear he had competition from other media activists. Take the Tea Party Tax Day Protests, a coordinated series of rallies held across the nation on April 15, 2009. In their study of the Tea Party, Theda Skocpol and Vanessa Williams likened conservative media's role in those rallies to that of "cheerleader" and "megaphone." They mapped the extensive reportage and celebration of the event on Fox News. On-air personalities like Greta Van Susteren, Sean Hannity, and Neil Cavuto headlined events around the country. But no one was more front and center than newly arrived Fox News host Glenn Beck.[46]

Beck earned his stripes as a radio host in the 1980s. He had little interest in politics, dealing with untreated addiction and mental illness until he entered a period of recovery and religious awakening in the mid-1990s. When it came to politics he was an autodidact as well as a late convert, reinventing himself as a conservative talk host in 2000 with the launch of the *Glenn Beck Program*. The radio show, which combined morning-zoo zaniness with impassioned political appeals, went national in January 2002, quickly gaining an audience that trended younger than that of other conservative hosts. In 2006 Beck added television to his lineup. After establishing himself as a popular host on CNN Headline News, he made the leap to Fox News in January 2009.[47]

It was from his new perch at Fox News that Beck began to branch out into political activism. When his radio show first started, he hosted a number of rallies across the country in support of the Iraq War and the American military. Those rallies were one-off, political gatherings unsupported by any longer-term organizing. With the rise of the Tea Party, Beck took on a more central role in the conservative movement. In March 2009, in response to the election of Barack Obama, Beck launched the 9/12 Project. The name reflected Beck's desire to recapture the spirit of national unity that presided the day after the September 11 attacks. The project coincided with the emergence of Tea Party activism, and over time the two movements merged.

The role Glenn Beck and other media personalities played in the development of the Tea Party went further than "cheerleader" and "megaphone." Skocpol and Williams concluded that conservative media "helped to orchestrate the Tea Party, breaking down the barriers between media and movement that have usually been so challenging for protestors to navigate." Indeed, they designated "the conservative media complex" a core component of the Tea Party movement. And increasingly of the Republican Party: Fox News served as a revolving door of commentators-cum-candidates, as well as an obligatory stop for candidates seeking to woo the conservative base. "You don't win Iowa in Iowa," Dick Morris proclaimed on *Fox & Friends* in advance of the 2012 Iowa caucuses. "You win it on this couch. You win it on Fox News." The political consultant with a penchant for wildly wrong-headed predictions had stopped-clocked his way into an accurate assessment of the relationship between conservative media and Republican politics in the twenty-first century.[48]

That Fox News was a billion-dollar industry mattered, too. By 2008, the Republican primary process had started to function not only as a race for the nomination but as a pundit audition process. Sarah Palin may not have won the vice presidency in 2008, but she walked away with a $1 million contract with Fox News. That kind of money introduced a new set of incentives into politicians' decision to undertake a presidential run. It also has the potential to shape the positions they take on the campaign trail, as a certain amount of ideological integrity and populist verve is required to make the leap to conservative media. This lack of space between movement and media has been a defining feature of postwar conservatism. What makes the second generation of media activists so different is that they have collapsed the space between media and party politics as well. By 2009, conservative media activists were commandeering both the national political conversation and the Republican Party.[49]

Some commentators, including a number of libertarians and conservatives, worried about the growing influence of conservative media on Republican politics. The first to properly theorize this new development was Julian Sanchez, a libertarian writer reflecting on "the closing of the conservative mind." He used the term "epistemic closure" to describe "the construction of a full-blown alternative media ecosystem . . . worryingly untethered from reality as the impetus to satisfy the demand for red meat overtakes any motivation to report accurately." His argument triggered considerable analysis of the conservative media's role in movement and party politics. It even teased out inadvertent examples. On RedState.com, a diarist demonstrated Sanchez's point in his denunciation of it. "When you are at war, while it is important to get facts right . . . it is also important to inspire the troops and to do so by distilling the realities of the fight into useful information. I frankly don't know if every statistic in Goldwater's *Conscience of a Conservative* was correct or not. Nor do I know if every statistic or number in Reagan's *A Time for Choosing* speech in 1964 was correct. I DON'T CARE. I know the facts were in the ballpark, and more importantly, the principles were timeless and correct." It was an epistemological claim: accuracy mattered, but ideology mattered more.[50]

David Frum, a conservative writer for the *Wall Street Journal*, *Weekly Standard*, and *National Review*, as well as a speechwriter for George W. Bush, believed conservative media had created a set of perverse incentives for the Republican Party that doomed it to electoral defeat. Writing after Mitt Romney's loss in the 2012 election, Frum diagnosed the GOP's problem as one not of leadership but of "followership." And the followership problem—the reliance on the most ideological members of the base to shape the party's agenda—was at heart a media problem. "The media culture of the U.S. has been reshaped to become a bespoke purveyor of desired facts," Frum argued. While he insisted this was happening for liberals as well as conservatives, he begrudgingly conceded "the Republican and conservative knowledge system does seem more coordinated than the liberal system—and even further removed from reality." Conservatives, in other words, had built an iron-clad media system, and in doing so had trapped themselves in a system of misinformation. Good, at times, for movement cohesion and organized outrage, but not so good when reckoning with the real world.[51]

Comedian Stephen Colbert, whose *O'Reilly Factor* spoof, *The Colbert Report*, satirized right-wing political punditry, captured this phenomenon when he coined the word "truthiness." Named the "word of the year" in 2005 by the American Dialect Society, truthiness signified a world in which certainty was valued over inquisitiveness, emotion over information. Liberals delighted in the word as shorthand for the conservative knowledge system. Truthiness, though, described something larger than conservatism. Its definition suited any ideological system and would have been just as apt for the first generation of media activists as the second. (*None Dare Call It Treason*, so highly acclaimed by the right and abjured by everyone else, could have served as Exhibit A for postwar truthiness.) The difference was that by the mid-2000s, truthiness had become a dominant mode of communication within conservative and Republican circles, and it was interfering in the party's policymaking as well as its electioneering. (Karl Rove's 2004 statement about Iraq captures this well: "We are an empire now, and when we act, we create our own reality.")[52]

Nowhere was this more on display than in the Fox News studios on election night 2012. With the exception of a few weeks surrounding the first presidential debate with Republican nominee Mitt Romney, polls showed an Obama advantage for months leading up to the election. In response, conservative media activists began to question not the weakness of their messaging but the accuracy of the polls. It was a moment of ideological ossification: believing it impossible for Obama to win reelection, a significant section of conservative leadership, driven by media personalities, rejected the most reliable indicators of the November vote. Nor did the stubborn unwillingness of the polls to yield to their cries of bias soften their stance. As vote totals rolled in on election night, former Bush adviser and Fox News contributor Karl Rove, speaking with host Megyn Kelly, laid out Romney's path to victory. Kelly paused, pursed her lips, then asked the devastating question: "Is this just math you do as a Republican to make yourself feel better or is it real?"[53]

It was indeed therapeutic math, but Rove either couldn't see it or wouldn't acknowledge it on camera. When Fox News called Ohio for Obama, effectively signaling the election had gone to the Democrats, Rove erupted in frustration, demanding the network undo the call. In part this was strategic. Rove knew how critical it had been in 2000 that Fox News called Florida for George W. Bush, triggering the other networks to do the same.

It was too early—too many votes were in dispute, a month-long recount followed—but that early call had created the impression of a Bush victory. Rove was loath to give the Democrats that advantage. But his understanding of the Ohio vote as a squeaker—of the entire election as a toss-up—reflected how inside the bubble he was. When the dust cleared on election night, Obama had been reelected, and nearly every conservative commentator in the country was left to explain how they had gotten it so wrong.

That moment triggered a reexamination of the role of conservative media in American politics and culture, one that continues today. No doubt the second generation of conservative media activism has been a boon for the movement, helping draw the Republican Party to the right, to normalize claims of liberal media bias, and to reconfirm the media's leadership position among conservatives. But media activism has also developed into an industry worth billions of dollars. As a result, the incentives of the media are no longer always in line with the movement or the party. The first generation of activists never had to worry about confusing profit and principles: they had a dearth of the first and a surfeit of the second. The second generation has had a more difficult course to chart. Yet despite the fundamental differences between these generations of activists, they shared a faith that working through media was the surest path to political power.

Liberals agreed, and repeatedly tried to replicate conservatives' media successes. But their efforts largely failed. Air America, the liberal talk-radio network launched in 2004, folded just six years later. MSNBC, which in the mid-2000s adopted a more explicitly progressive identity, lagged far behind Fox News in both ratings and revenue. The problem with these liberal efforts was that they were copying the products of conservative media, but their target audience lacked both the ideological justification and the identity-based media habits that sustained conservative media for so long. Liberal efforts failed because they based their understanding of conservative media on the second generation without recognizing the longer history of activism that made Limbaugh and Fox News possible. However one views the relationship between conservative media and right-wing politics in the United States, whether as a critical component of conservative power or a millstone exacerbating the Republicans' followership problem, there is little doubt that understanding conservative media activism is critical to understanding politics and media in America today, an understanding that must begin not with the successes of the second generation but with the struggles of the first.

Notes

Preface

1. Fred J. Cook, "Hate Clubs of the Air," *Nation*, May 25, 1964.

2. A smattering of histories appeared before the 1990s, many of them by either sympathetic or antipathetic authors. Perhaps the most important (and still indispensable) of these is George Nash, *The Conservative Intellectual Movement in America Since 1945* (New York: Basic, 1976). Reagan's two terms in office, followed by the election of George H. W. Bush and Republican successes in 1994, signaled that conservatism was not dead-letter but in fact a vibrant and powerful political force. In the midst of that conservative resurgence, Alan Brinkley called for remedies for what he labeled "the problem of American conservatism" (the essay was first written in 1989 and published in 1994). Leo Ribuffo, in his response to Brinkley, sharpened the point by noting that there were very good histories of conservatism but that historians had "to 'mainstream' the copious good scholarship that already exists." Alan Brinkley, "The Problem of American Conservatism," *American Historical Review* 99 (April 1994): 409–429; Leo P. Ribuffo, "Why Is There So Much Conservatism in the United States and Why Do So Few Historians Know Anything About It?" *American Historical Review* 99 (April 1994): 438–449.

Still, it was easy to see that historians had analyzed liberalism and the left with much more care and attention than they did the right, and a new generation of historians took up Brinkley's cause with gusto. The first wave of histories tended to treat right-wing activism as a parallel of left-wing activism, focusing on grassroots organizing and political identity. The exemplar of this approach is Lisa McGirr, *Suburban Warriors: The Origins of the New American Right* (Princeton, N.J.: Princeton University Press, 2001).

Soon, though, modern conservatism was one of the fastest-growing fields of study in American history. The religious right received an enormous amount of attention, as did Republican politics, the Red Scare, and foreign policy. Southern conservatism and the politics of racism have also been the subjects of a number of excellent studies. Kim Phillips-Fein mapped these different historiographical trends, and directions for future study, in "Conservatism: A State of the Field," *Journal of American History* 98 (Dec. 2011): 723–743.

The historiography of conservative media is substantially smaller. Most studies emerged in response to the rise of Rush Limbaugh, focusing on the second generation of media activists. For the first generation, historians have tended to approach the subject through biographies and surveys of publications, tilted heavily—almost exclusively—toward *National Review*. See especially John Judis, *William F. Buckley, Jr., Patron Saint of the Conservatives* (New York: Simon and Schuster, 1988); David Frisk, *If Not Us, Who?: William Rusher, "National Review," and the Conservative Movement* (Wilmington, Del.: ISI, 2012); Ronald Lora and William Henry Longton, *The Conservative Press in Twentieth-Century America* (Westport, Conn.: Greenwood,

1999); Jeffrey Hart, *The Making of the American Conservative Mind: "National Review" and Its Times* (Wilmington, Del.: ISI, 2005); and William P. Hustwit, *James J. Kilpatrick: Salesman for Segregation* (Chapel Hill: University of North Carolina Press, 2011).

Messengers of the Right also builds on histories of political media, particularly radio activism. The most important of these include Alan Brinkley, *Voices of Protest: Huey Long, Father Coughlin, and the Great Depression* (New York: Knopf, 1982); Elizabeth A. Fones-Wolf, *Waves of Opposition: Labor and the Struggle for Democratic Radio* (Urbana: University of Illinois Press, 2006); Aniko Bodroghkozy, *Equal Time: Television and the Civil Rights Movement* (Urbana: University of Illinois Press, 2012); and Chad Raphael, *Investigated Reporting: Muckrakers, Regulators, and the Struggle over Television Documentary* (Urbana: University of Illinois Press, 2005).

3. Daniel Bell, *The End of Ideology: On the Exhaustion of Political Ideas in the Fifties* (Glencoe, Ill.: Free Press, 1960); "Text of President Kennedy's Commencement Address to Yale's Graduating Class," *New York Times*, Jun. 12, 1962.

4. Arthur Schlesinger, *The Vital Center: The Politics of Freedom* (Boston: Houghton Mifflin, 1949). Schlesinger later denied that his "vital center" described liberals in opposition to American conservatives and progressives but rather that it described American democracy in opposition to communism. Yet Schlesinger clearly had Henry Wallace and the left's criticism of the New Deal in his sights, and he comments at length about the failures of the American right and the American left in domestic as well as foreign policy matters. On media polling, see Gallup's 2014 Trust in Media poll. http://www.gallup.com/poll/176042/trust-mass-media-returns-time-low.aspx.

5. In making this argument, I am conceptualizing media as a site of epistemological production and reproduction. On objectivity, see Richard L. Kaplan, *Politics and the American Press: The Rise of Objectivity, 1865–1920* (New York: Cambridge University Press, 2002); Michael Schudson, *Discovering the News: A Social History of American Newspapers* (New York: Basic Books, 1978); and David T. Z. Mindich, *Just the Facts: How Objectivity Came to Define American Journalism* (New York: New York University Press, 1998).

6. "How Accurate Is America's News?" *Facts Forum News*, Apr. 1955, 28–29, 41, Box 93, Folder 13, Herbert A. Philbrick Papers, Library of Congress (hereafter LOC), Washington, D.C.

7. In the 1980s, political scientist Daniel Hallin mapped out three spheres of media coverage: the sphere of consensus, the sphere of legitimate controversy, and the sphere of deviance. Though many conservative media activists carved out a space in the sphere of legitimate controversy, they often found themselves pushed into the sphere of deviance, judged unworthy of receiving a hearing. Hallin, *The "Uncensored War": The Media and Vietnam* (Oxford: Oxford University Press, 1986).

8. Rusher to Buckley, Jul. 28, 1982, Box 122, Folder 3, William A. Rusher Papers, LOC.

9. David Frum, *Why Romney Lost (And What the GOP Can Do About It)*, (Newsweek eBook, 2012), ch. 2.

Chapter 1

1. Anthony Levieros, "U.S. Study Headed by Ex–New Dealer," *New York Times*, Aug. 19, 1953.

2. Philip Warden, "Ike Considers 2 Chicagoans for Labor Post," *Chicago Tribune*, Oct. 7, 1953. On the Notre Dame charges, see, for instance, Manion to Rev. Phillip Moore, Jan. 30, 1969, Box 36, Folder 5, Clarence E. Manion Papers, Chicago History Museum (hereafter CHM).

3. Anthony Levieros, "Government Study Board to Miss March Deadline; Extension Sought," *New York Times*, Feb. 14, 1954, 1.

4. Charles Postel, *The Populist Vision* (New York: Oxford University Press, 2007); Michael

Kazin, *The Populist Persuasion: An American History*, rev. ed. (Ithaca, N.Y.: Cornell University Press, 1998), ch. 2.

5. Gerald J. Baldasty, *The Commercialization of News in the Nineteenth Century* (Madison: University of Wisconsin Press, 1992).

6. Bob Ostertag, *People's Movements, People's Press: The Journalism of Social Justice Movements* (Boston: Beacon Press, 2006), 23–71; Frances Grace Carver, "With Bible in One Hand and Battle-Axe in the Other: Carry A. Nation as Religious Performer and Self-Promoter," *Religion and American Culture: A Journal of Interpretation* 9 (Winter 1999): 31–65; Harriet Jane Hanson Robinson, *Massachusetts in the Woman Suffrage Movement: A General, Political, Legal and Legislative History from 1774 to 1881* (Boston: Roberts Brothers, 1883).

7. Jean Folkerts, "Functions of the Reform Press," *Journalism History* 12 (Spring 1985): 24; Postel, *Populist Vision*, 62–67.

8. Edmund L. Starling, *History of Henderson County, Kentucky* (Evansville, Ind.: Unigraphic, 1887, 1965).

9. Michael McGerr, *A Fierce Discontent: The Rise and Fall of the Progressive Movement in America* (New York: Oxford University Press, 2003).

10. Ellen F. Fitzpatrick, *Muckraking: Three Landmark Articles* (Boston: Bedford, 1994); Doris Kearns Goodwin, *The Bully Pulpit: Theodore Roosevelt, William Howard Taft, and the Golden Age of Journalism* (New York: Simon and Schuster, 2013).

11. Andrew Porwancher, "Objectivity's Prophet: Adolph S. Ochs and the *New York Times*, 1896–1935," *Journalism History* 36 (Winter 2011): 186–195.

12. Kaplan, *Politics and the American Press*; Schudson, *Discovering the News*; Mindich, *Just the Facts*; Lynn D. Gordon, "Why Dorothy Thompson Lost Her Job: Political Columnists and the Press Wars of the 1930s and 1940s," *History of Education Quarterly* 34 (Autumn 1994): 281–303.

13. Thomas Nagel, *The View from Nowhere* (New York: Oxford University Press, 1986); Jay Rosen, "The View from Nowhere: Questions and Answers," *PressThink*, Nov. 10, 2010, http://pressthink.org/2010/11/the-view-from-nowhere-questions-and-answers/.

14. Anthony Arthur, *Radical Innocent: Upton Sinclair* (New York: Random House, 2006), chs. 3 and 4.

15. James Chace, *1912: Wilson, Roosevelt, Taft & Debs—the Election That Changed the Country* (New York: Simon and Schuster, 2004); Lewis L. Gould, *Four Hats in the Ring: The 1912 Election and the Birth of Modern American Politics* (Lawrence: University Press of Kansas, 2008).

16. Henry Regnery, *Memoirs of a Dissident Publisher* (New York: Harcourt, 1979), 3.

17. Ibid., 6–16.

18. Calvin Coolidge, "Address to the American Society of Newspaper Editors, Washington, D.C.," Jan. 17, 1925. For an overview of this period, see Katherine A. S. Sibley, ed., *A Companion to Warren G. Harding, Calvin Coolidge, and Herbert Hoover* (West Sussex: Wiley Blackwell, 2014).

19. William A. Rusher, *The Rise of the Right* (New York: Morrow, 1984), 15–31; Frisk, *If Not Us, Who?*

20. Frisk, *If Not Us, Who?* 9–16.

21. Clarence Manion, "Reminiscences of Clarence E. Manion: Oral History, 1976," interview, 1976, Oral History Research Office, Columbia University, New York.

22. Originally released as a pamphlet in 1926, the essay appeared in the *Notre Dame Lawyer* in early 1927. Clarence Manion, "What Price Prohibition?" *Notre Dame Lawyer* 2(3) (Jan. 1927): 73–94.

23. Manion to Sen. Smith W. Brookhart, Feb. 12, 1929, Box 1, Folder 3, Manion Papers, CHM.

24. *South Bend News-Times*, Aug. 7, 1933, Box 1, Folder 3, Manion Papers, CHM; Arthur Evans, "Democrats Act to Make Indiana 100 Per Cent Wet," *Chicago Tribune*, Jun. 22, 1932.

25. Clarence Manion, "The Constitutionality of New Deal Measures," *Notre Dame Lawyer* 9(4) (May 1934): 381–387.

26. Clarence Manion, "Reviewing Judicial Review," *Indiana Law Journal* 12(3) (Feb. 1937): 167–182. Description of state directors' duties comes from the *United States Government Manual* (Washington, D.C.: Office of Government Reports, 1939), 389. Manion defended the New Deal in forums like a mock national convention at Northwestern University, where he debated a Republican, an anti–New Deal Democrat, and a Socialist. Percy Wood, "Students Cheer and Boo in Best Political Style," *Chicago Tribune*, Apr. 25, 1936.

27. On Manion's 1938 election efforts, including the role of religion in preventing his nomination, see Box 78, Folder 2, Manion Papers, CHM. On the backroom machinations that ended with Van Nuys's renomination, see "M'Nutt Faction Backs Schricker for Senate Race," *Chicago Tribune*, Jun. 10, 1938; and Geoffrey Parsons Jr., "McNutt Boom Wins Van Nuys Renomination," *Washington Post*, Jul. 13, 1938.

28. Regnery, *Memoirs of a Dissident Publisher*, 17.

29. Ibid., 14–25.

30. Brinkley, *Voices of Protest*.

31. Richard Polenberg, "The National Committee to Uphold Constitutional Government, 1937–1941," *Journal of American History* 52(3) (Dec. 1965): 582–598.

32. David Witwer, "Westbrook Pegler and the Anti-Union Movement," *Journal of American History* 92(2) (Sep. 2005): 527–552. Combs quoted in "How Accurate Is America's News?" *Facts Forum News*, Apr. 1955, 28–29, 41, Box 93, Folder 13, Philbrick Papers, LOC.

33. Felix Morley, "An Adventure in Journalism," in *A Year of Human Events* (Chicago: Human Events, Inc., 1945), vii.

34. For recent scholarship on neutrality debates and the Roosevelt administration, see G. Kurt Piehler and Sidney Pash, eds., *The United States and the Second World War: New Perspectives on Diplomacy, War, and the Home Front* (New York: Fordham University Press, 2010); Lynne Olson, *Those Angry Days: Roosevelt, Lindbergh, and America's Fight over World War II, 1939–1941* (New York: Random House, 2013); and Andrew Johnstone, *Against Immediate Evil: American Internationalists and the Four Freedoms on the Eve of World War II* (Ithaca, N.Y.: Cornell University Press, 2014).

35. Taft quoted in Colin Dueck, *Hard Line: The Republican Party and U.S. Foreign Policy Since World War II* (Princeton, N.J.: Princeton University Press, 2010), 50; Clarence E. Wunderlin, *Robert A. Taft: Ideas, Tradition, and Party in U.S. Foreign Policy* (Lanham, Md.: Rowman and Littlefield, 2005), ch. 2.

36. Alan Brinkley, *The Publisher Henry Luce and His American Century* (New York: Knopf, 2010), 252–273.

37. Justus D. Doenecke, *In Danger Undaunted: The Anti-Interventionist Movement of 1940–1941 as Revealed in the Papers of the America First Committee* (Stanford, Calif.: Hoover Institution, 1990).

38. Richard Norton Smith, *The Colonel: The Life and Legend of Robert R. McCormick, 1880–1955* (New York: Houghton Mifflin, 1997), ch. 13; John E. Moser, *Right Turn: John T. Flynn and the Transformation of American Liberalism* (New York: New York University Press, 2005).

39. Justus D. Doenecke, "General Robert E. Wood: The Evolution of a Conservative," *Journal of Illinois State Historical Society* 71 (Aug. 1978): 162–175; Doenecke, *In Danger Undaunted*, 6–9.

40. Regnery, *Memoirs of a Dissident Publisher*, 13; Regnery to Buchanan, Oct. 16, 1991, Box 120, Folder B, Henry Regnery Papers, Hoover Institution (hereafter HI), Palo Alto, Calif.

41. Doenecke, *In Danger Undaunted*, 35.

42. Husband E. Kimmel, *Admiral Kimmel's Story* (Chicago: Regnery, 1955); Manion Forum Broadcast #219, "December 7, 1941—The 'Day of Infamy' of Franklin Roosevelt," Dec. 7, 1958. Manion Forum broadcast reprints are located in Boxes 81–87, Manion Papers, CHM.

43. Regnery, *Memoirs of a Dissident Publisher*, 28.

44. Clarence Manion, "Some Legal Aspects of American Sovereignty," *Notre Dame Lawyer* 20 (Sep. 1944): 1–10.

45. Clarence Manion, *The Key to Peace: A Formula for the Perpetuation of Real Americanism* (Chicago: Heritage Foundation, 1950).

46. Quoted in Walter Trohan, "Key to Lasting Peace: Americanism," *Chicago Daily Tribune Magazine of Books*, Feb. 4, 1951, H5. Manion received a favorable hearing at the *Los Angeles Times* as well; see Paul Jordan-Smith, "I'll Judge, You Be Jury," *Los Angeles Times*, Mar. 25, 1951, D5. Speech at Cornell University, Feb. 12, 1951, Box 1, Folder 10, Manion Papers, CHM.

47. Earl T. Barnes to Manion, Mar. 4, 1952, Box 2, Folder 1, Manion Papers, CHM; Manion ad for Democrats for Eisenhower Committee, Nov. 1952, Box 2, Folder 3, Manion Papers, CHM.

48. For Manion's reminiscence about the CIR, see Manion, interview, 55. Manion to commission members, Sep. 23, 1953, Box 64, Folder 5, Manion Papers, CHM; Pew to Manion, Oct. 12, 1953, Box 65, Folder 6, Manion Papers, CHM.

49. Clarence Manion, *The Conservative American: His Fight for National Independence and Constitutional Government* (New York: Devin-Adair, 1964); Manion Forum Broadcast #17, "To Save the Constitution—Pass the Bricker Amendment," Jan. 23, 1955. For details on the Bricker Amendment and opposition to the pact, see Samantha Power, *"A Problem from Hell": America and the Age of Genocide* (New York: Basic Books, 2002).

50. Earl Harding to Manion, Aug. 10, 1953, Box 64, Folder 2, Manion Papers, CHM; Marquis Childs, "Bricker Amendment: Eisenhower Sounds Alert," *Washington Post*, Jan. 16, 1954; Joseph Alsop and Stewart Alsop, "The Case of Dr. Manion," *Washington Post*, Jan. 29, 1954; "The Gold-Bricker," *Time*, Feb. 9, 1954.

51. Manion to supporters, Sep. 19, 1969, Box 1, Folder 1, Manion Papers, CHM; Manion to Eisenhower, Feb. 17, 1954, Box 74, Folder 11, Manion Papers, CHM.

52. Frisk, *If Not Us, Who?* 19–21.

53. Ibid., 22–26.

54. Ibid., 44–45.

55. Ibid., 55.

56. Rusher to Brent Bozell, Mar. 6, 1969, Box 11, Folder 13, Rusher Papers, LOC.

Chapter 2

1. Regnery, meeting notes, Dec. 7, 1953, Box 16, Folder 5, Regnery Papers, HI.

2. Regnery to Wood, July 24, 1953, Box 80, Folder 1, Regnery Papers, HI.

3. Felix Morley, "For What Are We Fighting?" *Saturday Evening Post*, Apr. 18, 1942, 9–10, 40, 42–43.

4. Felix Morley, *For the Record* (South Bend, Ind.: Regnery, 1979).

5. H. C. Engelbrecht and Frank Hanighen, *Merchants of Death: A Study of the International Armament Industry* (New York: Dodd, Mead, 1934); *Human Events* pamphlet, [n.d., likely 1946], Box 53, Folder 1, Regnery Papers, HI; Fulton Lewis Jr., "The *Human Events* Story," 1966, Box 114, Folder 4, Philbrick Papers, LOC.

6. Quoted in D. von Mohrenschildt, "William Henry Chamberlin, 1897–1969," *Russian Review* 29 (Jan. 1970): 3; "William Henry Chamberlin, RIP," *National Review*, Oct. 7, 1969, 1000–1002; William Henry Chamberlin, *The Confessions of an Individualist* (New York: Macmillan, 1940); Nash, *The Conservative Intellectual Movement*.

7. *Human Events* pamphlet.

8. "Statement of Policy," in *A Year of Human Events: A Weekly Analysis for the American Citizen*, ed. Frank Hanighen and Felix Morley (Washington, D.C.: Human Events, 1945), x–xi.

9. Ibid.

10. Felix Morley, "An Adventure in Journalism," in *A Year of Human Events*, vii–ix.

11. "The Who, What, How and Why of Your Washington News Service," *Human Events*, Apr. 21, 1961.

12. Felix Morley, "The Early Days of *Human Events*," *Human Events*, Apr. 27, 1974.

13. Morley to Regnery, Oct. 11, 1945, Box 126, Folder "Human Events," Regnery Papers, HI.

14. Regnery, *Memoirs of a Dissident Publisher*, 30–34.

15. Ibid., 26–41; Nash, *The Conservative Intellectual Movement*, 21–23; Frank Chodorov, *Out of Step: The Autobiography of an Individualist* (New York: Devin-Adair, 1962), 113–123; Regnery to Morley, Jul. 22, 1955, Box 53, Folder 1, Regnery Papers, HI; Regnery to Kirk, Feb. 25, 1953, Box 39, Folder 9, Regnery Papers, HI.

16. President's Report, Human Events, Inc., Sep. 13, 1948, Box 53, Folder 1, Regnery Papers, HI.

17. Regnery to Hanighen, Jun. 17, 1946, Box 31, Folder 11, Regnery Papers, HI.

18. Hanighen to Regnery, Jun. 19, 1946, Box 31, Folder 11, Regnery Papers, HI; Morley to Regnery, May 2, 1946, Box 53, Folder 1, Regnery Papers, HI.

19. Regnery to Morley, Mar. 17, 1947, Box 53, Folder 1, Regnery Papers, HI.

20. Morley to Regnery, Mar. 21, 1947, Box 53, Folder 1, Regnery Papers, HI; Morley to Regnery, May 15, 1947, Box 53, Folder 1, Regnery Papers, HI; Regnery, *Memoirs of a Dissident Publisher*, 36–37. The name change became official on Sep. 9, 1947.

21. Regnery, *Memoirs of a Dissident Publisher*, 36–41.

22. Though the phrase "marketplace of ideas" was not coined until 1953, the concept traces back (in American jurisprudence) to Justice Oliver Wendell Holmes's dissent in *Abrams v. U.S.* (1919), where Holmes discussed "free trade in ideas," and in British thought to John Milton's *Areopagitica* (1644) and John Stuart Mill's *On Liberty* (1859). For a history of "the marketplace of ideas," see Gregory Brazeal, "How Much Does a Belief Cost?: Revisiting the Marketplace of Ideas," *Southern California Interdisciplinary Law Journal* 21(1) (2011–2012): 1–46.

23. "Growth Toward What?" *Time*, Dec. 5, 1949; Regnery to Robert Reynolds, May 7, 1957, Box 56, Folder 8, Regnery Papers, HI.

24. Henry Regnery, "Henry Regnery: A Conservative Publisher in a Liberal World," Oct. 1971, Box 81, Folder 11, Regnery Papers, HI.

25. Buckley to Regnery, Nov. 21, 1967, Box 11, Folder 1, Regnery Papers, HI.

26. Judis, *William F. Buckley, Jr.*, 33–34. Judis's book remains the best biography of Buckley. It has more recently been joined by Linda Bridges and John R. Coyne Jr., *Strictly Right: William F. Buckley Jr. and the American Conservative Movement* (Hoboken, N.J.: Wiley, 2007); Lee Edwards, *William F. Buckley Jr.: The Maker of a Movement* (Wilmington, Del.: ISI, 2010); and Carl T. Bogus, *Buckley: William F. Buckley Jr. and the Rise of American Conservatism* (New York: Bloomsbury, 2011).

27. Judis, *William F. Buckley, Jr.*, 74–81; speech reprinted in appendix F of William F. Buckley Jr., *God and Man at Yale: The Superstitions of "Academic Freedom"* (Chicago: Regnery, 1951).

28. William F. Strube, Reader report, n.d., Box 10, Folder 14, Regnery Papers, HI.

29. Regnery to Buckley, May 14, 1951, Box 10, Folder 14, Regnery Papers, HI; Bogus, *Buckley*, 82. Bogus calculated the $19,000 the Buckleys contributed would be the equivalent of $155,000 in 2011 dollars.

30. McGeorge Bundy, "The Attack on Yale," *Atlantic*, Nov. 1951; Selden Rodman and Frank D. Ashburn, "'Isms' & the University," *Saturday Review*, Dec. 15, 1951, 18–19, 44–45.

31. William Buckley and Brent Bozell, *McCarthy and His Enemies: The Record and Its Meaning* (Chicago: Regnery, 1954).

32. On the need for new journals, see Nash, *The Conservative Intellectual Movement*, 211–233. Chamberlain and Regnery quoted on 214; Kirk's proposal quoted on 216. For information on the *Freeman, American Mercury*, and others, see Niels Bjerre-Poulsen, *Right Face: Organizing the American Conservative Movement, 1945–65* (Copenhagen: Museum Tusculanum, 2002), 102–106.

33. William F. Strube, Reader report, n.d., Box 10, Folder 14, Regnery Papers, HI.

34. Nash, *Conservative Intellectual Movement*, 221.

35. William Buckley, "Re: A New Magazine," [1954], Box 10, Folder 15, Regnery Papers, HI.

36. "Statement of Intentions," n.d., Box 10, Folder 14, Regnery Papers, HI.

37. Ibid.

38. Ibid.

39. Frisk, *If Not Us, Who?* 68–74; Buckley, "Re: A New Magazine."

40. Frisk, *If Not Us, Who?* 70.

41. Manion Forum Broadcast #101, "Conventions Appealed Only to Animal Appetites," Sep. 2, 1956.

42. Ibid.

43. Manion Forum Broadcast #1, "Revive American Independence," Oct. 3, 1954.

44. Telegram from William M. Blanton, Frank Cullen Brophy, Frank Buttram, et al., Aug. 2, 1954, Box 48, Folder 28, Regnery Papers, HI; B. K. Patterson to Henry Regnery, Aug. 5, 1954, Box 48, Folder 28, Regnery Papers, HI; Manion to sponsors, Aug. 2, 1954, Box 98, Folder 13, Manion Papers, CHM.

45. The *Manion Forum* audit showed 394 contributors for 1954, with contributions totaling just over $60,000. Manion Forum Broadcast #1, "Revive American Independence," Oct. 3, 1954; Manion Forum Agreement and Declaration of Trust, Box 81, Folder 7, Manion Papers, CHM; *Manion Forum* audits, Box 105, Folder 2, Manion Papers, CHM.

46. Regnery to Kirk, Feb. 10, 1956, Box 39, Folder 9, Regnery Papers, HI.

Chapter 3

1. Hutchings to Manion, Oct. 21, 1957, Box 88, Folder 5, Manion Papers, CHM.

2. Nelson Lichtenstein and Elizabeth Tandy Shermer, eds., *The Right and Labor in America: Politics, Ideology, and Imagination* (Philadelphia: University of Pennsylvania Press, 2012), 8–9. *Human Events* used the anticommunist line in the 1940s but switched tacks by the mid-1950s. For example, cf. Jul. 24, 1946, issue with that of Jan. 7, 1956.

3. "If That's How They Want It," *National Review*, Sep. 8, 1956, 4–5.

4. John Kenneth Galbraith, *American Capitalism, the Concept of Countervailing Power* (Boston: Houghton Mifflin, 1952).

5. The National Association of Manufacturers had long been opposed to the union shop. See H. W. Prentis Jr., Letter to the Editor, *Time*, May 27, 1940.

6. Craig Miner, "The New Wave, the Old Guard, and the Bank Committee: William J. Grede at J. I. Case Company, 1953–1961," *Business History Review* 61 (Summer 1987): 243–290.

7. Fones-Wolf, *Waves of Opposition*, 28.

8. William J. Grede letter, [Sep. 1955], Box 97, Folder 68, Manion Papers, CHM; Trevor K. Cramer letter, American Thermos Production Company, Sep. 8, 1961, Box 90, Folder 3, Manion Papers, CHM; T. A. Baker letter, Baker Specialty and Supply Company, Aug. 12, 1960, Box 90, Folder 15, Manion Papers, CHM; T. C. Terrell, M.D., letter, Terrell's Laboratories, Feb. 11, 1963, Box 96, Folder 47, Manion Papers, CHM.

9. Manion Forum Broadcast #9, "Sell the TVA Now," Nov. 28, 1954.

10. B. K. Patterson to Manion, Feb. 22, 1955, Box 98, Folder 12, Manion Papers, CHM.

11. Manion Forum Broadcast #39, "'Guaranteed Annual Wage'—A Gross Deception," Jun. 26, 1955.

12. Atkinson to Manion, Nov. 15, 1955, Box 88, Folder 8, Manion Papers, CHM; Manion Forum Broadcast #60, "Let the People Speak," Nov. 20, 1955.

13. For details on the boycott, see letters and clippings in Box 88, Folder 8, Manion Papers, CHM.

14. Milliken to Regnery, May 10, 1954, Box 51, Folder 13, Regnery Papers; Buckley quoted in Kim Phillips-Fein, *Invisible Hands: The Making of the Conservative Movement from the New Deal to Reagan* (New York: Norton, 2009), 80–81.

15. Hanighen to Regnery, Jan. 31, 1953, Box 27, Folder 16, Regnery Papers, HI; Milliken to Regnery, Feb. 22, 1955, Box 51, Folder 13, Regnery Papers, HI. Closing the plant in Dec. 1956 was a violation of the Taft-Hartley Act, but the Darlington mill did not reopen. "Union Seeks Reopening of Textile Plant," *Washington Post*, Jun. 10, 1957.

16. Milliken to Regnery, May 23, 1955, Box 51, Folder 13, Regnery Papers, HI. Milliken dismissed Riesel because he was "considered an objective reporter on labor."

17. Milliken offered to fund Pegler's writing; Milliken to Pegler, Jul. 19, 1955, Box 51, Folder 13, Regnery Papers, HI. On Pegler's union views, see David Witwer, "Westbrook Pegler and the Anti-union Movement," *Journal of American History* 92 (Sep. 2005): 527–552.

18. "'Pish and Piffle,'" *Time*, Apr. 23, 1934; "Donald R. Richberg, NRA Chief, Is Dead," *Washington Post*, Nov. 28, 1960; Regnery to Richberg, Jun. 14, 1955, Box 64, Folder 14 "Donald R. Richberg," Regnery Papers, HI.

19. Garrity to Richberg, Jun. 14, 1955, Box 51, Folder "Donald Richberg," Devin A. Garrity Papers, HI.

20. Garrity to Richberg, Jul. 6, 1955, Box 51, Folder "Donald Richberg," Garrity Papers, HI; Regnery to Hanighen, Jul. 5, 1955, Box 27, Folder 16, Regnery Papers, HI; Hanighen to Regnery, Aug. 3, 1955, Box 27, Folder 16, Regnery Papers, HI.

21. Richberg to Regnery, Aug. 31, 1955, Box 64, Folder 14, Regnery Papers, HI; Richberg to Garrity, Aug. 31, 1955, Box 51, Folder "Donald Richberg," Garrity Papers, HI. Regnery was even more sure he wanted Richberg after reading an article by him in *Human Events* on labor unions. Regnery to Richberg, Sep. 9, 1955, Box 64, Folder 14 "Donald R. Richberg," Regnery Papers, HI; Garrity to Richberg, Aug. 10, 1956, Box 51, Folder "Donald Richberg," Garrity Papers, HI. Garrity and Regnery, as the major conservative publishers, had overlapping business. For instance, Admiral Husband Kimmel originally offered his manuscript to Devin-Adair, who turned it down, before it was picked up by Regnery. See Kimmel to Regnery, Jul. 21, 1954, Box 39, Folder 5, Regnery Papers, HI.

22. Regnery to Harnischfeger, May 24, 1957, Box 28, Folder 6, Regnery Papers, HI. On Pew's relationship to *Human Events*, see Felix Morley to Regnery, Oct. 1, 1969, Box 58, Folder 1, Regnery Papers, HI.

23. Regnery to Harnischfeger, May 24, 1957, Box 28, Folder 6, Regnery Papers, HI.

24. Ibid.; Regnery to Harnischfeger, Feb. 1, 1957, Box 28, Folder 6, Regnery Papers, HI. "The big problem, of course," Regnery groused to Pew, "is to break through the monopoly the left has succeeded in winning over the communication of ideas in this country." Jul. 9, 1957, Box 60, Folder 21, Regnery Papers, HI.

25. Philip Dodd, "Richberg Warns of Labor Monopoly," *Chicago Tribune*, May 19, 1957, G4. The four-part series by Chesly Manly ran Jul. 21–24; the Richberg book played a prominent role in the first and final installments; Manly, "Union Counts Kohler Loss—11.3 Million," *Chicago Tribune*, Jul. 21, 1957, 1; Manly, "Richberg Sees Socialist Rule as Union Goal," *Chicago Tribune*, Jul. 24, 1957, 7. Regnery remarks on the "hysterical" label in a letter to Milliken, Jun. 10, 1957, Box 51, Folder 13 "Roger Milliken," Regnery Papers, HI, and calls it "a very unfavorable review" in a letter to Harnischfeger, May 24, 1957, Box 28, Folder 6, Regnery Papers, HI. The most critical review was Joel Seidman's in *Industrial and Labor Relations Review* 11 (Jan. 1958): 303–305. Less biting but still unfavorable reviews included John E. Hughes, *American Catholic Sociological Review* 19 (Jun. 1958): 167–170, and Philip Taft, *Political Science Quarterly* 72 (Sep. 1957): 468–469. "Reflections of a Chicago Publisher," Feb. 1964, Reel 24, Rusher Microfilm, LOC.

26. Quoted in Regnery to Leonard Read, Jun. 26, 1957, Box 23, Folder 2, Regnery Papers, HI; Regnery to Harnischfeger, Jul. 8, 1957, Box 28, Folder 6, Regnery Papers, HI; Regnery to Milliken, May 21, 1957, Box 51, Folder 13, Regnery Papers, HI; Regnery to James J. Kilpatrick, Aug. 27, 1957, Box 39, Folder 2, Regnery Papers, HI.

27. Read to Regnery, Feb. 28, 1957, Box 23, Folder 2, Regnery Papers, HI; Regnery to Read, Jun. 26, 1957, Box 23, Folder 2, Regnery Papers, HI; Regnery to Kilpatrick, Aug. 27, 1957, Box 39, Folder 2, Regnery Papers, HI.

28. Manion Forum Broadcast #152, "Dictatorship by Labor—A Formidable Threat," Aug. 25, 1957; quoted in Manion Forum Broadcast #155, "Supreme Court Aids Labor Monopoly," Sep. 15, 1957.

29. Manion Forum Broadcast #160, "The 'Labor Movement' in Action at Kohler," Oct. 20, 1957.

30. "Rehiring Ends for Strikers at Kohler Co.," *Chicago Tribune*, Oct. 4, 1960, 8; "Kohler Deadline Passes," *New York Times*, Oct. 4, 1960, 57; "Unhappy Birthday," *Time*, Apr. 18, 1955.

31. For instance, Kohler claimed there had been more than eight hundred instances of union violence in a speech he delivered to the Freedom Club of the First Congregational Church of Los Angeles. "History of Violence in Strike Told," *Los Angeles Times*, Apr. 18, 1956, 34; "Four Years & Stubbornness Have Torn a Town," *Time*, Mar. 17, 1958; "Deadlock Holds in Kohler Strike," *New York Times*, Aug. 22, 1954, 51.

32. Jonathan Mitchell, "Labor . . .," *National Review*, Nov. 19, 1955, 19; "If That's How They Want It," *National Review*, Sep. 8, 1956, 4–5; Letters to the Editor, *National Review*, Oct. 6, 1956, 23; Letters to the Editor, *National Review*, Dec. 29, 1956, 23; William Rusher, "N.R. Newsletter (Confidential)," Dec. 1959, Reel 4, Rusher Microfilm, LOC.

33. Manion Forum Broadcast #100, "Both Platforms Conceal Vital Issues," Aug. 26, 1956.

34. Telegram, Kohler to Mutual Broadcasting System, Oct. 19, 1957, Manion Papers, Box 88, Folder 5, CHM.

35. Smith insisted that Christian Political Action was not anti-Semitic, "unless being determined that the Christian institutions of a Christian nation should, *and shall*, be administered by Christians—is anti-Semitic." Smith to Manion, Oct. 28, 1957, Box 88, Folder 5, Manion Papers, CHM. Manion disavowed anti-Semitism: Manion to Mrs. Frank H. Gibbens, Jul. 10, 1963, Box 10, Folder 1, Manion Papers, CHM: "The statement that 'I do not like Jews' is a lie that my enemies toss out when they can't refute my arguments for Constitutional government. Some of my firmest supporters of the Manion Forum are Jews. I have never said or published an anti-Jewish statement in my life and will pay $100 to anybody who can produce any evidence of this alleged anti-Jewish statement. Only occasionally can I identify people who make such a charge. When I do I get an immediate retraction. I will immediately sue anybody for libel who charges that I am anti-Semetic [*sic*]."

36. Articles include those in the *New York Times*, *Los Angeles Times*, *Columbia (N.C.) State*, *Cincinnati Enquirer*, *Arizona Republic*, and *The (St. Joseph, Ind.) Record*. See clippings in Box 88, Folder 5, Manion Papers, CHM. The *Chicago Tribune* coverage ran daily from Oct. 19 through 22. Manion noted the number of reprints in Manion Forum Broadcast #161, "Kohler Censoring—Omen of Peril to Free Speech," Oct. 27, 1957. How many of these were bulk purchases is unclear.

37. "Kohler Speech Against Union Still Tied Up," *Chicago Tribune*, Oct. 20, 1957.

38. Quotations in this paragraph and those that follow are taken from Manion Forum Broadcast #161, "Kohler Censoring—Omen of Peril to Free Speech," Oct. 27, 1957.

39. Fulton Lewis Jr. called McCarthy's censure a "journalistic lynching party" in a broadcast the day of McCarthy's death; see Fulton Lewis Jr. broadcast reprint, May 2, 1957, Box 29, Folder "Joe McCarthy Various," Garrity Papers, HI.

40. On potential airtime for Reuther, see "Kohler Talk on Network Hits Snag," *Chicago Tribune*, Oct. 19, 1957.

41. On equal time and the Fairness Doctrine, see Susan L. Brinson, *The Red Scare, Politics, and the Federal Communications Commission, 1941–1960* (Westport, Conn.: Praeger, 2004); United States, Congress, House, *Legislative History of the Fairness Doctrine* (Washington, D.C.: U.S. GPO, 1968). Brinson focused mainly on the conflict between the FCC and the left but acknowledged that the FCC tangled with those on both the left and the right.

42. In discussing sanctions, Congress analyzed a recent FCC notice but could not with certainty ascertain the statement's intent, though said it seemed to suggest that Fairness Doctrine violations were not finable. Congress, *Legislative History*, 7.

43. Headlines listed appeared in the *Cincinnati Enquirer*, Nov. 3, 1957, 46; *Richmond*

News Leader, Nov. 5, 1957, 10; *Fort Wayne News-Sentinel*, Nov. 5, 1957, 6; clippings in Box 88, Folder 6, Manion Papers, CHM. Reprint from Manion Forum Broadcast #161, "Kohler Censoring—Omen of Peril to Free Speech," Oct. 27, 1959.

44. Flynt to Manion, Oct. 30, 1957, Box 88, Folder 5, Manion Papers, CHM.

45. *The Kohler Strike and Boycott Bulletin*, vol. 2, no. 237, Nov. 13, 1957, Box 88, Folder 6, Manion Papers, CHM.

46. "Third Anniversary Report to Supporters of the Manion Forum," Manion Forum Radio Network Ephemera, Wilcox Collection, University of Kansas, Lawrence (hereafter KU).

47. In a 1956 letter to supporters, Manion insisted, "Every speaker over our network has been 100 per cent Right Wing." He used the word more pointedly after the break with Mutual, when he informed supporters, "We are now building our own network—contracting with each station as a unit." Letter to supporters, Sep. 21, 1956, Box 97, Folder 42, Manion Papers, CHM; Letter to supporters, Dec. 13, 1957, Box 98, Folder 68, Manion Papers, CHM.

48. "Calling the ACLU," *National Review*, Dec. 14, 1957.

49. On *National Review* coverage, see "This Week," *National Review*, Mar. 15, 1958; and "This Week," *National Review*, Aug. 1, 1959, 228. Longer coverage appeared as well; see, for instance, L. Brent Bozell, "A Crown into the Hazard," *National Review*, Mar. 22, 1958, 272–273. On Kohler ad buys, see William A. Rusher, "N.R. Newsletter (Confidential)," Dec. 1959, Reel 4, Rusher Microfilm, LOC. On *Human Events* coverage, see William Moore, "UAW Violence in Kohler, Wisconsin," *Human Events*, Apr. 28, 1958; and Herbert V. Kohler, "The Penalty of Welfarism," *Human Events*, Dec. 22, 1961.

50. Jameson G. Campaigne, *Check-Off: Labor Bosses and Working Men* (Chicago: Regnery, 1961); Sylvester Petro, *The Kohler Strike: Union Violence and Administrative Law* (Chicago: Regnery, 1961). Petro appeared on the *Manion Forum* to promote his book *Power Unlimited: The Corruption of Union Leadership* (New York: Ronald Press, 1959), in Manion Forum Broadcast #266, "Union Monopoly Worse Danger than External Enemies," Nov. 1, 1959. Reviews of *The Kohler Strike*: Fred Witney, *Journal of Business* 34(3) (Jul. 1961): 403–404; M. S. Ryder, *Industrial and Labor Relations Review* 15(1) (Oct. 1961): 149–150; A. H. Raskin, "Who's Out for Whom?" *New York Times*, Mar. 12, 1961; J. G. Ackelmire, "Books in Brief," *National Review*, Apr. 22, 1961. On *Human Events* coverage, see Regnery to Petro, Apr. 27, 1961, Box 60, Folder 19, Regnery Papers, HI. On Kohler sales, see Regnery to Petro, Nov. 30, 1960, Box 60, Folder 19, Regnery Papers, HI.

Chapter 4

1. Marcom to Manion, Sep. 20, 1964, Box 15, Folder 6, Manion Papers, CHM; "Olive Louise Marcom," *San Luis Obispo Tribune*, Aug. 29, 2010.

2. Manion Forum Broadcast #22, "A Program for Patriots," Feb. 27, 1955, emphasis added; Manion Forum Broadcast #24, "Why Not End the Cold War?" Mar. 13, 1955; Thomas J. Anderson, "Straight Talk," Jul. 1959, Box 84, Folder 12, Thomas J. Anderson Papers, University of Oregon (hereafter UO); "Coming Soon: What You Can Do," *Human Events*, Nov. 17, 1960, Box 114, Folder 5, Philbrick Papers, LOC.

3. On Eisenhower's centrism and embrace of "modern Republicanism," see, for instance, Jim Newton, *Eisenhower: The White House Years* (New York: Doubleday, 2011); and Gary W. Reichard, *Politics as Usual: The Age of Truman and Eisenhower*, 2nd ed. (Wheeling, Ill.: Harlan Davidson, 2004). Morrie Ryskind, "A Visit from St. Nik," *National Review*, Aug. 29, 1959, 294.

4. Manion Forum Broadcast #255, "Khrushchev Visit—The Voice of Jacob But the Hand of Esau," Aug. 16, 1959; "Mr. Eisenhower Falls to the Summit," *National Review*, Aug. 15, 1959, 262–265; Anderson, "Straight Talk," Oct. 1959, Box 84, Folder 12, Anderson Papers, UO.

5. Admantios Polyzoides, "Scandinavia Hostility to Khrushchev Seen," *Los Angeles Times*, Jul. 21, 1959; Werner Wiskari, "Khrushchev Calls Off Plan for a Visit to Scandinavia," *New York Times*, Jul. 21, 1959; "'Spit in Face' Canceled Trip, Says Nikita," *Los Angeles Times*, Jul. 22, 1959.

6. "Americans Exhorted to Greet Khrushchev with 'Civil Silence,'" *New York Times*, Aug. 24, 1959. Ads ran in the *Wall Street Journal, New York Times*, and *Chicago Tribune*, among others.

7. Manion Forum Broadcast #257, "Khrushchev Visit a Symbol of Death," Aug. 31, 1957; "Khrushchev," *Human Events*, Sep. 23, 1959, News 1; "For the Record," *National Review*, Sep. 12, 1959, 315; Peter Kihss, "Anti-Red Groups Here Press Protests Against Khrushchev," *New York Times*, Sep. 11, 1959; "Black Cloth Selling Fast," *Chicago Tribune*, Sep. 12, 1959; N.R. Forum, Sep. 17, 1959, Reel 6, Rusher Microfilm, LOC.

8. On dyeing the Hudson, see Godfrey Hodgson, *The World Turned Right Side Up: A History of the Conservative Ascendancy in America* (Boston: Houghton Mifflin, 1996), originally quoted in Judis, *William F. Buckley, Jr.*; N.R. Forum, Sep. 17, 1959, Reel 6, Rusher Microfilm, LOC.

9. Manion to Senators Andrew F. Schoeppel and Thomas Dodd, telegram, Aug. 12, 1959, Box 5, Folder 6, Manion Papers, CHM.

10. *National Review* underlined this point with a cartoon labeled "Courtship: The Year of Our Lord 1959," which showed a blood-soaked Khrushchev kissing the hand of Columbia. This ran with Buckley's reprinted speech from the rally. "The Damage We Have Done to Ourselves," *National Review*, Sep. 26, 1959, 349–351. For coverage of the rally, see Peter Kihss, "2,500 Anti-Communists Rally; Mayor and President Scored," *New York Times*, Sep. 18, 1959.

11. William A. Rusher, "Now It Can Be Told," *National Review*, Jan. 27, 1989; Bozell to Manion, Aug. 17, 1959, Box 68, Folder 4, Manion Papers, CHM.

12. Rusher to Ferdinand Lathrop Mayer, Feb. 22, 1960, Reel 10, Rusher Microfilm, LOC; Rusher to Thomas Stalker, Jun. 9, 1960, Reel 27, Rusher Microfilm, LOC.

13. Leo Reardon to supporters, Mar. 1, 1958, Box 98, Folder 61, Manion Papers, CHM; Rusher to Edward V. O'Brian, May 8, 1961, Reel 12, Rusher Microfilm, LOC; Rusher to Mayer, Feb. 22, 1960, Reel 10, Rusher Microfilm, LOC.

14. M. Stanton Evans, *Revolt on the Campus* (Chicago: Regnery, 1961), 6.

15. Kirk to Regnery, Dec. 4, 1961, Box 40, Folder 1, Regnery Papers, HI.

16. Bjerre-Poulsen, *Right Face*, 164.

17. While not limited to those in college, these groups drew their support primarily from students. On the origins of YAF, see John A. Andrew, *The Other Side of the Sixties: Young Americans for Freedom and the Rise of Conservative Politics* (New Brunswick, N.J.: Rutgers University Press, 1997). Andrew focuses on YAF's origins in electoral politics.

18. William Buckley, "The Young Americans for Freedom," *National Review*, Sep. 24, 1960, 172; second quote from Hodgson, *The World Turned Right Side Up*, 95.

19. Quoted in Bjerre-Poulsen, *Right Face*, 166–167; Andrew, *Other Side*, 202.

20. Regnery to Milione, Oct. 6, 1960, Box 34, Folder 9, Regnery Papers, HI; Buckley to Milione, Sep. 1, 1960, Reel 8, Rusher Microfilm, LOC; Rusher to Milione, Oct. 6, 1960, Reel 8, Rusher Microfilm, LOC.

21. Jack Jury to Manion, Nov. 13, 1962, Box 6, Folder 10, Manion Papers, CHM; Rusher to Buckley, [n.d.], Reel 4, Rusher Microfilm, LOC.

22. One of Manion's correspondents took issue with the "only 5 per cent" comment. Doing the math for senior colleges, she determined there were about 240,000 professors in the United States, meaning, in Kirk's estimation, 12,000 of these would be communists, a number that troubled her deeply. Mary Love Collins to Manion, Feb. 8, 1963, Box 7, Folder 5, Manion Papers, CHM. A Manion correspondent bemoaned the harassment of Dr. Murray Lincoln Miller at Illinois State University and then shared his role in getting a professor at the same school fired for his communist leanings. Austin Mosher to Manion, Oct. 6, 1964, Box 16, Folder 2, Manion Papers, CHM. Russell Kirk, "The Tyranny of Professorial Rationalism," *National Review*, Feb. 12, 1963, 115.

23. Manion Forum Broadcast #385, "A Case History of Ultra-Liberalism on the Campus," Feb. 11, 1962.

24. Ibid.

25. Manion Forum Broadcast #381, "Conservative Upsurge Indicates Growing Anti-Communism," Jan. 14, 1962.

26. Manion to Milliken, Jan. 12, 1962, Box 6, Folder 3, Manion Papers, CHM; Fund-raising letter, Jan. 19, 1962, Box 99, Folder 46, Manion Papers, CHM; "New Campus Craze" ad, Manion Forum Broadcast #439, "The Union Shop vs. Civil Rights," Feb. 24, 1963.

27. Manion Forum Newsletter, vol. 2, no. 6, [n.d.], Box 85, Folder 2, Manion Papers, CHM.

28. Rusher to James L. Wick, Nov. 22, 1957, Reel 2, Rusher Microfilm, LOC; quoted in Harvey Bartle III to Rusher, Jan. 30, 1960, Reel 3, Rusher Microfilm, LOC; Charles Edison to Buckley, Sep. 29, 1959, Reel 5, Rusher Microfilm, LOC; Regnery to Kirk, Feb. 8, 1957, Box 40, Folder 1, Regnery Papers, HI.

29. Advertising prospectus, [n.d., likely 1962 or 1963], Box 109, Folder 1, Manion Papers, CHM.

30. Manion Forum Broadcast #523, "Young America Embraces Conservatism," Oct. 11, 1964; Frank Chodorov, "In Quest of a Moses," *Human Events*, Oct. 27, 1958; "Resounding YAF Rally," *Human Events*, Mar. 17, 1962; Fulton Lewis Jr., "Ohio YAF Plans Giant Rally," *Human Events*, Apr. 28, 1962; "The Week," *National Review*, Jun. 17, 1961, 370; "Next Phase Coming Up," *National Review*, Mar. 27, 1962; Rusher to Mrs. Joseph Ikerman, Sep. 12, 1961, Reel 8, Rusher Microfilm, LOC.

31. David R. Jones to Regnery, Dec. 31, 1964, Box 80, Folder 15, Regnery Papers, LOC; "The New Trend on Campus: Conservatism," *Human Events*, Sep. 14, 1957.

32. *Human Events* claimed a loss of $3,606, while *National Review* lost around $2,000. They fought for the money at an ISI meeting, but the organization rejected their claims. See James L. Wick to Rusher, Jun. 13, 1959, Reel 14, Rusher Microfilm, LOC; Rusher to Wick, n.d., Reel 14, Rusher Microfilm, LOC.

Chapter 5

1. Cies to Gina Manion, Sep. 16, 1961, Box 6, Folder 1, Manion Papers, CHM.

2. Daniel Bell, *The New American Right* (New York: Criterion, 1955); Seymour Lipset, *The Radical Right: A Problem for American Democracy* (New York: Columbia University Press, 1954); Clinton Rossiter, *Conservatism in America* (New York: Knopf, 1955); Richard Hofstadter, "The "Pseudo-Conservative Revolt," *American Scholar* (Winter 1954–55): 9–27.

3. For the history of the Birch Society, see D. J. Mulloy, *The World of the John Birch Society: Conspiracy, Conservatism, and the Cold War* (Nashville: Vanderbilt University Press, 2014).

4. "The Americanists," *Time*, Mar. 10, 1961. The *Los Angeles Times* series, written by Gene Blake, ran Mar. 5–9, 1961.

5. Hans Engh, *Nation*, Mar. 11, 1961, 209–211; "State Probing Birch Society, Brown Says," *Los Angeles Times*, Mar. 15, 1961.

6. "Senator Scores Group Calling Eisenhower a Red," *New York Times*, Mar. 9, 1961; "Richard Nixon Advises Caution in Combat Against Subversives," *Los Angeles Times*, Mar. 18, 1961.

7. Alan Barth, "Report on the 'Rampageous Right,'" *New York Times Magazine*, Nov. 26, 1961. Among the articles on the right: "The Ultras," *Time*, Dec. 8, 1961; Arthur Schlesinger Jr., "The 'Threat' of the Radical Right," *New York Times*, Jun. 17, 1962; Cushing Strout, "Fantasy on the Right," *New Republic*, May 1, 1961, 13–15. Books included reissues of Bell's *The New American Right*, updated with the title *The Radical Right* (Garden City, N.Y.: Doubleday, 1963); Rossiter's *Conservatism in America* (New York: Vintage, 1962); and new books: Arnold Forster and Benjamin Epstein, *Danger on the Right* (New York: Random House, 1964); Ralph E. Ellsworth and Sarah M. Harris, *The American Right Wing: A Report to the Fund for the Republic* (Washington, D.C.: Public Affairs, 1962).

8. Peter Braestrup, "Now Birch Society Polarizes the Right," *New York Times*, Apr. 9, 1961; quoted in Fred J. Cook, "The Ultras," *Nation*, Jun. 23, 1962, 565–606; "Who's Who in the Tumult of the Far Right," *Life*, Feb. 9, 1961. Strout's article "Fantasy on the Right" also creates a conservative hodgepodge.

9. Manion Forum Broadcast #425, "Beware of Left Wing Extremists Who Now Run Our Government," Nov. 18, 1962; *Dan Smoot Report*, no. 52, 1961, The Dan Smoot Report, Wilcox Collection, KU.

10. William Buckley, "National Review's Position," *New York Times*, Apr. 16, 1961; "Confidential Behind-the-Scenes Report," Independent American Ephemera, Folder 1, Wilcox Collection, KU.

11. McCaffrey to Buckley, Mar. 9, 1961, Reel 11, Rusher Microfilm, LOC.

12. Welch to Regnery, Dec. 1, 1952, Box 78, Folder 1, Regnery Papers, HI.

13. Goldwater would later come to regret this, as the press tagged the committee a "Birch front group" during the 1964 presidential election. "Goldwater Denies Knowing He Joined Birch Front Group," *New York Times*, Oct. 10, 1964; Information Concerning Henry Regnery Company, Box 81, Folder 16A, Regnery Papers, HI; Regnery to Robert E. Wood, Aug. 28, 1953, Box 80, Folder 1, Regnery Papers, HI; Buckley to Regnery, Feb. 1, 1962, Box 10, Folder 14, Regnery Papers, HI; "Notes and Asides," *National Review*, Jan. 25, 1959, 79; Independent American Forum Ad, *National Review*, Oct. 10, 1959, 405.

14. Welch to Manion, Nov. 25, 1959, Box 62, Folder 1, Manion Papers, CHM; Manion to Welch, Nov. 30, 1959, Box 62, Folder 1, Manion Papers, CHM; Manion to Welch, Aug. 3, 1961, Box 62, Folder 1, Manion Papers, CHM; Rusher to Bozell, Sep. 26, 1961, Reel 28, Rusher Microfilm, LOC. Rusher expressed frustration that *National Review* editors refused to publicize Manion's clubs because they believed he "was personally ambitious" and a member of the Birch Society. Rusher was not an enthusiastic Manion supporter—"Manion is no particular hero of mine"—but he believed the clubs could be useful.

15. Seventh Anniversary Progress Report, 1961, Box 85, Folder 7, Manion Papers, CHM.

16. Manion to Welch, Aug. 3, 1961, Box 62, Folder 1, Manion Papers, CHM; Manion to Talbert, Aug. 16, 1961, Box 56, Folder 4, Manion Papers, CHM.

17. Quoted in memo to Conservative Clubs, "News from Conservative Clubs," n.d., Manion Forum Ephemera, Folder 1, Wilcox Collection, KU; Memo to Conservative Clubs, "Your Reading Program," n.d., Manion Forum Ephemera, Folder 1, Wilcox Collection, KU.

18. Memo to Conservative Clubs, "You *Can* Beat the Managed News Game," n.d., Manion Forum Ephemera, Folder 2, Wilcox Collection, KU.

19. Memo to Conservative Clubs, "Influencing Public Opinion: What a Conservative Club Can Do," n.d., Manion Forum Ephemera, Folder 2, Wilcox Collection, KU.

20. "'Conservative' Better Hurry," *Knoxville Journal*, Aug. 8, 1961, clipping in Manion Forum Ephemera, Folder 1, Wilcox Collection, KU; Manion Forum Newsletter, Nov. 1961, vol. 1, no. 8, Box 85, Folder 2, Manion Papers, CHM; "Responses" quoted in Manion to Rev. Richard Ginder, Aug. 10, 1961, Box 6, Folder 1, Manion Papers, CHM; Seventh Anniversary Progress Report, 1961, Box 85, Folder 7, Manion Papers, CHM; Manion to Hub Russell, Sep. 12, 1961, Box 68, Folder 8, Manion Papers, CHM; Reardon to sponsors, Jul. 20, 1962, Box 99, Folder 31, Manion Papers, CHM.

21. Manion to Welch, Aug. 3, 1961, Box 62, Folder 1, Manion Papers, CHM; Rusher to Manion, Jul. 25, 1961, Reel 11, Rusher Microfilm, LOC.

22. McCaffrey to Buckley, Mar. 9, 1961, Reel 11, Rusher Microfilm, LOC; Bogus, *Buckley*, 198–221.

23. Rusher memo to Buckley, Bozell, James Burnham, Willmoore Kendall, Frank Meyer, and Priscilla Buckley, Apr. 3, 1961, Reel 4, Rusher Microfilm, LOC.

24. Ibid.

25. Ibid.

26. Manion to Thomas J. Davis, Feb. 26, 1964, Box 61, Folder 1, Manion Papers, CHM;

Manion to Milliken, Jan. 12, 1962, Box 6, Folder 3, Manion Papers, CHM; Welch quoted in James E. Clayton, "John Birch 'Antis' Point Unwelcome Spotlight," *Washington Post*, Mar. 26, 1961.

27. William Buckley, "The Uproar," *National Review*, Apr. 22, 1961, 241–243.

28. "Charges Reds Began Attack on Birch Group," *Chicago Tribune*, Apr. 2, 1961; Manion quoted in Rusher to Harry L. Bradley, May 8, 1961, Reel 4, Rusher Microfilm, LOC; Welch quoted in Rusher to Kenneth D. Robertson Jr., May 1, 1961, Reel 12, Rusher Microfilm, LOC; Courtney to Manion, May 11, 1961, Box 5, Folder 12, Manion Papers, CHM.

29. Manion to Milliken, Jan. 12, 1962, Box 6, Folder 3, Manion Papers, CHM; Manion to Welch, Jul. 14, 1961, Box 62, Folder 1, Manion Papers, CHM.

30. Manion to Welch (confidential), Sep. 27, 1961, Box 61, Folder 4, Manion Papers, CHM; "Conservatism—Real and Unreal," *Wall Street Journal*, Aug. 14, 1961; "Warn Birch Quiz Can Backfire," *Chicago Tribune*, Apr. 6, 1961.

31. Rusher memo to Buckley, Burnham, Meyer, William Rickenbacker, and Priscilla Buckley, Jan. 30, 1962, Reel 4, Rusher Microfilm, LOC.

32. Manion to Milliken, Jan. 12, 1962, Box 6, Folder 3, Manion Papers, CHM; Rusher memo to Buckley et al., Apr. 3, 1961, Reel 4, Rusher Microfilm, LOC.

33. Buckley, "The Question of Robert Welch," *National Review*, Feb. 13, 1962, 83–88; Bozell to Rusher, Feb. 23, 1962, Reel 3, Rusher Microfilm, LOC; "Rabble Rousers" quoted in Thomas A. Stalker to Rusher, Feb. 19, 1962, Reel 13, Rusher Microfilm, LOC; Milliken to Welch, Feb. 12, 1962, Box 6, Folder 3, Manion Papers, CHM; Milliken to Rusher, Mar. 12, 1962, Reel 9, Rusher Microfilm, LOC; James Lewis Kirby Jr. to Rusher, Mar. 19, 1962, Reel 8, Rusher Microfilm, LOC; Rusher to Buckley, Feb. 28, 1962, Reel 4, Rusher Microfilm, LOC; Rusher to Buckley, Feb. 26, 1962, Reel 4, Rusher Microfilm, LOC; Rusher to Buckley, Feb. 20, 1962, Reel 4, Rusher Microfilm, LOC; Rusher to Arnold S. Anderson, Mar. 28, 1962, Reel 3, Rusher Microfilm, LOC.

34. William Rickenbacker memo to Bozell, Buckley, Priscilla Buckley, Burnham, Kendall, Meyer, and Rusher, Apr. 14, 1962, Reel 12, Rusher Microfilm, LOC; Virginia Gourdin to Buckley, Mar. 12, 1962, Reel 8, Rusher Microfilm, LOC; Schlafly to Buckley, Feb. 8, 1962, Box 6, Folder 3, Manion Papers, CHM.

35. Rusher to Buckley, Feb. 20, 1962, Reel 4, Rusher Microfilm, LOC.

Chapter 6

1. Matthew Dallek, *The Right Moment: Ronald Reagan's First Victory and the Decisive Turning Point in American Politics* (Oxford: Oxford University Press, 2000), ch. 1.

2. "Text of Kennedy's Palladium Speech," *Los Angeles Times*, Nov. 19, 1961.

3. David Wise, "Kennedy Assails Rightists," *Boston Globe*, Nov. 19, 1961; Tom Wicker, "Kennedy Asserts Far-Right Groups Provoke Disunity," *New York Times*, Nov. 19, 1961; "Ike Denounces Extremists of Right Wing," *Chicago Tribune*, Nov. 24, 1961.

4. "Washington Wire," *Wall Street Journal*, Aug. 17, 1962; Manion Forum fund-raising letter, Aug. 31, 1962, Box 99, Folder 29, Manion Papers, CHM.

5. Fred J. Cook, "Hate Clubs of the Air," *Nation*, May 25, 1964.

6. Ibid.

7. Ibid.

8. Manion Forum letter to sponsors, Dec. 7, 1962, Box 99, Folder 19, Manion Papers, CHM.

9. Heather Hendershot, *What's Fair on the Air?: Cold War Right-Wing Broadcasting and the Public Interest* (Chicago: University of Chicago Press, 2011), 26–64.

10. Mabeth E. Smoot, "The Dan Smoot Story," *Dan Smoot Report*, Jun. 1961, Box 70, Folder 1, Regnery Papers, HI; Hendershot, *What's Fair on the Air?* 65–67.

11. Mabeth Smoot to Devin Garrity, Apr. 15, 1960, Box 20, Folder 1, Garrity Papers, HI; Manion to Lewis, Jul. 22, 1963, Box 10, Folder 2, Manion Papers, CHM; Manion to Fred F.

Loock, Aug. 10, 1965, Box 74, Folder 14, Manion Papers, CHM; Manion to Lewis, Aug. 9, 1965, Box 20, Folder 1, Manion Papers, CHM.

12. Drew Pearson, "Right-Wing Radio-TV Probed," *Washington Post*, Dec. 10, 1965; Lloyd Flugum to Manion, Apr. 15, 1964, Box 14, Folder 2, Manion Papers, CHM; Lewis M. McKay Jr. to Manion, Box 9, Folder 3, Manion Papers, CHM.

13. D. B. Lewis was a major sponsor for Hargis, Manion, and Dan Smoot. Hargis repeatedly invited Manion, Paul Harvey, and others to his conventions, but they purposefully declined. Hargis to Reardon, Apr. 26, 1965, Box 18, Folder 6, Manion Papers, CHM; Manion to Harvey, Jul. 12, 1966, Box 23, Folder 1, Manion Papers, CHM. On "kook stations," see Recommendations for Cancellation, [n.d.], Box 25, Folder 2, Manion Papers, CHM. Rusher to All Concerned, Jan. 15, 1962, Reel 4, Rusher Microfilm, LOC.

14. Congress, *Legislative History*, 9–15.

15. Ibid., 19.

16. Ibid., 20–21, 23–24.

17. Ibid., 6, 18.

18. Manion column, Nov. 1, 1963, Box 108, Folder 4, Manion Papers, CHM; FCC 63-734 ("Stations' Responsibilities Under Fairness Doctrine as to Controversial Issue Broadcasting"), 28 Fed. Reg. 7962 1963.

19. FCC 63-734 ("Stations' Responsibilities Under Fairness Doctrine as to Controversial Issue Broadcasting"), 28 Fed. Reg. 7962 1963. On southern media and civil rights, see Steven D. Classen, *Watching Jim Crow: The Struggles over Mississippi TV, 1955–1969* (Durham, N.C.: Duke University Press, 2004). On the FCC's response to southern media's civil rights coverage, see Kay Mills, *Changing Channels: The Civil Rights Case That Transformed Television* (Jackson: University Press of Mississippi, 2004).

20. On the Citizens' Council radio program, see Stephanie R. Rolph, "Courting Conservatism: White Resistance and the Ideology of Race in the 1960s," in *The Right Side of the Sixties: Reexamining Conservatism's Decade of Transformation*, ed. Laura Jane Gifford and Daniel K. Williams (New York: Palgrave Macmillan, 2012), 21–39. For more on the role of race in the development of conservatism, see Joseph E. Lowndes, *From the New Deal to the New Right: Race and the Southern Origins of Modern Conservatism* (New Haven, Conn.: Yale University Press, 2008).

21. On objectivity, see Kaplan, *Politics and the American Press*; Michael Schudson, *Origins of the Ideal of Objectivity in the Professions: Studies in the History of American Journalism and American Law, 1830–1940* (New York: Garland, 1990); Mindich, *Just the Facts*; Russell Kirk, "Study of Current Events: Can It Be Objective?" *Human Events*, May 31, 1969; and "'Life' Goes to a Strike," *National Review*, Jun. 1, 1957.

22. Manion Forum Broadcast #474, "Do You Really Want Federal Censorship for Your Local Radio?" Oct. 27, 1963.

23. FCC 64-611 ("Applicability of the Fairness Doctrine in the Handling of Controversial Issues of Public Importance"), 29 Fed Reg. 10416–10427 1964; Congress, *Legislative History*, 5; Ben Waple to Arthur I. Boreman, Dec. 16, 1963, Box 66, Folder 12, Manion Papers, CHM; G. H. Thompson to Manion, Oct. 6, 1963, Box 11, Folder 5, Manion Papers, CHM; Manion to H. R. Gross, Oct. 15, 1963, Box 11, Folder 6, Manion Papers, CHM.

24. Manion Forum Broadcast #462, "The Unlimited Dangers of a Limited Test Ban Treaty," Aug. 4, 1963; Manion Forum Broadcast #463, "The Risks Involved in the Test Ban Treaty," Aug. 11, 1963; Manion Forum Broadcast #466, "The Test Ban Treaty: 'A Covenant with Death and an Agreement with Hell,'" Sep. 1, 1963; Letter to contributors, Sep. 21, 1956, Box 97, Folder 42, Manion Papers, CHM.

25. Billy James Hargis, "New Frontier Threatens Freedom of Speech," *Christian Crusade*, Sep. 1963, 24–25, Box 96, Folder 4, Philbrick Papers, LOC; M. Stanton Evans, "At Home," *National Review Bulletin*, Jan. 21, 1964, 6; Manion Forum Broadcast #474, "Do You Really Want Federal Censorship for Your Local Radio?" Oct. 27, 1963; "Wadsworth to Head New Test Ban Group," *New York Times*, Jul. 19, 1963, 2; Wilda Parnell to Al Hill, Oct. 14, 1963, Box 11,

Folder 5, Manion Papers, CHM; FCC 64-611 ("Applicability of the Fairness Doctrine in the Handling of Controversial Issues of Public Importance"), 29 Fed Reg. 10419 1964.

26. Manion to John Bell Williams, Sep. 30, 1963, Box 11, Folder 4, Manion Papers, CHM; Wilda Parnell to Al Hill, Oct. 14, 1963, Box 11, Folder 5, Manion Papers, CHM.

27. Reuther Memorandum, Dec. 19, 1961, Box 116, Folder 4, Manion Papers, CHM. The Kennedy administration did, in fact, use the IRS in ways consistent with the Reuther memo. The Ideological Organizations Project (IOP), launched prior to the memo's circulation, sought to strip both right-wing and left-wing groups of their tax-exempt status. On the right these groups included the Birch Society, Christian Crusade, and Life Line. The existence of the IOP remained secret until the Church Committee hearings in 1975. For a detailed analysis of the IOP, see Andrew, *Other Side*, 157–163.

28. Hargis, "New Frontier Threatens Freedom of Speech." Hargis learned of the memo from the 1963 book *The Far Right* by Donald Janson and Bernard Eismann. Introduction to the Reuther Memorandum, Manion Forum, n.d., Box 116, Folder 4, Manion Papers, CHM.

29. "Coincidence or Not," *National Review*, Nov. 5, 1963, 382–384.

30. "New Guide to AFL-CIO Radio & TV," *Machinist*, Aug. 22, 1963, 7, Box 96, Folder 4, Philbrick Papers, LOC.

31. Manion Forum Broadcast #474, "Do You Want Federal Censorship for Your Local Radio Station?" Oct. 27, 1963; Manion Forum Broadcast #478, "Congress Versus the FCC," Nov. 24, 1963; Manion Forum Television Broadcast #48, "Freedom of Speech Is in Jeopardy," n.d.

32. For an excellent discussion of the role of "public interest" in the regulation of radio, see Hendershot, *What's Fair on the Air?* 16–20, 89–93.

33. Manion Forum Broadcast #474, "Do You Want Federal Censorship for Your Local Radio Station?" Oct. 27, 1963.

34. Manion Forum Television Broadcast #48, "Freedom of Speech Is in Jeopardy," n.d.

35. Manion Forum Broadcast #449, "The 1963 Wheat Referendum: A Squeeze Play on America's Farmers," Guest: Robert J. Dole, May 5, 1963; Bob Dole to John Cavanaugh, Oct. 29, 1963, Box 12, Folder 1, Manion Papers, CHM; John G. Tower to Hobart K. McDowell, n.d., Box 12, Folder 3, Manion Papers, CHM.

36. Manion Forum Broadcast #478, "Congress Versus the FCC," Nov. 24, 1963.

37. FCC 64-611 ("Applicability of the Fairness Doctrine in the Handling of Controversial Issues of Public Importance"), 29 Fed Reg. 10416–10427 1964.

38. "Radio Station Fined by Federal Agency," *New York Times*, Jul. 28, 1961. New FCC policy came about in large part as a result of payola scandals, which led the FCC to revoke licenses because of programming practices for the first time in 1960. "Monitors for TV," *New York Times*, May 22, 1960. In discussing sanctions, legislators determined that while the FCC's stance was unclear, the legislative history suggested Fairness Doctrine violations were not finable. Congress, *Legislative History*, 7.

39. Manion to Owen Ayres, Nov. 13, 1963, Box 12, Folder 3, Manion Papers, CHM; "Coincidence or Not," *National Review*, Nov. 5, 1963, 382–384.

40. See, for instance, Manion Forum Broadcast #454, "The Menace of Managed News: Is the Image of the President More Important than the Truth?" Jun. 9, 1963; and Hanson W. Baldwin, "Managed News: Our Peacetime Censorship," *Atlantic Monthly*, Apr. 1963, 53+.

41. Letter to supporters, Oct. 15, 1963, Box unknown, Folder unknown, Manion Papers, CHM; Manion Forum Weekly Column, Nov. 11, 1963, Box 108, Folder 4, Manion Papers, CHM; "The Winds Are Ablowin'," Address by William B. Arthur to the Public Relations Society of America, Feb. 13, 1974, Box 156, Folder 8, Jameson G. Campaigne Papers, HI.

42. Letter to supporters, Oct. 15, 1963, Box unknown, Folder unknown, Manion Papers, CHM; Letter to supporters, Nov. 7, 1963, Box unknown, Folder unknown, Manion Papers, CHM; Wilda Parnell to Larry Wilson, Oct. 22, 1963, Box 67, Folder 1, Manion Papers, CHM; George K. Culbertson to Manion, Feb. 23, 1965, Box 18, Folder 2, Manion Papers, CHM; "A Constitutional Government Under God," Address by Tom Anderson to the National Defense Committee, Apr. 20, 1970, Box 80, Folder 4, Anderson Papers, UO.

43. W. D. Sutherland to Manion, Oct. 1, 1963, Box 11, Folder 5, Manion Papers, CHM; Lyons to Manion, Jan. 10, 1968, Box 66, Folder 9, Manion Papers, CHM.

Chapter 7

1. Rusher to Buckley, Mar. 9, 1972, Box 121, Folder 5, Rusher Papers, LOC.

2. Forum to supporters, May 20, 1963, Box 101, Folder 7, Manion Papers, CHM.

3. Regnery to Buckley, Jul. 15, 1952, Box 10, Folder 14, Regnery Papers, HI; *National Review*, Nov. 19, 1955, 1; Clarence Manion, "This Is Where I Came in," *American Opinion*, Apr. 1960, 17–22; Undated letter to supporters, Folder 2, Manion Forum Ephemera, Wilcox Collection, KU.

4. Chesly Manly, *The Twenty-Year Revolution: From Roosevelt to Eisenhower* (Chicago: Regnery, 1954), 261–264.

5. Smith, *The Colonel*, 512–514; "Publisher Active in G.O.P. Affairs," *New York Times*, Apr. 2, 1955.

6. "Publisher Active in G.O.P. Affairs."

7. "Sloppy Citizenship," *Time*, Nov. 16, 1942; "Fish Weights Race for Senate Seat," *New York Times*, Aug. 27, 1952; "Fish Plans 'States' Rights' Political Unit," *New York Times*, Sep. 22, 1954; Fish to For America, Sep. 21, 1954, Box 2, Folder 8, Manion Papers, CHM.

8. "Charts New Plan for America Unit," *New York Times*, Nov. 20, 1955.

9. Manion to Justus D. Doenecke, Oct. 7 and 22, 1974, Box 45, Folder 9, Manion Papers, CHM.

10. "Tax Rebellion Leader," *New York Times*, Oct. 16, 1956; "Ex-Tax Chief Opposes Tax (Now He Tells Us)," *New York Times*, Feb. 19, 1956.

11. Manion Forum Broadcast #54, "An American Party for the American People," Oct. 9, 1955; Manion Forum Broadcast #13, "Is Our Compulsory Old Age Insurance an Actuarial Fraud?" Dec. 26, 1954.

12. "New Party 'Drafts' U.S. Ex-Tax Chief," *New York Times*, Aug. 29, 1956; "Tax Reform Party Sets Rally Oct. 15," *New York Times*, Oct. 4, 1956; "Andrews Planning Week-End Campaign," *New York Times*, Oct. 17, 1956.

13. Judis, *William F. Buckley, Jr.*, 127–129.

14. Judis, *William F Buckley, Jr.*, 144–146; William Buckley, "Reflections on Election Eve," *National Review*, Nov. 3, 1956.

15. "The Party of Protest," *Wall Street Journal*, Oct. 17, 1956; Sam M. Jones, "The States' Rights Ticket," *National Review*, Oct. 27, 1956; "Why the South Must Prevail," *National Review*, Aug. 24, 1957.

16. "Andrews Reports Gains," *New York Times*, Oct. 18, 1956.

17. Third Anniversary Report, n.d., in Manion Forum Radio Network, Ephemera, Wilcox Collection, KU.

18. Reardon to supporters, Dec. 12, 1958, Box 98, Folder 42, Manion Papers, CHM; Envelope for Nov. 28, 1958, fund-raising letter, Box 98, Folder 44, Manion Papers, CHM.

19. Robert E. Wood to Hubbard Russell, Jan. 28, 1959, Box 69, Folder 4, Manion Papers, CHM; Jim Johnson, "Orval Faubus Can Be Elected President," Apr. 1959, Box 69, Folder 4, Manion Papers, CHM.

20. Johnson, "Orval Faubus Can Be Elected President."

21. Manion to J. Bracken Lee, Sep. 21, 1959, Box 70, Folder 1, Manion Papers, CHM; Manion to Howard Buffett, Mar. 27, 1959, Box 69, Folder 4, Manion Papers, CHM. Manion and Hub Russell dined with Faubus in early 1959 and scratched out a plan, but Manion abandoned his work for Faubus when he began working closely with Goldwater.

22. Elizabeth Shermer, "Origins of the Conservative Ascendancy: Barry Goldwater's Early Senate Career and the De-legitimization of Organized Labor," *Journal of American History* 95 (Dec. 2008): 678–709; "Remember the Mastodon," *Washington Post*, Apr. 10, 1957. Manion claimed that Goldwater's appearance on the *Forum* on May 12, 1957, was the senator's first

appearance on a national radio program. Manion to Russell Bennitt, Jul. 10, 1963, Box 10, Folder 1, Manion Papers, CHM.

23. Brent Bozell, "Death Throes of a Proud Party," *National Review*, Jan. 31, 1959, 487; "The Big Fight," *Human Events*, Dec. 28, 1957; James Wick, "Rating Your Members of Congress," *Human Events*, Oct. 20, 1958; Barry Goldwater, "The Future of Republicanism," *Human Events*, Jan. 28, 1959; Barry Goldwater, "The Epithets of Wayne Morse: A Challenge to Senatorial Dignity," *Human Events*, Jul. 22, 1959; Barry Goldwater, "Wanted: A More Conservative GOP," *Human Events*, Feb. 18, 1960.

24. Notes from meeting of Goldwater, Manion, and Hubbard Russell, May 15, 1959, Box 69, Folder 4, Manion Papers, CHM.

25. Wood to Manion, Apr. 22, 1959, Box 69, Folder 4, Manion Papers, CHM; Pulliam to Manion, Jun. 1, 1959, Box 69, Folder 5, Manion Papers, CHM; William B. Wright to Manion, Jul. 16, 1959, Box 69, Folder 7, Manion Papers, CHM; Manion to Frank Brophy, Jul. 28, 1959, Box 70, Folder 1, Manion Papers, CHM.

26. Buckley to Manion, Sep. 24, 1959, Box 70, Folder 1, Manion Papers, CHM; Smoot to Hubbard Russell, Oct. 13, 1959, Box 70, Folder 2, Manion Papers, CHM.

27. Frank Brophy laid out these reasons in a letter to Bozell when proposing the project on Manion's behalf. Brophy to Bozell, Jun. 18, 1959, Box 69, Folder 5, Manion Papers, CHM; Manion to Milliken, Jun. 18, 1959, Box 69, Folder 5, Manion Papers, CHM.

28. Manion to Clifford Ward, May 5, 1960, Box 70, Folder 5, Manion Papers, CHM; "Goldwater Book Reaps Financial, Political Hay," *New York World-Telegram*, Apr. 26, 1960, Box 72, Folder 1, Manion Papers, CHM; Bozell to Manion, Aug. 17, 1959, Box 68, Folder 4, Manion Papers, CHM; Manion to Frank Brophy, Sep. 1, 1959, Box 68, Folder 4, Manion Papers, CHM; Manion to Milliken, Jan. 29, 1964, Box 68, Folder 4, Manion Papers, CHM.

29. Manion to Buckley, Sep. 28, 1959, Box 68, Folder 4, Manion Papers, CHM; Buckley to Manion, Oct. 2, 1959, Box 68, Folder 4, Manion Papers, CHM.

30. Quoted in Shermer, "Origins of the Conservative Ascendancy," 701.

31. Initial sales numbers from "Goldwater Book Reaps Financial, Political Hay." John Chamberlain, "The Humane Base of Conservatism," *Wall Street Journal*, Jun. 2, 1960; George Morgenstern, "Harsh Facts, Hard Sense on the Perils to Liberty," *Chicago Tribune*, Apr. 17, 1960; Frank S. Meyer, "A Man of Principle," *National Review*, Apr. 23, 1960, 269–270; Barry Goldwater, "Platform for a Free America," *Human Events*, Apr. 14, 1960.

32. Sales numbers from *Wall Street Journal*, as mentioned in Bozell to Manion, Oct. 12, 1960, Box 72, Folder 1, Manion Papers, CHM.

33. Reardon to supporters, Apr. 12, 1960, Box 89, Folder 9, Manion Papers, CHM.

34. Knowland was appointed to the Senate in 1945 upon the death of Hiram Johnson and won his first race in 1946. Jenner also initially served as an appointed senator for a few months at the end of 1944 to fill Frederick Van Nuys's seat; 1946 was the first time he ran for and was elected to a Senate seat.

35. Gary W. Reichard, *Politics as Usual: The Age of Truman and Eisenhower*, 2d ed. (Wheeling, Ill.: Harlan Davidson, 2004).

36. Regnery to Wood, Dec. 10, 1953, Box 80, Folder 1, Regnery Papers, HI.

37. Manion promoted the ACA on his show; see, for instance, Manion Forum Broadcast #387, "Mobilizing for Freedom: Co-operation Between Conservative Groups Means Victory," Feb. 25, 1962; Rusher to Gerrish Milliken, Oct. 24, 1960, Reel 9, Rusher Microfilm, LOC; and James Wick, "Rating Your Members of Congress," *Human Events*, Dec. 2, 1959, 1–4. *Human Events* repeated this process with the Committee on Political Education's scores in 1960. James Wick, "Rating Your Members of Congress," *Human Events*, Nov. 10, 1960, 557–560.

38. "The Week," *National Review*, Apr. 11, 1959; Manion Forum Broadcast #387, "Mobilizing for Freedom: Cooperation Between Conservative Groups Means Victory," Feb. 25, 1962.

39. Judith G. Smith, *Political Brokers: Money, Organizations, Power, and People* (New York: Liveright, 1972), ch. 2.

40. John J. Synon, "The ACA-Index: How to Trap a Demagog," *Human Events*, May 26, 1960, 1–4; John J. Synon, "You Bet I'm a Republican," *Human Events*, July 28, 1960, 315–316. Background on Synon in Hustwit, *James J. Kilpatrick*, 124–126. Hustwit wrote, "Calling someone like Synon a segregationist would be kind," noting he published literature on scientific racism and "always took the most radical stances against civil rights." Schadeberg ad, *Human Events*, Nov. 24, 1961, 801.

41. Synon, "You Bet I'm a Republican"; "There Is a Difference—Back Home," *National Review*, Nov. 5, 1960.

42. In addition to Moreell, Major General Thomas A. Lane appeared on the program once he assumed the presidency of the ACA. Manion Forum Broadcast #711, "Protection of Person and Property: When Government Reneges—Responsibility Reverts to the Individual," May 19, 1968. Notes from ACA Luncheon Meeting in New York, Nov. 14, 1961, Reel 8, Rusher Microfilm, LOC.

43. "Questionnaire for Congressional Candidates," Box 74, Folder 14, Manion Papers, CHM.

44. For example, see Manion Forum Broadcast #97, "Income Tax—Path to Totalitarianism and Tyranny," Aug. 5, 1956; and Manion Forum Broadcast #316, "Design for Abolishing the Income Tax," Oct. 16, 1960.

45. Reardon to supporters, Apr. 12, 1960, Box 89, Folder 9, Manion Papers, CHM; Manion Forum Broadcast #305, "Manion Forum Congressional Questionnaire a Nationwide Sensation," Jul. 31, 1960.

46. Manion Forum Broadcast #305, "Manion Forum Congressional Questionnaire a Nationwide Sensation," Jul. 31, 1960.

47. Ibid.; Manion Forum Broadcast #299, "On Vital Issues, Candidates Must Be 'Put on the Spot,'" Jun. 19, 1960.

48. "What You Can Do," *Human Events*, Nov. 10, 1960, 17; Regnery to Sylvester Petro, Apr. 27, 1961, Box 60, Folder 19, Regnery Papers, HI.

49. "*Human Events* to Hold Political Action Conference," *Human Events*, May 5, 1960.

50. "Make Reservations Now for Human Events Summer Conference," *Human Events*, May 12, 1961, 301; PAC ad, *Human Events*, Jun. 29, 1963, 208; "Political Action Conference Tapes Now Ready," *Human Events*, Feb. 3, 1962, 87.

51. Garrity to Wick, Jan. 21, 1963, Box 36, Folder H, Garrity Papers, HI; Regnery to Wick, Jan. 12, 1962, Box 32, Folder 1, Regnery Papers, HI.

52. McCaffrey to Buckley and Rusher, Jan. 7, 1963, Box 17, Folder 1, Rusher Papers, LOC.

53. Wick to Regnery, Jan. 21, 1963, Box 32, Folder 1, Regnery Papers, HI; Cabell Phillips, "Right-Wing Rally Hails Goldwater," *New York Times*, Jul. 13, 1963, 13; "Human Events Conference Postponed," *Human Events*, Jan. 11, 1964, 4.

Chapter 8

1. Heibel to Manion, Mar. 2, 1963, Box 8, Folder 2, Manion Papers, CHM; "That Other Subversive Network," *Solidarity*, Jan. and Feb. 1963, Box 8, Folder 2, Manion Papers, CHM.

2. "That Other Subversive Network," *Solidarity*, Jan. and Feb. 1963.

3. Rusher to Brent Bozell, Mar. 6, 1969, Box 11, Folder 13, Rusher Papers, LOC.

4. Rusher, *The Rise of the Right*, 89; Rusher to Buckley, Oct. 5, 1960, Reel 27, Rusher Microfilm, LOC.

5. Rusher to Bozell, Mar. 23, 1961, Reel 3, Rusher Microfilm, LOC; Rusher memo, Apr. 3, 1961, Reel 4, Rusher Microfilm, LOC.

6. Barry Goldwater, "The Forgotten American," *Human Events*, Jan. 27, 1961; Robert Novak, "Goldwater's Image," *Wall Street Journal*, Jan. 11, 1961.

7. Willmoore Kendall, "Quo Vadis, Barry?" *National Review*, Feb. 25, 1961, 107–108, 127.

8. On Bozell's political transformations in Spain, see Daniel Kelly, *Living on Fire: The Life of L. Brent Bozell Jr.* (Wilmington, Del.: ISI Books, 2014), ch. 6.

9. Rusher to Buckley, Feb. 17, 1961, Reel 28, Rusher Microfilm, LOC.

10. William Rusher, "Suite 3505," *National Review*, Aug. 11, 1964.

11. This discussion of the 1964 Draft Goldwater drive and Suite 3505 is drawn from Rick Perlstein, *Before the Storm* (New York: Hill and Wang, 2001), ch. 10, and Rusher, "Suite 3505." Clif White chronicled the committee's activities in *Suite 3505: The Story of the Draft Goldwater Movement* (New Rochelle, N.Y.: Arlington House, 1967).

12. Rusher, "Suite 3505"; Goldwater quoted in Perlstein, *Before the Storm*, 190.

13. Manion Forum Broadcast #48, "A Second Political Party Is in Order," Aug. 28, 1955; "At Last—A *Chance* for a *Choice*," Manion Forum Ephemera, Folder 2, Wilcox Collection, KU.

14. These restrictions on campaigning were relaxed in 1981 (see IRS's Rev. Rul. 81-95, 1981-1 C.B. 332) and mostly done away with as a consequence of *Citizens United v. Federal Election Commission* (2010).

15. Manion to Hubbard Russell, Aug. 2, 1963, Box 10, Folder 3, Manion Papers, CHM.

16. Walter Lippmann, "Goldwater After California," *Washington Post*, Jun. 4, 1964.

17. Jonathan M. Schoenwald, *A Time for Choosing: The Rise of Modern American Conservatism* (Oxford: Oxford University Press, 2001), 154; E. W. Kenworthy, "Goldwater Gains in Drive for Unity," *New York Times*, Jul. 30, 1964.

18. James J. Kilpatrick, *Richmond News-Leader*, reprinted in the *Economic Council Letter*, Aug. 1, 1964, Box 56, Folder 4, Regnery Papers, HI; Manion Forum Newsletter, vol. 4, no. 21, Box 85, Folder 2, Manion Papers, CHM; Manion to Frank DeGanahl, Sep. 24, 1964, Box 16, Folder 1, Manion Papers, CHM; J. G. Bell to Manion, Oct. 29, 1964, Box 16, Folder 5, Manion Papers, CHM.

19. *Economic Council Letter*, Aug. 1, 1964, Box 56, Folder 4, Regnery Papers, HI; Schlesinger, *The Vital Center*, 207.

20. "Goldwater Seeks to End G.O.P. Rift over 'Extremism,'" *New York Times*, Aug. 10, 1964; Don Irwin, "Goldwater Won't Seek Support of Extremists," *Los Angeles Times*, Aug. 13, 1964; "subversive list" quoted in "Excerpts from News Conferences by Eisenhower, Goldwater and Rockefeller," *New York Times*, Aug. 13, 1964; "told right straight out" quoted in T. Coleman Andrews to Manion, Jun. 30, 1964, Box 58, Folder 8, Manion Papers, CHM.

21. Rusher to William Runyeon, Mar. 17, 1964, Box 31, Folder 1, Rusher Papers, LOC; Judis, *William F. Buckley, Jr.*, 228–230.

22. Charles Mohr, "Goldwater Bars Klan Aid; Confers with Eisenhower," *New York Times*, Aug. 7, 1964; Douglas Dales, "Rockefeller Denies That He Will Stump for National Ticket," *New York Times*, Aug. 8, 1964; Robert J. Donovan, "Goldwater Making Progress in Giving GOP Unified Look," *Los Angeles Times*, Aug. 9. 1964; Russell Freeburg, "Ike's Policies Adopted by Goldwater," *Chicago Tribune*, Aug. 13, 1964; quoted in "Conciliation at Hershey," *New York Times*, Aug. 13, 1964; Alistair Cooke, "Goldwater in Retreat from Extremism," *Guardian*, Aug. 13, 1964; Editorial cartoon, *Washington Post*, Aug. 13, 1964.

23. Maria L. Stille to Manion, Aug. 14, 1964, Box 15, Folder 4, Manion Papers, CHM; Manion to W. A. Price, Aug. 31, 1964, Box 15, Folder 1, Manion Papers, CHM; Manion to Mr. and Mrs. Peter Fino, Aug. 19, 1964, Box 15, Folder 5, Manion Papers, CHM.

24. Sheehan to Manion, Oct. 7, 1964, Box 16, Folder 2, Manion Papers, CHM; Jameson G. Campaigne to Karl Hess, May 27, 1964, Box 8, Folder "November 1 to November 30, 1964," Jameson G. Campaigne Papers, HI; John P. Shanley, "'Hello, Lyndon!' Joins Campaign at Democratic Parley Next Week," *New York Times*, Aug. 21, 1964.

25. The manuscript would become Jameson G. Campaigne's *Check-Off*; it was ghostwritten by Jean Kellogg. Regnery to Morley, Jan. 24, 1961, Box 58, Folder 1, Regnery Papers, HI.

26. "Goldwater: A Portrait in Words and Pictures," *Human Events*, Jan. 25, 1964; William Rusher, "A Man Who Stands Tall," *National Review*, Jul. 28, 1964, 656–657.

27. Regnery to Morley, Jan. 24, 1961, Box 58, Folder 1, Regnery Papers, HI; Regnery to Frank Meyer, Aug. 20, 1964, Box 51, Folder 5, Regnery Papers, HI; Regnery to H. W. Luhnow, Sep. 28, 1964, Box 76, Folder 4, Regnery Papers, HI.

28. Laurence Stern, "Watchdog Group Calls Campaign 'Most Bitter,'" *Los Angeles Times*,

Oct. 22, 1964; Thomas O'Neill, "Literati at Work," *Baltimore Sun*, Oct. 11, 1964; "Illegitimate Power Study Widely Read," *Chicago Tribune*, Aug. 30, 1964.

29. Clarence Petersen, "Hatchets with Soft Cover Sheaths," *Chicago Tribune*, Oct. 4, 1964; John Stormer, *None Dare Call It Treason* (Florissant, Mo.: Liberty Bell, 1964), 27.

30. Phyllis Schlafly, *A Choice Not an Echo* (Alton, Ill.: Pere Marquette, 1964), 25–26, 115, 78.

31. J. Evetts Haley, *A Texan Looks at Lyndon: A Study in Illegitimate Power* (Canyon, Tex.: Palo Duro, 1964), 103, 56, 54.

32. On California numbers, see Campaigne to Otto Von Habsburt, Aug. 17, 1964, Box 11, Folder 11 "August 1 to August 31, 1966," Campaigne Papers, HI. On the book's influence on the primaries, see Manion to Bonner Fellers, Jun. 15, 1964, Box 81, Folder 7, Manion Papers, CHM; and Manion to Fred Schlafly, Jun. 1, 1964, Box 79, Folder 1, Manion Papers, CHM. Orange County activist Cathy Sullivan quoted in McGirr, *Suburban Warriors*, 136.

33. The red-baiting anecdote comes from Perlstein, *Before the Storm*, 477.

34. Perlstein, *Before the Storm*, 479.

35. Regnery to Manion, Jun. 2, 1965, Box 48, Folder 27, Regnery Papers, HI; Regnery to Manion, Jun. 29, 1965, Box 48, Folder 27, Regnery Papers, HI.

36. Regnery to H. W. Luhnow, Sep. 28, 1964, Box 76, Folder 4, Regnery Papers, HI.

37. "Information Concerning Henry Regnery Company," Mar. 24, 1965, Box 81, Folder 16, Regnery Papers, HI; "devastating blow" quoted in Regnery to Crane, June 21, 1965, Box 17, Folder 8, Regnery Papers, HI; Regnery to Manion, June 2, 1965, Box 48, Folder 27, Regnery Papers, HI.

38. Rosemarie Tyler Brooks, "GOP Convention, 1964 Recalls Germany, 1933," *Chicago Defender*, Jul. 18, 1964; *Saturday Evening Post* quoted in "Campaign Reflections by a Family Magazine," *National Review*, Oct. 6, 1964, 854.

39. Bruce Galphin, "Pop Literature of the Radical Right," *New Republic*, Oct. 10, 1964, 22–25; Andrew Sinclair, "None Dare Call It Reason," *Guardian*, Oct. 27, 1964; Robert E. Segal, "Right Wing Paperbacks Impress the Gullible," *American Israelite*, Oct. 29, 1964; Virginia Pasley, "Politics in Print," *Newsday*, Oct. 17, 1964.

40. David Wise, "Cattleman Hurls Right at LBJ," *Boston Globe*, Sep. 13, 1964; Pasley, "Politics in Print"; Jack Anderson, "A Smear-Johnson Book," *Washington Post*, Sep. 20, 1964; "Texan's Book on Johnson Is Still at Top," *Chicago Tribune*, Oct. 15, 1964.

41. Stan Evans, "The Pamphleteers Return," *National Review*, Nov. 3, 1964, 981–982.

42. "Bailey Protests Books," *Christian Science Monitor*, Oct. 10, 1964; Burch quoted in Nan Robertson, "'Smear' Tactics Alleged by G.O.P.," *New York Times*, Oct. 15, 1964; Laurence Stern, "Watchdog Group Calls Campaign 'Most Bitter,'" *Los Angeles Times*, Oct. 22, 1964.

43. "L. A. Policeman Suspended for Political Work," *Los Angeles Times*, Sep. 16, 1964; John D. Leonard, "'Treason' Book Brings Bass-Lash in N.H.," *Boston Globe*, Oct. 7, 1964; "Elmira President Picketed over a Right-Wing Booklet," *New York Times*, Oct. 29, 1964; Murray quoted in Walter Carlson, "Right-Wing Book Arouses Campus," *New York Times*, Oct. 31, 1964; "Utah Official Bans Weekly from Capitol," *Chicago Tribune*, Oct. 29, 1964.

44. Thomas O'Neill, "Literati at Work," *Baltimore Sun*, Oct. 11, 1964.

45. Cabell Phillips, "Major Political Scandal Looming in the Bobby Baker Case," *New York Times*, Jan. 25, 1964.

Chapter 9

1. "Choice, Not Revolution," *New York Times*, Nov. 5, 1964.

2. Ibid.

3. James Reston, "What Goldwater Lost," *New York Times*, Nov. 4, 1964; Henry Regnery to Wilhelm Roepke, Nov. 10, 1964, Box 65, Folder 6, Regnery Papers, HI.

4. Regnery to Roepke, Nov. 19, 1964, Box 65, Folder 6, Regnery Papers, HI; Manion to Mrs. Rogers Follansbee, Nov. 4, 1964, Box 16, Folder 6, Manion Papers, CHM.

5. James W. Jeans, State Chairman, Citizens for Goldwater-Miller (IL), to Manion, n.d., Box 17, Folder 2, Manion Papers, CHM; Manion to Norman L. Cotton, Nov. 30, 1964, Box 17, Folder 1, Manion Papers, CHM; Manion Forum Broadcast #528, "26,900,000 Conservative Voters: Will They Be Deprived of Their Civil Rights?" Nov. 15, 1964. See also Ina Palmer Morrison to Manion, Dec. 2, 1964, Box 17, Folder 2, Manion Papers, CHM; Louis H. Bean and Roscoe Drummond, "How Many Votes Does Goldwater Own?" *Look*, March 23, 1965, 75–76.

6. Hargis to Manion, Apr. 2, 1964, Box 14, Folder 2, Manion Papers, CHM; Manion Forum pamphlet, [1965], Box 109, Folder 1, Manion Papers, CHM; Rusher to Buckley, Feb. 6, 1967, Reel 33, Rusher Microfilm, LOC.

7. Rusher to Buckley, Mar. 3, 1965, Reel 31, Rusher Microfilm, LOC; Ralph E. Gray to Manion, Jul. 24, 1966, Box 26, Folder 4, Manion Papers, CHM.

8. Manion Forum Audits, Box 106, Folder 3, Manion Papers, CHM; Audit Bureau of Circulations, Box 110, Folder 4, Rusher Papers, LOC; Regnery to John L. Ryan, May 19, 1965, Box 56, Folder 5, Regnery Papers, HI; Regnery to M. Stanton Evans, Aug. 5, 1965, Box 21, Folder 16, Regnery Papers, HI.

9. On *Manion Forum Footnotes*, see, for instance, Manion Forum Broadcast #936, "The Future of Freedom: Self-Government Cannot Be Maintained by Those Who Are Ignorant of Its Principles," Sep. 17, 1972. Examples taken from Footnotes 72, 163, and 1632.

10. Quoted in Sidney Blumenthal, *The Rise of the Counter-Establishment: The Conservative Ascent to Political Power* (New York: Union Square, 1986; repr. 2008), 25. On television audience, see Manion to Lester Varn Jr., Oct. 29, 1969, Box 102, Folder 1, Manion Papers, CHM; and Manion to Lewis, Aug. 9, 1965, Box 20, Folder 1, Manion Papers, CHM.

11. Lewis to Manion, Jun. 22, 1965, Box 19, Folder 4, Manion Papers, CHM; Manion telegram to Lewis, Jun. 25, 1965, Box 19, Folder 4, Manion Papers, CHM; Lewis to Manion, Jun. 28, 1965, Box 19, Folder 4, Manion Papers, CHM.

12. Dye to Manion, Jul. 19, 1967, Box 33, Folder 4, Manion Papers, CHM; "Texas Businessman Heads Group Seeking Control of CBS Network," *Human Events*, Aug. 7, 1965.

13. Rusher to J. R. Hancock, Aug. 6, 1965, Reel 32, Rusher Microfilm, LOC; Paul Harvey, "Conservatives Seek Control News Media," *Florence* (Ala.) *Times*, Sep. 21, 1965.

14. Regnery to John L. Ryan, May 19, 1965, Box 56, Folder 5, Regnery Papers, HI.

15. Regnery to William Mullendore, Jul. 1, 1965, Box 55, Folder 2, Regnery Papers, HI; Regnery to Ferdinand Mayer, Apr. 5, 1965, Box 50, Folder 9, Regnery Papers, HI.

16. McCaffrey to Rusher, Jan. 20, 1983, Box 57, Folder 7, Rusher Papers, LOC.

17. McCaffrey to Buckley, Mar. 8, 1968, Box 57, Folder 7, Rusher Papers, LOC; Anne Edwards, "The Story of the Conservative Book Club," *Human Events*, May 20, 1967.

18. McCaffrey to Lewis L. Strauss, Mar. 28, 1963, Reel 17, Rusher Microfilm, LOC.

19. William Buckley, "Neil McCaffrey, RIP," *National Review*, Dec. 31, 1994; McCaffrey to Regnery, Oct. 19, 1977, Box 47, Folder 7, Regnery Papers, HI.

20. McCaffrey to Rusher, Nov. 5, 1964, Reel 19, Rusher Microfilm, LOC.

21. Peter Bart, "Right Wing Group in Campus Appeal," *New York Times*, Feb. 6, 1966; Ted Loeffler, "Constructive Action Special Report, Confidential," April 1966, Constructive Action, Inc. Ephemera, Folder 1, Letters, Wilcox Collection, KU.

22. Alf Regnery to Henry Regnery, Dec. 9, 1965, Box 80, Folder [Young Americans for Freedom], Regnery Papers, HI.

23. Ibid.

24. Loeffler to Regnery, Jun. 2, 1966, Box 16, Folder 5, Regnery Papers, HI.

25. Constructive Action pamphlet, "Serving the Nation's Business & Professional Men," Constructive Action, Inc. Ephemera, Folder 2, Brochures, Wilcox Collection, KU.

26. "Dispel Apathy" calendar, 1965, Box 109, Folder 1, Manion Papers, CHM.

27. Manion Forum pamphlet, [1965], Box 109, Folder 1, Manion Papers, CHM.

28. Manion Forum letter to subscribers, Nov. 17, 1964, Box 16, Folder 7, Manion Papers, CHM; *National Review*, Dec. 15, 1964, 1089.

29. Manion to Francis S. Spence, Nov. 27, 1964, Box 17, Folder 1, Manion Papers, CHM.

30. Douglas C. Morse to Manion, Mar. 24, 1965, Box 18, Folder 4, Manion Papers, CHM; Manion to Morse, Mar. 26, 1965, Box 18, Folder 4, Manion Papers, CHM; Memo to sponsors of Dean Manion's events, May 18, 1965, Box 19, Folder 1, Manion Papers, CHM.

31. "The Question of Robert Welch," *National Review*, Feb. 13, 1962, 87.

32. Meeting notes, n.d., Box 76, Folder 9, Manion Papers, CHM. Overall, ten states were represented at the meeting. Manion to George S. Montgomery Jr., Feb. 1, 1965, Box 18, Folder 1, Manion Papers, CHM.

33. NFCO Press Release, n.d., Box 76, Folder 9, Manion Papers, CHM.

34. Meeting notes, n.d., Box 76, Folder 9, Manion Papers, CHM.

35. "Confidential Preliminary Report on the A.C.U.," n.d., Box 131, Folder 8, Rusher Papers, LOC.

36. Ibid.

37. "The Question of Robert Welch."

38. Memo, Rusher to Buckley, James Burnham, Frank S. Meyer, William Rickenbacker, and Priscilla Buckley, Aug. 26, 1965, Reel 32, Rusher Microfilm, LOC.

39. Ibid.

40. Ibid.

41. Memo, Rusher to Buckley, Burnham, Meyer, Rickenbacker, and Priscilla Buckley, Sep. 24, 1965, Reel 32, Rusher Microfilm, LOC.

42. Ibid.

43. Ibid.

44. Ibid.

45. "Coast Republicans Reject Support of Birch Society," *New York Times*, Sep. 12, 1965; Samuel Lubell, "Republicans Divided on John Birch Issue," *Los Angeles Times*, Sep. 20, 1965; "Reagan Criticizes Birch Society and Its Founder," *Los Angeles Times*, Sep. 24, 1965; Robert Barkdoll, "Birch Society Rejected for Role in GOP," *Los Angeles Times*, Oct. 1, 1965. Goldwater quoted in William F. Buckley Jr., *Getting It Right* (Washington, D.C.: Regnery, 2003), 296.

46. For subscription cancellations, see, for instance, Heinsohn to Buckley, Nov. 2, 1965, Box 54, Folder 13, Manion Papers, CHM. On donation withdrawals, see Rusher to Buckley, Jan. 26, 1966, Reel 33, Rusher Microfilm, LOC. Courtney quoted in "Free Men Speak" letter, Oct. 29, 1965, Independent American Ephemera, Folder 4, Wilcox Collection, KU.

47. Herber to Manion, Oct. 6, 1965, and Manion to Herber, Oct. 8, 1965, Box 20, Folder 5, Manion Papers, CHM.

48. J. W. Reeves to Manion, Oct. 15, 1965, Box 20, Folder 6, Manion Papers, CHM; Manion to Perry Fleagle, Sep. 29, 1965, Box 20, Folder 4, Manion Papers, CHM.

49. Tom Buckley, "When Good Birchers Get Together," *New York Times*, Jun. 5, 1966, 48+.

Chapter 10

1. Brent Bozell, "Letter to Yourselves," *Triumph* (Mar. 1969): 11–14. For more on Bozell and *Triumph*, see Kelly, *Living on Fire*; and Mark D. Popowski, *The Rise and Fall of "Triumph": The History of a Radical Roman Catholic Magazine, 1966–1976* (Lanham, Md.: Lexington, 2012).

2. "Khrushchev's Visit Defended by Nixon," *New York Times*, Sep. 21, 1959.

3. Judis, *William F. Buckley, Jr.*, 279.

4. John Herbers, "Romney Attacked Goldwater Race as Keyed to South," *New York Times*, Nov. 29, 1966; Richard Nixon, *RN: The Memoirs of Richard Nixon* (New York: Grosset & Dunlap, 1978), 265; Joseph Egelhof, "Rocky Urges Governors to Rebuild G.O.P.," *Chicago Tribune*, Nov. 5, 1964; Earl Mazo, "A 'Spoilsport,' Too," *New York Times*, Nov. 6, 1964.

5. Robert Novak and Rowland Evans, "Fifty Bucks from Buckley," *Washington Post*, Oct. 15, 1965.

6. "Mr. Nixon's Reply," *National Review*, Apr. 5, 1966, 304.

7. Ibid.

8. Patrick J. Buchanan, *The Greatest Comeback: How Richard Nixon Rose from Defeat to Create the New Majority* (New York: Crown Forum, 2014), 22; "Nixon Sees Conservatives Here and Opens Lines Useful for 1968," *Washington Post*, Aug. 25, 1966; Robert Novak and Rowland Evans, "Inside Report: Nixon's Shoreham Meeting," *Washington Post*, Sep. 7, 1966.

9. Judis, *William F. Buckley, Jr.*, 280.

10. E. J. Dionne, *Why Americans Hate Politics* (New York: Simon and Schuster, 1991, repr., 2004), 191.

11. Lee Edwards, *Reagan: A Political Biography* (San Diego: Viewpoint Books, 1967); Ronald Reagan, *The Creative Society: Some Comments on Problems Facing America* (New York: Devin-Adair, 1968); Garrity to Captain and Mrs. R. W. Orrell, Jun. 25, 1968, Box 25, Folder O, Garrity Papers, HI; quoted in Garrity to Mrs. Bruce Smith, Sep. 17, 1968, Box 25, Folder S, Garrity Papers, HI; Garrity to A. C. Wedemeyer, May 24, 1968, Box 25, Folder W, Garrity Papers, HI.

12. "Operation 1968," *National Review*, Oct. 17, 1967, 1116; Buckley quoted in Judis, *William F. Buckley, Jr.*, 280.

13. Hart, *The Making of the American Conservative Mind*, 179.

14. Quoted in Frisk, *If Not Us, Who?* 218–219.

15. "The Nixon Path," *National Review*, Oct. 8, 1968, 992–993.

16. Straight Talk Broadcast #113, Box 82, Folder 3, Anderson Papers, UO; John Ashbrook, "And Anyway Is Wallace a Conservative?" *National Review*, Oct. 22, 1968, 1048–1049; Frank S. Meyer, "The Populism of George Wallace," *National Review*, May 16, 1967, 527; William F. Buckley Jr., "Nixon vs. Wallace," *National Review*, Oct. 22, 1968, 1080.

17. Meyer, "The Populism of George Wallace"; William Buckley, "An Hour with Wallace, Part One," *National Review*, Mar. 12, 1968, 258–259; Ashbrook, "And Anyway Is Wallace Conservative?"; Barry Goldwater, "Don't Waste a Vote on Wallace," *National Review*, Oct. 22, 1968, 1060–1061, 1079.

18. Victor Gold, "The Rise and Stand of George Corley Wallace," *Human Events*, Jan. 27, 1968, 7–9.

19. Manion Forum Broadcast #732, "Wallace Would Ask Congress to Curb Supreme Court: Third Party Candidate Defines Areas of Jurisdiction to Be Returned to States," Oct. 13, 1968.

20. John G. Whinery to Manion, Sep. 9, 1968, Box 103, Folder 6, Manion Papers, CHM; Irvin Scheller to Manion, May 8, 1968, Box 32, Folder 1, Manion Papers, CHM.

21. Manion to Robert D. Love, Oct. 29, 1968, Box 30, Folder 5, Manion Papers, CHM.

22. Buckley fundraising letter, Mar. 4, 1969, Box 113, Folder 4, Rusher Papers, LOC; Manion Forum Broadcast #737, "Landslide Against Liberalism: Who and What Caused Nixon's Nomination and Election," Nov. 17, 1968.

23. Crane to Manion, Sep. 30, 1968, Box 29, Folder 1, Manion Papers, CHM; Manion to Crane, Oct. 8, 1968, Box 29, Folder 1, Manion Papers, CHM.

24. "What Is Nixon's Policy?" *National Review*, Feb. 25, 1969, 158, 160.

25. "Statement of Intentions," Box 10, Folder 14, Regnery Papers, HI; Kephart to Rusher, Mar. 6, 1969, Box 41, Folder 9, Rusher Papers, LOC.

26. Rusher to Bozell, Mar. 6, 1969, Box 11, Folder 13, Rusher Papers, LOC; Rusher to Kephart, Mar. 10, 1969, Box 41, Folder 9, Rusher Papers, LOC.

27. Manion to Mary Love Collins, Feb. 25, 1969, Box 33, Folder 3, Manion Papers, CHM; D. B. Duval, "The Ordeal of Otto Otepka," *National Review*, Dec. 30, 1969, 1335; Manion Forum Broadcast #756, "Perseverance Pays off for Otto Otepka," Mar. 30, 1969; "Otepka Vindicated," *Human Events*, Mar. 15, 1969, 163.

28. Manion to John G. Whinery, Sep. 18, 1968, Box 103, Folder 6, Manion Papers, CHM; Manion to R. F. Hicky, Jan. 14, 1970, Box 37, Folder 5, Manion Papers, CHM.

29. Judis, *William F. Buckley, Jr.*, 328–331.

30. "We Suspend Our Support," *Battle Line*, Aug. 1971, 8, Box 32, Folder 11, Philbrick Papers, LOC. The signers present at the Jul. 26 meeting were Jeffrey Bell and John L. Jones of the American Conservative Union; Buckley, Rusher, James Burnham, and Frank S. Meyer

of *National Review*; Anthony Harrigan of the Southern States Industrial Council; J. Daniel Mahoney of the New York State Conservative Party; Allan H. Ryskind and Thomas S. Winter of *Human Events*; Neil McCaffrey of the Conservative Book Club (and former PR man for *National Review*); and Randall C. Teague of Young Americans for Freedom.

31. Manion Forum Broadcasts #877 and 878, "Please, Mr. President: Read About One Man's Trip to Peking," Aug. 1 and 8, 1971; Manion Forum Broadcast #881, "Retreat— Decline—Collapse: The Current Trend in American Foreign and Defense Policies," Aug. 29, 1971; Manion Forum Broadcasts #892 and 893, "Playing with Matches: The Long Range Aspects of Present U.S. Foreign Policy," Nov. 14 and 21, 1971.

32. Judis, *William F. Buckley, Jr.*, 331–332.

33. "We Suspend Our Support"; Holmes Alexander, "Conservatives Feel Gulled by Nixon Record at Home Plus China Visit," *Bangor (Me.) Daily News*, Aug. 9, 1971; Manion Forum Broadcast #377, "Patriotic Groups, Such as Manion Forum Conservative Clubs, Can Preserve Freedom," Dec. 17, 1961; Manion to Ashbrook, Jan. 4, 1972, Box 58, Folder 10, Manion Papers, CHM; Telegram, Ashbrook to Manion, Feb. 21, 1972, Box 58, Folder 10, Manion Papers, CHM.

34. "In Re New Hampshire," *National Review*, Dec. 31, 1971, 1449; "The Ashbrook Candidacy," *Human Events*, Jan. 21, 1972, 18–22; "The Importance of Ashbrook's Candidacy," *Human Events*, Feb. 5, 1972, 1, 6; George F. Hobart, "John Ashbrook of Ohio: Conservative Candidate for President," *Human Events*, Feb. 5, 1972, 11–14; "Ashbrook's Race," *Indianapolis News*, Jan. 4, 1972; "Ashbrook Picks Up Support of Loeb in New Hampshire," *New York Times*, Dec. 22, 1971. *Human Events* endorsed Ashbrook more than once. The first time was just after he announced his candidacy. "Why Ashbrook Primary Race Is Necessary," *Human Events*, Jan. 8, 1972, 3.

35. Manion to Frank deGanahl, confidential, Jan. 24, 1972, Box 41, Folder 3, Manion Papers, CHM; Rusher to Buckley, Feb. 9, 1972, Box 121, Folder 5, Rusher Papers, LOC.

36. John Pierson, "An Ultraconservative Campaigns to Return Nixon to 'Right' Path," *Wall Street Journal*, Dec. 28, 1971; George Lardner Jr., "Nixon 'Allstars' Take Spotlight Around Florida," *Washington Post*, Mar. 10, 1972. James J. Kilpatrick made a similar argument when dissecting Ashbrook support: "Conservatives Can Back Nixon or They Can Stay Home and Sulk," *Los Angeles Times*, Jan. 4, 1972.

37. John Ashbrook, "A Conservative Looks at the Nixon Record," *Human Events*, Jan. 8, 1972, 8–9; Manion Forum Broadcast #946, "The Second Time Around: Conservatives Must Exert Their Influence During the Next Four Years," Nov. 26, 1972.

38. Manion to Burch and Ray Bliss, Feb. 17, 1965, Box 18, Folder 2, Manion Papers, CHM; "Capitol Briefs," *Human Events*, Sep. 27, 1969.

39. The Magruder memo made waves when it was revealed in late 1973 after investigations into the Watergate cover-up were well underway. All three would end up serving jail time for other activities during the Nixon administration. Paul W. Valentine, "White House Plans for Offensive Against the Press Revealed," *Washington Post*, Nov. 2, 1973; "Memos on the Media," *Washington Post*, Dec. 3, 1973; Steven J. Simmons, *The Fairness Doctrine and the Media* (Berkeley: University of California Press, 1978), 219.

40. Fred Schlafly to Manion, Aug. 5, 1971, Box 79, Folder 5, Manion Papers, CHM.

41. Marjorie Hunter, "Agnew Says 'Effete Snobs' Incited War Moratorium," *New York Times*, Oct. 20, 1969; "Nixon Divorces Himself from Agnew Stand," *Hartford Courant*, Oct. 22, 1969; "Mr. Agnew: No Longer a Laughing Matter," *Washington Post*, Oct. 21, 1969; "Mr. Agnew Doesn't Understand," *New York Times*, Oct. 21, 1969; William F. Buckley, "Agnew: He Spoke Strongly, But Was He Wrong?" *Los Angeles Times*, Oct. 24, 1969; Barry Goldwater, "Double Standard on Free Speech," *Los Angeles Times*, Nov. 2, 1969; James J. Kilpatrick, "Agnew's Speech Will Make Him a National Hero," *Los Angeles Times*, Nov. 7, 1969; "Agnew Defends 'Punchy Language,'" *New York Times*, Oct. 27, 1969.

42. Robert B. Semple Jr., "Assent: Agnew Calls for Protest Against TV," *New York Times*, Nov. 16, 1969.

43. Max Frankel, "Agnew's Speech: Three in One," *New York Times*, Nov. 15, 1969; Richard Harwood and Laurence Stern, "Sneers at Vice President Won't Dispel Doubts About Media's Performance," *Washington Post*, Nov. 19, 1969; William Greider, "Public Backs Agnew Blast at Networks," *Washington Post*, Nov. 15, 1969; Tom Wicker, "The Tradition of Objectivity in the American Press—and What's Wrong with It," *Proceedings of the Massachusetts Historical Society* 83 (1971): 83–100.

44. Edward S. Herman and Noam Chomsky, *Manufacturing Consent: The Political Economy of the Mass Media* (New York: Pantheon Books, 1988).

45. Manion Forum Broadcast #795, "Hanky-Panky: Liberal News Manipulators Are Caught with Their Scripts Down," Jan. 4, 1970; Manion to Clayton Kirkpatrick, Jan. 1, 1970, Box 55, Folder 3, Manion Papers, CHM; Manion Forum Broadcast #805, "We Shall Overcome: Free Flow of News and Good Sense of a Free People Will Insure Nation's Survival," Mar. 15, 1970, Manion Papers, CHM; Draft of suggested letter for Vig. List, n.d., Box 107, Folder 2, Manion Papers, CHM.

46. Frisk, *If Not Us, Who?* 244; *Human Events* insert card, "How Much News Is Being Withheld from You?" attached to Robert D. Kephart to Manion, Mar. 22, 1971, Box 107, Folder 2, Manion Papers, CHM; Stephen J. Ganslen to Rusher, Nov. 6, 1972, Box 41, Folder 9, Rusher Papers, LOC; Arlington House catalogue, Fall 1970, Arlington House Publishers Ephemera, Wilcox Collection, KU.

47. Thomas L. Winter to "Dear Fellow American," Committee to Combat Bias in Broadcasting Ephemera, Wilcox Collection, KU.

48. Edith Efron, "Why Speech on Television Is Not Really Free," *TV Guide*, Apr. 11, 1964, clipping in Box 67, Folder 1, Manion Papers, CHM; Edith Efron, "There *Is* a Network News Bias," *TV Guide*, Feb. 28, 1970, reprinted in *Human Events*, Mar. 14, 1970.

49. Quoted in David Brock, *The Republican Noise Machine: Right-Wing Media and How It Corrupts Democracy* (New York: Crown, 2004), 18.

50. Efron to Buckley, Jun. 4, 1971, Box 121, Folder 4, Rusher Papers, LOC; Memo, Buckley to Frank Meyer, Priscilla Buckley, Warren Steibel, WAR, McCaffrey, James Buckley, Jun. 17, 1971, Box 121, Folder 4, Rusher Papers, LOC.

51. "The News Twisters," *Firing Line*, Sep. 1, 1971, Program #S0026; John Chamberlain, "Edith Efron's Murderous Adding Machine," *National Review*, Nov. 5, 1971, 11. The Nixon administration's involvement in Efron's book is detailed in Brock, *The Republican Noise Machine*, 26–33.

52. Manion to Rusher, May 21, 1974, Box 61, Folder 4, Manion Papers, CHM.

53. "Behind the Lines" transcript, Show #127, Box 212, Folder 8, Rusher Papers, LOC; Kephart to Manion, Mar. 22, 1971, Box 107, Folder 2, Manion Papers, CHM.

54. Michael T. Kaufman, "Reed Irvine, 82, the Founder of a Media Criticism Group, Dies," *New York Times*, Nov. 19, 2004; Manion Forum Broadcast #1099, "Monitoring the News: 'Accuracy in Media' Scores in Combating Inaccurate and Biased Reporting," Nov. 2, 1975.

55. Manion Forum Broadcast #1099, "Monitoring the News," Nov. 2, 1975; Raphael, *Investigated Reporting*, 214.

56. Raphael, *Investigated Reporting*, 90–98.

57. Ibid., 213–217.

58. Footnote 927, Jan. 6, 1976, Box 86, Folder 6, and Footnote 1273, May 4, 1977, Box 86, Folder 9, Manion Papers, CHM.

59. William B. Arthur, "The Winds Are Ablowin'," Feb. 13, 1974, Box 156, Folder 8, Rusher Papers, LOC; Frisk, *If Not Us, Who?* 190–192.

60. Winter to Rusher, May 25, 1978, Box 101, Folder 1, Rusher Papers, LOC.

61. Manion Forum Broadcast #975, "An Abuse of Power: Freedom of the Press Is Not a License to Commit Acts of Suppression and Oppression," Jun. 17, 1973. Right-wing commentator Tom Anderson echoed this sentiment in his newsletter "Straight Talk," arguing that networks had too much power, which they used to promote leftist goals like the Watergate investigations. Anderson, "Straight Talk," Dec. 27, 1973, Box 86, Folder 6, Anderson Papers, UO.

62. Harvey to Manion, Jul. 3, 1973, Box 43, Folder 8, Manion Papers, CHM; Manion to Harvey, Jul. 11, 1973, Box 43, Folder 8, Manion Papers, CHM; Regnery, letter to the editor, "Press Self-Deceiving," *Chicago Tribune*, May 23, 1973; Manion Forum Broadcast #987, "The Genesis of Watergate: Liberals Lowered the Boom When Nixon Began to Exercise His Mandate," Sep. 9, 1973.

63. "Watergate as Power Struggle," *National Review*, Jul. 6, 1973, 721–723; Jenkin Lloyd Jones, "Liberals Using Watergate to Reverse '72 Election Mandate," *Human Events*, Jul. 21, 1973; "Apertura a Sinistra?" *National Review*, Aug. 3, 1973, 823–824, 826; "Watergate as Softener," *National Review*, Aug. 3, 1973, 820–821, 823; Manion Forum Footnote #287, Box 85, Folder 10, Manion Papers, CHM; "Will Watergate Push Nixon to the Left?" *Human Events*, May 12, 1973, 1, 6; "Watergate Is Reversing 1972 Election Mandate," *Human Events*, Aug. 4, 1973, 1, 6.

64. "'Cox's Army' Spells Trouble for Nixon and GOP," *Human Events*, Aug. 4, 1973, 3; "Capital Briefs," *Human Events*, Sep. 1, 1973, 2; "Nixon v. Agnew," *National Review*, Oct. 12, 1973, 1139.

65. This is not to suggest that they jettisoned the old interpretations, as is evident in "Watergate Report: End of Phase One," *National Review*, Nov. 7, 1975, 1218, 1220–1221. Buckley mentioned executive power earlier in "On Reducing Nixon's Power," *National Review*, Jun. 8, 1973, 650–651, but did not focus strictly on Watergate; Manion Forum Broadcast #1052, "No. 11490: Implementation of Nixon's Executive Order Would Mean 'Rule by Decree,'" Dec. 8, 1974; William Rusher, "An End to Imperial Presidencies," *National Review*, Aug. 30, 1974, 959.

66. Rusher to Rickenbacker, Aug. 28, 1975, Box 76, Folder 6, Rusher Papers, LOC.

Chapter 11

1. Manion Forum Broadcast #1000, "A Manion Forum Milestone: Prominent Americans Pay Tribute to Dean Manion on 1000th Consecutive Weekly Broadcast," Dec. 9, 1973.

2. Garrity to John W. Blodgett Jr., Jun. 11, 1974, Box 40, Folder "John W. Blodgett, Jr.," Garrity Papers, HI.

3. Henry Regnery, "How Henry Regnery Company Became Contemporary Books, Inc.," n.d., Box 127, Folder "Plotnick, Harvey," Regnery Papers, HI.

4. Ibid.

5. Ibid.

6. Ibid.

7. Regnery to Schlamm, Aug. 22, 1971, Box 67, Folder 21, Regnery Papers, HI; Regnery, "How Henry Regnery Company Became Contemporary Books, Inc."

8. Regnery, "How Henry Regnery Company Became Contemporary Books, Inc."

9. Richard D. Reddick to Manion, Jun. 26, 1975, Box 49, Folder 11, Manion Papers, CHM; Winter to Regnery, Jan. 26, 1972, Box 32, Folder 1, Regnery Papers, HI.

10. On the increase in *National Review*'s postal costs, see N.R. fund-raising appeal, Jul. 1979, Box 113, Folder 3, Rusher Papers, LOC.

11. Winter to T. A. Bolan, Jun. 9, 1975, Box 41, Folder 9, Rusher Papers, LOC.

12. Rusher to Buckley, Feb. 19, 1976, Box 121, Folder 9, Rusher Papers, LOC; Rusher to Buckley, Mar. 16, 1976, Box 121, Folder 9, Rusher Papers, LOC.

13. Rusher to Kilpatrick, Jun. 2, 1975, Box 48, Folder 6, Rusher Papers, LOC; 1971 subscriber survey, Box 109, Folder 4, Rusher Papers, LOC; Audit Bureau of Circulations reports, Box 110, Folders 4–6, Rusher Papers, LOC.

14. Buckley fund-raising letter, 1970, Box 113, Folder 5, Rusher Papers, LOC.

15. Jones to "Dear Friend," Sep. 4, 1972, Box 123, Folder 3, Rusher Papers, LOC.

16. Rusher memo to editors, Jan. 22, 1973, Box 123, Folder 4, Rusher Papers, LOC.

17. Ibid.

18. Rusher memo to editors, Apr. 30, 1973, Box 123, Folder 4, Rusher Papers, LOC.

19. Manion Forum audits, Box 106, Folder 4, Manion Papers, CHM.

20. Memo, Emmett Mellenthin to Manion, Jul. 18, 1969, Box 107, Folder 2, Manion Papers, CHM; Roy Rivenburg, "Apocalypse Now?" *Los Angeles Times*, Sep. 9, 1994.

21. Memo, Emmett Mellenthin to Manion, Jul. 18, 1969, Box 107, Folder 2, Manion Papers, CHM

22. Ibid.

23. Ibid.

24. Manion to R. N. Hoerner, personal, Oct. 6, 1969, Box 102, Folder 1, Manion Papers, CHM.

25. Dennis Frame to Mellenthin and Bruce Eberle, Jul. 8, 1976, Box 104, Folder 3, Manion Papers, CHM.

26. Rusher to Rickenbacker, Aug. 28, 1975, Box 76, Folder 6, Rusher Papers, LOC.

27. Ibid.

28. William Rusher, *The Making of the New Majority Party* (Ottawa, Ill.: Green Hill, 1975); Rusher to Winter, Feb. 10, 1975, Box 41, Folder 9, Rusher Papers, LOC.

29. *Daytona Beach Sunday News-Journal*, Feb. 17, 1975.

30. Evans to Reagan, draft, [1975], Box 133, Folder 3, Rusher Papers, LOC.

31. Loeb to Rusher, May 22, 1975, Box 53, Folder 3, Rusher Papers, LOC.

32. Rusher to Buckley, Mar. 16, 1976, Box 121, Folder 9, Rusher Papers, LOC.

33. Details on party splits in Rusher to Buckley, Feb. 19, 1976, Box 121, Folder 9, Rusher Papers, LOC.

34. Rusher to Buckley, Feb. 19, 1976, Box 121, Folder 9, Rusher Papers, LOC.

35. Buckley to Rusher, n.d., Box 121, Folder 8, Rusher Papers, LOC; Rusher to Evans, May 21, 1975, Box 133, Folder 3, Rusher Papers, LOC.

36. Evans to Don Lipsett, Apr. 18, 1974, Box 133, Folder 3, Rusher Papers, LOC.

37. Memo, Rusher to Buckley, Jun. 21, 1973, Box 121, Folder 6, Rusher Papers, LOC; Memo, Rusher to the editors, Aug. 1, 1973, Box 123, Folder 4, Rusher Papers, LOC; Memo, Rusher to the editors, Aug. 23, 1973, Box 123, Folder 4, Rusher Papers, LOC; Memo, Rusher to Buckley, Dec. 2, 1974, Box 121, Folder 7, Rusher Papers, LOC.

38. Rusher to Buckley, Mar. 16, 1976, Box 121, Folder 9, Rusher Papers, LOC.

39. Rusher syndicated column, "New Majority Party Unlikely Now," Jul. 24, 1977.

40. Van Allen Brady, "A Milestone in Publishing," *Chicago Daily News*, Feb. 2, 1963, Box 81, Folder 16, Regnery Papers, HI.

41. Regnery to Henry Salvatori, Jan. 6, 1977, Box 67, Folder 4, Regnery Papers, HI.

42. "A Proposal to Establish a New Publishing Firm," 1972, Box 134, Folder 1, Regnery Papers, HI.

43. Regnery to Welch, Sep. 20, 1978, Box 78, Folder 1, Regnery Papers, HI; Regnery to J. William Cuncannan, Jan. 21, 1981, Box 85, Folder "Defrees and Fiske," Regnery Papers, HI.

44. Pamphlet for Gateway Editions Ltd., [1977], Box 76, Folder 2, Rusher Papers, LOC; Buckley to Regnery, Aug. 17, 1978, Box 56, Folder 8, Regnery Papers, HI; Minutes, annual meeting of Gateway Editions, Dec. 1, 1978, Box 24, Folder 11, Regnery Papers, HI.

45. Regnery to Don Lipsett, Jan. 4, 1978, Box 45, Folder 8, Regnery Papers, HI; Minutes, annual meeting of Gateway Editions, Dec. 1, 1978, Box 24, Folder 11, Regnery Papers, HI.

46. Bob Secter and Tom Paegel, "270 on L.A.-Bound Jet Die," *Los Angeles Times*, May 26, 1979; "DC-10 Tragedy: Flaws, Loopholes," *Los Angeles Times*, Jul. 13, 1979.

47. Regnery to Vittorio E. Kostermann, May 18, 1988, Box 110, Folder K, Regnery Papers, HI.

48. "Starr Stations Acquire a Publishing Company," *Broadcasting*, May 18, 1970, 34; Edwin McDowell, "Outlet Books Buys Arlington," *New York Times*, Jan. 31, 1982; William Buckley, "Neil McCaffrey, RIP," *National Review*, Dec. 31, 1994, 18.

49. Rickenbacker to Regnery, Feb. 8, 1979, Box 64, Folder 18, Regnery Papers, HI.

50. Cross to John W. Blodgett Jr., Dec. 27, 1976, Box 40, Folder JWBJ, Garrity Papers, HI;

Garrity to Blodgett, Feb. 9, 1977, Box 40, Folder JWBJ, Garrity Papers, HI; Loeb to Cross, Jan. 27, 1981, Box 47, Folder [unlabeled], Garrity Papers, HI.

51. Note on Arthur I. Bovine to Manion, Jun. 27, 1964, Box 15, Folder 1, Manion Papers, CHM.

52. Manion to Thomas H. Anderson, Sep. 28, 1966, Box 21, Folder 5, Manion Papers, CHM; Stephen Wermiel, "Conservative's Nomination to U.S. Appeals Court Spurs Debate over Quality of Reagan-Era Judges," *Wall Street Journal*, Jun. 23, 1986.

53. Lyons to Manion, Oct. 14, 1975, Box 49, Folder 6, Manion Papers, CHM; Schlafly to Clarence and Gina Manion, Oct. 17, 1975, Box 49, Folder 10, Manion Papers, CHM.

54. Manion Forum Broadcast #1288, "Respite, Recollections and Resolution: The Road to Redemption Is Rough," Jul. 8, 1979.

55. Manion Forum Broadcast #1294, "A Final Look Back: The Fruits of the Soil of God's Creative Purpose," Aug. 19, 1979.

56. Gina Manion to Florence M. Mollan, Aug. 19, 1979, Box 75, Folder 1, Manion Papers, CHM; Manion Forum Broadcast #1294, "A Final Look Back: The Fruits of the Soil of God's Creative Purpose," Aug. 19, 1979.

Chapter 12

1. Reagan speech reprinted in *National Review*, Dec. 31, 1985, 127–129.

2. "Human Events: The White House Gets 24 Copies," *New York Times*, Oct. 25, 1981.

3. *National Review* fund-raising letter, 1982, Box 113, Folder 7, Rusher Papers, LOC; Rusher to Buckley, Mar. 9, 1981, Box 122, Folder 2, Rusher Papers, LOC.

4. Campaign to Becki Klute, Aug. 14, 1980, Box 170, Folder 1, Campaigne Papers, HI; Rusher retirement speech, Dec. 9, 1988, Box 111, Folder 6, Rusher Papers, LOC.

5. Robert Heckman to Rusher, Oct. 31, 1980, Box 173, Folder 10, Rusher Papers, LOC.

6. The starting point for understanding the New Right is the following: Alan Crawford, *Thunder on the Right: The "New Right" and the Politics of Resentment* (New York: Pantheon, 1980); and Robert W. Whitaker, ed., *The New Right Papers* (New York: St. Martin's, 1982). For more, see Bruce J. Schulman, *The Seventies: The Great Shift in American Culture, Society, and Politics* (Cambridge, Mass.: Da Capo Press, 2001), 193–217; Donald T. Critchlow, *The Conservative Ascendancy: How the GOP Right Made Political History* (Cambridge, Mass.: Harvard University Press, 2007); Adam Clymer, *Drawing a Line at the Big Ditch: The Panama Canal and the Rise of the Right* (Lawrence: University Press of Kansas, 2008); Bruce J. Schulman and Julian E. Zelizer, eds., *Rightward Bound: Making America Conservative in the 1970s* (Cambridge, Mass.: Harvard University Press, 2008); and Sean Wilentz, *Age of Reagan: A History, 1974–2008* (New York: Harper, 2008), ch. 2.

7. Richard Viguerie, "A Pattern That Disturbs," *Boston Globe*, Dec. 23, 1980; Bruce Buursma, "Reagan's Dismayed Fans Plan Holy War," *Chicago Tribune*, Feb. 1, 1981.

8. William Rusher, "Taking Issue with the Anti-Reagan Conservatives," *Human Events*, Nov. 26, 1983.

9. Pat Buchanan, "O'Connor Choice: *Why*, Mr. President?" *Human Events*, Aug. 1, 1981; Richard Viguerie, "Court Choice Could Be Devastating," *Los Angeles Times*, Jul. 14, 1981.

10. "Judge O'Connor, Cont'd," *National Review*, Aug. 7, 1981; John McLaughlin, "Summer Potpourri," *National Review*, Aug. 6, 1982.

11. Buchanan, "O'Connor Choice: *Why*, Mr. President?"; Viguerie, "Court Choice Could Be Devastating."

12. See, for instance, James Graham Wilson, *The Triumph of Improvisation: Gorbachev's Adaptability, Reagan's Engagement, and the End of the Cold War* (Ithaca, N.Y.: Cornell University Press, 2014), 129–142.

13. Cato, "Letters from Washington," *National Review*, Dec. 31, 1987; Phillips and Viguerie quoted in Hedrick Smith, "The Right Against Reagan," *New York Times*, Jan. 17, 1988; Pat

Buchanan, "Has Conservative Hour Passed?" *Human Events*, Jan. 2, 1988.

14. William F. Buckley Jr., "Veni, Vidi, Victus," *National Review*, Mar. 17, 1972, 258–262; Tom Sherwood and Molly Moore, "Viguerie, Other Conservative Fund-Raisers Face Leaner Times," *Washington Post*, May 11, 1985; "Loss of Liberal Foes Hurts Fund Raisers," *Washington Post*, Jan. 21, 1986; Lloyd Groe, "The Graying of Richard Viguerie," *Washington Post*, Jun. 29, 1989.

15. Thomas B. Edsall, "Head of Conservative PAC Quits in Dispute with Board," *Washington Post*, Sep. 1, 1987; Bob Davis, "The Republican Convention 1996," *Wall Street Journal*, Aug. 15, 1996; "Bloodhound on the Press's Trail," *Christian Science Monitor*, Jun. 27, 1991.

16. William Rusher, *The Coming Battle for the Media: Curbing the Power of the Media Elite* (New York: Morrow, 1988), 32; Frisk, *If Not Us, Who?* 390–392; "A Calm, Well-Lettered Ideologue," *St. Louis Post-Dispatch*, May 24, 1988.

17. "Exhibit A" quoted in Reginald Stuart, "An F.C.C. for the Common Man," *New York Times*, May 25, 1985; "who are we" quoted in Sally Bedell, "An F.C.C. Chief in an Era of Broadcasting Change," *New York Times*, Feb. 22, 1983; "article of faith" quoted in "A New View on FCC Role," *Boston Globe*, Mar. 26, 1981.

18. FCC 85-495 ("Inquiry into Section 73.1910 of the Commission's Rules and Regulations Concerning the General Fairness Doctrine Obligations of Broadcast Licensees"), adopted Aug. 7, 1985, published in Federal Communications Commission Reports, 102 FCC 2d, 1986, 145–253.

19. Steve Daley, "FCC Unplugs 'Fairness Doctrine' After 38 Years," *Chicago Tribune*, Aug. 5, 1987.

20. "The Hush Rush Law," *Wall Street Journal*, Sep. 1, 1993.

21. Val Adams, "Joe Pyne Wields a 'Fist' on Radio," *New York Times*, Mar. 8, 1966; "Joe Pyne, 44, Dies," *New York Times*, Mar. 3, 1970; "Bob Grant, a Combative Personality on New York Talk Radio, Dies at 84," *New York Times*, Jan. 3, 2014; Transcript, *Rush Limbaugh Show*, Jan. 2, 2014, http://www.rushlimbaugh.com/daily/2014/01/02/a_few_words_about_the_great_bob_grant.

22. On the rise of FM, see Christopher H. Sterling and Michael C. Keith, *Sounds of Change: A History of FM Broadcasting in America* (Chapel Hill: University of North Carolina Press, 2008).

23. Carl Quintanilla and Richard Gibson, "'Do Call Us': More Companies Install 1-800 Phone Lines," *Wall Street Journal*, Apr. 20, 1994; Andrew L. Yarrow, "The Revolution Wrought by Toll-Free Calls," *New York Times*, Feb. 12, 1987.

24. Claudia Puig, "Rush Limbaugh Gives Liberals the Business, Gets Plenty Himself," *Los Angeles Times*, Nov. 25, 1989; Lewis Grossberger, "The Rush Hours," *New York Times*, Dec. 16, 1990.

25. Zev Chafets, *Rush Limbaugh: An Army of One* (New York: Sentinel, 2010), 62–66.

26. There are three biographies of Ailes, two critical and one authorized: Kerwin Swint, *Dark Genius: The Influential Career of Legendary Political Operative and Fox News Founder Roger Ailes* (New York: Union Square Press, 2008); Gabriel Sherman, *The Loudest Voice in the Room: How the Brilliant, Bombastic Roger Ailes Built Fox News—and Divided a Country* (New York: Random House, 2014); Zev Chafets, *Roger Ailes: Off Camera* (New York: Sentinel, 2013).

27. Rick Du Brow, "Rush to the Right on TV," *Los Angeles Times*, Sep. 11, 1992; Chafets, *Rush Limbaugh*, 57–60.

28. Chafets, *Rush Limbaugh*, 80–84.

29. Blumenthal, *The Rise of the Counter-Establishment: From Conservative Ideology to Political Power* (New York: Times Books, 1986); Robin Finn, "Run the Country? No. He Just Wants to Rouse It," *New York Times*, Oct. 25, 2002; Nicholas Lemann, "Fear Factor," *New Yorker*, Mar. 27, 2006; Geraldine Fabrikant, "For Once He Says, 'Don't Take My Advice,'" *New York Times*, Aug. 18, 2002; Chafets, *Rush Limbaugh*; Mark Leibovich, "Being Glenn Beck," *New York Times Magazine*, Oct. 3, 2010.

30. Swint, *Dark Genius*, 115–118; Sherman, *Loudest Voice*, 141–157.

31. On Ailes and Murdoch's relationship, see Sherman, *Loudest Voice*, 171–186; and Swint, *Dark Genius*, 141–154.

32. Clifford J. Levy, "Mayor Can't Force Cable Firm to Add Channel, Judge Rules," *New York Times*, Nov. 7, 1996.

33. Jim Rutenberg, "Audience for Cable News Grows," *New York Times*, Mar. 25, 2002; Lorne Manly, "Advertising," *New York Times*, Apr. 3, 2002.

34. Diane Eicher, "The Growing Reach of King Kong: How Clear Channel Created a Radio, Concert Behemoth," *Denver Post*, Nov. 11, 2001. On the history of Clear Channel, see Alec Foege, *Right of the Dial: The Rise of Clear Channel and the Fall of Commercial Radio* (New York: Faber and Faber, 2008).

35. John Halpin, James Heidbreder, Mark Lloyd, Paul Woodhull, Ben Scott, Josh Silver, and S. Derek Turner, "The Structural Imbalance of Political Talk Radio," Jun. 21, 2007, https://cdn.americanprogress.org/wp-content/uploads/issues/2007/06/pdf/talk_radio.pdf.

36. David Streitfeld, "Publisher Adds to Conservative Empire," *Washington Post*, Dec. 2, 1993.

37. Richard Bernstein, "A Publisher of Conservative Books Complains," *New York Times*, Jul. 19, 1993; David Streitfeld, "Writers of the Right," *Washington Post*, Dec. 20, 1994.

38. Julie Bosman, "Publisher's Foray to the Right," *New York Times*, Sep. 27, 2010.

39. Tim Arango, "At National Review, a Threat to Its Reputation for Erudition," *New York Times*, Nov. 17, 2008; Howard Kurtz, "Buzz on the Right," *Washington Post*, Dec. 26, 2000.

40. David Karpf, *The MoveOn Effect: The Unexpected Transformation of American Political Advocacy* (Oxford: Oxford University Press, 2012).

41. Lawrie Mifflin, "At the Fox News Channel, the Buzzword Is Fairness, Separating News from Bias," *New York Times*, Oct. 7, 1996.

42. David Remnick, "Day of the Dittohead," *Washington Post*, Feb. 20, 1994.

43. "The Leader of the Opposition," *National Review*, Sep. 6, 1993; Robin Toner, "Election Jitters in Limbaughland," *New York Times*, Nov. 3, 1994.

44. Katharine Q. Seelyes, "Republicans Get a Pep Talk from Rush Limbaugh," *New York Times*, Dec. 12, 1994.

45. Adam Nagourney, "After Tussle on G.O.P. Title, an Apology to Limbaugh," *New York Times*, Mar. 3, 2009.

46. Theda Skocpol and Vanessa Williams, *The Tea Party and the Remaking of Republican Conservatism* (Oxford: Oxford University Press, 2012), 121; Susan Page, "Who Speaks for the GOP?" *USA Today*, Jun. 10, 2009.

47. Leibovich, "Being Glenn Beck."

48. Anna Fifield, "Fox Leads Hunt for Right's Champion," *Financial Times*, Dec. 12, 2011; Skocpol and Williams, *Tea Party*, 87.

49. Skocpol and Williams, *Tea Party*, 123; Brian Stetler, "Fox News Takes Two Potential Candidates Off Air," *New York Times*, Mar. 3, 2011.

50. Julian Sanchez, "A Coda on Closure," *Julian Sanchez*, Apr. 22, 2010, http://www.juliansanchez.com/2010/04/22/a-coda-on-closure/; "Hogan," "Epistemic Nonsense," Apr. 22, 2010, http://www.redstate.com/2010/04/22/epistemic-nonsense-count-me-on-team-levin/.

51. David Frum, *Why Romney Lost (And What the GOP Can Do About It)* (Newsweek eBook, 2012), ch. 2.

52. Ben Zimmer, "Truthiness," *New York Times Magazine*, Oct. 17, 2010; Ron Suskind, "Faith, Certainty, and the Presidency of George W. Bush," *New York Times Magazine*, Oct. 17, 2004.

53. Elspeth Reeve, "Rove's War with Fox's Nerds: The Backstory," *Atlantic Wire*, http://www.thewire.com/politics/2012/11/roves-war-foxs-nerds-backstory/58804/.

Index

Acknowledgments

A book this many years in the making accrues many debts, and a full accounting would likely be as long as the book itself. I received significant financial support for this project from Columbia University, Natalie and Howard Shawn, the University of Virginia's Miller Center, the United States Studies Centre at the University of Sydney, and the Hoover Institution. That funding was vital for my research and writing, and I am deeply grateful for the support.

I also benefited from a long line of remarkable teachers. First and foremost, Ray Haberski sparked in me a love of history that has never dimmed, and he remains a mentor and, more important, a friend. At Columbia, I was surrounded by thoughtful and generous scholars, including Alan Brinkley, Betsy Blackmar, Ira Katznelson, Sarah Phillips, Michael Janeway, Casey Blake, Eric Foner, and Victoria deGrazia. Tom Sugrue and Michael Kazin, my series editors at Penn Press, provided thoughtful and incisive comments on the proposal, and their advice has made this a much stronger book.

I had the privilege of working in two rich interdisciplinary environments, first at the Miller Center and then at the United States Studies Centre. My colleagues at both places are too numerous to list, but the supportive and challenging communities they created made my work far better. Likewise my colleagues at the University of Miami spent long lunches helping me untangle my ideas, and I will always be grateful for their support and encouragement. My Sydney colleague Tom Switzer not only read the manuscript in full but has encouraged me as a writer almost from the moment we met. My thanks and love to Carrie Hyde, who has read more drafts of my work than I can count.

In the earliest days of this project, I worked with a cohort of scholars who quickly transformed from colleagues to friends. My special gratitude to April Holm, who helped me when my doubts about this project were greatest. Neil J. Young has been my daily writing companion for years now, cheerleading, reading drafts, and holding me accountable on days when writing even a single sentence seemed like the most insurmountable obstacle.

My peerless editor Bob Lockhart at Penn Press deserves a paragraph all to himself. He has constantly pushed me to think in ever more creative ways throughout the writing of this book. He has shepherded this project from the day we huddled together over a skeletal outline to the final printed book, and I am profoundly grateful for his faith in this work and in me as an author.

This project has been part of my life for years, absorbing so much time, energy, and attention, and throughout it all I have received unending support from my family and friends. My mom has been there through it all, allowing me to take over the dining room with towering piles of books and stacks of file folders. Her help and love made this book possible.

The idea for *Messengers of the Right* came from the lively political debates that broke out any time my dad and I were in the same room together. I inherited my love of politics from him, as surely as I inherited his blue eyes and freckled skin. He died in 2009, when this project was still in its infancy, but he was so excited about the work I was doing. This book is many things, but at its core, it is an act of love and remembrance.

CPSIA information can be obtained
at www.ICGtesting.com
Printed in the USA
LVHW021504050819
626562LV00002B/434/P